HOW THE COUNTRY HOUSE BECAME ENGLISH

STEPHANIE BARCZEWSKI

REAKTION BOOKS

To the Moissons:
Heather, John, Kate, Claire, Ed and William,
who represent the best of Englishness,
parce qu'il y a du français mélangé dedans.

Published by
Reaktion Books Ltd
Unit 32, Waterside
44–48 Wharf Road
London N1 7UX, UK
www.reaktionbooks.co.uk

First published 2023
Copyright © Stephanie Barczewski 2023

All rights reserved

No part of this publication may be reproduced, stored in a retrieval system or transmitted, in any form or by any means, electronic, mechanical, photocopying, recording or otherwise, without the prior permission of the publishers

Printed and bound in Great Britain by
TJ Books Ltd, Padstow, Cornwall

A catalogue record for this book is available from the British Library

ISBN 978 1 78914 760 5

CONTENTS

Introduction:
Englishness and the Country House *7*

1 Violence and the Country House, I:
The Reformation *35*

2 Violence and the Country House, II:
The Civil War *75*

3 Reflections on the Non-Revolution in England *119*

4 No Such Thing as a British Country House *168*

5 The Empire Does Not Strike Back *216*

6 Fog in Channel *252*

Conclusion *307*

APPENDICES *319*
REFERENCES *331*
FURTHER READING *376*
ACKNOWLEDGEMENTS *378*
PHOTO ACKNOWLEDGEMENTS *381*
INDEX *382*

Introduction: Englishness and the Country House

It may seem odd for an author who previously wrote a book about the importance of the British Empire to the economics and the material culture of country houses to have now written one about the relationship between those same houses and Englishness.[1] This book arose, however, from a sense that I was not done with researching and writing about country houses after I published *Country Houses and the British Empire, 1700–1930* in 2014. That book showed both the financial and cultural impact that the Empire had on the country-house landscape. Over 1,500 houses were funded by imperial profits, and many more displayed objects imported from Britain's colonies or reflected imperial influence in other ways. These houses were found in all parts of the British Isles, with the highest concentrations in Scotland and in England around the port cities of London, Bristol and Liverpool. The book thus took the 'maximalist' side in the historiographical debate over the impact of the Empire on the British metropolis.[2]

Although I have not wavered from the conviction that the Empire had a significant cultural impact on Britain, at the same time I felt that I had only been able to tell one part of the story of the place of the country house in British culture. For although the Empire had been of major importance both financially and materially, it had not had a significant impact on the architecture and design of the country house. Only a handful of houses featured even a hint of an architectural style imported from one of Britain's colonies. This absence caused me to think more carefully about why this insularity and resistance to external influence persisted, and what this meant for British culture. At the same time as I was beginning to think along these lines, in January 2013 then Prime Minister David Cameron announced in his 'Bloomberg speech' that Britain would hold a referendum on its continued membership of the

European Union. Although the speech certainly received ample news coverage, there was little sense at the time of the power of the forces that Cameron had unleashed. 'Brexit', as it soon came to be known, consumed British politics for the next seven years, and remains far from resolved, though on the very day that I wrote these words Britain formally left the European Union. Brexit has forced scholars to reconsider both the trajectory of British history as it relates to the external world and the nature of British identity. Or 'identities', because the results of the referendum revealed significant disparities in the attitudes of the four nations that comprise the United Kingdom. Wales voted narrowly to leave, Northern Ireland narrowly to remain and Scotland much more decisively to remain. But it was England, where 53.4 per cent of voters opted to leave, which determined the outcome. The leave vote in the rest of the United Kingdom combined totalled 2.9 million, while in England alone almost 15.2 million votes were cast for leave. This stunning turn of events demonstrated the often-overlooked importance of English nationalism in determining the course of British history. This book was thus originally a result of that 'Brexit moment'. Whatever one's opinion of that moment, from the perspective of the historian it opened up new questions about British history and England's role within it.

I see, therefore, my two books on country houses as complementary. In recent years the Empire has very much dominated British history. One objective – and result – of this 'imperial turn' was to diminish the importance of the traditional nation-state (in this case both Britain and its constituent nations) as the primary scholarly frame of reference.[3] Although its early advocates sought to detail how the Empire had made its presence felt in the British metropolis, which, in the words of Antoinette Burton, left 'intact the sanctity of the nation itself as the right and proper subject of history', the next phase attempted to identify the 'interdependence' of 'national/imperial formations in any given historical moment'.[4] Burton argued for a recognition of how 'tenuous the stability of "national" culture really is', as the nation itself is 'precarious, unmoored and, in the end, finally unrealizable'.[5] In short, she asserted that the nation should no longer be the key category of scholarly analysis. In combination with its predecessor, however, this book contends that empire and nation must be understood as two parts of a whole. It reasserts the importance of the nation-state as a category of historical enquiry *alongside* empire and argues that in Britain's case one cannot be understood without the other.

As England was the hegemonic national power within the British Isles and the administrative hub of the British Empire, the imperial turn diminished it as a category of academic study and analysis more than the other parts of the British Isles. At the same time, the rise of 'four nations history' further decentred – and therefore diminished – England's place within British history. Andrew Mackillop writes: 'By recalibrating the dynamics of metropolitan cohesion with an emphasis on composite integration rather than linear, centre-led assimilation, the four nations model better captures the British-Irish Isles' four-hundred-year-old tendency towards alternating phases of greater unity and new forms of heterogeneity.'[6] This historiographical trend meant that the role of England as a discrete national actor was decreased. Mackillop continues: 'A criticism which can be levelled against much of the four nations scholarship to date . . . is that it is actually only three nations which garner attention. In an ironic role reversal, . . . England gets left out repeatedly.'[7] I am in no way, to be very clear, arguing for a return to the Anglocentrism of the past. I am, however, endorsing Mackillop's point that England should be understood 'as a nation in and of itself rather than as the automatic centre-point of the British Empire or the United Kingdom of Britain and Ireland'.[8] In other words, England must be considered as a separate entity alongside Scotland, Wales and Ireland.

This book therefore attempts to formulate an English history that takes into account its full complexity, riven as it is with tensions and contradictions. In particular, it is a history that celebrates order and stability, yet is filled with disruption and violence, in the form of religious strife and civil war. And it is a history that often embraces insularity and xenophobia but has been shaped in fundamental ways by engagement with the other nations of the British Isles, Europe and the wider world. By showing how country houses embody these contradictions, it will show at the same time how country houses came to be seen as embodiments of Englishness.

The English Country House

In 1950, Christopher Hussey declared in *Country Life*: 'The majority of English country houses are not really comparable with continental counterparts. The ideals and ways of life that they express, though superficially similar, differed so radically from those of France or Italy, for example, that they have to be accepted as *sui generis*.'[9] Hussey was writing at a time when such assertions of the national identity of the country house had become more urgent due to the perceived possibility of their extinction. In the first half of the twentieth century, country houses were sold and demolished in two great waves, one after the First World War and another after the Second. In England as many as 1,200, or around one in six, houses were lost forever.[10] In addition to the financial pressures that such houses faced in a world in which agricultural rents were no longer a reliable source of income, and taxation of the upper classes was required to pay for the welfare state, by the 1960s they faced cultural change – a more socially equal and ethnically diverse postwar Britain – that threatened to render their place in the nation's heritage obsolete. In hindsight, however, there was no serious danger, as a bevy of cultural institutions, most prominently the National Trust, came to the rescue of the country house.[11] These houses now form an important link between heritage and national identity, a partnership that has played a leading role in nation-building and the development of nationalism in western Europe since the nineteenth century. This link occurs because the establishment of a collective identity for any social group (in this case the citizens of a nation) requires a common understanding of its origin and shared experience, which is necessary to create a sense of unity, solidarity and shared purpose.[12]

National heritage, however, is not politically neutral, and in England it has in recent years typically been seen as conservative. In *On Living in an Old Country*, published in 1985, during and very much shaped by the Thatcher years, Patrick Wright asserted that English ideals of historic preservation emerged in the late nineteenth century from an 'aesthetic and neo-pastoral impulse which turns into a demand for preservation as it recoils from the rampant urbanity of a brutal industrial capitalism'.[13] A century later under Margaret Thatcher:

> Though presented as a historically formed legacy, the idea of 'national heritage' could be suffused with contemporary class assumption or imperial nostalgia. It could be aligned with a racist perspective, or wrapped around Westminster as the epicentre of the unitary British state. It could be invoked against a host of vividly imagined present-day bogeys: Europe, modernism, immigration, socialism and the welfare state.[14]

In this context the country house became not only conservative but Conservative, as part of what Wright terms the 'perfect naturalization of a hegemonic view of the nation which has needed special preservation in the years of progressive taxation and state-led social reform'.[15]

For Wright, the 'nation' in question was emphatically England, as the 'culture wars' of the 1980s and '90s transformed 'British' into a more progressive and forward-looking identity and 'English' into a more nostalgic and backward-looking one. This was endorsed by Tony Blair's *New* Labour, with its 'Cool Britannia' sloganeering, disdain for the party's socialist history and emphasis on the future over the past. In such a world, the English country house would appear to be doomed to relegation to the realm of nostalgia, its visitors ever-older and more politically reactionary. This perspective was shared by observers on both sides of the political spectrum. Andrew Marr has written:

> In rare moments of cynicism, tramping round a grand country house and trying to stifle a rising sense of proprietorial pride in somebody else's ancestors, I reflect that this instinctive, conservative view of England has been greatly helped by the fact that the buildings remain, and the people die. The National Trust ... is able to represent to the modern English, and millions of tourists, a country of wood panelling, brick towers, vast avenues and a few peach-cheeked families as seen by Gainsborough and Reynolds.[16]

Writing from a different political perspective, Roger Scruton also had little time for the conventional presentation of the country house by the heritage industry. He complained that 'the countryside is now scattered with aristocratic corpses, varnished over and preserved in their dying postures.'[17]

Even as they are frustrated by it, however, these commentators acknowledge the power of nostalgia. In 2016 nostalgia for a lost English past played a prominent role in the Brexit debate. Two days before the referendum, Sam Jacob, professor of architecture at the University of Illinois at Chicago, wrote:

> We now are at the border of Brexitshire, and if we choose to enter we'll find it a place where fiction runs backwards into reality. A place where we might cast ourselves as *Downton Abbey*

characters in a pseudo-Britain manufactured from a scrapbook of historical misquotes. Vote Leave is a vote for a theme park instead of a country.[18]

In their post-Brexit analysis, Edoardo Campanella and Marta Dassù note:

> Brexiteers benefited from the rather nostalgic atmosphere that characterized Britain at the time of the referendum. Inadvertently, the culture and entertainment industries lent a helping hand to the Leave camp in nationalizing the history of the United Kingdom and in propagating nostalgic feelings for a time when it was the fulcrum of the world. In the years ahead of the Brexit referendum there was a proliferation of films, TV series, books and art exhibitions that showcased Britain's glorious past and celebrated Englishness in its purest form. With their visual gorgeousness, they contributed to the idealization of bygone times, primarily showing the positive aspects of eras that were no less chaotic and destabilizing than the current one.[19]

Both Jacob (explicitly) and Campanella and Dassù (implicitly) invoke *Downton Abbey*, the wildly popular television series that appeared on ITV from 2010 to 2015 and then became a hit film in 2019. With a country house – in real life Highclere Castle, the Earl of Carnarvon's home in Hampshire – as its narrative centrepiece, *Downton* began as a more or less realistic look at the decline of the British aristocracy in the early twentieth century. It did not, however, allow that story to be told in full, as the Crawley family never actually lost their landed estate despite repeated threats to its continued ownership. It was as if its creator, Julian Fellowes, sought to rewrite the past in a manner that would permit the continued survival of the social, cultural and political attitudes of a century ago, rather than tracing their real-life decline. As a result, historians had little patience with the series: Simon Schama dismissed it as 'servicing the instincts of cultural necrophilia'.[20]

To be sure, Fellowes was sufficiently clever to cloak his yearning for a past in which the aristocracy still dominated British life beneath more modern sensibilities. *Downton*'s female characters were stronger than their male counterparts, and the show displayed an anachronistically tolerant attitude towards homosexuality. In this sense, it mirrored

Fellowes's argument for Brexit: regressive views concealed in modern guise. 'History has been moving for hundreds of years towards government that is answerable to the people,' he argued in 2015, 'and suddenly we have done an about-turn and we've gone back to the Austro-Hungarian Empire. I don't think that's the right direction.'[21] Ironically, a show that was supposed to be about aristocratic decline ended up garnering a peerage for its creator.

Downton demonstrates that nostalgia is not innocent: there is a fine line between admiring the aesthetics of a lost world and endorsing its values.[22] Yearning for an (imagined) past can have real political consequences in the present. James Raven writes:

> The cultural comfort food of a *Downton Abbey* . . . carries a political undertow in which current perceptions of the imperilled are implicitly contrasted with safe versions of the past. Perceived threats to national identity by immigration or European interference, for example, are transferred to parallel threats to constructed and imagined 'heritage'.[23]

To be sure, nostalgia as a component of political culture is far from unique to England. It is a characteristic of conservative and populist political movements throughout the Western world, as Donald Trump's 2016 campaign slogan 'Make America Great Again' demonstrates.[24] Campanella and Dassù, however, argue that

> only in the United Kingdom, given its historical legacy, was this phenomenon so ripe that it contributed to a highly temporally regressive decision such as Brexit. The tiny majority of the highly polarized British population who voted Leave and were brainwashed with nostalgic national myths of past glories did not just want divorce from Brussels. They wanted to return the United Kingdom to a time when the country was fully sovereign and simultaneously able to play a global role.[25]

The prominent place of nostalgia in English identity is in part because England is the only constituent nation of the British Isles in which national decline plays a prominent role in its present-day self-perception.[26] Northern Irish identity is fundamentally shaped by the dynamics of the struggle between nationalism and unionism, while the identities of

Scotland and Wales are bound up in efforts to maintain cultural and some degree of political independence, which means that for them national decline is predominantly fuel for separatist arguments, as the economic advantages of being conjoined with England have diminished. But in England, the perception of decline is central, and has played a prominent role in (English) national politics in recent decades. In the 1960s, writes Michael Kenny, Enoch Powell became an 'important and destabilizing force in British politics' because of his 'ability to reach into Labour's working-class vote in a period of relative economic decline'. He was able to accomplish this because 'he spoke directly to feelings of anxiety about national identity', which involved blaming immigrants for importing 'rival cultural traditions and practices'. In the process, he 'raised the spectre of a populist nationalism fixated upon the recovery of an older England'.[27] Camilla Schofield also reminds us of Powell's significance in defining England's postcolonial national identity.[28] Powell saw Englishness as something timeless and immutable. In 1961 he told the Royal Society of St George that the 'nationhood' of England had been 'unaffected' by empire, so that when the 'looser connections which had linked her with distant continents and strange races fell away', the 'continuity of her existence was unbroken':

> For the unbroken life of the English nation over a thousand years and more is a phenomenon unique in history, the product of a specific set of circumstances like those which in biology are supposed to start by chance a new line of evolution. Institutions which elsewhere are recent and artificial creations appear in England almost as works of nature, spontaneous and unquestioned.[29]

This definition of Englishness could not withstand demographic diversification, however, and thus Powell's conceptions of English nationhood became increasingly racialized, as he infamously expressed in his 'Rivers of Blood' speech in 1968. His views were not dissimilar from the 'Make England Great Again' politics that motivated many of the voters who opted to leave the European Union in 2016.

Country houses, in this context, have become symbols of the world we have lost, a world in which England was the core of the most powerful nation in the world. Scruton writes:

They are visited by hordes of curious tourists for whom these places, rather than any parliament or palace, breathe the mysterious magic whereby power becomes authority, and authority power. They are memorials to the force that maintained English society and English politics in being, and which became incarnate in them, as part of the landscape. They are the last signs of what England was like, when those who governed it also dwelled in them.[30]

The association of conservative politics, nostalgia and English national heritage that is apparent in the present-day cult of the country house is not, however, as straightforward as the above assessment suggests, for English nostalgia has never been exclusively conservative.[31] Instead, English culture has produced, as Michael Kenny notes, a 'varied stock of national mythologies, a number of which have been of considerable resonance for the left', including examples such as the Norman yoke and Robin Hood that feature a non-conservative yearning for a lost past.[32] In his landmark *The Making of the English Working Class* (1963), E. P. Thompson saw the formation of working-class identity in the late eighteenth century as lying in a desire to restore the purported rights of the 'free-born Englishman'.[33] If there is a dominant conservative discourse of national heritage, it has thus often been challenged, something which emerges particularly clearly in the relationship of the English landscape to national identity, the subject of the next section.

Country Houses and the English Landscape

The connection between country houses and English identity is closely related to ideas of the 'national' landscape.[34] To be sure, many nations celebrate their landscapes, but David Lowenthal argues that this impulse is particularly strong in England.[35] 'Nowhere else is landscape so freighted with legacy,' he notes, 'nowhere else does the very term suggest not simply scenery and *genres de vie*, but quintessential national virtues.'[36] Some parts of England, however, have been celebrated more than others. In 1973 Raymond Williams wrote:

> So much of the past of the country, its feelings and its literature, was involved with rural experience, and so many ideas of how to live well, from the style of the country house to the simplicity

of the cottage, persisted and even were strengthened, that there is almost an inverse proportion, in the twentieth century, between the relative importance of the working rural economy and the cultural importance of the rural idea.[37]

In his assessment of the impact of the pastoral tradition upon English culture, Peter Parker concurs: 'The English landscape defines English poetry (from Wordsworth's "Daffodils" to Edward Thomas's "Adlestrop"), English painting (Constable and Turner) and English music (Elgar and Vaughan Williams). There are of course other, urban Englands, but the increasingly mythic rural one persists as an idea.'[38] We might add other writers – Samuel Taylor Coleridge, Thomas Hardy, John Masefield, Rupert Brooke and the subject of Parker's book, A. E. Housman – to this list.

The link between national identity and the English landscape in its modern sense was first forged around 1800.[39] It was the result of two factors. First, the Romantic movement embraced nature as a source of artistic inspiration and spiritual renewal. Although the Romantics emphasized 'sublime' landscapes, such as the Lake District, that conveyed drama and danger, they also helped to transform attitudes towards the gentler parts of England. In the 1820s the poet John Clare described 'real happiness' as 'to stand and muse upon the bank of a meadow pool fringed with reed and bulrushes and silver clear in the middle on which the sun is reflected in spangles'.[40] Scotland and Wales had their mountainous northern regions to celebrate, but as most of England lacked such dramatic features, a more pastoral vision of the national landscape prevailed there.

The second factor that helped to link England's pastoral landscape with national identity was the increasing distance between the lives of most English people and rural life, which in consequence became easier to idealize. Jane Bingham writes:

> An important factor in changing attitudes to the countryside was the rapid industrialisation of Britain. As the nation's towns and cities became increasingly crowded and polluted, so the pleasures of the countryside grew in comparison. Wealthy city dwellers longed to escape to the country – at least for a long weekend – and the arrival of the railway made this a reality.[41]

Introduction: Englishness and the Country House

That desire to 'escape to the country' caused parts of England that had previously gone unappreciated to become the focus of celebration. Even the Romantics had not much loved the Cotswolds: William Cobbett had dismissed the region in the 1820s as 'a very poor, dull and uninteresting country'.[42] By 1900, however, the Cotswolds had come to be identified as a quintessentially English landscape, thanks largely to their ability to be interpreted as embodying continuity and a connection to the past that was unbroken by the intrusion of modernity.[43] In 1894 James John Hissey described 'that delightful old world, primitive, and picturesque region. It is a bit of real old England set in the midst of the new.'[44] In 1909 Spencer Edge wrote of his tour through the Cotswolds:

> As the first village came into view I was amazed at its beauty. Each house, perfect to the chimney-stack, struck me as something unique; and it was not until I had ridden slowly through several villages, each as perfect as the last, that the truth dawned on me – here was mediaeval England, in all save its inhabitants![45]

Such views would appear to support Martin Wiener's claim in *English Culture and the Decline of the Industrial Spirit* (1981) that a prominent strain of English culture from the mid-nineteenth century onwards was hostility to modernity as displayed through industrialization and urbanization. Wiener argued that this pastoral and backward-looking Englishness was responsible for a national failure to embrace economic modernity, and thus at least in part for Britain's twentieth-century decline as a great power.[46] His argument has been much disputed, but he is correct to identify an increasing strain of pastoralism in English culture in the late nineteenth century.[47] This was at least in part a reaction to industrialization and urbanization, the worst excesses of which – urban squalor, dangerous working conditions and factories spewing pollution – drew horrified responses from observers from the 1840s onwards. By the final decades of the nineteenth century these concerns had grown into a full-fledged panic as the medical examinations of prospective recruits for the Anglo-Boer War revealed serious physical deficiencies that were attributed to the transition from rural to urban living.

In the interwar years H. V. Morton and other writers toured and waxed eloquent about the countryside, utilizing the motor cars that had recently become available to a much broader range of people.[48] The lavishly illustrated 'Face of Britain' guidebooks produced by B. T. Batsford between 1936 and 1952 contributed further to this hagiographic view of rural England, as did the Shell guides with their contributions from John Betjeman and John Piper.[49] As that consciously arch-Englishman Stanley Baldwin put it in 1924, 'To me England is the country, and the country is England.'[50] Baldwin dressed in tweed and made sure his photographers frequently showed him with his pipe tightly clenched in his teeth. It did not matter that one of his grandparents was Scottish and another Welsh; that he spoke good French, passable German and could read Russian; or that he did not know the first thing about farming. (His family's wealth came from iron and steel.) Nor did it matter that by the mid-1920s most British people had lived in towns for three-quarters of a century.[51] Baldwin knew what sort of image voters wanted. And he was right: when the Second World War began, no civil defence action was more urgent than the dispatch of artists around the country to draw and paint rural scenes before they were destroyed by German bombs. Called 'Recording Britain', the project was really about England: only eighty of the more than 1,500 paintings it produced were of Wales, and none were of Scotland, which had to wait until a separate scheme was launched in 1942.

The English landscape is, however, capable of expressing a broader range of values than an insular and backward-looking nostalgia.[52] In the first half of the nineteenth century, the era of Peterloo, Chartism and the 'Hungry 40s', Elizabeth Helsinger finds that 'rural scenes' were

> the site of a contest for the possession and definition of the country – in both local and national senses. Conflicting meanings of the land [were] invoked in a struggle for cultural representation, which is also a struggle for political representation. Nostalgia is a luxury the embattled rural scene does not often afford in these years.[53]

Peter Mandler, too, argues that the dominance of rural ideals of Englishness was not as complete as Wiener suggests; instead, he finds that by 1900 England was an urban nation and was comfortable identifying itself as such.[54] David Matless writes that the emergent movement for landscape preservation in the interwar years sought 'to ally preservation and progress, tradition and modernity, city and country in order to define Englishness as orderly and modern. The common identification of preservation with nostalgia and anti-modernity does not hold here.' Matless finds that between 1918 and the 1950s there was a 'powerful historical connection between landscape, Englishness and the modern'. Even the 'most obviously nostalgic and conservative' expressions of pastoralist values in English culture could therefore 'have a complexity, either through exhibiting non-nostalgic/conservative traits, or because neither nostalgia nor conservatism are simple phenomena'.[55]

What emerges, therefore, is a complex picture of the place of the rural landscape in ideas of English national identity. Paul Readman describes this complexity as 'ideological hetereogeneity':

> While most Englishmen and women lived in towns and cities from the mid-nineteenth century on, discourses of rural Englishness remained integral to their experience of modernity. Embodying continuity with the past, these discourses constituted an important means by which a recognizable, historically rooted understanding of national identity was articulated at a time of significant social, economic and technological change ... Yet their prevalence should not lead us to conclude that English culture was somehow anti-modern, permeated by a reactionary, conservative-nostalgic mindset. On the contrary, the conceptualization of rural landscape as national heritage was compatible with a wide range of ideological perspectives – not least those avowedly progressive in complexion – and was accommodated within, and indeed supportive of, the English experience of modernity.[56]

How, then, do country houses fit into these complex – and at times contradictory – assessments of England's heritage as it relates to ideas of the national landscape?

The Ideology of the Country House

To be sure, country houses slot easily into a conservative, backward-looking vision of English heritage. They were owned exclusively by wealthy people, either those born to upper-class status or those aspiring to it, and by people who were almost always male and white. By definition, they were located in the countryside, away from urban centres. And certainly, some of the impetus behind their preservation, particularly in the decades after the Second World War, came from the political right and was motivated by regret for the passing of a pre-democratic age. In 1947 James Lees-Milne, then leading the National Trust's Country House Committee, felt little enthusiasm for the fledgling welfare state as he negotiated the acquisition of the Brockhampton Estate in Herefordshire:

> This evening the whole tragedy of England impressed itself upon me. This small, not very important seat in the heart of our secluded country, is now deprived of its last squire. A whole social system has broken down. What will replace it beyond government by the masses, uncultivated, rancorous, savage, philistine, the enemies of all things beautiful? How I detest democracy. More and more I believe in benevolent autocracy.[57]

Country houses are, however, capable of expressing more diverse social values and more complex versions of Englishness. Jon Stobart writes that 'when exploring a country house, we all too easily lose sight of history as a process. The country house is often viewed as a stable end product rather than an ongoing process of change.'[58] This 'process of change' encompasses a wide range of social and cultural values: the installation of Chinese wallpaper in the eighteenth century as a covering for Elizabethan wood panelling, for example, reveals the presence of empire in metropolitan culture. We should not assume, then, that country houses always reflect social and political conservatism. Libby Purves points out how the television show *Upstairs, Downstairs* (1971–5) 'pulled off a brilliant double ... by feeding both the sentimental attachment Britain has to lords and ladies and upright Scottish butlers, and the leftie instinct to side with downtrodden parlour-maids and betrayed maidens'.[59] (*Downton Abbey* repeated this formula, with its focus on the Crawleys *and* their servants.) The author Kazuo Ishiguro explains how he deliberately tried to reorient the country-house novel away from conservative nostalgia in *The Remains of the Day* (1989):

> The kind of England that I create ... is not an England that I believe ever existed. I've not attempted to re-produce, in an historically accurate way, some past period. What I'm trying to do there ... is to actually rework a particular myth about a certain kind of mythical England. I think there is this very strong

idea that exists in England at the moment, about an England where people lived in the not-so-distant past, that conformed to various stereotypical images. That is to say, an England with sleepy, beautiful villages with very polite people and butlers and people taking tea on the lawn. Now at the moment, particularly in Britain, there is an enormous nostalgia industry going on with coffee table books, television programs, and even some tour agencies who are trying to recapture this kind of old England. The mythical landscape of this sort of England, to a large degree, is harmless nostalgia for a time that didn't exist. The other side of this, however, is that it is used as a political tool ... It's used as a way of bashing anybody who tries to spoil this 'Garden of Eden'. This can be brought out by the left or right, but usually it is the political right who say England was this beautiful place before the trade unions tried to make it more egalitarian or before the immigrants started to come or before the promiscuous age of the '60s came and ruined everything.[60]

Here, Ishiguro simultaneously acknowledges the existence of a myth of pastoral, conservative Englishness and points to the ways in which such mythology can be 'reworked' for other political purposes. As Mandler writes, 'The story of the country house is, like the story of the nation itself, a story of change: changing economic and political arrangements, which bring with them changing attitudes to the national history, and a changing relationship between the nation and its historic ruling class.'[61]

Prior to 1900, country houses were still economically productive and the seats of political power and social prestige. Their emergence as popular tourist sites in the early nineteenth century, as Elizabeth Bennet's visit to Mr Darcy's Pemberley in *Pride and Prejudice* (1813) illustrates, was thus not the product of nostalgia for a lost world of hierarchy and wealth – because that world was not yet lost.[62] Instead, it was part of a process of creating a broadly shared sense of national heritage. In the early nineteenth century, the 'first great age of country-house visiting', the country house was

> caught up in the drive to recover a truly popular and national history ... In this period, the older stately homes were popularized as symbols of the common national history shared by all

classes, in contrast to the newer, showier homes that represented recent aristocratic exclusivity. The older houses were viewed ... not as private homes but as common property: they were the 'mansions of England', not merely of their aristocratic owners.[63]

In the final decades of the nineteenth century, however, social and economic forces combined to make the admiration of country houses and their owners more problematic. After 1873 the global agricultural depression compelled the great landowners to focus on the economic viability of their estates as never before.[64] In such an environment, country houses threatened to absorb too high a share of profits from the land. A wave of sales – of furnishings, art and sometimes the houses themselves – ensued. In other cases, the owners decamped and rented their houses to tenants, or sold off their land piecemeal in an effort to generate sufficient funds to maintain their houses and pay the staff required to run them. The demise of country houses as the backbone of the English rural economy led to a decline in public interest, while an increasingly progressive system of taxation, expressed most clearly in David Lloyd George's 'People's Budget' of 1910, threatened to finish what the agricultural depression had started. Not yet seen as part of the distant past but no longer part of the present, country houses occupied an uncertain position in evolving conceptions of what belonged to English heritage.

Even as they struggled financially, however, few owners were willing to make the case for public funds to maintain them as 'national treasures', for fear that this would send them down a slippery slope to public ownership. Instead, they 'modernized': more great estates were sold and financial portfolios were diversified, while those who could not stomach a future in a more egalitarian England decamped to the Empire. Country-house tourism plummeted: Chatsworth, which had received over 100,000 visitors annually in the 1870s, was only seeing 11,000 by the 1930s.[65] After 1945 the evolving place of the country house in English national heritage was shaped not only by the slow but undeniable erosion of the class system, but by Britain's changing position in the world. Peter Kalliney argues that

> the threat, and later the actuality, of imperial decline ... forced the English to overhaul this set of national symbols, moving swiftly from the concept of an extensive British authority to an

intensive national exceptionalism. This process ... resulted in a radical material and ideological transformation of the English landscape, a rethinking of not only national symbols but domestic space itself. In the absence of an imperial expanse, the English turned inward, confronting the loss of colonial sovereignty by renovating an indigenous geography. When imperialism could no longer guarantee material security, military self-confidence, or political stability, domestic space became the site through which the nation staged its cultural distinctiveness and attempted to manage its social contradictions.[66]

This 'indigenous geography' was not, however, exclusively rural, as the 'pastoral idyll became more and more unworkable ... as a setting through which to explore contemporary (rather than historical) cultural particularity'. Instead, writers 'began turning to urban settings to rethink the boundaries of an indigenous cultural polity'.[67]

In such an environment, it might be assumed that the relevance of the country house as a vessel for national values would continue to recede, but in fact the opposite occurred. E. M. Forster in *Howards End* (1910) and Evelyn Waugh in *Brideshead Revisited* (1945) reimagined the country-house novel as a vehicle for analyses of social change; although the two authors take very different views of the erosion of social hierarchy, they both cite it as 'a distinctive marker of English peculiarity'.[68] One reason why Waugh so loathed social change was that he feared it would lead to the demise of the country house. But in the preface to a new edition of *Brideshead* in 1959, he conceded that he had been wrong:

> It was impossible to foresee, in the spring of 1944, the present cult of the English country house. It seemed then that the ancestral seats which were our chief national artistic achievement were doomed to decay and spoliation like the monasteries in the sixteenth century. So I piled it on rather, with passionate sincerity.[69]

What Waugh had missed a decade earlier was that a new impetus had created momentum for country-house preservation: a desire for increased public access to green space. Although – or perhaps because – these efforts were often opposed by landowners, they also brought country houses into alignment with the same progressive political agenda that had threatened to destroy them. Interwar countryside planning was not the product of a nostalgic desire to recapture the 'world we have lost' in the face of fears of urban degeneration and class conflict, but a modern and democratic effort to make the natural environment more accessible to the British public. It proceeded from the same complex mix of motives as did the contemporary garden-city movement, which, as Standish Meacham describes, was led by both 'traditionalists as they celebrated the Englishness of a beneficent countryside and its hierarchical community' and 'progressives as they celebrated the liberal Englishness that encouraged direct intervention by enlightened individuals and the state'.[70]

Into this mix arrived the National Trust. The Trust is often assumed to be innately conservative in its political orientation, but as Raphael Samuel reminds us, it emerged in the 1890s from a context in which 'rural preservation and revival' was a 'progressive cause, one which found many of its most ardent supporters and exponents at the radical end of the political spectrum'.[71] Two of the Trust's three founders, Robert Hunter and Canon Hardwicke Rawnsley, were Christian Socialists and fierce defenders of rights to common land against enclosure; the third, Octavia Hill, was ambivalent about, and often critical of, the rights of private-property owners. As a result, the Trust in its early decades was 'associated in many landowners' minds with radical attacks on the great estates'.[72] The progressive spirit underlying the Trust's preservation efforts lasted well into the interwar period: as late as the mid-1930s, 'the rescue of doomed country houses was thought to be more of a Labour than a Conservative cause'.[73]

By the interwar years, it was possible to argue that country houses were national treasures rather than elite preserves. Hussey asserted in 1935 that because England, unlike other European countries, still had a functioning aristocracy, its country houses were not empty relics but rather 'a national possession to which there is a no parallel in the world'.[74] There was still, however, the matter of persuading the English public to provide the necessary funds to ensure the houses' survival. After the Second World War, this issue became even more urgent, as the requisition of hundreds of houses for military and other wartime uses caused massive damage, far more than resulted from enemy bombardment. Postwar austerity was a forbidding economic climate in which to contemplate their repair, and the late 1940s and '50s saw another rash of demolitions.

At the same time, however, the election of a Labour government in 1945 – somewhat counter-intuitively – proved a crucial step in ensuring the long-term future of the country house. After their wartime experience, people were less wary of government intervention in their economic and social lives, and more willing to accept policies that would impose greater control over the national landscape:

> The war undoubtedly triggered a revived idealization of the traditional landscape and of agriculture in particular. This does not mean, however, as is sometimes too readily assumed, that the identity of ordinary town dwellers became more wrapped up in a rural fantasy. In fact the idealized agricultural landscape was in many ways more distant from their lived experience: it was a place designed not for them but for countrymen, an educational and touristic asset to be visited by the mass of English people, but not inhabited by them.[75]

This new appreciation for the countryside was the complement of a new desire for urban planning that would make England's cities healthier and more habitable; it was all part of creating a 'land fit for heroes' in a way that had not occurred after the First World War, a 'people's peace' as a reward for a 'people's war'. The confidence of English people that resulted from the significant civilian contribution to the victory meant that they no longer took a deferential view of the great estates. Instead, they were prepared to claim them as part of their national birthright.

Landowners who had viewed the prospect of a Labour government with dismay and trepidation were thus pleasantly surprised. In 1946 the Chancellor of the Exchequer, Hugh Dalton, created the National Land Fund (NLF), which transferred land from private to public hands, with a healthy £50 million initial endowment, raised from the sale of surplus war equipment.[76] Dalton made a key decision to use some of this endowment to aid the National Trust, which he saw as doing 'fine work' in making the countryside accessible to ordinary people. He was more interested in land than in houses, while the Trust was nervous about conceding its autonomy to dependence on public finance, but in the end the marriage proved a happy one, and one that was crucial to the transformation of the country house into a national cultural asset. For the first time, country houses had been 'deemed a worthy target of public expenditure', in part simply because they were being transferred into public hands.[77] The Trust, now essentially a hybrid public-private body, used the NLF to acquire several houses, beginning with Cotehele in Cornwall in 1947.[78] The following year the Attlee government established a committee chaired by the retired civil servant Sir Ernest Gowers to explore further the question of preserving historic houses. Its report, issued in 1950, proposed providing grants and loans to owners, with the proviso that they would have to offer some public access to their houses. This resulted in the Historic Buildings and Ancient Monuments Act (1953), which made funds available to both the National Trust and private owners, creating the system that largely still funds the preservation of historic buildings today. The Act was passed by a Conservative government, but not with great enthusiasm. If beleaguered country-house owners expected increased generosity from the Tories, traditionally the party of the landed classes, they were disappointed. The relevant ministers associated the Gower report with quasi-socialist central planning and had little sympathy for the plight of the owners or their houses. Harold Macmillan, then Minister of Housing and Local Government, declared that 'the fact must be faced that the mode of life for which these notable houses stood [is] doomed.'[79] The preservation of country houses therefore remained largely a left-wing policy.

By the end of the 1950s around three hundred houses were open to the public, with the most popular drawing over 100,000 visitors a year.[80] This surge of interest was fuelled by another of England's periodic bouts of fear that the countryside was under threat. The pace of postwar urban and suburban development caused many English people to seek out the countryside, a desire which the 'never-had-it-so-good' affluence of the era permitted them to indulge. There was still, however, a debate about the place of country houses in the heritage environment, as it was not clear whether their value lay in their role as functioning residences, museums of a faded way of life or as archaic buildings that should be repurposed in ways that would allow greater enjoyment of the natural landscape. As historic buildings, country houses were now forced to compete with other parts of the built environment – urban and industrial sites in particular – for precious heritage-preservation resources. Despite all the progress that had been made in securing the future of country houses since the war, anxiety over their fate peaked in 1974, when the Victoria and Albert Museum put on an intentionally polemical exhibition entitled 'The Destruction of the Country House'.[81] To help make the case for the preservation of the country house, the exhibition's catalogue abounded with strident proclamations of its national uniqueness. James Lees-Milne described it as 'England's unique contribution to the visual arts' and declared that 'English country houses, whether palaces or manors, epitomize English history.'[82] John Harris opined that 'nowhere in the world are there so many country houses as in England, matchless for the astonishing variety of their styles and the richness of their collections and furniture.'[83] These tactics proved successful: the public response to the exhibition helped convince Harold Wilson's Labour government to scrap a new Wealth Tax that would have presented a serious challenge to the financial viability of those country houses still in private hands, and to exempt country houses, along with land and important works of art, from the Capital Transfer Tax.[84]

Today, few people would seriously question the right of country houses to occupy a place in England's national heritage, as they have become immensely popular as tourist sites.[85] In the 1970s, 270,000 people visited National Trust properties annually; by 2017 the number of visitors had surged to 26.6 million. Membership in the Trust now stands at an all-time high of 5.2 million.[86] These ever-increasing visitors are not all old and white, and they are not all seeking traditional interpretations of the history of the country house that emphasize their architecture and furnishings or the biographies of their elite owners. Since the 1970s, when the National Trust acquired Erddig in North Wales specifically because it contained an extensive archive – documents, paintings and photographs – depicting the lives of its servants, the display of life 'below stairs' has become one of the most emphasized aspects of the presentation of country houses. As Erddig's example illustrates, visitors now prefer a more thorough understanding of how lives – both of elite owners and domestic servants – were lived in the houses to an emphasis on their architectural or aesthetic merits.

These newer modes of presenting country houses are not, however, necessarily more democratic or left-wing. Though Samuel sought to defend heritage from critics on the left (like Patrick Wright), he conceded that a more progressive vision was not merely a matter of depicting the history of common people:

> People's history may have unwittingly prepared the way for more Conservative appropriations of the national past. Its preference for the 'human' document and the close-up view has the effect of domesticating the subject matter of history, and making

politics seem irrelevant – so much outside noise. Its very success in rescuing the poor from the 'enormous condescension of posterity' has the unintended effect of rehabilitating the past, opening the nation retrospectively to the excluded. The focus on 'domestic budgeting' and poor people's survival strategies underwrites the values of good housekeeping. The recycling of old photographs – a feature of the 'new' social history – also provides subliminal support for Conservative views of the past. It is difficult to think of the family in terms of oppression and insecurity when photographs testify to its stability and grace.[87]

These words were written in the 1990s, but as Owen Hatherley has recently observed, 'It sounds as if Samuel is anticipating not only the speeches of David Cameron, but the televisual world of *Call the Midwife* and *Downton Abbey*, where we are asked to admire a strong, struggling but basically deferent working class that knows its place.'[88] Even so, it is undeniable that country houses are now presented as heritage sites in very different ways from those of a few decades ago.

The country house as a living entity is no longer a viable proposition; it is now a component of England's heritage. Indeed, the very factors that ended its career as an engine of economic and agricultural activity ultimately proved its salvation, as the end of its role as the home of the English upper classes allowed it to become a more flexible heritage site.[89] For if heritage discourse must conform to contemporary conceptions of national identity, it does not mean that those conceptions are fixed, not only over time but in any particular moment.[90] Heritage is as much a product of the present as the past; the place of the country house in England's national heritage is a response to the cultural needs of the moment. Even if it must be *perceived* as historically accurate, that place has more to do with its role as part of what Walker Connor calls 'sentient or felt history' – meaning it is intuitive, emotive and non-rational – than historical reality, and is thus always subject to reinterpretation and change.[91] It is also subject to debate as 'people do not passively absorb the messages presented to them; they engage in a process of negotiation whereby certain aspects will resonate with their version of nationhood while other aspects will not.'[92]

This summary of the place of the country house in English national heritage argues that the established place it now holds is not, and never has been, exclusively the product of a backward-looking nostalgia. It is far more complex. And if the country house today represents many aspects of English heritage, it is because in the past it has reflected many dimensions of English history. The next section will explore those dimensions in greater detail.

The Contradictions of Englishness

England has no unique legal status; any laws that apply to it also apply to Wales. Being English is therefore a matter of ethnicity or self-definition rather than a matter of formal citizenship. This has at times been problematic in British culture, because, as Catherine Hall has noted, 'ethnicities have been constructed as belonging to "others", not to the norm which is English.'[93] And even when there have been attempts to define Englishness, they have often not only been disconnected from reality – most nationalisms are, after all, to one degree or another – but the complete opposite of it. England, for example, produced 'Little Englandism', with its attendant hostility to imperial expansion and all things foreign, at a time when it contained around 80 per cent of the population of the United Kingdom, when it was the place from which the largest empire the world had ever known was governed and when it was the dominant European power. England was, in other words, imagining itself as the diametric opposite of what it actually was, a reverse image of itself.

This book will explore the tensions and contradictions of English identity in two halves. The first half, consisting of three chapters, explores the contradiction in English identity between the celebration of continuity and a reality of violent disruption. Timothy Garton Ash asserts that English history is

> above all a story of continuity, by contrast with the fickle mutability of the continent, with its constantly changing regimes and borders and monarchs and constitutions; a story of the slow, steady, organic growth of institutions, of Common Law, Parliament and a unique concept of sovereignty, vested in the Crown in Parliament.[94]

Or as Krishan Kumar puts it, English identity is premised on

> an assumption of a continuity so seamless that the past dissolves insensibly into the present, making the distinction between past

and present both difficult and pointless. Continuity knits the past to the present; it creates an organic whole which confronts the future with the resources of a thoroughly mastered and assimilated history.[95]

In this view of a 'seamless' transition from past to present, England first came into being as a separate and clearly defined political and territorial entity in the reign of Alfred the Great.[96] Parliament emerged in the Middle Ages as a unique political institution which distinguished England from Continental monarchies, and one that proved capable of adapting to change, first the transition from absolutism and later to demands for increased democracy.[97] The sixteenth century saw a 'Tudor revolution in government', as G. R. Elton termed it, which saw the creation of a modern bureaucratic state.[98] The system of government that emerged from all this was sufficiently flexible and resilient to withstand the subsequent transition from monarchy to oligarchy to democracy without revolution. It adapted gradually to a changing political universe, in contrast to the violence and upheaval which occurred on the Continent. Country houses embody this continuity. Catherine Palmer points to 'their power and potency as signs of Englishness, because their physical durability ensures that what they represent will also survive, further reinforcing the notion that there are fixed and unchanging aspects of nationness passed down from one generation to the next'.[99]

Even if England has managed to progress from feudalism to democracy without revolution, however, English history is punctuated by episodes of massive disruption and violence.[100] Although it did not reach the same heights of mutual atrocity as it did on the Continent, the Reformation was an extremely violent event in England. Peter Marshall observes:

> Thousands died in the convulsions of 1549, and blood was spilled in encounters between armies fighting for religious causes in every decade between the 1530s and 1570s: after the Pilgrimage of Grace (a rising in the north of England against Henry VIII's break with Rome in 1536–37); during Wyatt's Rebellion (against Mary I in 1554); and in the Rising of the Northern Earls (a Catholic attempt to overthrow Elizabeth I in 1569–70). Over the same period and beyond, hundreds more were put to death for opposing the state's religious policies.[101]

An estimated 200,000 people, many of them civilians, died in the English Civil War. This represented around 3.7 per cent of the English population at the time, significantly larger than the percentage who died in the First World War (1.7 per cent) or Second World War (1 per cent). The Glorious Revolution was far from bloodless, not only in Scotland and Ireland, but in England as well. Steven Pincus reminds us that 'there was extensive mob violence throughout England in late 1688, violence that terrified local populations and resulted in extensive damage to property and individuals, violence that was on the same scale as the violence in France subsequent to July 1789.'[102] The Jacobite rebellions of the first half of the eighteenth century were responsible for around 3,000 deaths.

Country houses reflect these moments of disruption in English history. The Dissolution of the Monasteries, the subject of Chapter One, from the 1530s onwards represented the largest transfer of land in England since the Norman Conquest; dozens of houses were built from the ruins of monastic complexes, not only at the time but for decades and even centuries afterwards. The Civil War, examined in Chapter Two, not only resulted in massive fines which Royalist landowners had to pay in order to recover their estates from confiscation and sequestration, but increased taxes, falling rents and costly property damage. In the late seventeenth century, the English upper classes used their houses to display their opinions of the Glorious Revolution, and those on the losing side later to display (often secretly) their Jacobitism. In the late eighteenth and early nineteenth centuries, however, the contrast with revolutionary France led English culture to embrace continuity as a political ideal. This transition and the way in which this was embodied by the castle-like country houses of the era forms the subject of Chapter Three.

The second half of this book, also consisting of three chapters, will explore insularity and looking outward. In Chapter Four I consider England's relations with its nearest neighbours. At varying points from the Middle Ages through to the early modern era, the borders between England and Wales and England and Scotland were points of tension and at times open conflict. This shaped the country houses that were built near them, with the border with Scotland in particular requiring defensible houses right through to the end of the seventeenth century. At the same time, however, the houses on either side of both borders often shared more characteristics with each other than they did with houses elsewhere in their respective nations.

The relationship between country houses and the British Empire, the subject of Chapter Five, was equally complex. England's first efforts to establish overseas colonies in the late sixteenth and early seventeenth centuries generated curiosity and excitement about the economic and other advantages that such efforts might produce. This curiosity and excitement was reflected in contemporary country houses through the appearance of representations of American Indians in wood and plaster. As the population of British settlers in the colonies grew, however, a new imperative emerged for a shared sense of cultural identity between colonial and metropolitan elites. Country houses in the colonies therefore began to imitate the architectural trends of the metropole, as Palladianism and Neoclassicism came to be transimperial styles. After the loss of the American colonies the situation altered once again. With the Empire now containing a very large number of non-white subjects who were ruled by a small number of white settlers, soldiers and administrators, the need was for modes of cultural expression which could convey hierarchy and English superiority. The emphasis was now on creating a sense of difference rather than similarity between colonial and metropolitan buildings, including the houses of the respective elites. In this period, the colonies were not sources of ideas which were worthy of assimilation into traditional English modes of building. Instead, the Empire functioned as a source of wealth to fund the purchase or construction of houses and of objects brought back to display as loot, trophies or exotic curiosities.

Chapter Six focuses on the relationship between English country houses and the European continent. In the sixteenth century English culture both embraced and resisted the new ideas emanating from mainland Europe which were lumped under the heading of the 'Renaissance'. These ideas, which often looked back to classical civilization as the main sourcebook of European culture, were adapted and moulded over the next two centuries, culminating architecturally in English Palladianism. At the same time, the owners of country houses showed off their wealth and erudition through the collection and display of art acquired on the Grand Tour. The nineteenth century, however, saw a movement towards neo-gothic and neo-Tudor architectural styles which referenced English history, as well as criticism of some foreign styles, French influences in particular, for their cosmopolitanism and associations with parvenu and Jewish owners. These trends culminated in the vernacular revival and Art and Crafts movements of the late nineteenth and early twentieth centuries.

The four centuries which this book covers therefore saw a gradual consolidation of the idea of the country house as an embodiment of an ever-narrower form of Englishness. This Englishness was based upon a fallacious but powerful sense of continuity of political development without violent disruption, and it took an increasingly insular view of England's relations with its neighbours, the Empire and continental Europe. The fact, however, that country houses in the past expressed very different views of English identity shows that they are capable of expressing different aspects of it as well as how it evolves over time. Country houses are therefore more than mere vessels for a conservative, nostalgic view of English identity; this version of them has only emerged in the last century. The process of how country houses, once they became 'English' (that is, embodiments of continuity and insularity), became some of the most popular heritage sites in England has been well documented.[103] This book will instead explain how they came to possess the attributes that permitted them to be identified as 'English' in the first place.

1
Violence and the Country House, 1: *The Reformation*

The standard version of English history emphasizes continuity over sudden change, and stability over upheaval. This narrative first emerged as a conscious national ideal in the early 1790s, when Edmund Burke contrasted the stability of the English political system with the violence that was convulsing France. As Yuval Levin writes, Burke argued that

> The traditions embodied in England's social and political institutions (what he describes as 'the English constitution'), built as they are on the model of natural generation, are the best means available for his countrymen to reach a transcendent standard for government. He acknowledges that the constitutional tradition does not speak with one voice and cannot be traced back to a simple set of original principles that rely on man's beginnings to define his rights. But it does offer, in the norms it builds up, though always with exceptions, an approach by degrees to a real standard beyond mere convention. This view is neither natural-law philosophy nor a standard-less utilitarianism. Grounded in Burke's natural model of change, this approach respects traditional practices not because they began a long time ago but because they have survived and evolved, through a process of trial and error, for a long time.[1]

This belief that peaceful, gradual, constitutional change was preferable to revolutionary upheaval became the cornerstone of modern British conservatism, an ideology which has dominated British politics for the last two-and-a-half centuries. Even the mainstream British left generally shunned calls for revolutionary change.

The prevalence of this argument has resulted in a recasting of English history to fit this view. This recasting contends that by the 1720s political stability had been achieved under Sir Robert Walpole's Whig oligarchy. It was preserved by the Reform Act of 1832 and further strengthened by successive Acts in 1867, 1884–5 and 1918, which gradually extended the franchise to all adult men and most women without need for the revolutions and upheavals that plagued Continental countries. This is the view celebrated by conventional depictions of the English country house. Jonny Yarker writes that the country house

> tended to be a conservative space where the strategies of collecting and display were specifically motivated by a desire to emphasise continuity: political continuity, following the ruptures of the seventeenth century; familial continuity, given the importance of the hereditary principal [sic] in the parliamentary system; and perhaps most importantly, the continuity of a single family in a single geographical locality.[2]

Yarker's reference to the 'ruptures of the seventeenth century', however, is a reminder that before 1700 England was seen by many foreign observers, and even some of its own citizens, as 'a failed state: a discomfiting byword for seditious rebellion, religious extremism and regime change'.[3] This chapter will focus on the Reformation and its impact on the country house. In the late 1530s the Dissolution of the Monasteries led to the largest transfer of land since the Norman Conquest, as many former monastic buildings were converted to secular and residential use. Catholics created hiding places and secret chapels in their houses for priests after Queen Elizabeth 1 banned them from England, while others had their property seized after they joined religious rebellions intended to restore their faith.

The Violence of the English Reformation

Baddesley Clinton in Warwickshire was first built in the fourteenth century, but the present house dates from the 1520s, after the estate was acquired by the Ferrers family. Oxburgh Hall in Norfolk, another moated manor house, was begun in 1485, when its owner Sir Edward Bedingfeld obtained a licence to crenellate. Both houses are often cited as perfect examples of English manor houses, the relatively small and often fortified houses occupied by the English gentry from the late Middle Ages to the early seventeenth century.

In the late nineteenth and early twentieth centuries manor houses enjoyed what Jeremy Musson calls 'cult status': 'The older manor houses and smaller country houses of the pre-industrial age were admired for a variety of qualities: their Englishness, their sense of rural retreat and the beauty of weathered and ancient fabric.'[4] As Musson describes, this 'cult' reflected the contemporary search for an architectural embodiment of English national identity. At a time of tremendous social and economic change, the manor house represented a 'continuing way of life'.[5] The Englishness of manor houses was contrasted with the foreign styles of larger and grander houses. In an essay from 1907 that won the Chancellor's Prize at Oxford University, Geoffrey Scott wrote that the manor house was 'the most English product of our architecture'.[6] In 1910 B. T. Batsford published P. H. Ditchfield's *The Manor-Houses of*

Baddesley Clinton in Warwickshire, a late medieval manor house whose apparent continuity is belied by its violent history, relating to its ownership by a Catholic family after the Reformation.

England, a forerunner of its guides to rural England in the interwar period. Ditchfield described the manor houses of the Tudor era as

> some of the most perfect examples of English domestic architecture that our land ever possessed. The style was essentially English. Though Henry VIII brought over foreign artificers, who were employed to assist in the construction of his palaces and in designing decorations for the mansions of the great, the native masons and builders were engaged on these lesser houses, and wrought in simple fashion, clinging to the traditional style which they had loved and reverenced.[7]

Manor houses were seen as quintessentially English because they embodied a sense of continuity in which England was seen to pass gradually and peacefully from older, less settled forms of governance to the constitutional monarchy which had led the nation to its height of global power in the Victorian era. Krishan Kumar summarizes this traditional narrative of English history:

> The English can congratulate themselves on an orderly evolution, at least since the seventeenth century. Their revolution, and its attendant disorders, are far enough back in time to be decently buried. The 'Whig interpretation' of their history, which became the national myth, stresses progress through continuity and gradual change, rather than abrupt shifts and revolutionary convulsions. Despite the disruptions of the industrial revolution, despite the wholesale replacement of a rural by an urban way of life, despite the rise to global dominance and its subsequent demise, there was a sufficient approximation to reality in the Whig interpretation of English developments to make the English look complacently on themselves and their history.[8]

In English literature, manor houses are often presented as symbols of this continuity. H. G. Wells writes in *Tono-Bungay* (1909) of the fictional Bladesover:

> I find in Bladesover the clue to all England. There have been no revolutions or abandonments of opinion in England since the days of the fine gentry, since 1688 or thereabouts, the days when

Bladesover was built; there have been changes, dissolving forces, replacing forces, if you will; but then it was that the broad lines of the English system set firmly ... The fine gentry may have gone; they have indeed largely gone, I think; rich merchants may have replaced them, financial adventurers or what not. That does not matter; the shape is still Bladesover.[9]

Here Wells encapsulates how in the early twentieth century manor houses were seen to embody England's early development of a stable central government, because they allowed the upper classes to abandon fortified residences in favour of houses designed primarily for comfort. The late medieval and early modern manor house, wrote Sir Lawrence Weaver in *Country Life* in 1927, 'marked the security of English life', while houses elsewhere in the British Isles and in Europe continued to bristle with defensive features, reflecting the failure of their nations to achieve political stability.[10]

Many things about this view, however, were wrong, as its primary purpose was to conform to contemporary conceptions of English identity. The stripping of fortifications from English houses was a reflection of the weakness rather than the strength of the central government. English kings of the fifteenth and sixteenth centuries demanded these changes so as to prevent overmighty subjects from threatening their authority. And more to the point here, English history has featured serious disruption as well as stability. The subject of this chapter, the Reformation, was an extremely violent event in England, even if it did not reach the heights of mutual atrocity that occurred on the Continent. This violence was reflected in country houses, including the changelessness of Baddesley Clinton and Oxburgh Hall. Although their physical form remained relatively unaltered from the early sixteenth century onwards, this was not because English history was peaceful and non-violent, but because the bitter prejudice against Catholics which led to them being subjected to fines and additional taxation meant that their owners never had sufficient wealth to rebuild them. This knowledge is relevant when we consider these houses today. What appears to embody continuity in fact reflects one of the most violent and disruptive moments in English history.

REFORMATION HISTORIOGRAPHY HAS long been divided between 'traditionalists', who see the Reformation as a sharp, thorough and brutal break with what came before, and 'revisionists', who see it as more gradual, less comprehensive and less disruptive. One camp of traditionalists has argued that the Reformation was swiftly imposed from above by a newly powerful Tudor monarchy and state apparatus; G. R. Elton contended that 'by 1553 England was almost certainly nearer to being a Protestant country than to anything else.'[11] A different version of the 'rapid Reformation' thesis came from A. G. Dickens, who argued that it emerged from below as popular support for religious change grew in the late medieval and early Tudor eras.[12]

In the 1980s and '90s, however, the idea of a sudden Reformation, from above or below, was challenged. Revisionist scholars argued that the late fifteenth- and early sixteenth-century Catholic Church was not moribund, corrupt or lacking in committed adherents, but rather a flourishing and dynamic institution. Protestantism, meanwhile, garnered support in cities and towns, but it struggled in rural areas because it depended heavily on the written word, and in the countryside literacy rates were low.[13] Nicholas Tyacke sums up the revisionist view of a 'markedly piecemeal' Reformation: 'Religious change came about only gradually and largely because of the manoeuvrings of a section of the political elite; such was the enduring strength of Catholicism that Protestantism remained for long a sickly plant, its survival far from assured.'[14]

These revisionist arguments, however, threatened to transform the Reformation into such a protracted process that it barely had an impact at all. And so in the early 2000s a 'post-revisionist' view arose which combined elements from both traditional and revisionist scholarship. As Peter Marshall writes, post-revisionists see the English Reformation 'as a gradual yet profound cultural transformation rather than as the swift Protestant victory of traditional historiography or as the long-drawn-out and remarkably successful Catholic rearguard action portrayed by 1980s revisionism'.[15] In other words, although it was more gradual than the traditionalists would allow, the Reformation nonetheless represented a clear break with the past.

This historiographical debate represents the relatively narrow concerns of academic specialists, but it has broad implications for English history as a whole. This is because in the traditional Whig view the Reformation was a foundational event, as it swept away the superstition of the Middle Ages and made possible the emergence of a world governed by rational principles. It also produced, as Elton argued, a system of modern governance which would ultimately lead to the triumph of liberal democracy without need for violent revolution. 'We have been given', writes Christopher Haigh:

> a history of the progressives and the victors in which those men, ideas and issues seen as leading towards the final Reformation result are linked together in a one-sided account of change. The Reformation in England thus appears, in the pages of 'Whig' historians, as an inexorable process, a necessary sequence unfolding easily to a predetermined conclusion: the medieval Church was in decline, the laity was anticlerical, Lutheran ideas were readily accepted, a centralizing state espoused reform, superstition was attacked and, after a brief Marian fiasco, a finally Protestant England was recognized in the legislation of 1559.[16]

There followed a long but inexorable march towards enlightened ideas of religious pluralism and tolerance of other faiths, as enforced belief gave way to individual freedom of choice. This was the spiritual parallel of England's abandonment of absolute monarchy and embrace of parliamentary sovereignty; both trajectories marked England as distinct from – and superior to – its European neighbours.

A revisionist Reformation which was contingent on a complex 'series of conflicts and crises' and not the inevitable product of the unique qualities of the English character therefore challenges some of the most basic premises of English history.[17] An English Reformation caused by a random alignment of events cannot reflect an underlying English commitment to orderly historical progress or a resistance to tyranny. A revisionist Reformation was not an orderly march of reason, but a cacophony of negotiation and argument in which individual people from the top to the bottom of society were suddenly forced to choose which side they were on, leading to a fractious disunity in which believers branded their fellow citizens who did not agree with them as heretics.[18]

With such ideas dominating people's thoughts and actions, it is not surprising that violence often ensued; execution and martyrdom were logical consequences, even noble ends, in a world in which the eternal was seen as far more important than the earthly. Tudor monarchs executed around 57,000 people for religious reasons. Marshall writes:

> People were willing to die, and to kill, because they rightly believed that momentous, unprecedented, and perhaps irreversible

transformations were taking place. For good or ill, England's first exit from a European union, anchored on the church, rather than the Treaty of Rome, was a hard, not a soft one.[19]

This was part of a more general violence of retributive 'justice' in the sixteenth and early seventeenth centuries. Between 1530 and 1630, between 600 and 1,200 criminals were executed each year, adding up to a total of around 75,000, a greater rate of executions per conviction than at any other time in English history and fifteen times higher than it was in the eighteenth century, about which much more has been written regarding the eagerness of English justice to impose capital punishment for minor crimes.[20] The Reformation added to this pre-existing system of judicial violence.

Priest Holes

All of this religious rupture and violence played itself out in particular physical settings, which became imbued with meaning for both sides. The English landscape, both natural and man-made, became a battleground – sometimes literally – of competing religious beliefs. Alexandra Walsham writes:

> The landscape was a crucial forum in which confessional identities were forged. It was the setting for encounters and clashes for members of competing creeds, who fought for control over disputed locations. The rival legends and myths, rituals and customs that accumulated around these places over the course of the period became one of the ways in which men and women cemented their sense of belonging to the different churches and sects that were the end-products of the religious fracturing of the British and Irish realms.[21]

An example of these contested spaces is the priest holes found in country houses, which were created in response to the intensified efforts of the Elizabethan state to stamp out recusancy in the final decades of the sixteenth century. An analysis of National Trust properties, the Historic England database and other relevant sources identifies 128 extant houses with definite or likely priest holes, the survivors of an estimated four to five hundred which once existed.[22] (See Appendix 1.)

They are found in every region of England, but are clustered in an arc curving from west of London up to the Peak District, with the heaviest concentrations in the Thames Valley, the Cotswolds and the southern West Midlands. Smaller clusters are found on the south coast of Sussex and Hampshire and in East Anglia, Lancashire and North Yorkshire and Durham. There are few in the Southwest, the East Midlands and Cumbria. It is possible that the vagaries of preservation and survival have led to the disappearance of priest holes in those latter regions, but their geographic distribution today reflects the concentrations of Catholic gentry in England in the decades after the Reformation.[23] West Sussex, southeast Hampshire, the West Midlands, Lancashire, the North and West Ridings of Yorkshire and Durham all had high levels of elite recusancy.[24]

As physical artefacts, priest holes are highly evocative and symbolic. They call to mind a time when Catholics had to live in the shadows, keeping the continuing practice of their faith secret from the authorities, with dire and even deadly consequences if they failed. We should, to be sure, exercise caution about embracing too fully, or at least exclusively, a view of Catholic history as what Peter Marshall and Geoffrey Scott

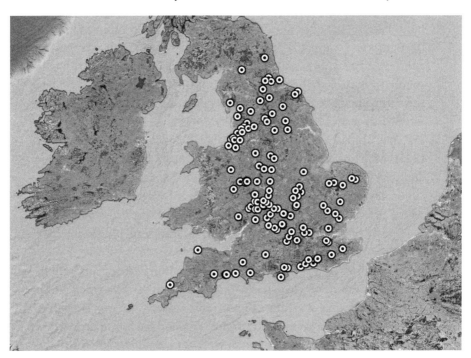

Houses containing priest holes, 1570–1620.

term 'recusant history': 'a story of resistance and refusal, of separation and survival'. Recent scholarship has emphasized 'the variety of ways in which Catholics were integrated into mainstream society and the extent to which Catholicism itself should remain integral to the master narrative of national history throughout this period'.[25] Not all Catholics, in other words, were recusants, in the sense that they actively resisted the growing power and prevalence of Protestantism; many found ways to coexist and even flourish in an increasingly Protestant English state.[26] This was particularly true on a local level, where the need for neighbours to get along meant that there was 'a process of negotiation and accommodation that sustained a pragmatic underpinning for many communities in the face of religious upheaval, often in contradiction of official church and state policies'.[27] But even so, some Catholics remained steadfast in their determination to maintain their faith and not to conform even outwardly; a count in 1603 recorded 8,590 committed recusants, out of an estimated 40,000 Catholics in total.[28]

Priest holes reflect a real history of official efforts to suppress Catholicism by aggressive – and at times violent – means and of recusant resistance. In a world in which Catholics were forced to transfer their religious practices from the public to the private sphere, upper-class households became key sites of recusant worship.[29] Country houses became the venues for some of the most violent episodes of confrontation between determined recusants and the representatives of state authority who sought to extinguish their faith. By the mid-1580s, around three hundred priests had managed to make their way back into England; in response, in 1585 Elizabeth I declared any priest found in England who had been ordained abroad a traitor, and his hosts felons. As a result, thirty-three priests were executed, eight died in prison, around fifty were incarcerated and sixty more were banished or fled to the Continent.[30]

In desperation, English Jesuits began identifying potential safe houses where priests might be concealed. The principal promulgators of this scheme were the Jesuit superior William Weston, until his arrest in 1585, and his successor Henry Garnet. Within a decade there were almost three hundred priests sheltering in secret hiding places in Catholic houses in nearly every county in England.[31] The earliest priest holes, which date from around 1580, were simple spaces, just large enough to conceal a man, that were hidden under the floorboards and accessed by a trap door. In 1588, however, the joiner and Jesuit lay brother Nicholas Owen began designing more ingenious hiding places. Owen was careful

Violence and the Country House, 1: The Reformation

Harvington Hall, Harvington, Worcestershire (late 16th century), contained eight priest holes created by Nicholas Owen, who was tortured to death after being arrested in 1606.

to use different designs and forms so that if one was discovered it would not give away the location of the others. He avoided placing his hides along outside walls, so that they could not be discovered by measuring to identify discrepancies between exterior and interior dimensions, and he often burrowed into solid masonry rather than framing the voids in wood. Owen's inventiveness is best seen in Harvington Hall in Worcestershire, which had eight priest holes, and Hindlip Hall in the same county, which had eleven. Owen worked mainly in the Midlands, while in the North the most skilled designer of priest holes was the priest Richard Holtby. After Owen was arrested at Hindlip and tortured to death in 1606, few new priest holes were built.

Many priest holes were never used for their intended purpose, although some were later pressed into service during the Civil War, while some functioned as intended and prevented those who hid in them from being arrested. A few, however, became the scene of some of the most violent episodes of the English Reformation, as the priests caught in them were sentenced to grisly punishments. Edmund Campion, who led the first Jesuit mission to post-Reformation England in 1580, was discovered hiding in a priest hole at Lyford Grange, then in Berkshire, the following year. Imprisoned in the Tower of London, he was tortured on the rack before being convicted of treason and hanged, drawn and quartered. In 1588 the priests Nicholas Garlick and Robert Ludlum were found hiding in the walls of Padley Hall in Derbyshire, the seat of the

Fitzherbert family, and were taken to Derby, where they, too, were hanged, drawn and quartered.[32] In the late sixteenth century the aforementioned Baddesley Clinton was owned by Henry Ferrers, a noted antiquary and a Roman Catholic, or at least a Catholic sympathizer. In 1588 he rented Baddesley to Anne and Eleanor Vaux, the daughters of the 3rd Lord Vaux, an ardent Northamptonshire Catholic.[33] The Vaux sisters used their inherited wealth to rent houses in order to conceal Catholic priests; it is unclear if Ferrers was aware that they hired Owen to build hiding places for up to a dozen in Baddesley. In October 1591 Father Garnet directed a group of Jesuit priests to meet him at Baddesley. The morning after their arrival, priest-hunters arrived and spent four hours searching the house, but found nothing, while the priests stood shivering in several inches of water in a hidden cellar space. But for three of the priests the respite was only temporary, as they were later caught and executed for treason. Father Garnet was sentenced to death in 1606 after it was revealed that Robert Catesby had confessed the plans for the Gunpowder Plot to him.

In 1594 the priest John Cornelius was arrested at Chideock Castle in Dorset after the searchers heard him coughing; he was hanged at Dorchester three months later.[34] When Owen was discovered at Hindlip in 1606, he was hiding in one of his own priest holes with the priest Ralph Ashley. Although their place of concealment was not discovered, hunger forced them to emerge on the fourth day. A contemporary source recorded:

> Three dayes had whollie bin spent, and no man found there all this while. But upon the fourth day, in the morning, from behinde the wainscot in the Gallerie, came foorth two men of their owne voluntarie accord, as beeing no longer able there to conceale themselves: for they confessed that they had but one Apple betweene them, which was all the releefe they had received during the time they were thus hidden.[35]

Owen's fate we know; Ashley, along with Garnet and another priest who was at Hindlip, Edward Oldcorne, were sent to the Tower of London to be tortured before they were returned to Worcester for trial. They were convicted of treason and executed.

Out of the hundreds of priest holes in England, only a small percentage were the scenes of such religious violence. The existence of so many others, however, means that the possibility of such violence was very real. In the late sixteenth and early seventeenth centuries priests and recusants lived under a constant threat that the heavy hand of the English state would fall upon them. The traditional view, which sees the Elizabethan settlement as part of a Whiggish march towards religious moderation, is contradicted by these increasingly ferocious efforts to curb recusancy. Although a degree of toleration was shown to Catholics who outwardly conformed, those who continued to resist were granted no mercy.

This Elizabethan state violence was, however, inflicted almost exclusively upon priests, while the owners of the houses in which they hid were subjected to fines or other monetary punishments, as the government used their disobedience to bring additional revenue into its coffers. Other country-house owners were stripped of their property due to their participation in rebellions against the Reformation such as the Pilgrimage of Grace (1536–7) and the Rising of the North (1569). This, too, was a form of state violence produced by the upheaval of the Reformation which had a direct impact on country houses.

Religious Rebellions and Property Confiscations

Until the late sixteenth century the Petworth estate in Sussex was a minor southern outpost of the Percy family, Earls of Northumberland, whose primary seat and power base lay far to the north at Alnwick Castle in Northumberland. Over the previous centuries, the Percys had proved extremely adept at currying royal favour. After arriving in England with William the Conqueror, they stuck closely to the sides of their kings. Petworth was acquired in 1151 as a gift to Jocelin de Louvain, half-brother of Henry I's widow Queen Adeliz and husband of Agnes de Percy, co-heiress to the family's estates. Their participation in wars against the Scots and the French in the late thirteenth century and the fourteenth earned them elevation to the earldom of Northumberland in 1377.

In the politically chaotic century that followed, however, the Percys revealed a more rebellious side. They initially backed Henry Bolingbroke's usurpation of the throne from Richard II, but they gradually grew disenchanted with him. The 1st Earl's son, Henry, forever immortalized as Shakespeare's 'Hotspur', was killed at Shrewsbury after rebelling against the king in 1403, and his father died at Bramham Moor five years later after he allied with the Scots. Both the 2nd and 3rd Earls died in the Wars

The famous west front of Petworth House, Petworth, West Sussex. The Earls of Northumberland would never have relocated their primary seat from their power base in the North of England had they not been compelled to by Elizabeth I, who wanted to keep a close eye on them after their participation in the Rising of the North.

of the Roses. The 4th Earl regained royal favour when he abandoned Richard III on Bosworth Field in 1485 and transferred his allegiance to Henry VII. The 5th and 6th Earls lived lavishly and stayed out of politics, but the latter's brother Thomas Percy was attainted and executed for his participation in the Pilgrimage of Grace in 1537. Because the 7th Earl was Thomas's son and because he retained his allegiance to the Catholic faith, he did not succeed to his title and estates until Mary I's reign. Elizabeth I permitted him to retain his recently regained status, but she compelled him to live at Petworth so that she could keep an eye on him. She was right to be wary: in 1569 he and the 6th Earl of Westmorland led the Rising of the North, which sought to install Mary, Queen of Scots on the throne. When the rebellion failed, Northumberland fled to Scotland, but he was captured by the Earl of Morton, who three years later ransomed him to the English government for £2,000, and he was beheaded at York soon afterwards. The earldom passed to his brother Henry, who had been imprisoned in the Tower of London since 1571. Elizabeth granted his release two years later, but he was ordered to remain at Petworth and forbidden to travel to his northern estates, while she continued to enjoy their income by preserving the family's attainder. None of this succeeded in compelling the 8th Earl's loyalty, or perhaps it drove him back into disloyalty. Reverting to the Catholic faith after the attainder was finally lifted in 1576, the 8th Earl dabbled in various plots to put Mary, Queen of Scots on the throne. In 1584 he was charged with treason and returned to the Tower. Eighteen months later he was found dead in his cell from a bullet wound; the official explanation was suicide, but it is more likely that he was murdered.

Having been compelled to live there, the 8th Earl began to transform Petworth from a minor possession into the seat of one of the most powerful families in England. He spent £4,500 carrying out repairs to the buildings, renovating the chapel and expanding the lodgings so that the house could accommodate the Percy family's enormous household.[36] The 9th Earl had even grander plans, which he had devised while – probably unfairly – imprisoned in the Tower as a Gunpowder Plot conspirator from 1605 to 1621. The 9th Earl's plans for Petworth would have cost a staggering £25,000, but after his release he contented himself with relatively minor improvements to the existing building.[37]

A much more significant programme of rebuilding was carried out in the late seventeenth century. The heiress to the estate, Elizabeth Seymour, already twice widowed at the age of sixteen, took as her third husband Charles Seymour, the 6th Duke of Somerset, whose pretensions and arrogance would earn him the nickname the 'Proud Duke'. With the combined wealth of two of the largest fortunes in England, he decided to build a house which could compete with the royal palace that Louis XIV was building at Versailles. He hired a French architect (possibly Daniel Marot or Pierre Puget) or an English one who was familiar with French ideas, and brought in the most highly skilled artisans in the country, including Grinling Gibbons, John Scarborough and Samuel Foulkes. The most obvious result was Petworth's famous west front, three storeys high and 98 metres (322 ft) long.

Petworth's splendour is a long way, in both time and style, from the 1530s. But it is nonetheless a physical reminder of the impact of the Reformation on the world of the country house. It would never have been built had the Percys not, because of their Catholicism and support for Mary, Queen of Scots, been forced to transfer their primary seat from Northumberland to Sussex by Elizabeth I. Today, Petworth's monumental west front gazes impassively out over the South Downs. Its formidable hauteur, however, conceals the turbulent history that led to its construction; beneath its superficial stability lies a violent and disruptive past.

THE PERCYS WERE SUFFICIENTLY powerful to be able to retain their property, but other rebellious families suffered the wrath of the Elizabethan state in ways that negatively affected their estates. Traditional views argue that the state's capacity for violence was most obvious in Ireland, which was seen by its Tudor rulers as being inhabited by barbarians who required civilizing, by force if necessary. Some Irish historians, however, have recently emphasized that the difference between Tudor England and Tudor Ireland was less marked than is often supposed, as both were characterized by what Rory Rapple describes as 'rebellion, coercion, violence, insurrection, and vigorous non-state political association'.[38] Similarly, Brendan Kane notes that 'state-on-subject, and even subject-on-subject violence enacted through use of the law, in England was endemic and extreme enough to justify seeing violence in Ireland as existing along a spectrum of "ordinary" violence characteristic of early modern England and Britain.'[39] According to Malcolm Smuts:

> At both an ideological and a practical level, the Elizabethan commonwealth had at least as much to do with combatting threats to its leaders' ideas of godliness and civility as with the pursuit of collective benefits through counsel, rhetoric and co-operation. To understand the true character and scope of the monarchical republic we need to pay more attention to its use of repression and organized violence.[40]

In times of 'emergency' this state-sponsored violence was intensified still further by the apocalyptic views produced by religious divisions. Rebellions against the rising Protestant tide therefore provoked sharp reactions which were 'characterised by terrific violence'.[41] Historians' fixation upon burnings at the stake and grisly forms of torture, however, obscures the way in which Elizabethan state violence was directed not only against the rebels but against their property, which meant that it had a significant impact on country houses. While ordinary offenders were often executed, the wealthy and powerful were able to avoid death through fines and property confiscations. P. R. Cavill observes:

> Treason was punished by a uniquely severe form of forfeiture. Unlike in cases of heresy and felony, both real and personal property was forfeit exclusively to the crown; moreover, confiscation extended to lands which the offender had held in fee

tail (a restricted form of descent) and also to those lands that were held by others in trust.[42]

In constant need of money, Tudor governments were eager to strip their wealthy subjects of their assets.

Not surprisingly, then, forfeiture of property was a common punishment imposed upon well-off subjects who rebelled for religious reasons. In 1536, in reaction to Henry VIII's policies towards religious foundations, the Pilgrimage of Grace began in the East Midlands and spread to the North of England. Its causes have been much debated, with some historians arguing that it was 'an authentic expression of the grievances of the north as a whole' against the Henrician regime, and therefore more founded in economic and social issues than a reaction against Henry VIII's religious policies. Recent studies, however, have emphasized the Pilgrimage's religious motivations. Diarmaid McCulloch concludes that 'religious and political protest' was at the core of the rebellion, and asserts that 'seeing it in any other light was the problem of late-twentieth-century historians incapable of believing that religion mattered to ordinary people in Tudor England'.[43] The rebellion had both common and elite participants; the role of the latter has been a source of debate, as some historians see them as taking a leading role but others contend that they intervened to restore order and only feigned being on the side of the common people.[44] This view reflects how the motives of elite landowners for joining the rebellion were complex, but among them was a desire to protect their property from damage. 'Many leading gentry became leaders of the hosts', McCulloch writes,

> because they saw it as a form of damage limitation: as local magistrates, they had a duty to maintain order, and in the face of huge demonstrations and no means of coercion at their disposal, this was the only route left to them. There was good reason for them to fear popular violence, at least against property if not against life.[45]

What they neglected to consider, however, was that their property was also in danger from a vengeful Tudor state, as the noblemen sent to oversee the trials of the participants determined that 'the execution of a head of house for treason was an attainder of the whole house and its lands.'[46] Sir Stephen Hamerton owned land stretching from Lancaster to York, all of which was forfeit when he was attainted and executed in 1537. The property lost included the manor of Slaidburn in Lancashire and Wigglesworth Hall and Hellifield Peel in North Yorkshire, although the family managed to recover some of it in the 1570s.[47] Sir Robert Constable was stripped of his lands, including his family seat at Flamborough Castle in Yorkshire, and hanged in chains at Hull in 1537. Flamborough was never occupied again and gradually fell into decay.[48] Sir John Bulmer was executed and attainted and so lost Wilton Castle and his house at Lastingham, both in North Yorkshire, although his nephew regained them in 1547.[49] John Scrope, 8th Baron Scrope, gave sanctuary to Adam Sedbar, Abbot of Jervaulx Abbey and supporter of the rebellion, at Bolton Castle after Sedbar fled from Henry VIII's forces. When the King's Commissioners arrived, Scrope fled to Skipton, while Sedbar was apprehended and subsequently hanged, drawn and quartered. The king ordered Bolton Castle to be burned, although Scrope managed to regain possession and carry out repairs a few years later.[50]

Sir Francis Bigod remains one of the more complex figures to join the Pilgrimage of Grace. As a Protestant of puritanical inclination, he was not an obvious participant, and indeed the rebels drove him from his seat at Mulgrave Castle in Yorkshire to Hartlepool, where they attempted to lynch him. He found common ground with his captors, however, over the issue of royal intervention in religious affairs, and thereafter launched a rebellion of his own in January 1537. It was almost immediately suppressed, and Bigod was hanged at Tyburn in June. His attainder meant that his family was stripped of both Mulgrave and Settrington House, his other Yorkshire estate. His son Ralph managed to lift the attainder in 1549 and to recover Mulgrave, but Settrington had been given to the Countess of Lennox and was permanently lost.[51] Unlike Bigod, Thomas Darcy, Baron Darcy of Darcy, was a vocal opponent of the Reformation, but his actions during the Pilgrimage of Grace remain a source of debate. In his capacity as guardian of Pontefract Castle, Darcy requested reinforcements, but when they were not forthcoming he surrendered the castle to the rebels and joined them, although his main objective appears to have been to prevent bloodshed by persuading both sides to disband their forces. After the uprising was quelled, Darcy was arrested and executed for treason. His property, including his estate at Temple Newsam near Leeds, was seized and he was attainted posthumously in 1539. His son eventually succeeded in restoring his title, but

Violence and the Country House, 1: The Reformation

he never recovered his father's estates.[52] Another landowner whose estates were affected by the Pilgrimage of Grace was Darcy's cousin John Hussey, 1st Baron Hussey of Sleaford, who was executed at Lincoln in 1537. Henry VIII ordered Hussey Tower, his brick tower house near Boston in Lincolnshire, to be destroyed; it was never recovered by his family and remains in ruins today.[53]

So angered by Thomas Cromwell's religious reforms that he led a conspiracy to usurp the throne, Henry Courtenay, 1st Marquess of Exeter, was executed and attainted, and his family was stripped of their Devon estates. Tiverton Castle was granted to the Earl of Bedford, although it was recovered after the accession of Mary I. Okehampton and Colcombe Castles were abandoned and fell into decay; their lands were incorporated into the Duchy of Cornwall.[54] Henry Pole, 1st Baron Montagu, met with the same fate, losing both his life and his manors in Buckinghamshire at Ellesborough, which Henry VIII sold for £623 to Sir John Baldwin, Lord Chief Justice of Common Pleas, and Medmenham, which Edward VI granted in 1553 to Sir Thomas Palmer.[55] Also caught up in the conspiracy was Sir Nicholas Carew, who was attainted and executed in 1539. His family forfeited their property in Surrey, including Carew Manor, which was granted to the Darcy family in 1552, and the manor at Bletchingley, which had formerly belonged to the Duke of Buckingham and which Carew had been granted after serving on the jury that convicted Buckingham of treason in 1521. Their lands in Lincolnshire, Northamptonshire, Northumberland, Sussex and Kent were later recovered.[56]

In 1554 Sir Thomas Wyatt launched a rebellion against Mary I's proposed marriage to Philip II of Spain. Wyatt's father had served as ambassador to Spain in the 1540s, and his young son, although raised a Catholic, was turned against the faith by the Spanish Inquisition. His seat at Allington Castle in Kent was seized; it fell into disrepair and remained a ruin until it was restored in the early twentieth century.[57] The rebels also targeted landed property, as they had threatened to do in the Pilgrimage of Grace. They besieged Cooling Castle in Kent, owned by Wyatt's uncle George Brooke, 9th Baron Cobham, and attacked it using two cannon which they had captured in a previous encounter with a force hastily assembled by the Duke of Norfolk. The castle was badly damaged, and Cobham decided to abandon it. He transferred his principal seat to Cobham Hall, to which he added two wings in the 1580s; as at Petworth, the very physical form of the house, which was rebuilt in the seventeenth century and modified several times since, stands as a monument to the impact of the upheavals of the sixteenth century on the English country house.[58]

Launched in 1549 in Norfolk, Kett's Rebellion was primarily a protest against agricultural enclosure, although it had religious aspects as well. Its leader, Robert Kett, had led the efforts to preserve Wymondham Abbey from destruction after the Dissolution. Henry VIII had granted part of Wymondham's land and assets to John Flowerdew, a local lawyer, and part to the town. Kett rallied the local parish to offer Flowerdew a fair price for his half so that they could use the abbey church for their services, but he refused and began dismantling the church. The bad blood between Kett and Flowerdew lingered, and in 1549 the rebels tore out some of Flowerdew's hedges.[59] In a further demonstration of their opinion of the Dissolution, the rebels also targeted Mount Surrey, the Earl of Surrey's estate on the outskirts of Norwich, which stood on the site of St Leonard's Priory. They occupied the site and used the house to incarcerate their prisoners.[60]

Recusant rebelliousness faded after Elizabeth I's accession to the throne, but there was one last major uprising. In 1569, as we have already seen, the Rising of the North was led by the Percy and Neville families, whose heads, the Earls of Northumberland and Westmorland, were the most powerful regional magnates. Their motives were complex: in addition to their continued adherence to the Catholic faith, they wanted to protect their local authority from royal incursion and supported the claim of Mary, Queen of Scots, to the throne. The response from Elizabeth I was swift and sharp: over six hundred rebels were executed and the royal army marauded across the North of England after the leaders fled to Scotland. The quasi-feudal vice-like grip of the northern nobility was never regained after the campaign of royal retribution targeted their property; Krista Kesselring writes that 'the disobedient were to pay for their sins not just with their lives but also with their goods.'[61]

The motive for this form of punishment was not merely retribution, as Elizabeth and her advisors were determined to use the rebellion both to improve the royal finances and to ensure that the northern nobility was brought firmly to heel. Kesselring notes:

> Concerns for profit rather than straightforward vengeance shaped the resolution of the conflict; pardons and punishment became commodities to be bartered and exchanged ... While the rebellion briefly posed a serious threat to Elizabeth's government, the

queen quickly turned it to her financial and political advantage. Ensuring that the disobedient paid in money as well as in blood, the queen sought to use their assets to secure the goodwill of others in the governing elite. She thus left the families of prominent rebels with little land but much incentive to conform. The suppression of the rebellion did not just give expression to royal power. Nor did it merely further the ascendancy of the Protestant faith over the Catholic. It also increased the capital at the disposal of the crown in concrete, practical ways.[62]

The suppression of the rebellion was therefore immediately followed by a campaign to identify the most desirable rebel property. While executions were concentrated among the rank and file, propertied rebels were punished with attainder, fines and confiscation. In 1571, 58 men were attainted, giving Elizabeth the right to seize their property. We have already learned the fate of the Earl of Northumberland; Charles Neville, 6th Earl of Westmorland, fled to Flanders. His two main residences, Brancepeth and Raby Castles in County Durham, were confiscated and never recovered. In total, Elizabeth acquired land worth £5,300 a year – the largest single accumulation of property to come into royal hands during her reign – from the rebels; she now owned more land in Durham than anyone save the Prince Bishop.[63] These penalties would continue to have an impact for generations to come. Kesselring writes:

> For the families of the rebels ... the crown's policy of exploiting the rebellion for all its economic and political value had dire results that left them more firmly at the Queen's mercy. Children obviously lost their paternal inheritances, and in theory at least the children of those formally attainted lost any maternal inheritance they may have expected: attainder corrupted the blood, not just of the guilty individual, but also of any offspring born before the event.[64]

But if some men lost property as a result of religious rebellions against the Tudor state, others gained. In 1545 the wool merchant Edmund Hall was granted several properties in Lincolnshire, Nottinghamshire and Rutland that had previously belonged to men attainted for their participation in the Pilgrimage of Grace. The proceeds from these properties would contribute to the building of the family seat, Greatford Hall in

Lincolnshire, around 1610.[65] After the Rising of the North, the men who had helped to put it down demanded to be rewarded for their efforts. Thomas Cecil, the eldest son of Elizabeth's chief advisor William Cecil, 1st Baron Burghley, wrote to his father that 'there are diverse gentlemen that mean at the end of this journey to crave in recompense of their chargeable journey at the Queen's majesty's hands some preferment of such of those goods and livings as are by reason of this rebellion forfeit.' Some went so far as to send itemized lists of the exact property they wished to receive.[66] Sir John Forster had already amassed a substantial property portfolio by acquiring land that had been owned by the dissolved monasteries. A veteran of the wars with Scotland, he was quick to offer his military expertise to aid in suppressing the rebellion and was rewarded with property worth £500 a year.[67]

In some cases the recipients of property confiscated from rebellious subjects used it to express their support for the government and its religious policies. After the Pilgrimage of Grace began in Lincolnshire, Henry VIII commissioned Charles Brandon, 1st Duke of Suffolk, to assemble a force in East Anglia and use it to suppress the rebellion. After this had been accomplished, several monks from two religious houses, Barlings and Kirkstead Abbeys, were executed, and the abbeys themselves were closed and their land and buildings given to Brandon, whom Henry had asked to take up residence in Lincolnshire as his regent in order to ensure that there would be no repeat of the uprising. Brandon established a local base of operations at Tattershall Castle, an impressive brick tower house which had been in royal hands since the death without heir of its builder Ralph Cromwell, 3rd Baron Cromwell, in 1456. Brandon's main embellishment to Tattershall was to build a large new tilt-yard in order to show off his martial prowess, as he was one of the most skilled jousters in England.[68] He then set about converting Barlings and Kirkstead from religious to secular use. At Barlings he built a new residential complex to the southwest of the former cloister. The cloister and the abbey church were deliberately left as features of a 'ruin garden'. Although the evidence for Kirkstead is less clear, there appears to have been a similar 'ruin garden' there as well. Paul Everson and David Stocker assert that Brandon's intent was to transform these hubs of 'resistance to religious change' to palatial residences for himself in his capacity as the king's vice-regent. In doing so, he sent an emphatic political message: any hint of rebellion would be crushed by the Tudor state.[69]

A similar conversion of monastic buildings for political purposes may have occurred at Tilty Abbey in Essex, where

> detailed earthwork surveys . . . have revealed that significant remodelling of the landscape east of the claustral ranges took place after the Dissolution, with the establishment of a series of platforms and paths. These, it is argued, were carefully placed to provide scenic walks and well-placed vistas of the ruins, maximizing the visual effect of the former church.

The site's new owner Thomas Audley was, in his capacity as Lord Chancellor, actively involved in suppressing the Pilgrimage of Grace and for punishing the ringleaders. It is possible, then, that he, like Brandon, 'wished to deliberately showcase the fate of a dissolved abbey through his creation of a ruined landscape'.[70]

Country houses therefore played a variety of roles in religious rebellions in the Tudor era. The rebels targeted them in order to express their grievances, while the Crown regarded them as valuable assets to be seized as punishment for disobedience. Once order had been restored, those converted from monastic sites could be used to display the state's political authority and new religious supremacy. The closure of Barlings, Kirkstead and Tilty Abbeys were merely early examples of what was about to sweep across England on a much larger scale.

The Dissolution of the Monasteries

Between 1536 and 1540, every one of England's 850 religious foundations was closed, ultimately resulting in the transfer of around a third of the land in the country from the Catholic Church to the Crown.[71] James Clark describes the degree of religious, social and economic disruption the Dissolution entailed:

> The number, variety and distribution of [monastic] properties made dissolution a disturbance of social and economic life in every region, urban and rural. As a shockwave shared countrywide, it recalled only moments in the remote past, the Black Death, nearly 200 years distant, or the conquest of the Normans another three centuries beyond that ... Nowhere [else in Europe] was the vowed life extinguished in just four years.[72]

A few decades earlier, there was little indication that such a change was coming. Both Henry VII and Henry VIII in the early years of his reign had been supporters and promoters of religious foundations, even if more from a desire to bolster the security of the newly established Tudor dynasty than personal piety. Even when Cardinal Wolsey first began to exert pressure on religious foundations in the early 1520s, he intended to bring about reform, not destruction. Henry VIII's divorce and assertion of supremacy over the English Church provoked little dissent. Protests were muted even in the mid-1530s, when Thomas Cromwell's commissioners began to carry out visitations in order to evaluate assets and issue injunctions demanding changes in longstanding practices.

Beneath this relatively placid surface, however, discontent was growing. This was dangerous, as any attempt at resistance led to more intense suppression. By Michelmas 1536 over two hundred religious houses had been closed. Although it was quickly quelled, the Pilgrimage of Grace was a warning that these changes were not popular among both the clergy and the laity. Some religious houses, still believing that the compact between Crown and Church could be restored, responded with obsequious demonstrations of conformity, but at the same time they began to hide, sell and even despoil their property to keep it out of the increasingly rapacious grasp of the Crown.[73] Their efforts were in vain: by the end of 1539 only fifteen houses remained in existence.

There were complex motives for this swift transformation of the religious landscape. Certainly, avarice played a role. The net income of the 525 monasteries that were listed in the *Valor Ecclesiasticus*, the survey of Church property and revenues carried out in 1535, was £136,360, which meant that it had a total value of around £3 million.[74] This represented a massive increase in royal wealth, given that up to that point Henry VIII's annual income was around £100,000 per year.[75] As an added incentive, Henry, in contrast to his father's careful management of the royal finances, spent lavishly on wars, palaces and entertainments, which meant that he was constantly in need of funds and, in spite of the revenues from the dissolved monasteries, died massively in debt. But others involved in the Dissolution were motivated by the genuine belief that Catholic buildings were the embodiments of a heretical religion. As they travelled across England shutting down religious foundations in the late 1530s, Henry VIII's commissioners often wrote about buildings with more vehemence and vitriol than they did about recusants. Clark observes:

In the few first-hand accounts [of the Dissolution] that survive, the human experience is largely obscured. The commissioners reported on the condition of buildings more often than on their residents. What they did write was brief and business-like... There was rarely any of the aggression which animated their dispatches about the churches and their altars. These attracted the language of punishment. Their people did not.[76]

But although they had been stripped of their contents, in particular their precious metals and stones, their occupants had been evicted and the bells and lead from their roofs had been removed, melted down and cast into ingots, the buildings still stood, as there was as yet no plan to dismantle them. The materials and fixtures were appraised but initially mostly left intact, with only occasional demolitions. In 1538 Cromwell hired the Italian engineer Giovanni Portinari to tear down the church and some other buildings of the Cluniac priory at Lewes in Sussex, so that he could erect a large house for his son Gregory on the site. On 24 March Portinari reported that the church had been 'plucked to the ground' after its walls were undermined.[77] This was, however, an usually swift decision, and may have been motivated either by the high value of the Caen stone or by 'this priory's historic role as the mother house of an order perceived as especially foreign'.[78] Elsewhere there was much uncertainty about what should be done with the physical remains of the religious foundations. Although a few of the more zealous king's commissioners set about defacing the structures, most proceeded with caution, wishing neither to stir up further anti-Reformation sentiment nor to unleash a frenzy of destructive reformism.

The question of how to proceed proved difficult for the Crown and its commissioners. As Margaret Aston writes, 'Converting buildings proved as difficult as converting worshippers.'[79] From the Crown's perspective, the initial discussion favoured 'conversion and continued use' rather than 'demolition and destruction'.[80] The assumption was that the majority of monastic lands would be retained by the Crown and leased rather than sold, in order to provide recurring income, although it was also intended to give grants of land to loyal subjects whom the king wished to reward: 234 grants were given in the first few years of the Dissolution, two-thirds of which went to peers and Crown officials.[81] Some went to civic grantees who converted the sites to public use, often as parish churches but also as commercial premises; Greyfriars and Blackfriars in London, for example, became warehouses for wine and herring.[82] Mayors and aldermen also harvested the materials in order to make improvements to local infrastructure such as town walls and roads. The majority of monastic grants, however, went to individuals. They were rarely given as freeholds, but rather extended existing lease arrangements between religious foundations and private tenants.[83] The general policy, writes Jane Whitaker, 'seems to have been to avoid raising rents, to protect existing tenancies and to favour local men in letting monastic properties, a business-as-usual approach which might best reconcile laymen to what had taken place'.[84]

As the financial pressure on Henry VIII increased, compounded by his decision to go to war with France in 1544, the need for ready cash became paramount, which led to the sale of over half of the confiscated monastic sites in the last five years of his reign.[85] In addition, the empty buildings had become the targets of looters and vandals. In 1542, when two commissioners went to investigate reports of looting at Hailes Abbey, they discovered 'a pattern of unauthorised yet systematic stripping of the site by the local population', in which 'windows, glazing bars, doors and even the trees and beehives in the precinct had been stolen away.'[86] The lead from the roofs was the first target, but the stone, too, was coveted, as it was often of the best quality, from Portland or even imported from Caen, and already cut into blocks. The Crown needed to dispose of these properties before their value decreased even further.

The new owners had several choices as to how to use these former monastic properties. They could sell the site on to another purchaser, sell off its most valuable assets, convert it to their own use as a residence or pillage the materials to build a residence elsewhere. Or they could hold on to the site until they decided what to do with it. The fate of monastic sites therefore varied enormously. Here, I am concerned with those which were converted, at the time or later, into large residences. I have identified 208 which fit this description. (See Appendix 2.)[87] They fall into two categories: houses which were converted from the existing monastic buildings and houses which incorporated stone and other materials taken from monastic sites.[88] The first category is by far the largest, comprising 189 of the sites.[89] Hugh Willmott, who has conducted the most detailed archaeological research on the conversion of monastic sites to country houses, emphasizes that these sites were extremely attractive not only to established landowners looking to expand their holdings, but to rising gentry seeking an opportunity to build an impressive residence cheaply:

> Whilst the fabric of the church and conventual buildings themselves represented an opportunity to make short-term gain through the sale of window glass, furnishing and even the building stone itself, perhaps their greater value lay in their ability to be transformed into new domestic dwellings, and at a fraction of the cost of building from new.[90]

Even before the first Act of Suppression had been passed, men with connections to the king or influential courtiers were lining up to request particular monastic properties. The suppression agent Sir Thomas Wriothesley, for example, began stockpiling stone with which to convert Titchfield Abbey in Hampshire to a house even before it had been officially dissolved and granted to him.[91]

Willmott describes the 'provincial gentry' as the biggest beneficiaries of the Dissolution. Their acquisition of a large proportion of monastic lands meant that on a local level there was less disruption than a more top-down view of the Dissolution might suggest. These men, Willmott continues,

> would have had extensive dealings with the monasteries, and in many cases were leasing manors, granges and tenements from them before the Dissolution. More often than not, the local gentry had been patrons of their local abbey or priory, and many of their dead would have been buried within their precincts, so it was perhaps understandable that they wanted to acquire the sites of the houses too.[92]

Most purchasers, in other words, had ties to the site they acquired, or at the very least were already a local landed proprietor; they were almost never parvenu carpetbaggers looking to set themselves up as grandees in an unfamiliar place.[93] Plotting the monastic sites that were converted to country houses on a map confirms this picture. The distribution conforms to existing patterns of settlement, with a denser concentration in the middle of the country and a thinning out on the northern, eastern and western peripheries. The map shows that the Dissolution did not lead to the building of country houses in new parts of England as

Religious foundations converted to country houses, 1530–1700.

monastic land became available, but rather increased their concentration in places where they were already fairly thick on the ground. There were, however, exceptions in which men sought to confirm their rise from urban trade to the gentry by acquiring a former monastic site. One example was Sir Thomas Leigh, a wealthy mercer from London who bought Stoneleigh Abbey in Warwickshire in 1561 and transformed it into an impressive residence.[94]

It might be argued that the concentration of country houses converted from monasteries simply reflects the location of monasteries prior to the Dissolution. This is not entirely true, however. There are notable gaps on the map in regions where there was a fairly dense concentration of monasteries, in particular in Norfolk, the far Southwest and the North.[95] In Norfolk, the paucity of conversions was due to the dominance of one landed magnate, Thomas Howard, 3rd Duke of Norfolk, who received the bulk of the grants. This was possibly because Norfolk, who remained loyal to the Catholic faith, was trying to protect the religious foundations, but he also may have been trying to expand his landholdings from his base of strength in the southern part of the county and along the north coast into the central and western zones, where he concentrated his acquisitions. The Crown was willing to support this agenda because it reduced the potential for aristocratic conflict in East Anglia by preventing rivals such as the Duke of Suffolk from challenging Norfolk's hold in the region.[96]

In the far Southwest, Henry VIII decided that the best option for disposing of the former monastic sites was to add them to the Duchy of Cornwall, which was held by his young son Edward, Prince of Wales. He therefore orchestrated an exchange of the Duchy's valuable manor of Wallingford in Oxfordshire for six manors once owned by Tywardreth Priory and seven once owned by Launceston Priory.[97] This was in addition to the lands confiscated from the 1st Marquess of Exeter that he had previously granted to the Duchy. In the North, the need to ensure that the potentially rebellious region remained under firm royal control meant that monastic property was granted to Henry VIII's most trusted subjects or to men whom he particularly wished to reward. In Yorkshire, for example, Fountains Abbey went to Sir Richard Gresham, Lord Mayor of London; Rievaulx Abbey to Thomas Manners, 1st Earl of Rutland, a close advisor to the king; Bolton Abbey to Henry Clifford, 1st Earl of Cumberland, who had remained loyal during the Pilgrimage of Grace; Byland Abbey to Sir William Pickering, Knight-Marshal to Henry VIII; and Jervaulx Abbey to Matthew Stuart, 4th Earl of Lennox, a leading Scottish nobleman who had supported the 'Rough Wooing', Henry VIII's attempt to marry his son Edward to Mary, Queen of Scots. St Mary's Abbey in York was simply dismantled. Only Easby Abbey was an exception: the 8th Baron Scrope was permitted to maintain his lease, despite the fact that his conduct during the Pilgrimage of Grace had been suspect; his rank was likely a factor in his being treated with such leniency. Yorkshire was therefore an exception to the acquisition of monastic property being dominated by local gentry. Instead, larger grants were made to a few high-ranking noblemen, in order to ensure that royal authority was secure.

The cost of transforming a monastic site to a residence could range from £500–600 to slap up some timber buildings to complement the existing abbot's lodging to many thousands for a more extensive reworking.[98] The simplest way to convert a monastic complex to a residence was to use the cloister, either the full quadrangle, which could serve as the basis for a house arranged around a courtyard, or the west range, where the abbot's lodging was usually found and which was relatively easy to convert to a comfortable secular dwelling.[99] Abbots' lodgings were increasingly luxurious in the early sixteenth century, in imitation of the most impressive secular houses. The lodgings at Fountains Abbey in Yorkshire, for example, featured a long gallery like those that were becoming fashionable in contemporary country houses.[100] In such conversions, the need to make use of the cloister walk, or the covered walkways that had ringed the interior of the cloister, contributed to the fashion for loggias and colonnades in the late sixteenth and early seventeenth centuries.[101] Not every owner took this approach, however. Another strategy was to use the monastic gatehouse, often a very large and grand structure, as the core of a new residence. This approach was taken at Beaulieu Abbey in Hampshire; Bottesford Preceptory in Lincolnshire; Cerne Abbey in Dorset; Hinton Priory in Somerset; Leicester Abbey in Leicestershire; and Wombridge Priory in Shropshire.

As the most visible reminder of the site's former purpose, the church was often targeted for rapid demolition. A frequent condition for the lease or sale of monastic buildings was that the new owner had to destroy the church and other important buildings in order to eliminate any possibility of it returning to religious use.[102] In a few cases, however, the church escaped this fate and was used as the basis for a substantial house. In 1537 the aforementioned Titchfield Abbey was one of the first monastic sites to be converted to a country house. Seeking a quick and easy solution, Sir Thomas Wriothesley refashioned the south front of the nave into a new gatehouse and entrance range.[103]

Buckland Abbey in Devon was sold in 1541 to Sir Richard Grenville the Elder. Over the next thirty years, three generations of Grenvilles continued to develop the house, using the church as the core of its structure. Formed from the crossing in the church's nave, the Great Hall stands atop the graves of the monks who were buried there.[104] The arch which led from the crossing to the south transept of the church, which the Grenvilles demolished so that a window could be inserted to bring more light into the hall, remains visible on the south front of the house today, and the crossing's four arches can still be seen on the top floor.[105] At Launde Abbey in Leicestershire, where Thomas Cromwell built a manor house for himself, part of the church was incorporated into the new chapel.[106] At Mottisfont in Hampshire, Sir William Sandys converted the nave, tower and south transept of the abbey church into the central block of his new house.[107] Using partitions and floors, Sir William Paulet divided the interior of the church at Netley Abbey in Hampshire

The east side of Buckland Abbey, Devon, which was converted to a residence after it was sold to Sir Richard Grenville in 1541. Unusually, the church rather than the cloister was used as the basis for the house; the arch which led from the crossing to the south transept is clearly visible in this image of the south front.

and inserted new windows and doors in order to transform it into a residence. When Sir John Byron converted Newstead Abbey in Nottinghamshire into a house in 1539, he demolished the nave but retained the facade of the church as a decorative feature adjacent to the house. It is unclear why Byron made such an unusual choice, but it may have been because he secretly retained his adherence to the Catholic faith despite his outward support for the Reformation. (Or perhaps he merely wanted to buttress the western side of the house.) Archaeological excavations in the 1950s revealed that Audley End in Essex, despite having been rebuilt in the early seventeenth century, still incorporated not only the western and southern cloister ranges but part of the church as well. The new house built by Richard Lee on the site of Sopwell Priory in Hertfordshire used the foundations and possibly some standing elements of the church.[108] Wilton House in Wiltshire, although converted to an Inigo Jones-style Palladian house in the 1630s, used the existing medieval alignments and stonework from Wilton Abbey for its walls. Monastic-era walling probably survives underneath the new fabric to at least the first-floor level, and archaeological investigations between 1988 and 1991 uncovered monastic carved doorways from the abbey's cloister.[109]

Some of these conversions took place decades and even centuries after the Reformation, demonstrating the lasting impact of the Dissolution on the country-house landscape. In the first decade of the seventeenth century, Blanchland Abbey in Northumberland was converted by the Forster family into a house, part of which survives today as a wing of the Lord Crewe Arms. Sir Thomas Pope, Treasurer of Henry VIII's Court of Augmentations and founder of Trinity College, Oxford, did not build a house on the site of Wroxton Abbey in Oxfordshire; instead his nephew William Pope did in 1618 after he inherited the house. Attorney-General during most of the Interregnum, Sir Edmund Prideaux purchased Forde Abbey in Dorset in 1649 and converted it to a residence. Pipewall Hall in Northamptonshire was built in 1675 with stone from the ruins of Pipewell Abbey.[110] The last country house to be converted from a monastic site was Thame Abbey in Oxfordshire. Acquired in 1547 by Sir John Williams, it later passed through marriage into the hands of the Wenman family. The ruins were used as simple farm buildings until the 1740s, when they were incorporated into an impressive Palladian house, possibly designed by William Smith of Warwick.[111]

A less popular, because considerably more expensive, option, was to remove stone and other materials from former religious sites and use them to build or remodel a house elsewhere. Thomas Cromwell converted the prior's lodging at Lewes Priory to an impressive house for his son Gregory, but the rest of the buildings, as we have seen, were demolished. They supplied stone for no fewer than five other nearby houses: Broyle Place, Clayhill House, Hangleton Manor, Kingston Manor and Southover Grange.[112] Sir Christopher Alleyne acquired Church Gresley Priory in 1556 and used the stone to build Gresley Hall. Fulke Greville removed stone from Alcester Abbey in Warwickshire and used it to rebuild Beauchamp Court, located less than a mile to the north. In the 1570s Edmund Brydges, 2nd Baron Chandos, used Winchcombe Abbey in Gloucestershire to supply stone for his rebuilding of Sudeley Castle. Some of the stonework from Chirbury Abbey in Shropshire was incorporated into Chirbury Hall, and some from Polesworth Priory in Warwickshire into Polesworth Hall.[113] On the one hand, these examples show how, as Donald Woodward has described, 'the recycling of buildings and their constituent materials was commonplace in pre-industrial society.'[114] But on the other, they show that the cost of demolition and the transport of recycled stone over any significant distance was prohibitive to all but the wealthiest builders: only 32 of the monastic sites which were converted to country houses adopted this approach.[115] All of them were located very near the monastic site which provided the materials, as it was immensely costly to transport stone. Only rarely was it moved more than a mile. Built as a hunting lodge for Sir Nicholas Poyntz, Newark Park in Gloucestershire used stone from Kingswood Abbey, which was about three miles to the west. It was also around three miles from Taunton Priory in Somerset to Poundisford Park, where after 1546 the merchant William Hill built a new house using its stone. Sir Edward Baynton transported the stone from Stanley Abbey in Wiltshire about six miles to his manor house at Bromham, and in the 1560s Sir William More brought stone about eight miles from Waverley Abbey near Farnham in Surrey to Loseley Park near Guildford.[116] Even the monarchy could not afford to move stone very far. In 1538, more than 3,000 tonnes of stone was transported three miles from Merton Abbey in Surrey to build Nonsuch Palace, and the following year a significant amount of stone was taken seven miles from St Radegund's Abbey near Bradsole to build Sandgate Castle near Folkestone in Kent.[117] R. L. Dickinson argues that 'demolition was far more rapid and extensive' in the Southeast, because there 'good building stone was comparatively rare and the population comparatively large', whereas in the North and West 'the reverse conditions prevailed', and so there was less destruction there.[118] My findings do not, however, bear this out. Of the examples of the removal of stone which I have identified, only two are in the Southeast: the aforementioned Loseley Park and Tortington Place in Sussex, which Roger Gratwick built in the late sixteenth century using stone from Tortington Abbey.

The demolition of monastic ruins was dangerous. The walls were undermined by digging beneath them, and when the building was ready for demolition the wooden props which temporarily supported them were burned or the walls blown up with gunpowder. Several accounts record that workmen were killed when the masonry fell prematurely. Sir Edward Baynton demolished Stanley Abbey in Wiltshire in order to provide materials for his new house at Bromham, but the attempt to undermine the transept of the church was halted when a sudden collapse crushed one of the workmen.[119] Binham Priory in Norfolk was granted to Sir Thomas Paston, who used some of the stone to build a new house

Shown here in a drawing by John Thirtle from the early 19th century, Binham Priory in Norfolk was given to the local magnate Sir Thomas Paston at the Dissolution. Paston used some of the stone to build a house at Wells. But when his grandson Edward attempted to demolish more of the buildings in order to build a new house on the site, a workman was killed by collapsing masonry. Edward Paston deemed this a bad omen and called a halt to the works. Sometime later, the seven western bays of the nave were converted to a parish church, which remains in use today.

in Wells, but when his grandson Edward attempted to demolish the remaining ruins in order to build a house on the site, a workman was killed by collapsing masonry and the project was abandoned.[120]

The continuing conversion of monastic sites into country houses gives some indication of the power of their physical presence even two centuries after the Reformation. Many country houses built long afterwards had features which revealed their origins as monastic buildings. Syon Abbey, now in west London, was converted to a country house for Edward Seymour, Duke of Somerset, between 1547 and 1552. It was then substantially remodelled by Robert Adam in the 1760s, but the basic form of the house continued to be determined by the configuration of the monastic buildings.[121]

We are left, then, with a complex picture of the impact of the Dissolution upon the built environment of England. On the one hand, it was immensely destructive, as the reformers carried out an 'all-consuming campaign against idolatry' which sought 'to eradicate telltale reminders of the Catholic past embedded in the rural and urban world'. In this campaign, 'the landscape itself came to be regarded as a repository of error and falsehood, an arena filled with sources of fatal infection to the souls of the faithful and dangerous provocations to divine wrath.'[122] In this frenzy of destruction, religious foundations – the most visible components of England's Catholic landscape – were swept away, but they remained as major physical features in the landscape. Clark continues:

> If they were of no other significance to their Tudor neighbours, the religious houses held some meaning as features of their landscape. They were never only scenery; for many they were the very substance of their own home. The houses of religion were the oldest of all in many places and to those living among them their physical presence defined the locality as much as any natural feature.[123]

Their presence went far beyond their religious role as places of worship. They served as waymarkers, navigational aids and lodgings for travellers; their orders provided much local infrastructure, by building bridges and roads and by managing fields, forests and waterways. It is not an exaggeration to say, as Clark does, that they 'moulded the landscape': in the countryside, they owned a large portion of the agricultural land and defined the boundaries between fields with walls, ditches and hedges, while in towns 'the house itself defined the scale and scope of the living space around it. The outline of the town and the profile of its buildings were drawn in response to the development of the conventual buildings and the precinct boundary.'[124] With their splendid materials and decoration, monastic buildings were sources of admiration and wonder which were filled with relics and treasures that drew both the faithful and the merely curious. In times of crisis they served as talismans which were believed to have the power to ward off evil and smite enemies. Their bells could be heard for miles and served as the official markers of time. And for elite families, religious houses loomed even larger, as they were repositories of patronage, sites of residence for younger sons and daughters sent into holy orders and, at life's end, places of interment.

Some of these roles changed with the Dissolution, but others did not. Very few sites were cleared quickly or completely; most were engaged in a lengthy process of transformation in which their physical shape altered only gradually:

> The Henrician regime succeeded in emptying the religious houses but not effacing them. When the old king died in January 1547, he left a monastic and mendicant landscape which in its principal features was for the most part unaltered from the scene that he had stepped into thirty-eight years before. This is not to claim that certain buildings had not been taken down. But they were the smallest fraction of the whole, and in most of the centres of population, the essential ensemble, the placement of conventual buildings within a wider residential, commercial and industrial setting was little changed. In outline they still appeared as the cornerstones of their neighbourhood just as they were known before the royal supremacy... Reassimilation and recycling unfolded so slowly that it was surely imperceptible to the passer-by. The abiding impression would not have been of savage ruin but strange abandonment.[125]

As they continued to stand empty or were converted to other purposes, and as English history continued to evolve around them, they acquired new cultural meanings. But the secularization of monastic sites did not entirely eradicate the memory of their former religious function. To be sure, English reformers often behaved in very iconoclastic, and therefore physically destructive, ways as they sought to strip monastic sites of all religious meaning. But the destructive impact of the Reformation was not always as thorough or aggressive as is often assumed. Sarah Tarlow writes:

> The traditional view of Reformation iconoclasm was that at the Reformation, a popular anti-Catholicism manifested itself in passionate iconoclastic destruction or mutilation of those artefactual and architectural objects which bore signs of 'Popish' idolatry... In fact, iconoclasm associated with the Reformations in Britain was mostly premeditated, highly directed and usually carried out coolly by people in positions of authority... Moreover, the extent and nature of Reformation iconoclasm has recently

been reassessed. Iconoclasm was neither so complete nor so extensive as had been previously suggested.[126]

Although some physical remnants of the pre-Reformation religious world were destroyed, others were converted to secular uses. This was particularly true of buildings, which were expensive and dangerous to destroy, and in demand for new purposes.

Secularization, however, did not mean that all of the previous meaning was stripped out of the building or its fragments. Most obviously, many monastic sites were converted to parish churches or even cathedrals and so maintained their religious function.[127] But what of the sites which were converted to secular use? People would have remembered their former purpose, and for some they would have retained their sanctity. David Stocker and Paul Everson distinguish between the 'functional' and 'iconic' reuse of architectural materials; the former is merely practical but the latter has a symbolic meaning which relates to its history.[128] In the contested context of Reformation England, however, that distinction was often blurred. Reformers could claim that physical structures were not inherently sanctified, but this did not mean that everyone, Protestant or Catholic, accepted that argument. Tarlow writes that 'rather than a wholesale acceptance or rejection of the Reformers' agenda, individuals and communities transformed and appropriated the Catholic past within the constraints and structures of the post-Reformation church to construct their own spiritual way of being.'[129]

Most owners of country houses that had been converted from monastic buildings treated the surviving structures merely as potential components of their plans for new residences and built new facades which concealed their former purpose. In this sense, Harriet Lyon writes, they 'became sites of forgetting the monastic past': 'By altering, adapting and appropriating monastic structures, the English gentry created not bleak reminders of what had been lost during the suppression, but powerful symbols of what had been gained.'[130] Lyon describes how contemporary antiquaries were complicit in these efforts to erase the previous histories of these houses, 'as a means of minimising the magnitude of the rupture engendered by the Dissolution'.[131]

These attempts at erasure, however, could not entirely conceal the massive impact of the Reformation on English country houses. Houses served as the primary refuges for the Catholic priests who returned to England after 1580 in contravention of Elizabethan law. Hiding places, or 'priest holes', were constructed in hundreds of houses. This meant that they became the sites of some of the most violent episodes of the English Reformation, as priests were hunted down, forcibly removed and subjected to grisly forms of torture and execution. Country houses were also the targets of religious rebellions, both by the rebels themselves and by Tudor governments looking to exact vengeance on disloyal subjects. A number suffered physical damage or were stripped away from their owners as a punishment for their participation in an uprising. In the late 1530s the Dissolution of the Monasteries saw the transfer of a massive amount of religious property into private hands, and the conversion of many monastic sites into country houses. This process was undeniably immensely destructive. It was also a uniquely English, or at least English and Welsh, manifestation of the iconoclasm of the Reformation; there was no equivalent to the Dissolution in Scotland or Ireland. Maurice Howard writes:

> The political decisions that swept away centuries of monasticism in a few short years have been portrayed as a swift and violent change the like of which is unparalleled in English history and a form of imposed governmental tyranny. Although violence also attended reform movements across northern continental Europe, the particular progress of the Dissolution in England is not really like that of any other reformed country, including that of the nearest kingdom, Scotland.[132]

The change was less abrupt than is often assumed, however. If the suppression of the monasteries was 'swift and brutal', the 'despoliation of the built heritage of the Church did not happen all at once'.[133] There was never any official governmental programme to destroy the sites entirely; rather, 'it was widely expected for the physical monastic fabric to continue in some form once the buildings had been sufficiently decommisioned, thus making the re-gathering of their religious communities impossible.'[134] Local and individual circumstances, not top-down policies, dictated the fate of most monastic sites, and this meant that they would be put to alternative uses. Only a handful suffered serious destruction at the hands of zealous reformers; some were quickly converted to gentlemen's residences, while others were used for civic purposes or languished for decades or even centuries as they were gradually pillaged for stone and other building materials. On the one hand, these conversions were a means of eradicating the religious associations of the sites, and thus conformed to the reformist agenda. But on the other, they did not totally destroy the site, but usually preserved some buildings. As we have seen, the decisions as to which buildings to preserve and which to destroy could be made merely for reasons of cost and efficiency, but they could also send a particular message about the new owner's opinion of the Reformation. Some owners, for example, chose to destroy the church as the most visible reminder of the pre-Reformation world, but a few, such as Sir John Byron at Newstead, may have deliberately preserved it as an indication of their continuing loyalty to the Catholic faith. And whatever Byron's intent, observers may have interpreted it differently; a devout Protestant might have seen the facade standing alone without the rest of the building as a symbol of the destruction, rather than the survival, of Catholicism.

Monastic-sites-turned-country-houses thus remained as repositories of memory of the Reformation. To be sure, the authorities and other defenders of the Reformation in the late sixteenth century and the seventeenth desired them to be seen as 'the continuation of the legacy of the government's wider campaign against monasticism and the most visible and tangible symbols of its triumph over Catholic error and corruption. For those who sought to perpetuate the Henrician vision of the Dissolution, ruins functioned as sites of memory for admonition of posterity.'[135] But there was no way to ensure that everyone would see them in such a light; rather, they were interpreted in a variety of ways according to individual beliefs and attitudes. Walsham writes:

> The reformation of the landscape was double-edged . . . If defaced monasteries, shrines, chapels, wells and other topographical landmarks had the potential to become places of near veneration by the hotter sorts of Protestants, they also served to stir up intense feelings of regret and embarrassment in those who saw them as testimonies to puritan excess and sectarian sacrilege. In turn these emotions fostered an impulse to reconsecrate spaces polluted by profane use. At the same time they provided a powerful focus for the continuing resistance of the Catholic community to the efforts of the Tudor and Stuart Church and State to drive it into total extinction. The very sites that were the victims of reformed rites of violence were therefore imbued with renewed spiritual potency.[136]

This tension was exacerbated during the Civil War, when puritan iconoclasm reached its apex of intensity.[137] It would unleash a cascade of violent acts towards people and property which were motivated by political disagreement, as the next chapter will describe.

2

Violence and the Country House, II: *The Civil War*

Sandwiched between Chesil Beach and the Ridgeway Hills, Abbotsbury is one of the most attractive villages in Dorset. Its present-day beauty, however, stands in stark contrast to its history of violent upheaval. The village takes its name from the Benedictine monastery that was founded there in the eleventh century. It was dissolved in 1539 and leased to Sir Giles Strangeways, whose family had owned Melbury House, about fifteen miles to the north, since 1500. Strangeways converted part of the remains of the abbey to a residence, while some of the other buildings were dismantled. The stone was recycled into houses all over the village, including nearby Abbey House, which dates from the seventeenth century.

So far the story of Abbotsbury Abbey is one that occurred all over England in the decades after the Reformation, as dissolved monasteries were converted to houses by the local gentry. Abbotsbury's buildings, however, were to suffer another phase of destruction more than a century after they were first converted to secular use. At the time of the Civil War, Abbotsbury Abbey was owned by the ardent Royalist Sir John Strangeways. When in April 1643 a troop of Parliamentary soldiers demanded to occupy the house, Sir John's wife Grace refused, and so they forced their way in and plundered it. When they found hidden arms, they retaliated by inflicting £200 worth of damage and demanding that Grace Strangeways pay another £500 in ten days' time or the troops would 'take all away from the house and land'.[1] The following year Sir Anthony Ashley Cooper, a former Royalist who had recently switched sides and was now in command of Parliamentary forces in Dorset, marched from Dorchester with the intention of dislodging the Royalists from Abbotsbury once and for all. Thirteen men from the garrison, which was commanded by Sir John's son James, took refuge in the church but were quickly taken prisoner after what Ashley Cooper in his report called a 'hot bickering'. He then described what happened next:

> The business was extreme hot for above six hours; we were forced to burn down an outgate to a court before we could get to the house, and then our men rushed in through the fire and got into the hall porch, where with furse fagots they set fire on it, and plied the windows so hard with small shot that the enemy durst not appear in the low rooms: in the meantime one of our guns played on the other side of the house, and the gunners with fire balls and granadoes with scaling ladders endeavoured to fire the second story, but, that not taking effect, our soldiers were forced to wrench open the windows with iron bars, and, pouring in fagots of furse fired, set the whole house in a naming fire, so that it was not possible to be quenched, and then they cried for quarter; but we having bet [*sic*] divers men before it,

The village of Abbotsbury in south Dorset. The church in the centre of the image was the scene of a violent struggle during the Civil War, when Parliamentary forces attacked the Royalist defenders of Sir John Strangeways's nearby manor house. Bullet holes are still visible in the woodwork of the church's pulpit, and the house, which stood to the right of the church, was destroyed.

and considering how many garrisons of the same nature we were to deal with, I gave command there should be none given, but they should be kept into the house, that they and their garrison might fall together.

Although Ashley Cooper intended to allow the Royalists to burn to death, in retaliation for losing fifteen men in the assault, Colonel William Sydenham, who was fighting on the other side of the house, granted them quarter. As the prisoners were being escorted out, Cooper's men rushed in to plunder. Seeing that the flames were nearing the Royalists' powder store, their commanders tried to call them back, to no avail. The powder exploded with such force that it blew 'four score [Royalist prisoners] that were in the court a yard from the ground', but only two were seriously injured. Cooper's own men were not so lucky: 'We had hurt and killed by the enemy not fifteen, but I fear four times that number will not satisfy for the last mischance.' Abbey House, reported Ashley Cooper, 'is burnt down to the ground, and could not be saved'.[2]

Political and Religious Violence in Seventeenth-Century England

This violent incident shows how, after 1600, the religious divisions spawned by the Reformation combined with a fierce political argument over legislative and executive sovereignty, with a continuing impact on country houses. Abbotsbury was not the only English country house to experience the upheaval of both the Reformation and the Civil War. At least five other houses which had been converted from monastic sites were also damaged or destroyed in the strife of the seventeenth century: Godstow House in Oxfordshire; Leicester Abbey in Leicestershire; Lilleshall Abbey in Shropshire; St John's Abbey (Colchester) and St Osyth's Abbey in Essex.

These houses provide evidence that the seventeenth century was 'the most violent century of English history'.[3] An estimated 200,000 people died in the Civil War, or around 3.8 per cent of the English population at the time, significantly larger than the percentage who died in the First World War (1.7 per cent) or Second World War (1 per cent).[4] And as Abbotsbury demonstrates, this bloodshed was accompanied by massive damage to private property, as each side sought to deny its opponents the use of defensible structures and to exact revenge upon its enemies.

Some of this strife resulted from the ongoing conflict over religion. Recent studies of the English Reformation have emphasized its protracted character, arguing that it extended well beyond Henry VIII's reforms and even Elizabeth I's attempts to resolve the religious conflict that her father had unleashed. Peter Marshall observes:

> 'The Reformation' was once widely regarded as a historical event, initiated in Henry VIII's reign and essentially concluded within the space of three decades. But only a political and statutory Reformation can be considered in any way complete by the early part of Elizabeth I's reign, and then only with the benefit of hindsight.[5]

Some interpretations have stretched their chronological framework into the eighteenth and even the nineteenth centuries.[6] In this context, the exact moment when a quasi-permanent religious settlement was achieved in England is not directly relevant. What does matter, however, is, as Marshall continues, that the 'strict and artificial division of labor between historians studying the outcomes of sixteenth-century religious change and those looking into the origins of the civil and religious strife of the mid-seventeenth century has been pretty thoroughly eroded'.[7] In other words, 'civil and religious strife', and the violence that accompanied it, continued in England well into the seventeenth century, into the era of the Civil War and beyond. And given that the participants were often from the landed classes, it is not surprising that English country houses continued to reflect this in various ways.

In 1603 several prominent courtiers led a plot to replace James I with Arabella Stuart. The chief conspirator in the 'Main Plot', Henry Brooke, 11th Baron Cobham, was attainted and sentenced to death, but he was reprieved on the scaffold at Winchester and imprisoned in the Tower of London. His wife Frances was allowed to continue living at Cobham Hall in Kent until her death in 1628, although in 1613 James I granted the estate to Ludovick Stuart, 2nd Duke of Lennox.[8] Sir Walter Ralegh, another participant in the plot, was also imprisoned in the Tower and stripped of Sherborne Castle in Dorset, which was first given to James I's favourite Sir Robert Carr and then in 1617 sold to John Digby, 1st Earl of Bristol.[9]

An associated, or 'Bye', plot attempted to kidnap James and the Privy Council in order to force them to show greater tolerance towards Catholics. These conspirators were also punished by the loss of their landed property. Sir Griffin Markham was, like Cobham, reprieved at Winchester, but he was exiled to the Continent and his estates in Nottinghamshire, Essex and Cambridgeshire were granted to Sir John Harington. Bartholomew Brooksby forfeited his property in London and Leicestershire as well as the manor of Shillingstone manor in Dorset, but he was permitted to nominate Catholic friends as recipients of the grants and was subsequently pardoned. None of the conspirators in the 'Main' or 'Bye' plots of 1603 was executed; Mark Nicholls interprets this leniency as an indication that 'the balancing of mercy and justice remained an arbitrary process' in early Stuart England, but it is consistent with what occurred following the suppression of the Tudor plots discussed in the previous chapter.[10] James I, like Elizabeth before him, preferred to profit from – in wealth and patronage – the assets of conspirators against him rather than execute them.

Although the Gunpowder Plot of 1605 was a more dangerous affair and its main conspirators would be shown no such mercy, it too had a significant impact on property. The Gunpowder plotters operated from a network of country houses in the Midlands. On 3 November, two days before the attempt to blow up the Houses of Parliament, several conspirators spent the day at Grafton Manor in Worcestershire. One of them, Robert Wintour, was married to the daughter of Grafton's owner John Talbot, a prominent recusant. Although Wintour swore that Talbot had been ignorant of the plot, he was interrogated and Grafton was searched for incriminating documents. Nothing was found, but the furnishings were confiscated and sold. It took Talbot three years to recover their monetary value in compensation.[11]

One of the most fascinating stories of a house caught up in the Gunpowder Plot concerns Chastleton House in Oxfordshire. Chastleton was owned by Robert Catesby, who was from a prominent Catholic family and who ardently wished to see a Catholic monarch on the throne. After being wounded in the Earl of Essex's failed rebellion in 1601, he was imprisoned and fined 4,000 marks, or around £2,600. This hefty penalty was probably why he sold Chastleton to the wool merchant Walter Jones the following year. Jones, however, permitted Catesby to continue living at Chastleton, presumably allowing him an opportunity to repurchase the house. Instead, Catesby, a wild but undeniably charismatic character, became one of the leaders of the Gunpowder Plot and was killed while attempting to flee. Jones then decided to pull down Chastleton and build a new residence; the square stone house, possibly designed by Robert Smythson, which stands there today therefore would not exist without Catesby's plotting.[12]

Coughton Court in Warwickshire was connected to the Gunpowder Plot in several ways. Its owner Thomas Throckmorton was uncle to two conspirators, Catesby and Francis Tresham, and several others were relatives as well. At Catesby's behest, Sir Everard Digby rented Coughton in October 1605; he was supposed to use the house as his base of operations for organizing a 'hunting party' whose mission was to kidnap Princess Elizabeth, the daughter of King James I. Digby never arrived at Coughton, although his wife Margaret did. After Guy Fawkes was arrested in London, Catesby dispatched his servant Thomas Bates to warn her and the other conspirators gathered at the house after learning of the plot's failure. This group included the Jesuit superior Father Henry Garnet, the priest-hole builder Nicholas Owen, the Vaux sisters from Baddesley Clinton and several Jesuit priests.[13] The previous chapter described the fate of Garnet and Owen, who fled to Hindlip Hall in Worcestershire, where they were caught before being tortured and executed. Anne Vaux was also arrested after she was caught sending messages written in invisible ink to Garnet while he was imprisoned in the Tower,

Chastleton House, Oxfordshire, was caught up in the Gunpowder Plot. After its previous owner, the plot's leader Robert Catesby, was killed while attempting to evade arrest, Walter Jones built the new house seen here, starting in 1607.

but she was released. Other conspirators fled first to the Wintour family's Huddington Court in Worcestershire and then to Holbeche House in Staffordshire, which was owned by Stephen Lyttleton, who was sympathetic to their cause even though he probably had no prior knowledge of the plot. At Holbeche, several men were injured when a store of gunpowder exploded as they were attempting to dry it. The next morning, the High Sheriff of Worcester surrounded the house with two hundred men. Several conspirators, including Catesby, were killed, while the rest, including Robert Wintour's brother Thomas, were captured. Other houses which had links to conspirators in the Gunpowder Plot and were the scenes of searches and arrests after its failure included Kenilworth Castle, Clopton House and Bushwood Hall in Warwickshire and Harrowden Hall in Northamptonshire.

The Civil War

In the seventeenth century country houses thus continued to serve as meeting places for plotters against the Crown and occasionally as the sites of violent efforts to suppress the plots they hatched. The impact of these episodes paled in comparison, however, to that of the English Civil War. Large landowners found it very difficult to remain neutral; at the very least they were forced to contribute funds and men to one side or the other.[14] Most directly, the Civil War resulted in enormous physical destruction, either by damage incurred through sieges and battles or by the deliberate 'slighting' of buildings in order to render them unfit to be used for military purposes.[15] The war also affected the owners of landed property financially. Many Royalists had to pay substantial fines to recover their estates from confiscation and sequestration by Parliamentary forces, and they also lost the income from their property while it was sequestered. Rents fell as agricultural production was disrupted by the war, and taxes were increased to pay for keeping armies in the field. Another effect of the war was that many houses were neglected, as some landowners decided not to build or rebuild while the war continued.

When considering the damage to property during the Civil War, historians and archaeologists debate whether it resulted from religious, political or military motives. Certainly, a substantial amount of the religious iconoclasm of the mid-seventeenth century targeted buildings. Architectural iconoclasm had been a feature of the puritanical strain of English Protestant reformism from the outset.[16] The recent historiography examining the issue of iconoclasm in the English Civil War has emphasized its religious inspiration, despite attempts by its contemporary critics to depict it as carried out by marauding troops, vandals or other elements from outside the local community.[17] Much of this iconoclasm was sparked by Archbishop William Laud's campaign in the 1630s to restore church buildings to a pre-Reformation level of splendour and to place altars, communion tables and other furnishings in a way that seemed to mark a return to Catholic forms of ritual and hierarchy.

In other cases, however, the motivations for attacks on religious buildings were more complicated. Eccleshall Castle in Staffordshire was the palace of the Bishop of Lichfield and Coventry. In 1642 the bishop was Robert Wright, an anti-puritan with a reputation for corruption and self-aggrandizement. In early 1643 Charles I ordered the castle to be garrisoned, but its light fortifications proved no match for the Parliamentary forces who besieged it in October. The garrison surrendered after two months, and Eccleshall remained in Parliamentarian hands until it was slighted in 1647. Today only a single tower and some fragmentary ruins survive. It is tempting to conclude that the castle's destruction was due to Wright's religious views and personal unpopularity. Rachel Askew, however, argues that the archaeological evidence suggests that it was instead the result of an attempt by Sir William Brereton, an unpopular Parliamentary commander of puritanical leanings, to seize the castle for his own use after the siege had ended. Askew concludes that 'iconoclasm was not a simple phenomenon; the term itself masks a highly complex social discourse that, whilst being influenced by religion, could also be affected by other political and social factors.'[18]

So far, this discussion of the impact of the Civil War has focused exclusively on religious buildings, but what of their secular counterparts? Most of the fighting took place not in major set-piece battles, but in smaller local encounters. David Appleby observes:

> Most of the fatalities occurred not in momentous battles, but as a consequence of localized low-intensity warfare. Rival garrisons competed for local resources, mounting raids to plunder, disrupt and demoralize communities in enemy-held territory. Regional commanders routinely pooled resources to facilitate larger operations against obscure locations which the flow of war had momentarily imbued with strategic significance.[19]

This meant that buildings, including castles and country houses, frequently became temporary battle zones. Ronald Hutton and Wylie Reeves write that 'the characteristic military action' of the Civil War was 'an attack upon a fortified strongpoint'. These strongpoints could be towns, which offered goods and services to sustain garrisons, but they could also be castles and fortified houses, which were important for securing rural areas. This meant that the Civil War 'produced an unusual multiplication in the number of garrisons', in order to prevent local uprisings and to protect against sudden raids and 'flying columns which might occupy otherwise undefended centres of communication'. As a result:

> Successful field armies rarely cleared blocs of territory completely; usually they left isolated enemy strongpoints which were intended to be mopped up by local forces, or else planted garrisons themselves and then retired ... Most parts of England, Wales and even Ireland became chessboard patterns of rival fortresses, the larger of which developed networks of garrisons to hem in local enemies and starve them of supplies. After 1645 Parliament consciously wrecked or demolished most castles or houses which it took from enemy forces, to reduce the number of potential strongholds to a few key fortresses which it could easily control.[20]

In other words, both armies, but particularly Parliament's as the size of the area under its control increased, faced the problem of needing to hold down territory by garrisoning fortified sites, which limited its ability to wage offensive campaigns. It is therefore unsurprising that military leaders tried to reduce the number of garrisons by destroying potential strongpoints. Greenlands House in Buckinghamshire, for example, was levelled because its position beside the Thames allowed a garrison to intercept barges carrying supplies to London. Stapleton Castle, an Elizabethan manor house built inside a twelfth-century keep, was destroyed because it occupied a commanding position over the Lugg Valley in Herefordshire. In order to prevent it from being occupied by the Parliamentarians, the Royalist defenders demolished Godstow House when the defensive ring around Oxford was reduced in 1645.[21]

There were generally accepted rules of war in seventeenth-century England that defined appropriate conduct by soldiers regarding their treatment of enemy combatants and their property. Barbara Donagan writes:

> Rules of surrender were, of necessity, an intrinsic part of a soldier's education. They applied to individuals in the field and to defended places, whether castles, houses, churches, or towns. In the field, the life of a soldier who laid down his arms was presumed to be safe. In sieges, there was a crucial distinction between storm and surrender. If the besiegers were forced to storm, then anything short of rape or mutilation was permissible. If surrender had been negotiated, however, its terms should be binding.[22]

These codes of conduct applied to property as well. An order issued in 1642, for example, prohibited soldiers from burning buildings unless by direct command of their commanding officer.[23]

Such rules were often strictly adhered to. In January 1643 Parliament issued an order to search Hengrave Hall in Suffolk, which was owned by Mary Kytson, a Catholic who obeyed the law by practising occasional conformity. Her daughter Penelope, however, was the widow of Sir John Gage, a prominent Sussex recusant, and therefore she was a target of Parliamentary attention. Mary Kytson had settled Hengrave on Penelope's son Edward, which explains why Penelope was living there when around 35 men arrived and confiscated the contents of the armoury. Penelope reported that 'they made great apologies to me at theyr coming inne, saying they hoped I would pardon theyr unwilling employment, and that they wer forced to what they did.' The officers promised to write a letter to Mary Kytson apologizing for confiscating her property and assuring her that it would be well-treated.[24] In 1644 a Royalist soldier was hanged for looting Lanhydrock House in Cornwall, as its owner Lord Robartes had been given protection despite being a supporter of Parliament.[25] After the Royalist Philip Stanhope, 1st Earl of Chesterfield, garrisoned his house at Bretby in Derbyshire, the local Parliamentary commander Sir John Gell sent four hundred men to capture it. When cannon-fire failed to breach the earthwork defences, the Parliamentarians launched a frontal assault that forced the Earl and his men to flee towards Lichfield. The attackers broke into the house; their commanding officer Major Johannes Molanus entreated the Countess to 'give everye soldier halfe a crowne, for to have her saved from plundering'. When she refused, Molanus lowered the price to forty marks, but 'shee made the same answer, that shee had not monyes.' Even when Molanus said that they would advance her credit, 'if shee would promise to repay it them', she 'still refractorily and willfully said, that she would not give them one penny'. Only then did the soldiers finally plunder the house, and despite the Countess's obstinacy 'the said officers saved her owne chamber, with all the good therein.'[26]

Soldiers did not always behave so chivalrously, however. In August 1642 Parliamentary troops did considerable damage to Sir Richard Minshull's house at Bourton in Buckinghamshire, in defiance of their officers:

> Brushing aside the attempts of their officers to prevent it, the troops drank the wine in the cellars, burned Minshull's papers, tore the lead off the roof, dug up the floors in search of buried valuables and set fire to the house. Outside they broke down fences, killed sheep, destroyed fish ponds and cut down woods: one was killed falling through the dovecot roof while trying to destroy Minshull's pigeons.[27]

In early 1643 Giffords Hall, Sir Francis Mannock's house in Suffolk, was 'pillaged of all goods, and as is said not his writings spared ... nor his dogs'.[28] In 1642 Parliamentary troops removed five wagon-loads of arms and armour – a motley collection of old, rusty swords and pikes – from Knole in Kent, the home of the Royalist Sackvilles. The officer in charge, Colonel Henry Sandys, then proceeded to ransack the house; according to the steward's account of 'the hurtes dones', they broke forty locks and ripped gold thread from embroidered upholstery and cushions. The following year the house was requisitioned by the Central Committee for Kent, forcing the family to sell off their most valuable paintings and furnishings.[29]

Some Parliamentarians were appalled by the indiscipline of their troops. 'We are the most abominable plunderers,' wrote Richard Goodwin, MP for Buckinghamshire, in October 1642. 'I am ashamed to look an honest man in the face.'[30] But the Royalists were guilty too. The property of the Royalist Jermyn family, Torksey Castle in Lincolnshire, was seized by Parliamentary forces in 1645. A Royalist contingent marched from Newark and retook the house; it was badly damaged as a result and never lived in again.[31] Appleby writes of how the Civil War became increasingly marked by atrocity:

Far from being a genteel civil war, the conflict in England was pockmarked by acts of barbarity. By 1645 these had become increasingly frequent, driven by factors such as fear, revenge, xenophobia and anti-Catholicism. Having undertaken many assaults around England during three years of conflict, soldiers on both sides had become used to vicious hand-to-hand fighting in claustrophobic surroundings.[32]

Sieges were particularly prone to atrocities, as the besieging force was often frustrated by the long delay in taking a particular objective and the casualties incurred in attempts to storm it. This frustration often resulted in vengeful acts not only against the besieged, but against the buildings which they had defended. The Parliamentarians' efforts to take Hillesden, Sir Alexander Denton's house in Buckinghamshire, illustrate how intense such encounters could be. In early 1644 Hillesden was garrisoned by the Royalists with around 150 men and five guns. A surprise attack was repulsed in February, but in March a force of around 2,000 men, commanded by Sir Samuel Luke and Oliver Cromwell, arrived to take the house. The defenders had been busy: five hundred workmen had been impressed from the surrounding area to demolish houses in the village, build a mound for five cannon which were sent from Oxford, and fill the stables and outbuildings with earth and dung so that they could serve as defences. Even so, Luke and Cromwell's force swiftly overran the positions. The thirty or so French or Walloon soldiers among the defenders were immediately slaughtered, the women stripped of most of their clothing and the house plundered. Denton's livestock and wine were taken away, and the following day the house was burnt to the ground. Denton estimated the cost of the damage at £16,000.[33]

Because of their defensive capabilities, the most frequent target of attacks were castles, hundreds of which were destroyed or seriously damaged.[34] Here, too, the motives for destruction reflected the intertwining of religion and politics in the conflict. Early in the war, most of the damage was a direct result of the fighting, but later it was more often a deliberate act carried out for defensive purposes. The standard explanation is that, as Parliamentary forces tired of the endless sieges required to defeat Royalist garrisons, castles were slighted in order to prevent them from being used for military purposes in the future.[35] Stephen Porter writes:

Numerous country houses and castles were garrisoned at one time or another during the war, controlling large areas of the countryside, but also tying down considerable numbers of troops. Such structures in potentially strategic positions, which were fortified or could be adapted for defence, but could not be held because of a shortage of soldiers, were, in many cases, destroyed or so badly damaged that they would not provide a base for the enemy.[36]

The only alternative to leaving behind hundreds of defensible structures which potentially could have been reoccupied by Royalist forces would have been to garrison every captured castle, which was simply not feasible.

Matthew Johnson, however, has argued that mid-seventeenth-century castle destruction should instead be seen as the result of the early modern English state's efforts to eradicate the 'private strongholds' of overmighty subjects and to favour 'the middling sort of people, and more broadly... new ideas of moral and political order'.[37] Johnson cites as evidence the fact that it was not always defensive fortifications that were destroyed, but the parts of the castle that were 'most visible' to ordinary people and therefore the 'most potent' symbols of lordship. At Kenilworth Castle in Warwickshire, for example, the north face of the donjon was slighted even though it had little military purpose.[38] Lila Rakoczy, however, challenges 'the fallacy of the apocryphal monolithic "local community" that rose up against a "hated symbol of oppression" and reclaimed building materials for "local" use'. She argues that merchants, financiers and contractors followed both armies around England in order to acquire profitable materials for resale:

> Quite clearly, outside influences helped instigate, shape and profit from the destruction, and even 'local' purchases were demonstrably limited to those with influence, means and connections. For too many in the local community, the reality of destruction probably consisted of losing a higher paying job to a more skilled outsider, and watching the more 'well affected' – current and former mayors, aldermen and military officers from far away – profit from the dangerous labour of others.[39]

As an example, the Parliamentary officer Adam Baynes developed a profitable business in acquiring confiscated property and demolishing it so that the materials could be reused. One of his acquisitions was Holdenby House in Northamptonshire, where Charles I had briefly been held as a prisoner in 1647. Baynes purchased Holdenby in 1651 on condition that he would demolish it; he preserved one wing as a residence and used the stone to build three other houses in Northampton.[40] But in other cases the motives underlying demolition were indeed local, with Sheffield Castle, as Askew writes, a prime example:

> The slighting of Sheffield Castle acted as a microcosm of relationships within the town and country, reflecting the complex relationship between Earl, Parliament and townspeople both rich and poor. In this it was not alone; in the aftermath of conflict, the same negotiation was being conducted throughout the countries affected by war. The fate of castles were part of that negotiation and, just as the circumstances within each town was unique, so too was their destruction.[41]

Although conflicting, these arguments all see the slighting of castles as having broader social and cultural contexts, motives and meanings than mere military necessity. This begins to help answer another question: why were fortified houses such as Hillesden slighted as well as castles? To answer that question, I have identified and mapped 146 houses that were damaged or destroyed during the Civil War. (See Appendix 3.) This representative sample is probably only a small proportion of the total: Christopher Clay estimates that there were thousands of houses which were damaged or at least pillaged, with between 150 and 200 of them totally destroyed.[42] Ninety-five of the houses on my list (65 per cent) were damaged or destroyed by the Parliamentary side; thirty-six by the Royalists (24 per cent); and seven unlucky houses by both sides. I was unable to determine which side was responsible for the damage to eight houses. The fact that Parliamentary forces were responsible for a significant majority of the damage reflects the course of the war, as the Royalists were gradually pushed back and forced to wage a more defensive campaign.

The map shows that the highest concentration of these houses stretch in a diagonal line from Shrewsbury in the northwest to Reading in the southeast. This distribution reflects the geography of the conflict, in which Parliament quickly established control over Eastern and Southeastern England, with Royalist support concentrated in the North and

Violence and the Country House, II: The Civil War

Houses destroyed or damaged in the Civil War.

West, leaving the West Midlands and western Thames Valley as contested territory. The line of damaged and destroyed houses follows closely the shifting boundary between the zones controlled by each side, since for much of the war the Royalists controlled Wales and the Southwest, while the area controlled by Parliament gradually expanded from east to west and from south to north. In other parts of the country, the damage was less predictable. In East Sussex, for example, 'the pattern of rural life was hardly affected', but West Sussex saw considerable damage to property due to the fighting which occurred at Chichester and Arundel.[43]

The location of so many of the houses in the contested zone suggests that they were caught up in the fighting that was taking place nearby, and so the damage that they suffered must be in some sense considered military. Some fortified houses were better defended than castles: the Earl of Derby's Lathom House in Lancashire featured stone walls 1.8 metres (6 ft) thick and nine towers, all behind a moat 7.3 metres (24 ft) wide and 1.8 metres (6 ft) deep. After the Parliamentarians' demi-cannon and mortars failed to breach the walls in 1644, they abandoned the siege. The house was finally taken the following year by a larger force, but the garrison had to be starved into submission. It was stripped of its most valuable contents and razed to the ground.[44]

Attacks on country houses could be very violent events. In June 1643 the 1st Duke of Newcastle advanced with the intention of engaging the Parliamentary forces at Bradford, but the garrison at Howley Hall was in his path. Newcastle wrote afterwards that he demanded its surrender, but the commander, Sir John Savile:

> returned an uncivil answer, and that he would keep it despite our forces, whereupon we planted our cannon against that house, and environed it upon Wednesday the 21st of June in the afternoon, and next morning took it by assault, and in it the said commander-in-chief and all his officers and soldiers, about 245, some few whereof were slain, the rest taken prisoner.

According to the Duchess of Newcastle, Savile only narrowly escaped with his life: he was captured by an officer who 'resolved then to kill him', but Newcastle 'would not suffer him to do it saying, it was inhuman to kill any man in cold blood'.[45] In July 1645 a skirmish between Royalist attackers and the Parliamentary garrison at Barton Hall in Derbyshire resulted in dozens of men being killed or wounded. A local doctor named George Blagrave submitted a bill for his services in tending to the injured Parliamentarians and Royalist prisoners; it listed injuries such as 'a thrust in the arm with a tuck and a shott in the back'; 'a very sore cut in the forepart of his head which caused a piece of his skull the breadth of a half a crowne peace to [be] taken forth'; 'a dangerous cut over the eye ... and a sore thrust through the arm'; and a 'thrust and cut in the arme a very dangerous wound'.[46]

Further evidence of the violence of the efforts to attack and defend country houses comes from the appeals for assistance from wounded soldiers during and after the war. In 1649 James Cawverd submitted this petition to the Quarter Sessions in Derby:

> About 5 years agoe yor peticioner beinge souldier under the command of Coll. Randle Ashenhurst in the p'liament's service beinge one of a p'tie by order appointed to keepe the hall at Shallcrose: Mr Shallcrosse himself entringe the house and a

strong p'tie with him cutt and wounded most of the souldiers found in the house. Amongst whom yor peticioner receaved such cutts and wounds: that ever since he hath lost the use of his arme and to his utter undoeinge.[47]

After Lord Newport garrisoned High Ercall Hall in Shropshire with two hundred Royalist troops, it was besieged by the Parliamentarians three times between July 1645 and March 1646. More than five hundred Parliamentary soldiers were killed trying to take the house.[48] In 1663 Robert Mathew of Denbighshire in Wales petitioned the government for a welfare payment due to the wounds he had received while defending High Ercall:

> The said petitioner being a servant in Wroxeter, became a soldier under Lieutenant Lingham then in and under the command of Captain Nicholas Armour, Governor for the defence of the said house, where your petitioner continued for the space of four years from first to last. And therein, received many wounds in his body head, divers cuts in his body, and shot three times in both his arms, the one whereof he has no use of to this day.[49]

For both sides, the siege of a country house had particular symbolic resonance. As Hutton and Reeves note, withstanding a siege was celebrated in partisan propaganda. Parliamentarian narratives emphasized 'corporate dedication and mutual support'; their siege stories 'conveyed the impression of a complete social organism united in a common cause, operating as a microcosm of the nation'. On the Royalist side, however, the 'favourite narrative' was of 'the defence of a castle or, even better, a mansion by its aristocratic or genteel owner'. Such stories presented a view of a hierarchical society, with 'a monarchy upheld by its "natural" supporters, the aristocracy, with all the other ranks of the nation, down to the meanest kitchen scullion, united under its command to protect the traditional order'. Moreover, 'as the stronghold under attack was also a private home, its resistance could offer a fine symbol for the defence of personal property against a usurping and illegal power.'[50]

This symbolic meaning was often supported by the motives behind the decision to destroy a house, which transcended military expediency. In his study of the Civil War in the Midlands, Philip Tennant refers to the 'wanton destruction of a handful of midland England's finest seats'.

He cites as a 'deplorable example' Prince Rupert's attack on William Purefoy's Caldecote Hall in Warwickshire, which Tennant describes as a 'deliberate vindictive measure'.[51] After the Royalists occupied Campden House in Gloucestershire in 1645, the Parliamentarians marched out from Warwick and burned the Earl of Middlesex's Milcote House in revenge.[52] In his study of the Civil War in Oxfordshire, David Eddershaw writes that 'pillaging could ... be used as a form of punishment for those known to sympathise with the enemy.' He cites as examples the destruction of Fawley Court, owned by the Parliamentarian Bulstrode Whitelocke, by Royalist soldiers in November 1642. Whitelocke's books and papers were shredded and burnt; his bed linens stolen and mattresses slashed; his horses and hounds carried off; his fences pulled down; and his deer slaughtered or set free, except for one tame hind who was taken as a present for Prince Rupert. His children were subjected to a terrifying interrogation about his whereabouts. Whitelocke wrote about the incident:

> There was no insolence or outrage which such guests commit upon an enemy but these brutish soldiers did it at Fawley Court. There they had their whores, they spent and consumed in one night 100 loads of corn and hay, littered their horses with good wheat sheaves, gave them all sorts of corn in the straw, made great fires in the closes, and William Cook telling them there were billets and faggots nearer to them than the plough timber which they burned, they threatened to burn him ... Whatsoever they could lay their hands on they carried away or spoiled, and did all that malice and rapine could provoke barbarous mercenaries to commit.[53]

Although the house was not damaged on this occasion, two years later it was destroyed when it was caught in a crossfire of artillery.[54]

Sir William Russell was a Catholic and 'the dominant figure in Worcester royalism'. As an officer in the Royalist army he was responsible for the capture of Tewksbury in 1643, and as Governor of Worcester he refused entry to Parliamentary forces in September 1642.[55] This led to the Civil War's first skirmish at Powick Bridge, in which Prince Rupert's cavalry triumphed. Shortly afterwards, however, Worcester was deemed indefensible and the Royalist army returned to Shropshire. The Earl of Essex's army occupied the city for weeks, with brutal consequences for the inhabitants. Russell had fortified his moated manor house at Strensham, about thirteen miles south of Worcester, but Parliamentary forces quickly overcame the small garrison and ransacked the house and then rendered it unfit for occupation. Nevertheless, after Royalist forces moved back into Worcester after Essex's departure, they regarrisoned Strensham and strengthened the existing defences with artillery platforms on which were mounted light cannon. In 1645, however, the garrison surrendered without a fight, and the site was occupied by Parliamentary troops.[56] It is difficult to interpret the destruction of Russell's house at Strensham as anything other than retaliation for his actions before Powick Bridge and for his military service on the Royalist side. The house was not an important part of the moated site's defences, as is clear from the fact that the site continued to be garrisoned long after the house was destroyed.

When the king was at Liskeard in Cornwall in 1644, some local people complained to him that the Parliamentarians were plundering the countryside. He dispatched a force under Colonel Richard Neville, who learned from an informer that a group of Parliamentary soldiers had taken Boconnoc House, the seat of the Royalist Lord Mohun. Neville set out to dislodge them:

> Notwithstanding they had eighty men to guard them, as they were carousing they forced the doors upon them, killed the man that locked the door, broke in the house, took Colonel Aldridge who was governor of Aylesbury, the Lieutenant-Colonel, captain and one ensign of Essex his life-guard, another Lieutenant-Colonel, without the loss of any one of His Majesty's party.[57]

Eastwood Hall in Derbyshire was the home of the Reverend Emmanuel Bourne, rector of Ashover, who attempted to remain neutral, but his hand was forced when a contingent of passing Parliamentary troops demanded food. When he refused, they burned the house down.[58] The fortified manor house at Boarstall in Buckinghamshire was garrisoned by the Royalists, taken and garrisoned by the Parliamentarians in 1643, taken back by the Royalists in 1644 and then in 1645 unsuccessfully attacked by Parliamentary forces, who lost between 120 and 300 men. The Royalists then demolished most of the village in order to prevent the enemy from using it for defensive purposes. The Parliamentarians responded by laying siege to Boarstall in 1646; ten weeks later the garrison surrendered, after hearing that the king had fled from Oxford. The house was demolished in 1778, but damage from cannon fire is still visible on the surviving gatehouse.[59]

Basing House in Hampshire, which was owned by the Catholic Royalist John Paulet, 5th Marquess of Winchester, occupied an important strategic position guarding the main road to the west. Renaming it 'Loyalty House', Paulet garrisoned the house with 150 men and reinforced its defences. It was besieged by Parliamentary forces in 1643; by some estimates 2,000 men lost their lives in three attempts to storm the house, which was finally taken in 1645, after the Dutch siege engineer Colonel John Dalbier arrived with a force of seven hundred men. In the final assault on 10 October, Oliver Cromwell himself ordered a bombardment with heavy artillery. The walls were breached in two places, opening the way for an infantry assault. The Parliamentary troops slaughtered the garrison: an estimated 74 men (and one woman) were killed and two hundred taken prisoner. The contents of the house were plundered, including even the clothing of the occupants. They included the architect Inigo Jones, aged 72, who was carried out naked and wrapped in a blanket. In the chaos the house caught fire and was badly damaged; some of the prisoners had not yet been taken out and were burned to death. The next day, Cromwell ordered the charred remains of the house to be 'totally slighted and demolished'. The surviving bricks and other materials were offered to anyone who wanted to take them away. The Marquess and Marchioness of

'The Siege of Bazinge House', a woodcut by Wenceslaus Hollar, c. 1645. This image shows the fortifications and some of the physical damage that was inflicted upon the house during the siege, but it does not show its total destruction by Parliamentary troops afterwards, suggesting that Hollar felt that his audience might be uncomfortable with such violent acts.

Winchester were imprisoned in the Tower of London, and their children were taken away to be educated by Protestants.

Basing House was clearly a problem for the Parliamentary army, and so its destruction may be regarded as having been carried out for military reasons. But the frenetic violence which followed its capture shows that there were emotional forces at work as well. Cromwell did not want to devote resources to garrisoning Basing House, but he also used it as an example to deter other Royalists who might continue to resist. He was sanguine about the plunder and violence that accompanied the final assault, referring to it as 'good encouragement' for his troops.[60] Those troops, meanwhile, were motivated by a combination of frustrations stemming from the long siege and antipathy for the Catholic Royalists who defended the house. The Roundhead newspaper *Mercurius Civicus* printed this account by the one of the officers who led the final assault:

> The enemy, for aught I can learn, desired no quarter, and I believe that they had but little offered them. You must remember what they were: they were most of them Papists; therefore our muskets and our swords did show but little compassion, and this house being at length subdued, did satisfy for her treason and rebellion by the blood of the offenders.[61]

Even in the most war-torn parts of the country, then, the damage to houses was not entirely done for military reasons. Some houses, moreover, were spared, in some cases because there were fears that civilian opposition would lead to unrest following damage to the local economy. The Royalist commander Charles Lloyd admitted that he had abandoned his plans to destroy an unnamed house in the Southwest 'because it would have incensed the Countrey'. Some of the most impressive houses in England, including Cowdray House in Sussex, Chatsworth House and Hardwick Hall in Derbyshire, seem to have been preserved for similar reasons.[62] Other houses were saved because they were owned by influential men. Porter writes that when soldiers were 'faced with the prospect of destroying a country house of a powerful supporter of their own side ... [they] were wise to seek authority from their superiors before they carried out the task'.[63] Henry Harvey refused to permit his manor house at Bridgwater in Somerset to be demolished, which meant that the Parliamentarians were subsequently able to capture it and place a battery there when they attacked the town in 1645.[64] In 1644 the Royalist officer Sir William Campion wrote to Prince Rupert to inform him that he did not have sufficient men to leave a garrison at Chilton House in Buckinghamshire, and so 'my fancye that morning did much envite mee to set fyre to the house.' Rupert, however, ordered Campion only to demolish the outer walls and remove the doors; it is unclear why he decided that complete destruction was unnecessary, but it may have been because the house belonged to Sir John Croke, a colonel in the Royalist army.[65]

Not all of the damaged houses were in contested territory, as some were in the far Southwest, East Anglia or the North. These houses suffered deliberate 'slighting' as Parliamentary forces sought to eliminate isolated pockets of Royalist support. In other areas, loyalties were divided. Dorset lay between the Parliamentarian Southeast and Royalist Southwest, making it contested territory which was roughly evenly divided between king and Parliament. This made the local conflict particularly bitter and destructive. Richard Ollard writes:

> Some parts of England were more or less solid for one side or the other. This meant that the fluctuating fortunes of war caused comparatively little destruction. But where, as in Dorset, the gentry and towns were divided among themselves, the temporary triumph of one side meant a chance of getting one's own back on people who had ruined your house and estate, had smashed your furniture, staved the casks in your cellar.[66]

Sussex, too, was split, although a preponderance of its landowners supported the Parliamentary side. Desmond Seward writes:

> Climb Mount Caburn and you look down over the Glynde Reach, a tributary of the Ouse, dawdling through the Glynde Levels... Two great houses can be seen. That at Glynde, immediately below, belonged to a man who virtually ruled Sussex on Parliament's behalf during the Civil War and for a time under the Commonwealth. The other, in the distance on the far side of the Reach is Firle, home of a family from which came one of the most popular Cavalier commanders.[67]

Lancashire was split between a Royalist and Catholic north and west and a Parliamentarian and Puritan south and east.[68] Yorkshire, often characterized as broadly Royalist, was in fact split between a Cavalier

North Riding and a Roundhead East and West Ridings. Burton Constable Hall, the home of Henry Constable, 1st Viscount Dunbar, a 'hard-drinking, heavy-gambling papist', was therefore in the 'wrong' part. During the Civil War he gave substantial financial support to Charles I and took a commission as a colonel in the Royalist army; his three sons fought on the king's side as well. In 1645 he died of wounds received in the siege of Scarborough Castle. Burton Constable was sacked by Parliamentary troops and sequestered. Dunbar's widow was left virtually penniless and his eldest son John, £17,550 in debt from heavy fines, was forced into exile in the Netherlands.[69] Puritan-dominated Norfolk was Parliamentary territory throughout the war, but there were a few Royalist houses in the county. Oxburgh Hall was owned by the recusant and Royalist Sir Henry Bedingfeld, who raised troops for the king and sent his three sons to fight in the Royalist cause; one of them, John, was killed in the Battle of Worcester. Henry was imprisoned in the Tower from 1647 to 1649, and his estates were sequestered. In 1652 Oxburgh was sacked and burned.[70] It is difficult to claim that there was any military purpose to the damage to Burton Constable and Oxburgh, which was more likely the result of their owners having supported the wrong side.

The total amount of destruction of buildings in the Civil War was enormous. The Earl of Northampton wrote after the war that his houses Compton Wynyates and Castle Ashby had been reduced to 'almost waste', as they 'in these times of distraction have bin plundered and almost pul'd downe, and of late uninhabited, are daily fallinge into greater decay'.[71] In some cases, landed estates were pillaged for materials to rebuild damage to local buildings: in 1643 timber was cut from the Earl of Carnarvon's Wing estate in Buckinghamshire and used to repair damage to the village of Swanbourne, where the Royalists had burned down several dozen houses.[72] Michael Thompson writes:

> The alterations produced in the landscape or townscape recall those of the Dissolution of the Monasteries a hundred years before. It differed from the Dissolution in that a large number of the structures were already ruinous, and it was not associated with a massive transference of property, and in any case what had been transferred was returned at the Restoration. Nevertheless the destruction constitutes a part of the background to the great change that divides the seventeenth century into two such distinct halves.[73]

Rebuilding was expensive: an average-sized country house in the early seventeenth century cost £3,000 to £4,000, while larger houses could cost many times that.[74] In the most heavily damaged parts of rural England, it was well into the late 1650s and '60s before villages, churches and country houses were rebuilt. Highnam Court was severely damaged in the fighting around Gloucester in 1643 and not rebuilt until 1658.[75] Sudeley Castle in Gloucestershire remained a ruin until it was purchased and rebuilt by the Dent family in 1837.[76]

Warfare and plundering were not the only ways in which the Civil War damaged the physical fabric of country houses. They were also affected when they were fortified to withstand enemy attacks, and garrison troops caused damage as well. By early 1643, no fewer than six country houses in north Derbyshire were garrisoned by Parliamentary forces: Wingerworth, Chatsworth, Wingfield Manor, Sutton Scarsdale Hall, Renishaw Hall and Staveley. Of these, Wingerworth, Chatsworth, Sutton Scarsdale and Staveley had either been abandoned by or taken from Royalist families. Wingfield belonged to the Parliamentarian 4th Earl of Pembroke, but was taken by the Royalists later in 1643. It had been surrounded by a strong defensive wall, which proved impervious to Royalist cannon fire, but the garrison of 160 men decided to accept a Royalist offer to allow them to march away unharmed. The Royalists then built massive earthen bulwarks, parts of which are still visible today on the north side. After the Royalist cause suffered a major setback at Marston Moor in July 1644, however, the garrison at Wingfield was left isolated. Parliamentary forces besieged the house and brought in heavy demi-cannon to batter the walls. So stout were the defences that it took ten weeks to open a breach. The garrison of 220 was permitted to march out and return to their homes.[77]

The Royalist Sir Richard Fleetwood fortified Wootton Lodge in Staffordshire so formidably that the Parliamentary officer Sir George Gresley described it as 'one of the strongest places in that county, exceeding well provided of all necessaries and manned with such a company of obstinate papists, and resolute theeves, as the like were hardly to be found in the whole Kingdome'. Even so, it proved unable to withstand an attack by four hundred men and a troop of horse in 1643, and eighty men from its garrison were taken to Derby as prisoners.[78] The Royalist stronghold of Oxford was surrounded by a chain of garrisoned and fortified sites, including not only the castles at Banbury, Wallingford, Abingdon and Donnington, but manor houses:

Faringdon House was strengthened to protect the western approach and Gaunt House guarded the key crossing of the Thames above the city at Newbridge near Standlake. To the north of Oxford, Woodstock Manor, the old royal hunting lodge, was surrounded by earthworks, and on the vulnerable eastern frontier Bletchingdon, Boarstall, Brill, Shirburn and Greenland[s] House formed a chain of fortified outposts. Parliament too had its local strongholds. From the spring of 1643 it held Henley, and ...Phyllis Court was protected with earthworks and gun emplacements as a counterbalance to the Royalist Greenland[s] House a little distance away.[79]

In Worcestershire, the principal Royalist garrisons were stationed in the towns of Worcester and Evesham, which guarded the main river crossings of the Severn and Avon respectively, but the moated manor houses at Hartlebury to the north and Strensham to the south served as bases for mounted patrols, and temporary bases were also established at two other houses, Leigh Court and Madresfield.[80] The development of mobile artillery meant that the defensive capabilities of masonry walls were much reduced, and therefore new defensive structures had to be devised. These included lower and thicker walls which combined earthworks with brick or stone, interspersed with bastions, or arrowhead-shaped projections which allowed for a wide angle of fire while providing only a small target. Typically there was a bank, or glacis, in front of the defences which sloped down to a ditch or moat, with a clear field of fire on the other side.[81]

In some cases, physical reminders of this turbulent period remain. Strensham still features visible evidence of two concentric moats and a rampart with an artillery emplacement and bastions on each corner.[82] Basing House was defended by earthwork banks and three bastions.[83] Strensham and Basing both suffered long sieges, but other fortified houses never saw any serious action. Horsenden Manor in Lincolnshire was the home of the Royalist John Denham, surveyor of the king's parks and buildings. The house was seized by Parliament without a fight, and Denham did not recover it until after the Restoration. The defensive moat was later converted into a serpentine pond which remains a feature of the house's landscape garden.[84] Albright Hussey in Shropshire may have been fortified during the Civil War, which explains its peculiar west wing, with its top storey of Grinshill stone above lower storeys of brick.[85] Three Oxfordshire houses, Cornbury, Woodstock and Bletchington, were fortified, probably by the Royalists between 1642 and 1644, in order to form a defensive line north of Oxford. An earthwork is still visible about half a mile east of Cornbury.[86] At Houndhill near Barnsley in South Yorkshire, the boundary wall and two towers which were built to defend the Royalist garrison survive. These defences were damaged when Sir Thomas Fairfax led a contingent of Parliamentary troops in an attack on the house in 1643.[87] Rousham House in Oxfordshire was owned by the Royalist Sir Robert Dormer. He was in the process of building a new house when the Civil War broke out, and attempted to protect his property by boring holes in the woodwork surrounding the front door so that muskets could be fired through them. The holes, now filled with lead, are still visible today.[88]

Yet another way in which country houses were physically affected by the Civil War was by the interruption of their construction. In the 1630s Sir Francis Godolphin added a new north range inspired by Italian Renaissance principles to Godolphin House in Cornwall. On the east side, the toothings remain for a matching garden range, but the Civil War intervened. The Godolphins were staunch Royalists: Sir Francis sheltered the future Charles II during his flight to the Scilly Isles in 1646 and then accompanied him into exile in France. His estates in Cornwall and Norfolk were sequestered, and his full plans for Godolphin House were in consequence never realized.[89]

In the 1630s Richard Fletcher began to convert Hutton in the Forest in Cumbria from a medieval pele tower to a country house. One side of the forecourt features a 'grand, arcaded lodging range', but the matching range on the other side was never built, because Fletcher's son Henry, who inherited the house in 1637, was killed eight years later fighting for the Royalist side in the Battle of Rowton Heath. Henry's son George did not complete his father's design, but chose instead to rebuild Hutton's central range.[90] Sir Robert Dormer began building Rousham House in Oxfordshire in 1635, but construction was halted by the outbreak of the Civil War. His son repaired the damage inflicted by Parliamentary troops but otherwise left the house unfinished. In 1741 Sir Clement Cottrell-Dormer hired William Kent to add two wings to the now-truncated house, along with a magnificent Augustan garden.[91] Henry Killigrew began building Ince Castle in Cornwall in the 1630s; it was originally intended to have another storey, but construction was halted when Killigrew declared for the Royalists and the house was besieged.

Violence and the Country House, II: The Civil War

Richard Fletcher began to convert Hutton in the Forest in Cumbria from a medieval pele tower to a country house before the Civil War. He added an impressive arcaded lodging range to the forecourt and intended to add a matching one to balance it, but he died before he could complete his plans.

Surrendered without a fight, it was sold to Edward Nosworthy, the mayor of Truro. The additional storey was finally built after it was purchased by Sir Montague Eliot, 8th Earl of St Germans, in 1918.[92] Castle Ashby in Northamptonshire, the seat of the Earl of Northampton, had been undergoing an ambitious classicizing scheme since the mid-1620s, but while the family was away fighting in the Royalist cause a fire seriously damaged the east wing, and later the house was looted by the Parliamentarians. After the war the family chose to live at Compton Wynyates in Warwickshire and did not return to Castle Ashby until the end of the seventeenth century.[93] The construction of Weston Hall in Derbyshire was begun in 1633 when James I granted the estate to Anthony Roper, but after one wing and one bay of the central block were completed the building works were halted by the Civil War and never resumed. The fragment of the house, which survived despite being used as a barracks, is now a pub.[94]

Other houses were demolished after the war ended because their owners could no longer afford a large residence. The finances of Sir John Heydon, who had served as an artillery commander for Charles I, never recovered after he was declared delinquent in 1646, and four years later he began demolishing Baconsthorpe Castle in Norfolk so as to sell the

HOW THE COUNTRY HOUSE BECAME ENGLISH

Around 1650, the Royalist Heydon family partially demolished Baconsthorpe Castle in Norfolk in order to sell its stone. The outer gatehouse, visible in the centre of the image, was the only part of the house that continued to be occupied.

stone. Heydon converted the outer gatehouse to a house, which continued to be occupied until 1920.[95] The Royalist Spencer family of Yarnton Manor in Oxfordshire pulled down the north and south wings of the house in the 1660s, presumably because of the heavy fines they had been forced to pay.[96]

The Financial Impact of the Civil War

Built between the early sixteenth and early seventeenth centuries, Little Moreton Hall is one of Cheshire's most famous half-timbered houses. By the late nineteenth century Little Moreton's decaying state had become the subject of 'romantic allure', and it served as the inspiration for vernacular revival houses such as Hill Bark on the Wirral and Wightwick Manor in Staffordshire.[97] In a retrospective essay about the first one thousand issues of *Country Life* in 1916, Henry Avray Tipping described Little Moreton as a house where 'the hands of men and of time have been held back from doing real injury'.[98] Little Moreton's picturesque decay was, however, very definitely the product of an 'injury', as the Moreton family's fortunes never recovered from their support for the king in the Civil War. From the late seventeenth century onwards Little Moreton was rented to relatives or other tenants. The neglected house slowly crumbled, and by the 1790s letters from the estate manager were full of reports of collapsing chimneys and leaky roofs. In John Britton's *Architectural Antiquities of Great Britain* (1808), it was depicted by the artist John Sell Cotman with chickens strutting through the rooms.

A similar transition occurred at Sissinghurst Castle in Kent. Sissinghurst's 200,000 annual visitors almost all come to admire the garden, one of the most famous in England, and so immacutely kept that Adam Nicolson, whose father Nigel gave the house to the National Trust in 1967, complains that the Trust 'hates mud'.[99] Nigel Nicolson, writer and co-founder of the publishing house Weidenfeld & Nicolson, was the son of the writers Vita Sackville-West and Harold Nicolson, who, after they purchased Sissinghurst for £12,000 in 1930, spent another £17,000 transforming it from the derelict remnant of a great Elizabethan house to the embodiment of English horticultural enthusiasm.[100] Like Little Moreton, however, Sissinghurst has a more tumultuous history. Sir John Baker, who owned the house in the mid-seventeenth century, was a Royalist and Catholic; there is evidence that he converted a banqueting house in the garden to a Catholic chapel in the late 1630s.[101]

John Sell Cotman's drawings and paintings of Little Moreton Hall in Cheshire emphasized its picturesque decay, which was the result of the house having been rented out after the Royalist Moreton family lost much of their wealth in the Civil War.

He was with the king at Oxford in 1642 when his house, land and 'rich furniture in Covent Garden' were seized by Parliament; two years later Sissinghurst was raided and everything of value seized. The parkland also seems to have been stripped of its timber, as only two trees dating from earlier than 1644 survive today.[102] Baker's compounding fine to recover his property was initially set at £5,000 and later reduced to £3,000, but to pay even the smaller sum he had to mortgage all that he owned, which raised £2,760, allowing him to regain control of his estates in 1652.[103] Sissinghurst never recovered, however. Sir John was still heavily in debt when he died the next year, and his son followed in 1661, leaving no male heir. His four daughters married and moved to distant counties, and his widow went to live in London. Abandoned, Sissinghurst fell into decline; Horace Walpole visited in 1752 and described 'a park in ruins and a house in ten times greater ruins'.[104] In the 1760s it was leased by the government for use as a camp for French prisoners-of-war, whose letters describe vermin-infested rooms and a moat stinking with ordure. They had their revenge for these appalling conditions by pulling up the floorboards and destroying the fittings. The house's owner Sir Horace Mann was given £361 in compensation after they left, but he kept the money and pulled down the house, leaving only the gatehouse and the attached servants' quarters.[105]

Sissinghurst's decline shows that, for some English landowners, the destruction caused by the Civil War was not only physical but financial. After 1643 Parliament began increasing rates of taxation by five or ten times their previous level in order to pay for the war. The king did the same in the areas under royal control. In disputed areas, some landowners were required to pay taxes to both sides, in amounts that often far exceeded the rental incomes from their estates. This burden fell almost entirely on landlords, because tenants were entitled to deduct any taxes they paid from their rents.[106] The financial impact was magnified because rents were greatly reduced because of wartime disruption to agriculture, which was significant even in places far from the fighting.[107] The 'management and very maintenance of estates soon became well-nigh impossible as the war dragged on'.[108] Tenants and labourers were difficult to find as many men were on active service; markets and trade routes were thrown into disarray; estates were plundered by garrisons forced to live off the land; and deer were killed and timber cut down. The billeting of troops was particularly damaging, as they often wreaked havoc on the houses. Gayhurst Hall in Buckinghamshire had been the home of Sir Everard

Digby, one of the Gunpowder plotters, and when Parliamentary troops occupied the house, they scratched an 'X' and '1649' into the stonework of the porch, as a reference to the execution of Charles I.[109] The cost of losses caused by the war could add up to massive sums. The Duchess of Newcastle estimated that the Duke lost £45,000 in felled timber and tens of thousands of pounds more from stolen personal property from his estates. When this was added to the complete loss of rents while his property was sequestered and the amount of money he personally expended on supplying the king with troops, his total losses amounted to £950,000, equivalent to hundreds of millions of pounds today.[110]

The biggest problem for landowners was sequestration, which meant that their property was held as a punishment until a composition fine was paid to recover it. Sequestration was mostly used by Parliament against Royalists and Catholics; the former had their entire estates sequestered and the latter, even if they had not actively supported the king, two-thirds.[111] In the areas under Royalist control, the king also sequestered the property of his opponents. It is difficult to determine precisely what percentage of estates fell victim to sequestration, but the best estimate is around 4,000, or a quarter of all estates, with a much higher proportion in contested areas.[112] This had a major impact on upper-class finances, as Clay describes:

> Landowners whose incomes were even partly interrupted for a considerable period were likely to find themselves in financially deep water because it was difficult or impossible for them to reduce their outgoings to the extent that their incomes had been reduced. Even if they did cut down their living expenses to the bare minimum, economize drastically on the education of the younger children and postpone the marriage of the older ones, there were often other items over which they had no control. If debts or annuities were charged on their estates, the creditors or annuitants would not in the long run willingly abate their claims just because of the misfortunes of the debtor ... and they would keep careful account of unpaid arrears, which after a few years would begin to mount up to a frightening sum.[113]

As an example, Sir Peter Temple received no income from his Leckhampstead estate in Buckinghamshire from 1642 to 1647. This meant that he could not pay his creditors, and his steward John Pollard was imprisoned for debt in his stead because Temple was an MP and therefore had legal immunity. By the time of his death in 1653 Temple's debts had grown to £26,000, and Leckhampstead was in consequence handed over to his creditors.[114]

After 1646 the 'delinquent' owners of sequestered property could regain control of their estates by compounding for them, which typically amounted to a payment of between a tenth and two-thirds of the value of their estate. Although the way in which these fines were calculated meant that they were often reduced to no more than a year or two's income, four-digit sums were not unusual.[115] Even so, H. J. Habakkuk concluded that 'delinquents who were not already heavily indebted before the imposition of the fine found it easy to pay the fine without selling any land; they rode out the difficulties of the Interregnum with no obvious long-term effect.'[116] Some owners, however, were prohibited from compounding, because they were politically prominent and therefore excluded from being pardoned or because they were Catholic. Their property was sold under three Acts of Sale – which listed a total of 780 names – that were passed between July 1651 and November 1652. Other owners refused to compound out of principle or could not afford to; their property was also sold. Owned by the Catholic Dolman family, Badsworth Hall in Yorkshire was sequestered and sold for £8,600 to Sir John Bright in 1653.[117] Since 1472 the manor of Allerton in Lancashire had been held by the Lathom family, who built a new house there in the early seventeenth century. But the Lathoms were both Royalists and recusants, and the estate was sequestered by Parliament and never recovered. In 1654 it was purchased by John Sumner of Midhurst in Sussex.[118] Although most families eventually succeeded in regaining their lost estates, some never did.[119] Charles I's Secretary of State Sir Francis Windebank was forced to flee to France in 1640 when it was discovered that he had signed letters favouring priests and recusants; he died in Paris six years later. During the Interregnum, his estate at Haines Hill in Berkshire was confiscated and given to the Parliamentary supporter Richard Biggs.[120]

When the costs of lost rents, damage and fines were added together, the total losses were often in the thousands or even tens of thousands of pounds, the equivalent of millions in today's money and a financial blow which crippled many families for decades to come. Buying one's way back into favour was expensive: the Lucys of Charlecote Park in Warwickshire first supported the king, then Parliament, then paid a fine of £3,513 – equivalent to an entire year's income from their estates – to convince Charles II of their loyalty.[121] While the Lucys could afford such a sum, many landowners were forced to resort to extreme measures, such as heavy borrowing, strict economies of expense and substantially increased rents. The sale of land was a last resort, but in some cases it was unavoidable; Clay estimates that 15 per cent of the land owned by the actively Royalist gentry and aristocracy had to be sold to pay off debts and repair damage.[122] In 1654 the 6th Baron Sandys, impoverished after serving as an officer in the Royalist army, was forced to sell The Vyne in Hampshire to the lawyer Chaloner Chute.[123] Henry Rainsford suffered the indignity of selling Clifford Manor in Warwickshire to one of his tenants.[124] Farnborough Hall in Warwickshire had belonged to the Raleigh family since 1322, but after they supported the Royalist side in the Civil War their finances never recovered, and they were finally forced to sell in 1683.[125]

Other landowning families took a very long time to recover their lost property. The Royalist Sir Vincent Corbet was, as Richard Gough described in his history of the parish of Myddle in Shropshire (1701), 'putte to pay a great sume' to recover his Shropshire estates.[126] He had to sell some of his property, including Preston Hall in Preston Brockhurst, in order to afford the fine. The house was purchased by Samuel Wingfield, a lawyer from Shrewsbury, who demolished it and built a new five-bay residence. In the early nineteenth century the Wingfields began to shift their property interest southwest towards Onslow in Shropshire, and Preston was put up for sale in 1843.[127] The purchaser was Sir Andrew Vincent Corbet, a descendant of the seventeenth-century seller; it remains in the hands of the Corbet family today.[128]

Considering the overall impact of the Civil War on country houses therefore begins to move us away from a focus on military expediency as the sole – or even primary – motivation behind the enormous amount of destruction that they suffered. Some of the damage was financial and was motivated by vengeance upon enemies seen as heretics and traitors, and some by what Christopher O'Riordan terms 'simple opportunism': 'People took advantage of the disruption of civil society and the weakened political position of parliament's enemies, who were also often absent from their estates. As far as can be told from the scantier records, something similar happened on parliamentarians' estates in royalist-held territory.'[129]

Rising from the Ashes

Today the visitor to Kingston Lacy in Dorset encounters a beautiful house set in unspoilt countryside, but its peaceful and elegant appearance belies its turbulent history. Kingston Lacy was a royal estate granted temporarily to various supporters of the Crown until 1603, when James I gave it to Sir Charles Blount, 1st Earl of Devonshire, as a reward for his role in the pacification of Ireland. In 1636 Blount's son Mountjoy Blount, 1st Earl of Newport, sold Kingston Lacy to Sir John Bankes, who had risen from Cumbrian yeoman stock to become one of the most prominent and wealthiest lawyers in England. In 1630 Charles I had appointed him as Attorney General, a post worth around £10,000 a year. Five years later, Bankes began converting his professional success to landed status by purchasing the royal castle of Corfe on the Isle of Purbeck and then Kingston Lacy, about fifteen miles to the north, a year later.

As tension between king and Parliament mounted in the late 1630s, Bankes was not unsympathetic to the Puritan cause and tried to act as an honest broker between the two sides as the situation degenerated into open conflict. Nevertheless, having been appointed Chief Justice of the Court of Common Pleas in 1641, he was forced to carry out prosecutions of prominent Puritans, including the pamphleteer William Prynne, and to defend the Crown over ship money. He gave Charles generous personal donations to help his cause – a receipt for £525 for twenty horses is displayed in the drawing room at Kingston Lacy – and at the Salisbury assizes in 1643 he led the indictment of the leaders of the king's armed opponents.

Sir John paid a heavy price for his loyalty. In 1643 Corfe Castle was besieged by Parliamentary forces, but Sir John's wife Mary and a small garrison held out for six weeks. The Parliamentarians used a variety of tactics, including various siege engines and the placement of snipers in the tower of the parish church. When those failed, they bribed the men with alcohol and money; the first man over the wall was promised £20 (more than a year's wages), the second £19, and so forth, all the way down to £1 for the twentieth. But to no avail: the attackers fled when they met with rifle fire, stones and hot embers. Having suffered a hundred casualties, they slunk away. Two years later, Corfe and the Isle of Purbeck were the only Royalist strongholds left in Dorset. The Parliamentarians besieged Corfe for a second time, but they did not have sufficient forces

The Bankes family was forced to build a new house (top) on their Kingston Lacy estate after Corfe Castle (bottom) was destroyed in the Civil War. This drawing of Kingston Lacy by John Preston Neale shows the original house before it was rebuilt in the 19th century.

to launch a full-scale attack. Treachery, however, allowed them to take the castle almost bloodlessly. One of the garrison's officers took a £200 bribe to betray his erstwhile comrades. He left the castle and returned with what he claimed were reinforcements but in fact were Parliamentary troops: between 40 and 150 were admitted through a sally-port before the defenders grew suspicious and shut the gate, but it was too late. The garrison was granted quarter and 'Brave Dame Mary' was permitted to depart with the keys, which now hang over the fireplace in the library at Kingston Lacy. Because Corfe had proved such a formidable obstacle, £300 was immediately allocated for its demolition. Trenches were dug along the walls and under the towers in which gunpowder was detonated, but the castle was so strongly built that much of it remained standing.

From a distance, Corfe now looks like a romantic ruin which has crumbled gradually over time. A closer view, however, reveals the speed, extent and violence of its destruction: large holes were blown in the masonry and entire walls toppled over. The ruins were then plundered by local people; many of the buildings in the village today contain stone from the castle. Sir Walter Erle, a staunch Puritan, had commanded the Parliamentary forces in the first siege. After his efforts to use various siege engines failed to breach the walls, he ordered a frontal assault which failed and cost the lives of around a hundred of his men. After the battle, Erle was accused of having 'put on a bear's skin, and ... for fear of musket shot he was seen to creep on all fours on the sides of the hill to keep himself out of danger'.[130] He was subjected to a humiliating inquest which led to him being relieved of his command. To make matters worse, Royalist troops destroyed his house, Charborough Park, also in Dorset. It is therefore not surprising that when he saw an opportunity to profit from Corfe Erle took it. When he rebuilt Charborough in the 1650s he used stone and timbers taken from the castle ruins.[131]

The remainder of the Bankes family's property, including Kingston Lacy, was sequestered and its contents removed. Sir John did not live to see this, as he died in 1644. What remained of his estates and fortune passed to his eldest son, also named John, who was a minor at the time. Lady Bankes worked tirelessly over the next few years to pay the substantial fines required to regain their property, which she managed to do in 1647. John Bankes died in 1656, leaving Kingston Lacy to his younger brother Ralph, another successful lawyer. Ralph Bankes built the first great house there between 1663 and 1667. It was designed by Sir Roger

Pratt, one of the most influential architects of the second half of the seventeenth century. Brimming with optimism after the Restoration and aware of Continental developments from his travels in France and Italy in the 1640s, Sir Ralph Bankes harboured grandiose architectural ambitions. He commissioned Pratt to design his new house in the style of Inigo Jones, and was rewarded with a fashionable, compact, double-pile brick block, its hipped roof topped by a cupola. It was, as Michael Hill observes, 'about as modern a conception as possible in the 1660s'.[132] The destruction of Corfe Castle thus contributed to the building of two country houses, Charborough Park and Kingston Lacy.

A difference between the Dissolution of the Monasteries and the Civil War is that the former resulted in the building of numerous country houses which were converted from or built using materials from former monastic sites, whereas the latter led to the destruction of many houses. As Charborough shows, however, recycling and reuse also occurred during the Civil War. Some of the houses which were damaged or destroyed served as quarries for building materials. Devizes Castle in Wiltshire was captured after a siege by Parliamentary forces in 1645 and slighted three years later. Stone was quarried from the ruins and used for a number of local buildings.[133] Ursula, Lady Bertie, had inherited her late husband Sir Roger Bertie's house, Wenlock Priory in Shropshire. After the war, she sold tiles from the roof of Wenlock's tithe barn so that they could be used to re-roof the Market Hall at Bridgnorth, which had been damaged in a siege.[134] After Campden House was burned by the Royalists on Prince Rupert's orders in 1645, its stone found its way into numerous buildings in Chipping Campden, while the stables and Banqueting House were converted to residences.[135] Hampton Court in Herefordshire may have benefited from the need to protect church fittings from Puritan iconoclasm: a stained-glass window that was installed in its chapel in 1683 probably came from Hereford Cathedral.[136]

Some families, like the Bankeses, chose to abandon their demolished or damaged castles or houses, which necessitated the building of a new house or the improvement of an existing one. Sir Edward Baynton abandoned his house at Bromham in Wiltshire, which had been burned by the Royalists, and built a new residence a few miles away at Spye Park.[137] In 1645, Royalist soldiers burned down Wormleighton Manor in Northamptonshire, leaving only the gatehouse and part of the north wing still standing. Instead of rebuilding, the Spencer family moved twenty miles east to their secondary estate at Althorp, where they began

Rather than rebuilding Wormleighton Manor in Northamptonshire after it was destroyed by Royalist forces, the Spencer family moved 20 miles east to their other estate at Althorp and built a new house there. This watercolour by William Daniell shows the house after it was remodelled by Henry Holland between 1787 and 1792.

rebuilding the house in the 1660s. Remodelled again by Henry Holland from 1787 to 1792, it is still the seat of Earl Spencer. Althorp preserves some architectural elements from Wormleighton: in the seventeenth century oak panelling was taken from the old house and installed in the dining room, and in the nineteenth century some of its stained glass was installed in the chapel.[138] After Caus Castle in Shropshire was destroyed by Parliamentary forces in 1645, its owner Sir Henry Thynne chose to move his seat four miles southeast to Minsterley Hall, which his father Sir Thomas Thynne had acquired in 1636. As at Althorp, panelling was removed from the old residence and installed in the dining room of its successor.[139]

Other owners chose not to rebuild slighted castles and moved to more modern and comfortable houses instead. After Wardour Castle was badly damaged by the Parliamentarians, Lord Arundell abandoned it in favour of the smaller Wardour House, which served his family until a grander replacement was built in the 1770s. The Hastings family left Ashby de la Zouch Castle in Leicestershire and moved to their fortified house at Donington.[140] After an eleven-week siege, the Marquess of

Worcester's seat at Raglan Castle in Montgomeryshire was taken by Parliamentary forces in 1646. Thomas Fairfax ordered it to be destroyed, but this proved too difficult and so the walls were breached in order to render it indefensible. Instead of carrying out repairs, the subsequent owners, now elevated to the Dukes of Beaufort, allowed it to crumble into ruins and permitted their stewards to use the stone to repair other buildings on the estate.[141] In its place Badminton House in Gloucestershire, which the family had acquired in 1612, became their seat, even though nine-tenths of their property remained in Wales. The 1st Duke of Beaufort rebuilt the house between 1664 and 1691, doubling the length of the facade and adding a new east range. The 3rd and 4th Dukes would make further changes which produced the house that exists today.[142] Edward Conway, 2nd Viscount Conway, intended to use Conwy Castle in North Wales as his main residence, but after it was besieged by Parliamentary troops and slighted in 1645, he opted for Ragley Hall in Warwickshire instead; Ragley was rebuilt in the 1680s by his son, the 1st Earl of Conway.[143] Owned by the Puritan Robert Harley, Brampton Bryan Castle in Herefordshire was a Parliamentary stronghold in Royalist territory. It withstood a siege in 1643 but fell in a second one the following year. Already badly damaged by mines and artillery, it was sacked and burned, leaving it in ruins. Instead of rebuilding the castle, Harley used the compensation money from Parliament to replace it with a brick-and-sandstone mansion in the 1660s.[144]

What, then, was the long-term impact of the Civil War on landed society? Did the sequestrations and fines imposed on Royalists lead to large-scale and lasting changes in the landed elite? We must be careful not to exaggerate the ability of sequestration to inflict long-term damage on landowning families. A more serious issue, however, was the potential for the Civil War to turn a manageable debt, which many families had, into a spiralling financial crisis in which a great portion of their income had to be dedicated to servicing the debt. Although sales remained rare, many Royalist families experienced 'a period of impoverishment, denuded estates, possibly poor marriages for a generation or more'.[145]

The physical and financial damage of the Civil War lingered for decades. The Haydons of Cadhay in Devon were forced to take out large mortgages to pay the fines resulting from their support for the Royalist cause, and were eventually forced to sell the estate in 1736.[146] The Catholic and Royalist Bodenhams had owned the Rotherwas estate in Herefordshire since the fifteenth century. Along with their other property in Herefordshire and Wiltshire, it was sequestered in 1642 and confiscated in 1651. Sir Roger Bodenham managed to raise sufficient funds through land sales and loans to buy back most of the estate, but this left him in substantial debt. In the mid-1660s he tried to sell Rotherwas, which had sustained significant damage in the Civil War. He failed to find a buyer, but he did sell seven manors and three other properties between the 1650s and 1680s.[147] These sales allowed Bodenham to reduce his debt, but it was not until 1732 that his descendants managed to accumulate sufficient funds to replace the ruined timber-framed house with an eleven-bay brick mansion which was possibly designed by James Gibbs.[148]

The financial pressures imposed by the economic conditions of the Civil War and its immediate aftermath were not suffered only by Royalists. John Broad reminds us that 'many of the phenomena of war were ... politically indiscriminate and have been underrated in their effects on the whole of landed society'; the burden of 'falling rents, high taxes, war damage, disruption, and free quarter on landed society' fell on Royalists and Parliamentarians alike.[149] After Sir Edmund Verney was killed fighting on the Royalist side at Edgehill in 1642, his son Ralph took over the family estates in Buckinghamshire, including their seat at Claydon House in the Aylesbury Vale. He supported Parliament, but when he refused to sign the Solemn League and Covenant in 1643 he was forced into exile in France and his property was sequestered. He returned to England a decade later, but his income of £1,440 per year had been reduced to nothing between 1643 and the release of his property from sequestration in 1648, and he was hounded by his creditors. It was not until the 1750s that there were sufficient funds to rebuild Claydon, which by that point was a 'run-down and unimpressive sight'.[150] Although Royalists suffered more, the Civil War was therefore financially damaging to landowners on both sides.

Remembering – and Forgetting – the Civil War

The Civil War destroyed around 10,000 houses in England and Wales, leaving approximately one in every hundred people homeless.[151] These included as many as two hundred country houses. Some ruined houses stood for decades or even longer before they were cleared away.[152] Travellers around England could not help but notice all this destruction. In John Taylor's published account of his journey from London to

Land's End in 1649, he observed that Farringdon in Oxfordshire, formerly 'a good hansome Market Towne', had been turned 'into Ashes and Rubbidge', while in Exeter 'this mad fire of contention' had 'turned all into ruines, rubbidge, cinders, ashes and fume'. In 1649 the minister Ralph Josselin described Melford in Suffolk as 'plundered out desolate without inhabitant', and seven years later John Evelyn recorded in his diary that Colchester, once a 'fair towne', was 'now wretchedly demolished by the late siege'.[153]

What then was the long-term significance of all this damage to private property? Within historical memory studies, increasing attention has been paid to the Civil War.[154] Although much of this scholarship has focused on political ideology or death and injury to individuals, relatively little attention has been given to the destruction of property. At the time, however, it loomed large in public consciousness. Ann Hughes writes that 'in recounting the burdens of Civil War, the consciousness of familiar places disrupted was a frequent stimulus to remembering and recording.' Foremost among these memories of the disruption of physical space was the 'wanton destruction' which 'transformed the built environment'.[155] In civilian petitions for restitution or remuneration for destruction, requisition or plunder, 'the experience that features most frequently ... is that of property loss.'[156] The petitioners often complained that malice rather than military necessity had dictated the fate of their property; even if they were merely attempting to strengthen their case for compensation, the fact that such arguments were thought to be plausible is telling. Even after repairs were made, memories of what had existed previously and what had happened to it during the war lingered. Some place names recalled the war years. Pike House outside Manchester may have acquired its name from a company of pikemen who were billeted there.[157] Royal Fort House in Bristol received its name from the bastions that surrounded it during the Civil War; the 'Royal' designation was because it was Prince Rupert's western headquarters. Cromwell ordered the fort's demolition in 1655; the present house, built by the merchant and banker Thomas Tyndall, dates from around 1767.[158] Other memories recalled the violence of those years. Stories of ghosts haunting sites of destruction and bloodshed were common. 'By consciously connecting the appearance of spectral visions to sites of wartime violence', Imogen Peck writes, 'observers delineated these places as spaces where the events of the past continued to echo in the present.'[159]

Even during the war, there was an awareness that the physical scars of the conflict would later serve as reminders of a traumatic time. In 1646 the Committee of Both Kingdoms advised the Parliamentary Committee of Salop not to destroy High Ercall Hall after its bloody and destructive siege, because if 'all houses whose situation or strength render them capable of being garrisons should be pulled down', then 'there would ... be too many sad marks left of the calamity of this war'.[160] The victorious Parliament had good reason to try and conceal the massive damage its forces had caused, but even when that damage had been caused by Royalists, it could be regarded as an indication of a failure to defend persons and property. In Gloucester, which had withstood an extremely destructive siege by the Royalist forces, 'Parliament's supporters downplayed the material damage which the city had sustained.'[161] The emphasis was instead upon the city's providential deliverance by a force commanded by the Earl of Essex, which arrived just as Gloucester's supply of gunpowder was running out.

It was not only partisan interests who wanted to move beyond the trauma of the war years; there were also more personal reasons to eradicate traces of the conflict. Bulstrode Whitelocke was so eager to demolish the defences around Phyllis Court, his house in Oxfordshire, that he applied for permission in early May 1646, even before the city of Oxford had surrendered. Whitelock wrote that 'he thirsted after the end of the war, and was the most desirous to have garrison slighted because it was his own house.' He paid the garrison troops 6*d* above their wages and hired more men from the surrounding villages to get the job done as quickly as possible: 'He threw down the breastworks and made handsome walkes of them on two sides, digged down the Bullworkes, sent away the great guns and ammunition and gott pay for his soldiers, whom he pleased, butt the country more, to see his readiness to slight garrisons.'[162] The phrase 'butt the country more' conveys how it was not only Whitelocke but the local population that was ready to leave the war behind. That was easier said than done, however, as even today part of the moat survives at Phyllis Court.[163]

As time passed, the reasons to forget wartime destruction became more compelling, as memory of the war became entangled with the Restoration settlement of political and religious affairs. 'Immediately after the English civil wars and Interregnum', writes Matthew Neufeld, 'the majority of the political nation chose the option of deliberately neglecting the recent past.'[164] This attitude was codified in the Act of

Indemnity and Oblivion of 1660, which issued a general pardon for acts committed during the war that applied to all but regicide, murder, rape, buggery, piracy and witchcraft. Neufeld argues that the effort to erase the memory of the recent past was part of an effort to eliminate 'the puritan impulse from civil and spiritual affairs', because it was deemed necessary for 'the kingdom's peace, security and the survival of English Protestantism'. The goal was therefore not to 'encourage national reconciliation, but rather to secure religious peace and political stability for the future'.[165]

At the same time, Charles II tried to distance himself from being too closely associated with Catholicism, which had tainted the Royalist cause in the Civil War. The memory of the violence that had been inflicted upon Royalist country houses was in consequence affected by the need to purge any hint of popery. A case in point was the story of Shelford House in Nottinghamshire. In November 1645 a Parliamentarian force overwhelmed Shelford's Royalist garrison. Its commander Colonel-General Sydenham Poyntz ordered no quarter to be given, and perhaps four-fifths of the garrison of two hundred men was slaughtered before the order was rescinded.[166] There was a large percentage of French and Walloon soldiers in the Royalist garrison. 'It seems clear', Appleby writes, 'that Shelford's garrison had been treated more brutally because of the prevalence of foreign Catholics within its ranks.'[167] After the Restoration, Charles II wished to downplay the belief that Royalist forces had been comprised of a substantial proportion of 'popish foreigners', because he needed to present himself as the defender of the Anglican confessional state. The massacre at Shelford and destruction of Shelford House therefore received little attention. Even today, it is barely mentioned in accounts of the village's history. Appleby writes:

> Given that Shelford is still a small, close-knit community, it is strange that even long-established families appear to possess no discernible folk memory of the most important event in the village's history; neither are there any local ghost stories or commemorative place-names to parallel those found in abundance at other civil-war sites.[168]

Such efforts to distance the Stuart dynasty from the taint of popery were undermined in the mid-1680s, however, when it became apparent that Charles II's heir would be his Roman Catholic younger brother.

In the second half of the seventeenth century, then, views of the recent past continued to be heavily influenced by memories of the Civil War. Neufeld writes:

> Picturing the past through historical writing arose from a deep concern to show what the conflicted past meant for the present and the future. The overwhelming focus of histories was to establish a continuity of principles and personnel between the conflict-ridden past and a difficult present. These writings offered stories and images as prescriptive parallels of what had happened, and what might happen again, if readers ... did not act in light of their perspective on the past.[169]

The didactic message of these histories was that recent history proved that consensus was always preferable to conflict, and stability to chaos. Once this message took root, it opened up the possibility of new historical narratives which would treat the turbulence and violence of the previous two centuries as an aberration from the true course of English history. In these narratives, as we will see in the next chapter, country houses would play a key role in distancing English history from the disruption and violence of the sixteenth and seventeenth centuries.

3
Reflections on the Non-Revolution in England

The home of the Ingilby family since the early fourteenth century, Ripley Castle in North Yorkshire is an example of how English country houses were swept up in the chaos and violence of the sixteenth and seventeenth centuries. In 1568 Sir William Ingilby helped to suppress the Rising of the North, but two of his sons were among the rebels. Subsequently ordained a priest at the English seminary in Rheims, Francis Ingilby was captured and hanged, drawn and quartered at York in 1585.[1] His brother David continued to help Catholic priests move secretly around the North of England. They may have used Ripley as a hiding place: the 'Knight's Chamber' in the tower still contains a priest hole with a stone seat and a ventilation port.

In 1603 James VI of Scotland stayed at Ripley while on his way to London for his coronation as James I of England. With only four days' notice, Sir William Ingilby, grandson of his aforementioned namesake, hastily brought in plasterers to install a splendid new ceiling in the bedroom which James was to occupy; it featured crowned heads, the English lion and the Scottish unicorn in the king's honour. Despite this ostentatious display of loyalty, two years later Ingilby became one of the key Gunpowder plotters; nine of the eleven conspirators were his relatives or close associates. After the plot was foiled, Ripley was ransacked by the ardent recusant-hunter Sir Stephen Proctor of nearby Fountains Hall. Although Proctor found nothing, Ingilby continued to be under suspicion, and in 1611 he was brought before the Privy Council on a charge of high treason. A key witness, however, revealed that he had been bribed by Proctor to lie, and the prosecution's case collapsed. Ingilby escaped punishment, even though he was almost certainly involved in the conspiracy in some way.[2]

During the Civil War the Ingilbys were staunchly Royalist. After the Parliamentarian victory at the Battle of Marston Moor in 1644, Oliver Cromwell's army pursued their fleeing opponents, including the castle's then-owner, yet another Sir William Ingilby, to Ripley; the pockmarks from their musket-fire may still be seen on the gatehouse. According to legend, Sir William's sister Jane refused to allow the Parliamentarian troops to spend the night in the castle. Eventually a compromise was reached in which only Cromwell himself was permitted to sleep there, while his men made do with the village church. Jane guarded Cromwell all night at gunpoint; although she claimed that she needed to keep her pistols in order to defend her virtue, her real reason was that her brother was hiding in the priest hole in the tower. And the legend further has it that 'Trooper' Jane had also fled from the battlefield at Marston, where she had fought – supposedly in full armour – disguised as a man.[3] As Royalists, the Ingilbys suffered financial penalties during and after the war; Jane seems to have spent the years prior to her death at the age of only fifty in 1651 working on a farm near Ripley, probably to pay off the debts arising from the sequestration of the family's estates. At the time of the Glorious Revolution, the Ingilbys

Ripley Castle in North Yorkshire was caught up in the Rising of the North and the Civil War, and in 1688 its owner Sir John Ingilby fled to France with James II. Although a later Sir John Ingilby added new ranges to Ripley in the 1780s, the house retains the basic form of a sixteenth-century tower, a reflection of the financial struggles of the family due to their political views.

– unsurprisingly in view of their history – supported James II: Sir John Ingilby followed James into exile in France in 1688, where he possibly joined the disgruntled Jacobites crowded into the dilapidated chateau at Saint-Germain-en-Laye outside Paris.

Lingering Echoes: The Glorious Revolution

This account of the Ingilbys' fortunes from the mid-sixteenth century to the late seventeenth is a combination of family lore and known facts. Every detail may not be true, but the basic story of a family repeatedly thrown into turmoil by religious and political strife is accurate, and serves as a reminder that the Civil War did not fully resolve the religious and political issues over which it had been fought. Nor did the Restoration mark a return to royal-dominated government or achieve a permanent religious settlement. Instead, the failure of Charles II to produce a legitimate heir led to another debate over faith and sovereignty, which led to his brother James II's removal from the throne in 1688. Although the Glorious Revolution was not as devastating for English country houses as the Civil War, it nonetheless affected them, as their owners sought to display their partisan affiliations.

It is a standard feature of Whig history that the Glorious Revolution was largely 'bloodless', at least in England, but recent scholarship has challenged this view. Steve Pincus writes:

> The events of 1688 were far from peaceable. Although historians have long emphasised that events in Scotland and Ireland were hardly bloodless, they have underplayed how much violence pervaded everyday life in England itself. In 1688 and after, England as well as Scotland and Ireland ... were plagued by battles, rioting and property destruction that were eerily similar to the events following the fall of the Bastille in the following century. There were no great set-piece battles in England in 1688–9. There was, however, a good deal of violence involving James's army and what remained of his militia.[4]

All over England, townspeople attacked James's soldiers, revenue collectors and other royal officials. Catholics were, however, the most frequent targets. 'The Revolution of 1688–9 was certainly not bloodless in Catholic historiography and popular memory,' Pincus observes, as 'no region of England escaped anti-Catholic violence.'[5] Many of these attacks concentrated on property, not only Catholic churches but the homes and business of English Catholics. Sir Richard Bulstrode, who fled with James II to Brussels in 1688, heard that many Catholics had been killed and most Catholic houses in England had been 'pulled down'.[6] This was an exaggeration, but not a complete fabrication. Mobs roamed the streets of many English cities and towns and the lanes and villages of rural areas, looking for Catholic property to despoil.

A case in point was Edgbaston Hall outside Birmingham. Twelve days after William of Orange landed at Torbay on 5 November 1688, Henry Booth, 2nd Baron Delamere, rallied a thousand men in Cheshire in support of the Protestant cause. He raised more men in Manchester and then marched south to Birmingham, by which point his force had doubled in size. Outside the city, they stopped at Edgbaston Hall, where they intended to seize 'a great quantity of arms'. Edgbaston was the ancestral home of the Catholic Middlemore family, who had temporarily lost the estate during the Civil War when it was garrisoned by Parliamentary troops. At the Restoration it was returned to Mary Middlemore and her husband Sir John Gage, also a Catholic. When Delamere's men failed to find the arms, they burned the house to the ground. In retaliation, James II's supporter Lord Molyneaux threatened to burn Delamere's house, Dunham Massey in Cheshire, but was prevented from doing so 'when the county rose up to the number of 4 or 5000 men with such arms as they had to defend the house'.[7]

Other supporters of James II suffered financial losses when they followed him into exile. In 1536 Walter Strickland of Sizergh Castle in Cumbria had joined the Pilgrimage of Grace, but he was pardoned by Henry VIII and thereafter conformed, at least outwardly. The family prospered over the following decades, but in the early seventeenth century Sir Thomas Strickland imperilled their financial position in the short term by racking up substantial gambling debts and over the long term by marrying a Catholic, Margaret Curwen. When he died in 1612 she raised their seven children as Catholics. The eldest son and heir, Robert, commanded a Royalist regiment in the Civil War until he was captured by the Parliamentarians in 1644; Charles I rewarded him with a knighthood. He tried to prevent the loss of his estates by making them over to his son Sir Thomas, who had been granted his own knighthood after fighting for the king at Edgehill in 1642, thereby avoiding sequestration although not heavy fines. And even this small respite was short-lived: when both Sir Robert and Sir Thomas Strickland supported the king in the second Civil War, their estates were sequestered, necessitating another heavy fine to recover them. Sir Thomas's financial problems continued in the decades after the Civil War, while increasing anti-Catholicism made career advancement more difficult. He had been MP for Westmorland since 1661, but he was forced to resign when Catholics were expelled from the House of Commons in 1677. During the Popish Plot scare of 1678–9, Sizergh was searched for weapons.

Sir Thomas had high hopes that James II's accession to the throne would improve his prospects, as several members of his family were closely connected to the new king. Things seemed to be moving in his favour when his wife Winifred was invited to attend the birth of the Prince of Wales in June 1688 and was shortly thereafter appointed the child's Under-Governess. Sir Thomas was added to the Privy Council a month later. But then the Glorious Revolution intervened. Lady Strickland fled to France with the queen and prince in December 1688, and Sir Thomas followed soon afterwards. Lady Strickland was given an apartment in the chateau of Saint-Germain-en-Laye, but in 1692 Sir Thomas's ill health forced them to move to the English convent of Poor Clares in Rouen, where his half-brother was chaplain. Sir Thomas died there two years later, and Lady Strickland returned to Saint-Germain-en-Laye as Governess to the Young Pretender. When aged seven he was placed under the supervision of a Governor. She returned to England and began working to recover the family's lost property. Before leaving England, Sir Thomas had protected his estates by transferring them into a trust with two family servants as the trustees. This prevented Sizergh from being seized when Jacobite property was confiscated in 1696, and allowed Sir Thomas's eldest son Walter to reclaim it three years later. Lady Strickland returned to France in 1700 as a Bedchamber Woman to James II's queen Mary of Modena. There she acquired, or was given as gifts, several portraits of members of the Royal House of Stuart, which now hang in the Dining Room at Sizergh, along with a few pieces of porcelain, including a Japanese Imari soup tureen with silver mounts, also still at Sizergh.

The Stricklands continued to support the Jacobite cause in the first half of the eighteenth century; a cousin, Francis Strickland, was a close friend of Bonnie Prince Charlie and died on the retreat to Scotland during the 1745 rebellion. This meant that they were cut off from profitable government posts and sinecures, which prevented Sizergh from

Painted around 1710, Alexis Simon-Belle's portrait of Princess Louisa Maria Theresa Stuart (1692–1712), the youngest child of James II and Mary of Modena, was given by Mary to Winifred, Lady Strickland, while she was serving as a Bedchamber Woman at James II's court in exile in France.

being rebuilt. The fact that it still retains the basic form of a pele tower reflects the Stricklands' longstanding commitment to the Catholic faith and to the Stuart monarchy, and the impact of their loyalty on their finances.[8]

While James II's backers suffered financial decline, William III's reaped the rewards of their support for the new king. George Jeffreys already had a reputation for severity when James II appointed him his Lord Chancellor in 1685, but he became one of the most notorious judges in English history when he sentenced 170 people to death in the 'Bloody Assizes' which followed the Monmouth Rebellion that same year. He was therefore a prime target for public retribution during the Glorious Revolution. He attempted to flee, but was captured in a London tavern and died in the Tower of London in 1689. In 1706 the house that Jeffreys had built at Bulstrode Park in Buckinghamshire between 1676 and 1685 was purchased from Jeffreys's son by Hans Willem Bentinck, Baron Bentinck of Diepenheim and Schoonheten, a Dutch favourite of William of Orange who had accompanied him to England in 1688. Bentinck was rewarded with a bevy of sinecures and titles, culminating in his ascension to 1st Earl of Portland in 1689. 'That Portland benefited materially from the king's favour cannot of course be doubted,' write Hugh Dunthorne and David Onnekink in his *Dictionary of National Biography* entry. 'Royal generosity combined with the salaries of office to make him a rich man.'[9] His purchase of Bulstrode using the proceeds of his relationship with William III was 'a clear confirmation of the Williamite victory, a victory easily visible ... through Bentinck's rather unsubtle inclusion of a row of orange trees across the south front of the house.'[10]

Others less close to the court celebrated as well. Thomas Legh of Adlington Hall in Cheshire installed a new entrance gate and planted a lime avenue to commemorate William of Orange's arrival in England. The left side of the gate bears the inscription 'IW 1688' on its top bar.[11] A staunch opponent of James II, Thomas Erle of Charborough Park in Dorset fought in the Monmouth Rebellion in 1685 and was possibly involved in the planning of the Glorious Revolution. Decades later, his great-grandson Henry Drax, Whig MP for Wareham, inscribed above the entrance to the grotto which served as Charborough's icehouse: 'Under this roof in the year 1686 a set of patriotic gentlemen of this neighbourhood concerted the great plan of the Glorious Revolution.' This was an exaggeration, as William of Orange was not invited to England until the spring of 1688, but it is possible that informal meetings of some of James II's enemies were held there.[12] In 1690 while on his way to face James II at the Battle of the Boyne in Ireland, William III stayed at Gayton House on the Wirral Peninsula. The owner William Glegg later planted two evergreen oak trees, which he named William and Mary, in honour of the visit.[13]

Charles Lennox, 1st Duke of Richmond and Lennox, was the youngest of Charles II's seven illegitimate sons. In 1685, aged thirteen, he converted to Catholicism and three years later followed James II into exile and subsequently served in the French army as aide-de-camp to the Duc d'Orléans. 'All of this', writes Rosemary Baird with considerable understatement, 'did not look good in England.'[14] In 1692 Lennox converted back to Anglicanism and declared his support for William III, but this may have been merely a cosmetic gesture so that he could return to England. His wife Anne Brudenell's father, Lord Brudenell, had served two stints in the Tower, one in the 1670s for promoting popery and another in the 1690s on suspicion of Jacobitism. Even Richmond's own mother, Louise de Kérouaille, Duchess of Portsmouth, was worried he would turn Jacobite in 1714.

It is therefore not surprising that when Lennox inherited the title in 1723, he decided to make an ostentatious declaration of loyalty to the Hanoverian regime. He served as a patron for a project launched by the Irish opera impresario Owen Swiny (or McSwiny) to commission Italian artists to create a series of 24 paintings of allegorical tombs of recent English heroes, with a strong emphasis on the Glorious Revolution and with George I featured in the final painting in the sequence. Richmond purchased at least ten of the paintings for display in his seat at Goodwood House in Sussex. Baird writes that they were 'celebrations of the lives of the Whig faithful, who had so recently built the political structure on which the Hanoverian dynasty rested. The Duke was determined that there should be no doubt about his allegiance to the King.'[15]

These examples were obvious and deliberate attempts to inscribe partisan responses to the Glorious Revolution on the physical fabric of country houses. Other cases were more subtle. Dutch architectural influence in England, in the form of hipped roofs, flat pilasters and the use of brick as decorative material, had grown over the course of the seventeenth century.[16] After 1650 prominent English architects such as Roger Pratt, Hugh May, Robert Hooke and William Talman were influenced by Dutch models.[17] Christopher Wren looked to Dutch precedent in his rebuilding of the City of London's churches after the Great Fire, and his country houses, for example Tring Park in Hertfordshire (c. 1682–3), also incorporated Dutch elements.[18] The number of country houses that clearly showed Dutch influence was,

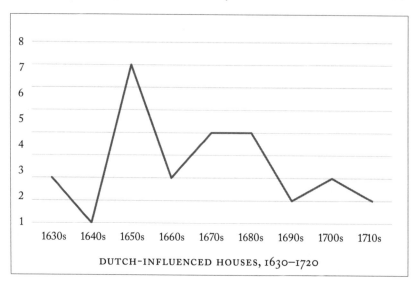

DUTCH-INFLUENCED HOUSES, 1630–1720

Delftware flower pyramid, c. 1693–4, at Dyrham Park in Gloucestershire. Made in the workshop of Adrianus Kocx in Delft, it is one of many Dutch objects in the house, a reflection of William Blathwayt's association with and allegiance to William III.

to be sure, never large, but there was a steady stream in the second half of the seventeenth century, with peaks in the 1650s and '70s.

After 1680, however, Dutch influences became less fashionable, suggesting that their appearances after the Glorious Revolution were likely to be expressions of political allegiance. Built between 1692 and 1704, Dyrham Park in Gloucestershire was designed by William Talman for William Blathwayt, William III's Secretary of State. Blathwayt filled the house with Dutch fashions: paintings by Dutch artists, leather wall-coverings and blue-and-white Delft tiles and vases. Outside, the gardens were in the formal and geometric Dutch style.[19] Oliver Garnett writes of the entrance hall:

> The Dutch character of Dyrham is clear right from the start. The Cromwellian chairs are covered with Dutch leather. The landscape paintings hanging on the walls are by minor seventeenth-century Dutch artists and still have their original Dutch-style

black frames. The tile pictures of exotic palms and pineapples flanking the fireplace were manufactured in Delft, and were inspired by a Dutch East India Company expedition to China.[20]

Blathwayt had gained much of his admiration for Dutch culture during his four years in The Hague as secretary to Sir William Temple, who was dispatched to negotiate the Triple Alliance among England, Sweden and the Dutch Republic as well as the marriage between Princess Mary, James II's eldest daughter, and William of Orange. But Blathwayt also wanted to pay tribute to his monarch by filling Dyrham with Dutch objects.

In the early 1680s Ford Grey was one of the leaders of the movement to exclude James II from succeeding to the throne. When that failed, he joined the Duke of Monmouth's Rye House Plot to kidnap and murder the king, and offered Uppark, his Sussex estate, to the Duke as a safe house until the plot was launched. The plot was unearthed and Grey dispatched to the Tower, but he plied his captor with fourteen bottles of claret and escaped back to Uppark, and from there on to Chichester, where he boarded a boat for Flushing. He returned to England in 1685 to serve as Monmouth's chief lieutenant in his short-lived rebellion; he and Monmouth were arrested shortly after they fled the battlefield at Sedgmoor. Monmouth was summarily executed, but Grey turned informer, which, with the addition of a £40,000 bond and other gifts to influential courtiers such as Lord Rochester, who received £1,700 'per Ann for ever out of Lord Grey's estate', saved his life.[21]

Grey avoided further trouble until the Glorious Revolution, when he immediately announced his support for William of Orange. He was rewarded with a seat on the Privy Council (1695) and appointments as a Commissioner for Trade (1696), First Commissioner of the Treasury (1699) and Lord Privy Seal (1700), as well as the titles of Viscount Glendale and Earl of Tankerville (both in 1695). Given the reversal of his fortunes – very much for the better – that William's accession had produced, it is not surprising that Grey celebrated his king when he began building a new house at Uppark shortly after the Glorious Revolution:

> Uppark is one of the finest surviving examples within a tradition of country-house building introduced to England from Holland in the 1660s by gentleman-architects like Hugh May and Roger

Reflections on the Non-Revolution in England

Uppark in West Sussex was built in a Dutch style by Ford Grey, probably to show his loyalty to William III, who had granted Grey, a strong supporter of the Glorious Revolution, a number of valuable government posts.

Pratt. Symmetry and simplicity are its hallmarks, and Uppark shares many of its other common features: a hipped roof with a deep cornice, dormer windows and tall chimneystacks; a central three-bay frontispiece set slightly forward, with a pediment which once contained the Grey coat of arms . . .; two principal floors separated by a plain string course, above a semi-basement; and steps up to a pedimented doorway on the south front leading into the principal room on the principal floor . . . Uppark is reminiscent of May's elegant domestic style, markedly Dutch in its use of brick with stone dressings.[22]

Another way in which country-house owners showed their support for the Glorious Revolution was by using classical mythology. As part of his rebuilding of Chatsworth House in Derbyshire in the early 1690s, William Cavendish, 4th Earl of Devonshire (after 1694 1st Duke of Devonshire), commissioned the French painter Louis Laguerre and the Italian painter Antonio Verrio to decorate the walls and ceilings of some of the most important rooms. A Whig in his partisan affiliation, Devonshire had been one of the 'Immortal Seven' who had invited William of Orange to England, and after William landed at Torbay he travelled around the country recruiting troops on his behalf. In the

Louis Laguerre's depiction of the assassination of Julius Caesar over the staircase in the Painted Hall at Chatsworth House in Derbyshire (opposite); and Antonio Verrio's ceiling for the staircase, entitled *The Triumph of Semele*, 1691 (above). Contemporary visitors would have seen the paintings as references to the Glorious Revolution.

Painted Hall where guests entered the house, Laguerre depicted the story of Julius Caesar, culminating in his assassination. Laurel Peterson notes that at the time 'Caesar would have been familiar as a symbol of the Stuart kings.' By featuring his assassination so prominently – the scene is directly above the staircase which guests must ascend to go further into the house – Devonshire wanted to signal 'the dismantling of a myth': 'The Painted Hall becomes a chilling reflection on the dangers of tyrannical absolutism, suggesting how unjust government leads to downfall.'[23]

Verrio's ceiling of the Great Staircase continues to convey Devonshire's political message. It depicts Cybele, the Greek and Roman 'mother of the Gods' who had become the subject of a cult of worship during the Second Punic War (218–201 BC), when a famine threatened to lead to a catastrophic defeat. The Sybilline oracle warned that the only way to stave off disaster was to import the *Magna Mater* from her home in Pessinos in the kingdom of Pergamum, a Roman ally. The king agreed, and the goddess was brought to Rome in the form of a black meteoric stone. The famine ended and Carthage was defeated. In late seventeenth- and early eighteenth-century England, when the upper classes were well versed in classical mythology, the story of Cybele was one of many myths that was drafted into contemporary political debates.

Verrio's painting of the Cybele myth at Chatsworth is intended to allude to Queen Mary II's role in the Glorious Revolution as the deliverer of the nation from the catastrophe of a Catholic, absolutist monarch. Mary, who reigned as joint sovereign with William until her death in 1694, is now all but forgotten as a focus of attention at the time, but in the years after 1688 she was a key figure in efforts to legitimize the removal of James II.[24] In Verrio's version:

> She presides over global prosperity; allegorical representations of the four continents offer products from their corners of the world. Below, representations of Hercules with the severed body of the hydra and the Erymanthian boar, painted in grisaille, fill the walls – symbols of William III, who use[d] the brawny demigod as his emblem. While Hercules alludes to the king's heroic efforts to depose a tyrant, above, the prosperous reign of a queen over the continents celebrates Mary II. Mary, the eldest daughter of James II, helped to legitimize the British rule of her husband William, and thus was a key component to the success of the Glorious Revolution.[25]

Lest there be any doubt that the painting referred to contemporary political events, Devonshire ensured that the meaning was clear. At the bottom of the painting:

> Fury appears in the midst of blind destruction, standing upon the symbols of religion and absolutist rule. Underneath his right foot lies a crozier and a golden miter with its lappets falling over the edge of the balustrade. With his left foot, Fury tramples the Latin Bible – 'DEUS' prominently inscribed at the top of the page. The jeweled crown and the scepter topped with a fleur-de-lys connect these religious symbols to the French monarchy ... This startling vignette representing the destruction of apparently Catholic symbols makes pointed reference to the contemporary events of the Revolution of 1688 ... On the ceiling of an important room in his country estate, [Devonshire] chose not simply a generalized celebration of the victory of virtue over vice, but rather hailed the triumph of Protestantism at the close of the seventeenth century. Since Verrio himself was Catholic, the duke almost certainly initiated and directed the scheme's strong anti-Catholic sentiment.[26]

Another example of the use of classical mythology to express support for the Glorious Revolution was at Boughton House in Lincolnshire, where Ralph Montagu, Baron Montagu of Boughton (after 1705 1st Duke of Montagu), commissioned Louis Chéron to paint the ceiling of the entrance hall in preparation for a visit by William III in 1695. Chéron depicted the marriage of Hercules and Hebe, which, as Gervase Jackson-Stops writes, was

> undoubtedly intended to symbolize the marriage of William and Mary. As Child of State in Holland, William had been depicted as the infant Hercules strangling the serpent, and Hercules was always his favorite mythological persona; Hebe, the daughter of Jupiter and Juno ... underlined Mary's status as the legitimate heir.[27]

Montagu's kinsman Charles Montagu, 1st Duke of Manchester, served as ambassador to Venice from 1699 to 1701 and again in 1707–8. He hired the Venetian stage decorator Giovanni Antonio Pelligrini to paint the lower level of the staircase hall of Kimbolton Castle in Cambridgeshire, which was remodelled to designs by Sir John Vanbrugh in 1707, with scenes of the triumph of Caesar 'a clear parallel to William III's later triumph'.[28] These houses were examples of the increasing didacticism of country-house iconography in the decades following the Glorious Revolution, as English politics became more partisan and owners more eager to display their allegiances. And it was Whigs such as Devonshire and Montagu who made the most determined efforts to 'adapt baroque court art to the exigencies of the post-revolutionary state'.[29]

A later example is Hanbury Hall in Worcestershire, where around 1710 Thomas Vernon commissioned Sir James Thornhill to decorate the staircase. The ceiling depicts a group of classical gods and goddesses, among which Mercury points to a printed portrait of Dr Thomas Sacheverell, which is floating through the air dangerously close to the torches of the Furies. Sacheverell was a clergyman of High Church principles who on Guy Fawkes Day in 1709 had given a fiery sermon attacking Catholics and, especially, Nonconformists. After the Whig government convicted him of sedition for contravening the revolution settlement of 1688 and suspended him from preaching for three years, riots broke out in London and other cities. Queen Anne, disenchanted with the progress of the War of the Spanish Succession, used the unrest as an

A detail from Sir James Thornhill's paintings for the staircase at Hanbury Hall in Worcestershire, 1710, showing Mercury pointing to a printed portrait of the High Tory Dr Thomas Sacheverell, who had delivered an incendiary sermon attacking Catholics and Nonconformists on Guy Fawkes Day the previous year.

excuse to replace her Whig ministers with Tories. A staunch Whig, Vernon, as Jeffrey Haworth and Gervase Jackson-Stops write, 'no doubt regarded Sacheverell as the blackest of traitors, fit only to be roasted and burnt to ashes by the torches of the Furies'.[30]

These country houses became sites for displaying partisan views of the Glorious Revolution. In the decades that followed, the ideology they expressed became dominant, as the Whigs enjoyed four decades of power. First, however, Whig dominance had to be secured by the failure of the Jacobite rebellion of 1715.

The Jacobite Rebellion of 1715

General James Edward Oglethorpe, the founder of the American colony of Georgia, hailed from a strongly Jacobite family. His father, Major-General Sir Theophilus Oglethorpe, was relieved of his rank after he remained loyal to James II in the Glorious Revolution; he retired to Surrey and purchased Westbrook Place. James Edward was the youngest of ten children and the fifth son; he was named after James II and his son James Francis Edward Stuart, the Old Pretender. His sisters were raised at the Stuart court in Saint-Germain-en-Laye, and his elder brother gave up the family estates and entered the Pretender's service. James Edward, however, joined the army and served the Hanoverians loyally for over three decades. In the early 1730s Oglethorpe proposed the founding of a new colony between Florida and South Carolina in order to provide opportunities for impoverished Britons. Keen to establish a buffer state to protect the colonies to the north from the threat of a Spanish invasion from Florida, King George II granted the charter. While Oglethorpe was in Georgia working to establish the colony, his sister Anne lived at Westbrook, and another sister, Eleanor Marquise de Mézières, visited frequently. The two sisters were involved in Jacobite plots and, anticipating a future rebellion, they built two miniature forts along a vineyard wall in Westbrook's garden. One of them, known as the 'Little Fort', is still there today.[31]

Although the Little Fort now seems hyperbolic, the Oglethorpe sisters were right to recognize that the Jacobite rebellions posed a threat to private property. After 1688, as we saw in the previous section, Whigs expressed their growing confidence in the décor of their country houses. They could do so because the revolution settlement came to be increasingly entrenched as the political norm, and although far from relegated to complete irrelevance, after 1720 the Tories were cut off from any prospect of power at Westminster.[32] The Jacobite rebellion of 1715 was the major factor in driving the Tories into the political wilderness. Although nowhere near the scale of the Civil War, the rebellion had a direct impact on country houses, some of which suffered collateral damage. Most of this damage occurred in Scotland, but a few English houses were also affected. Henry Prescott, Deputy Registrar of Chester Diocese, recorded in his diary in November 1715 that he was 'disturbed with Accounts of the barbarous behaviour of the soldiers in theire plunder of the popish gentlemen's houses'.[33] After the Jacobite Albert Hodgson was captured at the Battle of Preston in 1715, government troops sacked and burned his Lancashire house, Leighton Hall.[34] Clifton Hall Tower in Cumbria, a fifteenth-century pele tower, was occupied and plundered by the Jacobites before the Battle of Clifton Moor in 1745.[35]

Also reminiscent of what had occurred during the Civil War, the government carried out acts of retribution on those who had dared to rebel against it. Anyone who had taken up arms for the Jacobites or who had actively supported them was potentially subject to draconian penalties, including execution and forfeiture of property. Daniel Szechi writes:

> Early modern European governments were great believers in deterrence, and consequently everyone knew there was bound to be retribution in store for the Jacobite communities directly involved in the rebellion. Of these, the Scots had most cause for apprehension simply because the rebellion had started and ended there and they had clearly posed the greatest threat to the Whig regime's hold on power. Any opportunity to righteously punish the English Catholic community – the ancestral enemy of all good Whigs – was also bound to be of great interest to any Whig-dominated government in the early eighteenth century. The only questions concerned who and how many were to be punished.[36]

On the other hand, however, the Hanoverian Succession was new, and while not exactly precarious, it was not on as firm a footing as several decades later. The 1715 rebellion

> revealed serious faultlines in the political foundations of the new dynasty – a discontented Roman Catholic religious minority in Northern England, the willingness of former Privy Councilors like the Earl of Mar, Viscount Bolingbroke and the Duke of Ormonde, previously loyal to the Protestant Succession, to betray the new ruler for promises of power from his Stuart rival, bitter resentment in Scotland of the 1707 Treaty of Union, even amongst

otherwise loyal subjects of the new king, and the menacing broad appeal of Jacobite ideology to the Episcopalians of Scotland.[37]

Moreover, memories of James II's brutal repression of the Duke of Monmouth's rebellion in 1685 lived on as a reminder of Tory tyranny. The Whig government therefore had to take care not to seem overly harsh in its application of justice. In the end, only forty people were executed for participating in the rebellion, with another 638 transported to America. Because of the difficulty of trying Scots for crimes committed in Scotland under English law, English participants in the rebellion were punished more severely than their Scottish counterparts. Of the forty executions, only one was of a Scotsman, while the English leaders, along with Scots who had the misfortune to be captured in England, were taken to London for what Szechi describes as 'some suitably grim show trials', prior to which 'they were paraded through the streets on their way to Newgate and the Tower so as to allow the government's plebeian supporters to celebrate its triumph in a kind of grand charivari.'[38] One English peer was executed: James Radclyffe, 3rd Earl of Derwentwater, an illegitimate descendant of Charles II who had joined the rebellion along with his brother Charles. After his execution in February 1716, his property, totalling 3,500 acres, worth £93,000 and including Langley Castle and Dilston Hall in Northumberland, was seized by the government. Langley had long been a roofless ruin, but the 3rd Earl's son was permitted to continue living at Dilston until his death in 1731. In 1748 the estates were granted to the Royal Naval Hospital in Greenwich, and Dilston was demolished in the 1760s.[39] George Collingwood of Eslington Hall, also in Northumberland and worth £1,000 a year, was hanged, drawn and quartered in Liverpool the day after Derwentwater's execution. His property was confiscated by the Crown and sold in 1720 to Sir Henry Liddell for a bargain price of £21,131, out of which Collingwood's widow was granted a payment of £6,000, in addition to her jointure and annuities for her children.[40]

The public spectacle of these executions did not, however, produce the reaction the government intended. In particular, the young, handsome and charismatic Earl of Derwentwater earned the crowd's sympathy, and when the Northern Lights appeared over northern England shortly after his death it was widely interpreted as a sign of divine displeasure at the government's action.[41] The government was careful not to repeat the mistake of imposing sentences which were likely to be perceived as excessively retributive. The other English peer who was tried for high treason, William Widdrington, 4th Baron Widdrington, was sentenced to death but his punishment was first reduced to banishment to the American colonies and then in 1717 lifted entirely. He was placed under attainder, however, and his property was confiscated. Widdrington was living at Stella Hall in County Durham, an estate which he had acquired through marriage, because his own seat at Widdrington Castle in Northumberland had been damaged in a French raid in 1691. He was granted a £200 payment from the king and £400 a year from the income of his estates. In 1719 he petitioned for the latter to be increased to £700 to support his 'distressed family', but his plea was rejected by the House of Commons. Four years later he was granted £12,000 from the sale of Widdrington Castle, and in 1733 he was able to reacquire Stella after its purchaser, the York Buildings Company, was unable to turn a profit from the colliery that lay on the estate.[42] John Thornton was also reprieved from a sentence of death, but his estate at Netherwitton, which produced £1,353 in annual rents, was forfeited and sold in 1720 for £13,100 to Robert Stoddart of London. Friends of the Thorntons purchased it back from Stoddart, however, and then resold it to trustees of Thornton's young son Thomas.[43] George Gibson died in prison after being found guilty of participating in the rebellion. His estate, Low Hall in Northumberland, was forfeited and sold for £360 in 1720.[44]

The fates of Widdrington and Thornton signified the government's shift from targeting persons to targeting property as a means of punishing Jacobite rebels. A precedent had been set by the Jacobite war of 1689–91, when a large amount of property belonging to Jacobites in Ireland had been forfeited to the Crown, thereby reducing Catholic landholdings from 22 to 14 per cent of the total.[45] The rebels in 1715 were clearly aware of the potential consequences for their estates. When the Earl of Derwentwater tried to persuade William Errington, who owned Beaufront Castle in Northumberland, the adjacent estate to Derwentwater's Dilston, to join the rebellion, Errington initially attempted to dissuade him by walking him up a hill which overlooked Dilston and showing him what he would lose if the rebellion failed.[46]

Errington's prediction proved accurate. In 1716 a Commission for Forfeited Estates was established by Act of Parliament. Its purpose was

> to make good on the theoretical forfeiture of the estates of every rebel landowner in northern England and Scotland, and

specifically to seize the property of those individuals who had failed to heed the summonses to Edinburgh issued in August 1715 or were named in the Act of Attainder passed later in the year.[47]

In the ensuing effort to identify anyone with even the slightest sympathy for the Jacobite cause, a number of prominent politicians were targeted. Henry St John, 1st Viscount Bolingbroke, Secretary of State from 1710 to 1714, had flirted with Jacobitism not from principle but as a means of securing personal advancement and Tory power. When the rebellion of 1715 broke out, he was asked to surrender his papers and fled to France to avoid arrest. He was placed under attainder and his estates, including his manor in Battersea (now the site of Battersea Park), were confiscated. He was pardoned in 1723 but his property was not restored, and so he purchased an estate at Dawley near Uxbridge instead.[48] In contrast with Bolingbroke, the 2nd Duke of Ormond was a committed Jacobite. Most of his property was in Ireland, but when he was attainted he lost his estate at Richmond in Surrey as well. It proved, however, a mixed blessing for the Commissioners, who not only had to pay the taxes and carry out basic maintenance on the Richmond property after they evicted Ormond's tenant, the Duke of Grantham, but were forced to deal with a severe infestation of rats which required the intervention of the noted rat-catcher John Humphries. The estate was eventually purchased by the Prince of Wales for £6,000.[49]

In Scotland, where Jacobites were quickly transformed in the eyes of the public from 'deadly enemies in need of extirpation' to 'objects of contemptuous pity', the Commission's activities proved controversial.[50] In northern England, however, attitudes were less sympathetic:

> There its principal target was the Catholic community, and by a judicious mix of legal measures and the solicitation of information from disgruntled tenants, worried creditors, avaricious informers and greedy neighbours it was able to uncover not only the bulk of the landed property held by many wealthy landed Catholic families, but the lands and properties secretly dedicated to supporting the underground Catholic church in northern England and its support network of colleges and religious houses on the continent.[51]

The government blamed not only the rebels themselves, but the Catholic community more broadly. The Commissioners were permitted to seize property used to support 'superstitious practices' (that is, Catholicism), and informers were offered one-quarter of its value as an incentive to reveal what they knew of their neighbours' religious beliefs. This was, in other words, an effort to destroy the wealth and influence of the Catholic gentry by driving them into poverty. 'If they are divested of their estates ...', declared the Commissioners to the Treasury in 1717, 'the Roman Catholics in the northern counties must be completely destroyed.'[52] Catholic estates that were forfeited after 1715 included Cheeseburn Grange in Northumberland, owned by Sir Ralph Widdrington; Bavington Hall in Northumberland, owned by William Shafto; and Eccleston Hall in Lancashire, owned by Thomas Stanley. Already burned by government forces, Albert Hodgson's Leighton Hall in Lancashire was confiscated. Although a friend bought it back for him in 1722, he could not afford to rebuild it, and it remained a ruin until the 1760s.[53]

The effort to impoverish English Catholics was further strengthened by the Papists' Estates Act (1716), which required Catholic landowners to register their estates and income so that they could be assessed for a contribution 'to all such extraordinary expenses as are, or shall be brought upon this Kingdom by their treachery'.[54] English Catholics did not meekly acquiesce to such punitive measures. Led by the Duke of Norfolk, the leading Catholic peer, they petitioned for relief, but when none was forthcoming they turned to a variety of strategies to mitigate the worst consequences of the law: some delayed registering, others undervalued their property so as to reduce their financial liability and still others placed their estates in trust with friendly Protestants. William Shafto, for example, was able to solicit the help of his relative Admiral George Delaval to purchase Bavington when it was sold at auction in 1718.[55] The Forfeited Estates Commission was as a result often frustrated; the Commissioners complained to Parliament that many estates 'of a very considerable value' that were 'given and settled to popish and superstitious uses' were 'artfully screened by intricate trusts, and otherwise encumbered'.[56]

Szechi characterizes the government response to the 1715 rebellion in northern England as 'distinctly brutal' and concludes that 'it was a blow from which their community was to take decades to recover.'[57] Certainly, these measures were reasonably successful in eradicating Jacobite sentiment in the North of England; there would be much less sympathy to the Jacobite cause in the region in 1745. Historians debate, however, the effectiveness of these measures in permanently damaging the finances of Catholic families. On the one hand, Leo Gooch argues that over the long term the majority of Catholic landowners managed, through 'subterfuge or sheer effrontery', to preserve or fairly quickly regain their landed property.[58] On the other, Margaret Sankey concludes that

> despite some defiance and the interference of relatives who saved a handful of estates from passing out of family control through forfeiture, the Commission in England accomplished the government's aims. They crippled the northern Jacobites, redistributed their land to more trustworthy owners, mostly wealthy merchants from London in search of a relatively inexpensive way of moving into the landowning class, and impressed the government's authority on local tenants.[59]

For those Jacobites who managed to retain their property after 1715, expressions of political views which did not endorse the Williamite revolution were not merely defiant but treasonous. It was therefore necessary to express such views covertly, in ways that could only be understood by sympathizers. This poses a problem for identifying the remnants of Jacobite material culture today. Neil Guthrie writes: 'Concealing an overt Jacobite message could have been prudent in the face of potential legal penalities. While one ought to avoid over-enthusiasm in identifying Jacobite supporters, an eye that is both informed and critical may be able to discern Jacobite sentiments where they are ... expressed cryptically.'[60] The possibility that Chiswick House in London contained secret Jacobite iconography, despite Lord Burlington's ostensibly impeccable Whig credentials, has been much discussed by historians and art historians.[61] This shows the nature of the problem in a world in which Jacobite opinion could not be overtly expressed. Print and public speech were off-limits, which meant that 'objects, décor and material culture' assumed greater significance as means of communication. These were often found in country houses owned by Jacobites – because 'it required relative wealth to produce a grammar of wordless ... sedition through multiple objects or narrative décor.'[62] One example of such objects was a six-fold screen at Wallington House in Northumberland that reproduced illustrations from John Ogilby's 1659 edition of Virgil's *Aeneid*, which had been intended to promote the Restoration through its references to exile. Wallington's owner in the early eighteenth century was Sir William Blackett, who helped to plan the 1715 Jacobite rebellion.[63]

One of the most common ways to express Jacobite sentiments was through the possession and use of Jacobite glassware. Pittock observes that objects

> involving shared dining or drinking were often the most developed in their symbolism, for in the mutuality of food and drink lay an intimate exchange between host and guest in which political sympathy could be intensified through glass, ceramics and ultimately perhaps toasts or even songs . . . This kind of exchange was at the core of the milieux of live Jacobite memory, where commemoration of the past and plots for present and future could occupy the same space and time. Thus it is in Jacobite glass that some of the most developed micronarratives of Jacobite ambition are emplaced, and a syntax of symbols exist in clear relation to each other, sometimes themselves triggers for particular rituals to be carried out at certain stages of the evening or meal.[64]

At Chastleton, Henry Jones commissioned a set of eleven Jacobite wine glasses and two decanters which were engraved with the six-petalled Jacobite white roses and oak leaves.[65] Other examples were owned by the Leghs at Lyme Park in Cheshire and the Bedingfields at Oxburgh Hall in Norfolk. The largest collection that survives today was that of the Newdigates at Arbury Hall in Warwickshire.[66] Sir Philip Grey-Egerton kept his Jacobite glassware in a special cabinet at Oulton Park in Cheshire. In trusted company, it would be opened with great ceremony to reveal a 'tabernacle' portrait of an armoured Bonnie Prince Charlie.[67] Jacobite country-house owners also amassed a wide variety of other objects and relics, including locks of the hair of the Old and Young Pretenders and weapons used in battles against the Hanoverian state. Nunnington Hall in Yorkshire still possesses several Jacobite artefacts in its collection, including a blue garter that supposedly belonged to Bonnie Prince Charlie and a ring containing a lock of his hair.[68]

As Neil Guthrie notes, however, Jacobite material culture was 'not confined to relatively small objects', as 'Jacobite partisanship' also 'found its expression in buildings, décor and landscape gardening'.[69] Can we

Part of the set of Jacobite glassware at
Chastleton House in Oxfordshire, mid-18th century.

read Jacobite messages in architectural styles? Danny in Sussex was a sixteenth-century house owned by Henry Campion. In 1728 he hired John Sanderson to remodel it. The south front was classicized – 'a typical stately early Georgian job' – but inside the Elizabethan great hall was preserved, according to the authors of the Pevsner guide, because Campion was an 'arch-Tory and Jacobite' and was therefore 'faithful to tradition'.[70] Although there was no obvious 'Jacobite' country-house style, the Baroque and Rococo are sometimes cited as such, the former for its Continental associations and the latter for its characteristic 'disorder', which could be seen as an endorsement of the disruption of the existing Whig political order. Not all houses with Baroque exteriors or Rococo plasterwork on their interiors were owned by Tories, however, just as not all Palladian houses were owned by Whigs.[71] Care must also be taken not to interpret every potential Jacobite symbol as evidence of sympathy for the Stuart cause; not all oak trees planted on English – or even Scottish – estates in the late seventeenth and early eighteenth centuries referred to the famous tree in which Charles II had hidden at Boscobel.

Some trees did, however, have political meaning. Sir Richard Graham, Viscount Preston, was attainted and sentenced to death in 1691 for his support of James II. His life was spared and his children managed to reacquire the family's estates, including the aforementioned Nunnington

Hall. After inheriting the house, Graham's daughter Catherine, Lady Widdrington, planted a Scots pine – known in Catholic circles as a 'Charlie tree' – in a prominent position on top of a hill to show her continuing commitment to Jacobitism.[72] At Chastleton House in Oxfordshire, the Jacobite Henry Jones planted Scots pines in the garden, supposedly to act 'as a guide to Jacobite fugitives'.[73] In the 1750s Sir James Dashwood planted Scottish fir trees on his Kirtlington Park estate in Oxfordshire to display his continuing support for the Jacobite cause, even after the failure of the 1745 rebellion.[74]

It was the interiors, however, of country houses that were best suited for Jacobite display, for the simple reason that their seditious nature could be better concealed from the prying eyes of government spies. At Lullingstone Castle in Kent, the Jacobite Percival Hart installed a plasterwork rose in the ceiling which bore the inscription:

Kentish True Blue
Take this for a Token
That what is said here
Under the Rose is spoken.

In this context, 'True Blue' invoked loyalty to the rightful king, while 'under the Rose' possessed a double meaning: it referred not only to the Jacobite white rose, but to the need for Jacobites to conduct their activities clandestinely, or *sub rosa*.[75]

In 1734 Thomas Wentworth, 1st Earl of Strafford, commissioned James Gibbs to design an obelisk for the park of his Wentworth Castle estate in South Yorkshire. Although Strafford served as a minister under Queen Anne, he remained secretly loyal to the Stuarts, and after he left office on the Hanoverian Succession, he was involved in both the Atterbury and Cornbury Plots. In 1722 he was created a 'Lord Regent' by the Old Pretender, elevated to Duke of Strafford in his peerage and named commander of his forces north of the Humber. The inscription on the obelisk refers to how Strafford 'was one of the seven appointed by act/ of PARLIAMENT to be REGENTS of the/ KINGDOME during [two words damaged by stone scaling] the absence of the/ SUCCESSOR'. This ostensibly refers to his role as one of the Lord Justices who after the death of Queen Anne governed until George I reached England, but the absence of any clear identification of the 'successor' shows where Strafford's true loyalties lay.[76] Inside the castle, a plasterwork relief panel depicting Perseus by the Italian *stuccodore* Giuseppe Artari may have alluded to a young prince who had been unjustly deprived of his rightful inheritance.[77]

These expressions of Jacobitism in country houses were for the most part allusive and covert, so much so that today we often cannot be sure that they truly had any political meaning. The architect James Gibbs undeniably held Jacobite sympathies, but we will never know for certain whether the octagonal chapel at Orleans House in Twickenham that he built for the Scottish Tory politician James Johnston was *really* a half-joking allusion to James VIII, the royal name that the Old Pretender might have adopted had he succeeded to the Scottish throne.[78] What is clear is that Jacobite sympathies had to be displayed very cautiously.[79] An open statement of Jacobite sentiment was at Callaly in Nothumberland, owned by the Clavering family, where the saloon featured plasterwork oak leaves and two herons under an oak tree, a symbol of a 'lost paradise'.[80] But even that would not have been possible to prosecute.

The 1715 Jacobite rebellion therefore accelerated the use of country houses as sites for the expression of increasingly dominant Whig views, while other opinions were relegated to more secretive forms of display. Country houses no longer reflected strife, as they had done in the sixteenth and seventeenth centuries, but were instead beginning to express stability. This was the origin of their role as embodiments of the continuity that became a key component of English national identity over the next two centuries. For the rest of the eighteenth century, however, country houses would express this continuity not through overt displays of political partisanship, but more abstractly in their architectural style.

The Political Battle of the Styles

In the first half of the eighteenth century the victorious 'Whig' version of history was increasingly – and triumphally – expressed by the English elite in their houses, while alternative views, not only Jacobite but Tory, were forced into more covert forms of expression. After 1720 this unequal contest between opposing political views extended into a broader 'battle of the styles' between the classical and the gothic. English classicism was a response to a very different set of political and cultural circumstances than those of continental Europe: it conveyed partisan national and imperial values rather than promoting the power of the monarchy and the Church.[81] In this context, classicism, or more specifically English Palladianism, is often seen as a 'Whig' style which was used to embody a Protestant vision of national glory based on constitutional monarchy, global commerce and naval might. It was based upon a sense of restraint which contrasted with the cultural grandiosity of Catholic nations, where the Baroque prevailed as the main form of classicism in the early eighteenth century.

The juxtaposition of 'Whig' restraint against the ostentation of 'Tory' Baroque became less relevant in the decades after 1720. The divisions between Whigs and Tories which had evolved after the Restoration were based upon competing interpretations of England's political past, and in particular how these influenced the balance of power between Parliament and monarchy. But as the Glorious Revolution came to be broadly accepted by both sides, this ideological division was replaced by one between the 'Court' and 'Country' parties, with the latter made up of both Tories and 'Patriot' Whigs who opposed Sir Robert Walpole's lax sense of political morality. Since there was now broad agreement that England's history had resulted in a mixed government whose primary purpose should be the preservation of liberty, history was no longer a fundamental subject of debate.[82] Men from both parties could thus embrace Palladianism: 40 per cent of the subscribers to Campbell's *Vitruvius Britannicus* were Tories, and even Lord Burlington, although publicly a Whig, may have had secret Jacobite leanings.[83]

Palladianism's supremacy, however, was challenged by a revival of the gothic style, at first in the form of landscape garden features, with the 'Gothick Temple' at Shotover Park in Oxfordshire (1717) and 'Alfred's Hall' at Cirencester Park in Gloucestershire (1721) two of the earliest examples.[84] At Esher Place in Surrey (1732–3), William Kent expanded a medieval gatehouse into a battlemented residence for the antiquary Henry Pelham; and at Rousham in Oxfordshire (1737–41) he converted a mill into a gothic-style 'ruin' and built a gothic eyecatcher on a nearby hill. In 1741 James Gibbs added a large gothic 'Temple of Liberty' to the famous landscape garden at Stowe in Buckinghamshire.[85]

To some, the historicism of the gothic style meant that it embodied the traditional – in Whig eyes archaic – values of Toryism. Cirencester Park, the site of Alfred's Hall, was owned by the staunchly Tory Lord Bathurst.[86] Worse still, with its irregularity and refusal to adopt the symmetry and strict mathematical proportions of classicism, it had associations with the chaos of the previous century. But just as Tories could embrace Palladianism, so Whigs could embrace the gothic. Over the course of the seventeenth century a link had been forged between English liberty and the gothic architectural style. Influenced by the French Huguenot lawyer François Hotman's *Franco-Gallia* (1573) and refined through English texts such as Richard Verstegen's *Restitution of Decayed Intelligence* (1605), John Selden's *The Reverse of the English Janus* (1610), Nathaniel Bacon's *Historical and Political Discourse of the Laws and Government of England* (1647) and James Harrington's *The Commonwealth of Oceana* (1656), a view evolved that English liberty had been inherited from the Saxons, who elected their kings and limited their powers.[87] This liberty was seen as having been disrupted by the Norman Conquest, but it had been clawed back over the succeeding centuries. After 1688 this view was incorporated into the Whig interpretation of the Glorious Revolution, which held that the Magna Carta was not an innovation but a restoration of pre-1066 political rights, and that the execution of Charles I and the removal of James II were not revolutionary acts, but rather defences of ancient rights unlawfully usurped by tyrannous monarchs. 'No Nation has preserv'd their Gothick Constitution better than the English,' wrote the Whig historian and pamphleteer John Oldmixon in the 1720s.[88] More specifically, English liberty had been established by the Saxons, whose *witans*, or king's councils, were the precursors to the Parliament of the present day. In 1748, in a sermon celebrating the defeat of the Jacobite rebellion two years earlier, William Warburton, rector of Brant Broughton and Firsby and later Bishop of Gloucester, declared: 'When the fierce and free nations of the North dismembered and tore in pieces the Roman Empire, they established themselves in their new conquests, on one common principle of policy; in which, the Liberty of the People made, as it ought to do, the Base, and operating Power.'[89]

James Tyrrell, the owner of Shotover Park, where an early gothic temple had been built in 1717, was a friend of John Locke and had published his own version of Whig constitutional theory, the *Bibliotheca Politica* (1694). Michael Lewis writes that the temple

> was built just after the Hanoverian king George I ascended the throne in 1714, an event which caused England to brood over questions of national identity. A German-speaking Protestant now reigned, while the Catholic Stuarts threatened invasion and rebellion from Scotland: this could not help but throw into doubt every aspect of English religion, nationality and culture. The gothic assuaged these doubts, providing an assertive and

haughty symbol of national independence, untainted by association with the Roman Catholic courts of Europe, where baroque taste reigned ... English pedants could cheerfully associate the gothic with semi-legendary figures such as King Alfred or King Arthur. Likewise, they connected it not with Catholic cathedrals, but with secular buildings, above all sturdy castles.[90]

A similar political message may be ascribed to Gibbs's temple at Stowe. Intended to evoke the Magna Carta as a foundation of English rights, it was a key piece of the garden's 'Patriot Whig' ideology.[91] Michael McCarthy writes that Stowe's temple was 'a declaration of Protestant individualism against Catholic uniformity, and of the virtues of constitutional monarchy against the doctrine of the Divine Right of Kings'.[92]

It was not until the late 1740s, however, that Horace Walpole's Strawberry Hill became the first country house to embrace fully the gothic style.[93] This slow pace was because the merits of the gothic style were not yet universally accepted. In his *Essay on the History of Taste* (1759), Alexander Gerard compared it unfavourably to the classical:

> The profusion of ornament, bestowed on the parts, in Gothic structures, may please one who has not acquired enlargement of mind, sufficient for conceiving at one view their relation to the whole; but no sooner is this acquired, than he perceives superior elegance in the more simple symmetry and proportion of Grecian architecture ... WHERE refinement is wanting, taste must be coarse and vulgar.[94]

Even Walpole had reservations; he intended Strawberry Hill to be an expression of freedom from the strictures of classicism, not an advertisement for the gothic, which he critiqued for its 'unrestrained licentiousness'.[95] As a result, most gothic houses of the mid-eighteenth century merely used the style for detailing, such as crenellated rooflines, pointed or ogee-shaped arches, trefoils and quatrefoils, and fan vaulting.[96] William Kent's unrealized plan to rebuild Honingham Hall in Norfolk (1738) was essentially a Palladian design – a central block with two wings, but with crenellations and ogee-arched windows.[97] This reluctance to commit wholeheartedly to the gothic reflects the fact that its political associations remained complex. On the one hand, it could be used to make claims regarding the evolution of English liberty from the medieval era to the present, as the temples at Shotover and Stowe had done; on the other, the gothic continued to suffer from its association with Catholicism.[98] In contemporary gothic literature, castles and monasteries were frequently used as the settings for homosexual and other illicit acts committed by Catholics.[99]

After the Jacobite Rebellion of 1745, however, patriotic Protestants made a more determined effort to take control of the political meaning of the gothic. David Stewart writes that

> many gothic sham ruins ... were produced as attacks on England's Catholic and baronial past. Such sham ruins were not merely images of picturesque beauty, nor images of nostalgia; rather, they were monuments of ridicule and images of *just* destruction, commemorating the defeat of Charles Edward, the Young Pretender, by the forces of George II.[100]

In 1746 John Yorke, MP for Richmond, built the gothic Culloden Tower on his Yorkshire estate The Green to commemorate the Duke of Cumberland's victory over Bonnie Prince Charlie in the previous year.[101] Two years later Sanderson Miller added a gothic ruin to the garden of Hagley Hall in Worcestershire, whose owner George Lyttleton was a committed anti-Jacobite. Lord Hardwicke, who held similar political views, commissioned Miller to design another gothic ruin for the garden of Wimpole Hall in Cambridgeshire in 1753.[102]

The political meaning of the gothic was therefore consolidating. Although in the first half of the eighteenth century it had retained associations with Catholicism and Jacobitism, and thus with instability and disorder, it was now regarded as expressing opposition to Jacobitism and by extension a commitment to continuity and tradition. Alexandrina Buchanan writes:

> At a time when classicism formed the normal mode of building for all shades of political opinion and the erection of new buildings was used to symbolize authority, gothic or old buildings could be used to represent opposition to the governing power, either negatively or positively. When antique forms were used to express legitimacy, gothic could stand for chaos. When classicism was defined as foreign, illiberal, modern or grandiose, gothic could be seen as its converse.[103]

The Culloden Tower in Richmond, North Yorkshire, built by John Yorke in 1746 to celebrate the defeat of the Jacobite Rebellion.

With this transition in mind, we can now revisit the ruined monastic sites and castles that appeared in the previous two chapters.

Monastic and Castle Ruins in the Eighteenth Century

The Dissolution of the Monasteries had a significant impact on the history of the English landscape garden. By transferring a large amount of land from institutional and ecclesiastical ownership to private and secular hands, it altered the purpose for which this land was used. A significant proportion remained in agricultural cultivation, but the land immediately surrounding monastic sites, which had typically been used for the growing of food or medicinal plants for the residents, was now converted to ornamental gardens so as to display the new owner's wealth and status.[104] At Bindon Abbey in Dorset, for example, Sir Thomas Howard, second son of the 3rd Duke of Norfolk, used the monastic hydraulic system of sluices and channels to create an elaborate water garden after he acquired the property in the mid-1540s.[105]

The evolution of the English landscape garden since the Reformation is well known. The geometric gardens of the sixteenth and early seventeenth centuries gave way to the Baroque style, with the long, straight axes and symmetrical layouts that had been pioneered in France and the Netherlands. After 1720 the 'English landscape style' emerged. Less formal and intended to appear more natural, it featured rolling lawns, serpentine lakes and plantings of trees carefully selected for their colours. Classical temples, grottoes, Chinese bridges and other structures served as objects of interest for visitors as they strolled along gently curving paths. In the first half of the eighteenth century this increased informality was seen as reflecting an English commitment to liberty, in contrast to the strict formality of French gardens, which was perceived as embodying absolutism.[106] The English landscape garden therefore became a source of patriotic pride. Stephen Bending writes that 'the "English" aesthetic of variety in the garden, the rejection of geometrical form, [was] recognised as an image of the constitution and of Britons' inherent liberty.' Bending goes on to assert that this interpretation of the English landscape garden 'reinforces one of the central Hanoverian myths of the later eighteenth century, that of natural succession rather than revolution'.[107]

How then do former monastic sites fit into this interpretation of the landscape garden as an embodiment of the ability of the English constitution to reform itself without revolution? Most obviously, they became spaces where history played out, as the smaller, geometric gardens planted in the cloisters and other enclosed courts of converted monastic buildings gave way to the much larger-scale gardens of the eighteenth century, in which all the land surrounding the house became a feature. There was, however, a more symbolic link, as there is evidence that some early conversions of monastic sites to private residences included gardens intended to spotlight the ruined buildings. At Egglestone Abbey in County Durham, the garden appears to have been designed to make the ruined church an 'integral feature', and there may even have been a belvedere to provide a good view of it.[108]

These gardens, like those developed by Charles Brandon and Thomas Audley after the Pilgrimage of Grace, were probably statements of Protestant piety and political loyalty which were intended to celebrate the destruction of the Catholic religion in England and the establishment of royal supremacy over the Church of England. But as time went on and monastic ruins remained standing, they became focal points of conservationist and even nostalgic sentiment.[109] We must ask why so many owners chose to preserve the name of the religious foundation as the name of their new house if they were so eager to eradicate all memory of its pre-Reformation past. This practice continued long after the sixteenth century: in 1825 the Earl of Dudley constructed a new house called Priory Hall on a site located just to the northwest of the ruins of Dudley Priory in Staffordshire.[110] Other owners highlighted the religious history of their houses in more substantive ways. Woburn Abbey, the Earl of Bedford's seat in Bedfordshire, was first transformed into a house in the 1560s, but it underwent more extensive work in the 1630s, when it was in the hands of the 4th Earl. As Diane Duggan notes, 'the perpetuation of much of the Cistercian layout means that it can be confidently assumed that most of the buildings probably retained much the same usage' as they had in monastic times.[111] Moreover, the west range preserved 'elements from the former monastic design'; it is unclear why the 4th Earl made this decision given that his other improvements were in a classical style influenced by Inigo Jones, but Duggan suggests that it may have been because he 'wished to retain some monastic architectural ethos'.[112]

After he acquired Forde Abbey in Dorset in 1649, Sir Edmund Prideaux added new, complementary structures to its monastic buildings, creating in the process 'one of the earliest proto-romantic silhouettes' and a model for the gothic houses of the later eighteenth and nineteenth centuries.[113] Other owners had more ideological motives. Rowland

Wilson preserved Merton Abbey in Surrey and even defended it from damage by Parliamentary forces in the Civil War because he wanted 'to operationalise Roman Catholic remains for the acclamation of a Protestant triumph'.[114]

In other instances, the descendants of the men who had been granted monastic property by Henry VIII felt guilty about their ancestors' desecration of religious sites. Dore Abbey and land adjacent to his Holme Lacy estate in Herefordshire had been granted to John Scudamore, a friend of Thomas Cromwell. Scudamore demolished most of Dore's buildings, sold the materials and used the profits to rebuild the house at Holme Lacy in the 1540s. But his great-grandson, the 1st Viscount Scudamore, took a very different attitude to the site. Between 1632 and 1635 Scudamore built a new church on the foundations of the abbey church's choir and crossing, at a cost of £425. There are two explanations for why he undertook this costly project. The first is that he was frustrated that none of his children had as yet survived childhood, and so he decided that the cause of his misfortune was his family's desecration of a religious site. This explanation cannot be true, however, because Scudamore's son

Forde Abbey in Dorset, where Sir Edmund Prideaux added matching buildings to the existing monastic fabric in the mid-17th century, in the process creating a model for later gothic revival houses.

James was born in 1624 and did not die until 1668. The second explanation is therefore far more likely: Scudamore was close friends with the Bishop of London, and after 1633 Archbishop of Canterbury, William Laud, who was critical of Puritan iconoclasm and neglect of pre-Reformation religious buildings.[115] After consulting with Laud, who was engaged in the restoration of St Paul's Cathedral in London at the time, Scudamore 'clearly felt that it was his duty to God to restore churches'.[116] He may also, however, have been worried about the source of his landed property, as a significant portion had come from his great-grandfather's monastic acquisitions. Ian Atherton writes that in the mid-seventeenth century

> there was a developing concern that it was sacrilege to hold lands which had once belonged to the dissolved monasteries... Thomas Bayly, in a sermon in Sussex in 1640, warned that those who held former abbey land were guilty of sacrilege and would not prosper; others warned that the sacrilegious would be punished by the extinction of their family line.[117]

Scudamore had reason to be concerned: even if his son had survived, his first three children had died in infancy, and he seems to have been in financial difficulty around the time he decided to rebuild the church at Dore. He wrote to Laud to ask if he could sell the former monastic property, but Laud told him that it would be wrong to keep the profits. Instead, he opted to rebuild the church, to endow it with the surrounding manor and to resume the payment of tithes on his former monastic property.[118] In other cases, it was external observers who attributed guilt to the owners of former monastic sites. Thornton Abbey in Lincolnshire had passed through the hands of several owners before being granted to Sir Vincent Skinner in 1603. The antiquary Abraham de la Pryme recorded in his diary that the 'staitly' and 'delicate' residence that Skinner had adapted from its buildings had collapsed 'without any visible cause' and blamed the sacrilege that Skinner had committed in attempting to build on a former monastic site.[119]

Looking back during the upheaval of the seventeenth century, the destruction of monastic sites must have seemed all too familiar; it is not surprising that a strong sense of nostalgia emerged for the seeming serenity of the pre-Reformation past, especially when the causes of the contemporary chaos seemed to be much the same. Margaret Aston writes:

New zeal, new desolation, new nostalgia: where Henry VIII led others followed. The wrecking of the monasteries was but a beginning, and by the middle of the seventeenth century pietistic sackings of various kinds had piled up the causes for regret. The dangers of iconoclastic enthusiasm had been made all too evident.[120]

To be sure, for the vast majority of English people, this regret at the destruction of the monasteries did not extend to a desire to see the restoration of Catholicism, but it did produce a desire for change to occur without so much violence and physical damage. Antiquaries such as John Aubrey and William Dugdale lauded the beauty of monastic buildings and pointed out that more of them might have been converted to Protestant use. In their eyes, 'Henry VIII's reign seemed like a barbarous holocaust, cutting a brutal swathe through the English landscape and the ecclesiastical past.'[121]

After the Glorious Revolution, the significance of monastic ruins shifted yet again. In at least eight instances between the late seventeenth and early nineteenth centuries, ruins were incorporated into landscape gardens. These included Gisborough in Yorkshire, where the Chaloner family built a new house in the 1680s and incorporated the dramatic arch of the east end of the former abbey church into its garden. In 1717 John Aislabie began laying out a water garden which followed a natural stream through the grounds of his Studley Royal estate in North Yorkshire. After about half a mile, the visitor rounded a curve and encountered a dramatic view of the ruins of Fountains Abbey.[122] Around 1758 Thomas Duncombe built a walkway so that visitors could view the ruins of Rievaulx Abbey in Yorkshire.[123] At Bayham Abbey in Sussex, the Pratt family built a gothic villa in the 1750s which was situated to take advantage of the view of the ruins.[124] In the 1770s the 4th Earl of Scarborough hired Capability Brown to create a picturesque setting, 'with Poet's feeling and Painter's eye', for the ruins of Roche Abbey, which stood near his Sandbeck Park estate in Yorkshire.[125] In the mid-1820s the ruins of Dudley Priory in Staffordshire were incorporated into the garden of Priory Hall, a new dower house built by the Earl of Dudley.[126] Such usages of monastic ruins had not occurred since the sixteenth century, and so it must be regarded as a new fashion.[127]

Houses as well as gardens continued to display remnants of their monastic past. In the mid-eighteenth century, when Woburn was given

An aquatint from *c*. 1811 showing tourists enjoying a stroll through the water garden incorporating the ruins of Fountains Abbey.

a Palladian makeover by Henry Flitcroft, Horace Walpole complained that, because it still stood 'upon the foundations of old abbey', it was 'neither stately nor venerable'.[128] The house's pre-Reformation history was thus still apparent even then. In 1824 Sir Richard Colt Hoare of Stourhead in Wiltshire privately published a book about the three former monastic sites that he owned: Witham, Bruton and Stavordale. 'Even the dilapidated ruins of a Monastic Establishment excite our attention and respect', he wrote, 'and we become anxious to know its ancient state, and the many vicissitudes, which, during a long course of years, it may have experienced.' At Bruton, where no physical remains of the abbey were visible, he installed a stone tablet in 1822 in order 'to commemorate the former existence of a Monastic Establishment in this place'.[129]

Such uses of ruins are usually viewed as reflecting the influence of the picturesque, a concept which first appeared in the middle decades of the eighteenth century in reference to attempts to borrow principles from painting in the assessment and cultivation of landscape scenes. By the end of the century, the picturesque had come to be associated with romanticism and with more rugged and dramatic landscapes.[130] Monastic ruins played a key role in the creation of picturesque scenes. The owners and designers of gardens used ruined religious buildings to add drama to the vistas seen by guests as they strolled along the paths. But there was something more underlying their sudden popularity as landscape garden features than mere aesthetic concerns. From the perspective of the eighteenth century, as the chaos of the previous era receded into the rear-view mirror, they were cause for celebration of the triumph of liberty over tyranny and Protestant enlightenment over Catholic superstition. Sir Uvedale Price, a leading light of picturesque design, wrote in 1794 that 'the ruins of these once magnificent edifices are the pride and boast of this island; we may well be proud of them, not merely in a picturesque point of view – we may glory that the abodes of tyranny and superstition are in ruin.'[131] What had shifted since the nostalgic laments over ruined abbeys in the seventeenth century is that now the ruins were being celebrated, rather than regret being expressed for the loss of the pristine buildings they once were. The poet William Shenstone built several mock ruins on The Leasowes, his modest estate in Shropshire, in some cases using stones from the abbey of Halesowen. He wrote in his essay 'Unconnected Thoughts on Gardening' (1764) that 'a ruin . . . may be neither new to us, nor majestic, nor beautiful, yet afford that pleasing melancholy which proceeds from a reflection on decayed magnificence.' In 1772 the clergyman and travel writer William Gilpin criticized what he saw as William Aislabie's heavy hand in incorporating the ruins of Fountains Abbey into the water garden at Studley Royal. 'A ruin', Gilpin declared, 'is a sacred thing.'[132] Monastic ruins had become the end point of – and not a disruption to – England's political and cultural destiny.

By the second half of the eighteenth century, monastic ruins no longer signified a break with the past, but rather the culmination of a historical evolution that had led England to reach new heights of prosperity and global power, a situation for which the Protestant Reformation was an important – perhaps the *most* important – foundation. They were increasingly viewed in explicitly national terms, and for that reason seen as superior to classical ruins, even Roman ones in England. William Mason wrote in his poem *The English Garden* (1786):

> But Time's rude mace has here all Roman piles
> Levell'd so low, that who, on British ground
> Attempts the task, builds but a splendid lye
> Which mocks historical credence. Hence the cause
> Why Saxon piles or Norman here prevail:
> Form they a rude, 'tis yet an English whole.[133]

Buildings that had once been symbols of a heretical and treasonous 'foreign' faith were now celebrated for their embodiment of the continuity of English institutions. It was now even possible for English Catholics to participate in this interpretation of monastic sites without it seeming treasonous. In the early nineteenth century Thomas Weld, whose family had retained their Catholic faith after the Reformation, drew up plans to rebuild Bindon Abbey in Dorset in impressive gothic style, but he settled for an elaborate reworking of the garden. This included the construction of a number of gothic buildings, including the 'Abbey House', which featured a chapel used for Catholic worship on the first floor. The garden prominently featured the ruins of the medieval abbey, which 'would have acted as reminders of a lost age of faith'.[134]

Although they were not used for this purpose as frequently as were monastic sites, ruined castles also appeared in eighteenth-century landscape gardens. By 1735 the Arundell family had developed the ruins of Wardour Castle, which had been severely damaged in the English Civil War, into a landscape feature, before building a new house nearby in the late 1760s. The landscape architect Richard Woods created a wooded terrace which overlooked the old castle.[135] Castles, however, faced an obstacle to their incorporation into the progression of English history: their association with the 'foreign' Norman Conquest, which was alleged to have eradicated the liberties of the native Saxons. In the late eighteenth century English radicals embraced the notion of the 'Norman yoke', which claimed that the people of England had enjoyed liberties that were protected by laws and democratic institutions until they were stripped away by the Normans.[136]

The French Revolution, however, would do much to change this view of the castle as a foreign intrusion. Suddenly, young English gentlemen were prevented from going on the Grand Tour, which in consequence became less important as a rite of passage after the 1790s. Richard Wilson and Alan Mackley write that 'not only was much of the continent closed for years on end, but the wars stimulated the fiercest nationalism and a concentration upon elements more identifiably British in native culture.'[137] The destruction of the Bastille assumed great symbolic importance not only in France, where it represented the collapse of the 'Old Regime', but also in England, where castles both still stood and were being newly built, thereby representing the continuity (and hence the superiority) of the political and social system.[138] The architectural impact of the French Revolution on the architectural style of English country houses is very clear. The data chart shows a gradual increase in the number of gothic houses from the 1740s onwards, but then a dramatic spike once the war with France began in the 1790s.[139] As Geoffrey Tyack has written, 'Houses in the medieval style could express a shared sense of indigenous cultural values threatened, but not suppressed, by the might of Napoleonic France.'[140] In 1799 the antiquary John Carter wrote:

> In a day like the present, when the infernal dispensers of 'liberty and equality' are spreading their destroying power on so many realms, and when this country, the favoured nation of Heaven, has hitherto escaped the direful contagion; it behooves every Englishman to come forward to protect his King and Country, each in a way his ability enables him to perform, either by his person, his contribution, or his mental faculties; and I know of no way that can so well aid the general cause, as to stimulate my countrymen to think well of their own national memorials, the works of art of ancient times, and not to hold up any foreign works as superior to our own; and in particular the name of France should never be introduced, but to raise ideas of terror and destruction. Then will our ancient remains of art ... remind us of the heroic acts of those defenders of their country who brought perfidious France beneath their triumphant swords; remind us of our long race of sovereigns, the admiration and dread of surrounding nations, and remind us of our duty to our Creator, to ourselves, and to mankind.[141]

Here, Carter argues that the English constitution had evolved gradually, avoiding the sorts of violent disruptions that France was now experiencing. From this perspective, old buildings were the physical embodiments of the national superiority conferred by continuity. After 1789 continuity therefore became a marker of difference from France.[142]

These new patriotic associations of the gothic revival reflected its evolution from the early 'Strawberry Hill' phase to a new mode which consciously imitated the castle, although it had little concern with military defence. In 1802 the architect William Porden, while writing to the Earl of Grosvenor about his plans for Eaton Hall in Cheshire, advocated the gothic over the classical style 'on the score of preserving that Distinction of Rank and Fortune, which it is the habit of the age to diminish'.[143] The leading architect of this new mode of gothic was James

Wyatt, whose designs included Lee Priory in Kent (1785–90), Fonthill Abbey in Wiltshire (1796–1813), Belvoir Castle in Leicestershire (1801–30) and Ashridge Park in Herefordshire (1808–14). Of these, Fonthill was the most remarkable, with a cathedral-like, cruciform plan and a central octagonal tower topped by a 84-metre (276 ft) spire.[144] Similar in his approach to the gothic was John Nash, who designed his own residence, East Cowes Castle on the Isle of Wight (1798–1802), as well as six more castellated houses in England and four in Ireland between 1798 and 1811. Other prominent contemporary examples of castellated houses included Eastnor Castle in Herefordshire (Robert Smirke, 1812) and Goodrich Court in Herefordshire (Edward Blore, 1828).

These buildings were in keeping with the increased conservatism of the early nineteenth century. William Wordsworth, who had gone from supporter to opponent of the French Revolution, was financially supported by the Earl of Lonsdale, owner of Lowther Castle in Cumbria. He wrote of Lowther's 'ancient honour':

> Hourly the democratic torrent swells;
> For airy promises and hopes suborned
> The strength of backward-looking thoughts is scorned.
> Fall if ye must, ye Towers and Pinnacles,
> With what ye symbolise; authentic Story
> Will say, Ye disappeared with England's Glory![145]

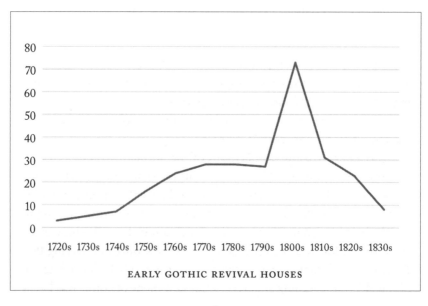

EARLY GOTHIC REVIVAL HOUSES

This was blatant fiction: Lonsdale's family fortune came from coal and dated back a mere half-century, while his peerage, granted in 1807, was even newer. Designed by Robert Smirke, Lowther Castle had been built between 1806 and 1814. But historical accuracy was not the point: Wordsworth was supporting the idea that continuity now defined English identity.[146]

The 'capture' of the medieval past as a way of indicating the continuity of English history was symbolized by Highcliffe Castle on the Dorset coast. Highcliffe was designed in the 1830s by William Donthorne for Charles Stuart, 1st Baron Stuart de Rothesay. Stuart, a prominent Regency-era diplomat, was magpie-like in his acquisitiveness as he looked to build his new house. While serving in St Petersburg in 1804 he acquired timber, and while minister in occupied Spain in 1808 he ordered bricks.[147] Even greater opportunities to acquire items for Highcliffe, however, presented themselves when he was appointed as British Ambassador to Paris in 1815. He would serve until 1824 and again from 1828 to 1831, when he was recalled for over-active engagement in French politics. Michael Hill writes that

> the timing of Lord Stuart's ambassadorship was perfect from the point of view of acquiring the many architectural artefacts that were becoming available: manor houses, abbeys and churches were vandalised or demolished during the revolution and it seems that the *ad hoc* demolition gangs were understandably keen to sell as soon as possible.[148]

Normandy's medieval abbeys and chateaux had suffered particularly badly during the French Revolution, but the architectural salvage of buildings all over France was a booming business in England in the late eighteenth and early nineteenth centuries. As a sale catalogue of 1791 proclaimed: 'Wars and Commotions are seldom favourable to the fine Arts, the late Revolutions in France and Flanders have deprived these countries of many inestimable Productions which otherwise, could never have been removed ... The Demolition of the Convents and Religious Houses has also contributed to this Collection.'[149] Known as the 'Wardour Street Trade', a number of dealers in architectural salvage set up shop off Oxford Street in London.[150] Stuart was not the only country-house owner to take advantage of the situation. The redundantly named Gregory Gregory filled Harlaxton Manor (1831) in Lincolnshire with what the garden designer J. C. Loudon described as 'an ample stock of vases, statues and other sculptural ornaments, and of rich gates and other iron work, collected by him in all parts of the continent after the peace of 1815'.[151] Nicholas Roundell Toke of Godinton Hall in Kent imported a number of pieces of ornamental woodwork from France in order to embellish the existing Elizabethan features of the hall, staircase and an upstairs chamber known as the Priest's Room. Fragments of continental church furnishings decorated Broomwell House near Bristol, while Weare Giffard in Devon and Snelston Hall in Derbyshire also featured Flemish architectural salvage, possibly from the same shipment.[152] A particularly popular type of French architectural salvage were *boiseries*, or ornately carved wood panelling. In 1824 Elizabeth, Duchess of Rutland, purchased *boiseries* for the 'Elizabeth Saloon' at Belvoir Castle which were supposed to have come from the apartments in the Grand Trianon at Versailles of Louis XIV's second wife, Madame de Maintenon.[153]

No one, however, was more enthusiastic in the pursuit of the treasures made available by the French Revolution than Stuart.[154] Twelve barges from Rouen carried back artefacts and stonework. These were unloaded at Lord Bute's Gap and carted up to Highcliffe. From Jumièges Abbey came a doorway, a set of carved wooden panels and various pieces of stonework which were installed in the Great Hall; a French observer reported that 'the English carried away for cash the sculptured remains of Jumièges', and that the cloister 'was thought to have departed ... with the family of the ambassador'.[155] From the church of St Vigor in Rouen came a Tree of Jesse window. And from the Manoir des Picarts de Radeval, a sixteenth-century manor house in Les Andelys, came an ornate gothic oriel window and a set of window surrounds. So intense was Lord Stuart's pillaging of France's architectural heritage that it prompted Victor Hugo to publish a scathing essay entitled 'Guerre aux démolisseurs' in 1825 and the archaeologist Arcisse de Caumont to found the Société des Antiquaires de Normandie in 1823, the precursor of the Service des Monuments Historiques, which still protects France's historical environment today.[156] Nor did Stuart confine his acquisition of French furnishings for his new house to the medieval era. He also obtained furniture and carpets from the sale of the possessions of the Napoleonic military hero Marshal Ney after Ney's execution by the victorious allies in 1815, as well as the Empress Josephine's bed from her palace at Malmaison, another bed with hangings supposedly embroidered by Marie

Antoinette and Gobelin tapestries rumoured to have been looted by Napoleon from the Knights of St John in Malta.[157]

There were obvious patriotic connotations to Stuart's enthusiastic plundering of so much French loot so soon after the conclusion of a war with France. But these items were more than mere military trophies. Even at the time, it was recognized that English identity was becoming increasingly based upon historical continuity, due to a heightened contrast with the French arch-enemy brought on by the attempts of the French Revolutionaries to erase the past – and demolish its physical remains – in order to bring new forms of governance and social organization into being. In 1821 the archivist and historian Francis Palgrave wrote:

> It is the English alone who labour to preserve the memory of the structures of Normandy, which are doomed to destruction by the disgraceful sloth and ignorance of the French. Whilst the owners of these noble structures are dull to their beauties and incapable of appreciating their value, we have made them English property.[158]

Here, Palgrave attributes England's superiority to its maintenance of physical links to the past. The French were so deficient in this regard, meanwhile, that the English had to intervene to save their heritage for them.

Palgrave's claims illustrate the increasingly nationalistic way in which architecture styles were viewed in England in the early nineteenth century. With their tendency to treat the gothic as pastiche by combining elements from radically different eras of the Middle Ages, early nineteenth-century castles such as Lowther infuriated serious scholars of gothic architecture like Carter, but he was not entirely free from a subjective perspective himself, as he viewed the gothic through an unabashedly nationalist lens.[159] In 1798 he wrote in the *Gentleman's Magazine*:

> Why have the minds of Englishmen, for these two centuries, been deluded to imitate the Roman and Grecian styles? What features have their boasted remains that we cannot parallel? For the extensiveness of their edifices, their grandeur, their elegance, their enrichments, view our cathedrals, and other attendant buildings. Is any one excellence that architecture boasts to be sought for in vain in our country? No, we may here find them all.[160]

Highcliffe Castle in Dorset, built in the 1830s for Charles Stuart, 1st Baron Stuart de Rothesay, incorporated stonework from medieval French buildings which Stuart had obtained while serving as ambassador to Paris.

Contemporary antiquaries, meanwhile, created a classification system for gothic architecture which bolstered efforts to define it as 'English'. In his *History and Antiquities of the Conventual and Cathedral Church of Ely* (1777), James Bentham decreed the rounded arch to be Norman and the pointed to be 'gothic', which meant that the gothic was 'an indigenous style', since it had not been brought to England by foreign conquerors.[161] Subsequent scholars divided the gothic into more precise evolutionary categories. In his *Treatise on the Ecclesiastical Architecture of England during the Middle Ages* (1811), John Milner argued that the gothic should be split into three 'Pointed Orders': an early crude but vigorous phase, a superior middle phase and a third phase which was corrupted by over-refinement. Six years later, Thomas Rickman developed Milner's tripartite classification further, by naming the three phases the 'Early English', the 'Decorated English' and the 'Perpendicular English', and by adding a fourth, earlier phase, the 'Romanesque'. This interpretation was based upon a different set of considerations from those of Milner, who had been concerned with moral advancement and decay. Rickman, in contrast, argued that there had been an evolution from Norman (that is, French) dominance to improvement and ultimately perfection – in the form of the Perpendicular – in English hands. He argued that the creation and evolution of the gothic style was driven by England, as English architects were 'prior to their continental neighbours' and produced work that was superior in its 'pure simplicity and boldness'.[162] This sense of the Perpendicular as both uniquely English and as the most superior form of the gothic has lasted until the present day.[163] English commentators could not claim that the gothic in its earliest form had been invented in England, but they could put forward Perpendicular 'as the one indisputedly national variant of it'.[164] The elevation of the Perpendicular to the highest form of the gothic meant that its use in a contemporary building became a form of patriotic expression. Toddington Manor in Gloucestershire (1819), the home of the amateur architect and Whig MP Charles Hanbury Tracy, imitated with scholarly precision the Perpendicular style.

Toddington, and certainly the cultural attitudes that determined its style, may have helped to inspire Charles Barry's design for the Houses of Parliament.[165] David Cannadine identifies a desire to express this continuity in visual form as the main reason why gothic or Elizabethan was designated the 'national' style in the competition to design the new Palace of Westminster after its predecessor was destroyed by fire in 1834. The new building, he writes, was 'meant to re-establish and reassert those visible ties to the nation's past that the fire had temporarily sundered':

> It would articulate a hierarchical image of the social and political order, stressing venerable authority, providential subordination and true conservative principles, and it would be the very antithesis of the classical style, which had become associated in the popular patriotic mind with the rootless anarchy and national enmity of revolutionary France.[166]

This was the view adopted by Colonel Julian Jackson in 1837, in responding to William Richard Hamilton's criticism of the choice of gothic for the new building. Hamilton regarded the classical style as embodying the progress of civilization, and the gothic as a step backwards into a world of fanciful romance and deliberate archaism. In rebutting Hamilton's views, Jackson asserted that as Parliament was where 'the affairs of state are discussed', it should be 'the rallying place of patriotism', and thus gothic was the appropriate style, as it was 'more national' than classical. 'We are intimate with gothic forms', Jackson wrote, 'and ... they constitute in our minds very positively, though perhaps unconsciously, a connecting link to this great chain of associations which bind us still more closely to our country.'[167]

Toddington Manor, Gloucestershire (1819), from F. O. Morris, ed., *A Series of Picturesque Views of Seats of the Noblemen and Gentlemen of Great Britain and Ireland* (1880).

THE RUINS OF MEDIEVAL buildings in England had come full circle since the Dissolution of the Monasteries in the late 1530s. In the immediate aftermath of the Dissolution, abandoned monasteries were seen as emblems of a heretical and treasonous faith, and accordingly became the targets of destructive iconoclasm. A century later, many castles were destroyed in the English Civil War, the most violent event in English domestic history. Even so, many medieval buildings survived and were converted to other purposes, pillaged for materials or allowed to crumble slowly into ruins. In the eighteenth century some of those which had reached that latter state were transformed into features of landscape gardens in the emerging English landscape style. This connected them to contemporary discussions of both the national distinctiveness (and hence superiority) of that style, as well as the relationship between gothic architecture and the English belief in liberty as a key marker of national identity, particularly in contrast with absolutist France. Buildings which had once been remnants of a traitorous faith or tyrannous royalty thus now served as repositories of English values. In the 1790s, in the wake of the French Revolution, the survival of medieval buildings, and the construction of new imitations of them, came to be seen as emblematic of England's ability to maintain political continuity, in contrast to the upheavals across the Channel. In this way, the physical remains of the most disruptive moments in English history now represented the stability of the English political system and its superiority to that of France.

4

No Such Thing as a British Country House

Sandon Hall in Staffordshire is a rare example of a British country house. At first glance Sandon is a conventional example of the Jacobethan houses of the mid-nineteenth century; Michael Hall describes it as 'unremarkably Jacobean in style', but he also notes that Sandon's one interesting design feature is the 'the attractive addition of Scottish strap work ornament around the windows and porch'.[1] The presence of those decorations is no accident, as Sandon was designed by the Scottish architect William Burn for the 2nd Earl of Harrowby, after the previous house was destroyed by fire in 1848. After rejecting a design from the classicist Thomas Cubitt, Harrowby turned to Burn, who had been a prolific designer of country houses in Scotland for three decades before moving his practice to England in 1844.

With his protégé David Bryce, Burn was the leading exponent of the Scottish Baronial style, which emerged in the first half of the nineteenth century as an embodiment of the Scottish cultural nationalism which was prevalent at the time. But Burn also worked in other popular styles of the mid-nineteenth century, including the Jacobethan and the Italianate. Burn was just starting to build his practice in England, and so he was content to let a prestigious client such as Harrowby make many of the decisions. In a letter from December 1848, he told Harrowby that there would be 'no material difference of expense between the Tudor and Italian styles', leaving the choice up to him. The following month, Harrowby showed Burn sketches of a Jacobethan-style house drawn by his eighteen-year-old son Lord Sandon. Burn agreed to the 'general idea' of a Jacobethan house, although he was compelled to 'take some liberty' with the sketches, as 'if fully carried out they would have led to an expenditure much beyond what is contemplated, and also . . . to a house considerably too long for the grounds.'[2]

Designed by William Burn for the 2nd Earl of Harrowby, Sandon Hall (1852) in Staffordshire combines English and Scottish architectural elements, making it a rare example of a 'British' country house.

Even though the question of the style for the new house had been resolved, the process of building did not go smoothly. Instead, Harrowby proved a difficult client who required Burn to make revision after revision to his plans. It was not until 1852 – four years after the fire – that the rebuilding began. Faced with constant interference from Harrowby, Burn became increasingly frustrated. In June 1855 he complained to Lady Harrowby that 'there are so many things done ... at Sandon, contrary to the advice I have given, and the drawings and suggestions I have submitted, I not only feel my presence there to be wholly useless, but as giving a sanction to arrangements and designs which my whole experience condemns.'[3] With his English practice now flourishing, he appears to have lost interest in the project. Paul Bradley notes that 'the fact that one of the fireplace "designs" was a brazen tracing from a book shows that ... there was some creative detachment ... on Burn's part.'[4] It seems likely that the Scottish strapwork appeared for the same reason: as Burn grew more disenchanted and so less committed to Sandon, he turned to design elements which he had used in the past. Rather than being the product of an attempt to create a truly British architectural style, the one house in England south of the Scottish Borders which can be identified as blending English and Scottish design elements resulted from a frustrated architect's irritation with his client.

THE CREATION OF ENGLISHNESS as an invented identity resulted in part from interactions with external entities. The next three chapters will explore three of these entities, beginning in this chapter with the other nations of the United Kingdom and followed by the British Empire and the European continent. For centuries, England was so dominant over the rest of the British Isles that there was little need to assert its identity in this context. Recently, however, national decline and the resurgence of Scottish, Welsh and Irish identities and political aspirations has altered this dynamic, and English nationalism has resurged, most obviously in the Brexit vote of 2016.[5]

In some ways, to be sure, the idea that there was no English nationalism before the 1970s is itself an expression of English nationalism. Colin Kidd summarizes this view:

> Until our recent discontents England had never succumbed to doctrinal nationalism. Absent from English history was the obsessiveness found in many countries across Europe about the recovery of authentic nationhood. Although the English have often been perturbed about the condition of England, they have rarely floated nationalist solutions to their problems.[6]

This attitude stems from the belief, mostly held on the political right, that the English are too stoic and unemotional for such flag-waving excess, and from a corresponding belief on the left that English nationalism is the exclusive province of National-Front-voting thugs. Both attitudes are inherently nationalist because they see the lack of English nationalism as a point of difference between England and other nations. Nationalism is seen as being for the Scots, with their Braveheart-inspired cries of freedom; or for the Welsh, with their dogged defence of their language; or for the Irish, with their terrorist bombs. The English, it is argued, have no need of such things.

England does, however, have country houses, which as the previous chapters have described embody the national character in various ways. British country houses, however, do not exist other than geographically as country houses located on the island of Britain. There is no such thing, in other words, as a British country-house style: there are styles distinct to the three nations on the island, with occasional forays of style over the border from one nation to another. Although English-style houses were built in Wales and Scotland, and occasionally Scottish-style houses were built in England, no hybrid style of architecture developed that was common to all three nations. This chapter will explore the reasons for that, concentrating on the defensive nature of the border zones between England and Wales and between England and Scotland well into the early modern era, which prevented the development of hybrid architectural styles.

The Borders as Battlegrounds

Welsh and Scottish country houses are usually assumed to have very different respective relationships to their English counterparts. In Wales, so the argument goes, the houses of the elite were virtually indistinguishable from those in England from an early date.[7] Peter Smith concludes that 'by the fourteenth century, if not before, the ultimate source of architectural ideas in Wales was the English court.' As evidence for this claim, Smith points to the spread of the Perpendicular style in Wales as an example of how 'the styles of the English court spread over Wales in precisely the same way as they spread over provincial England.'[8] Miles Wynn Cato contends that English dominance of Welsh architecture continued into the modern era:

> The rich in Wales were ... universally anglicised and the prosperous towns were those of the industrial areas which were then breaking away from the traditional Welsh culture to become anglicised ... There was no incentive or need for a school of professional architects in the Welsh rural community. Consequently the mansions of the country squires and the buildings of the anglicised towns are almost without exception English in inspiration ... In this respect, it is true to say that there is no Welsh architecture. Such buildings are the work of Welsh- or English-born architects working in a supra-national tradition which has not found a peculiar Welsh expression. Is there such an expression in any Welsh building? The answer is to be found in the dwelling-houses of the Welsh people.[9]

Scottish buildings, in contrast, have long been celebrated for their distinctive character. R. W. Brunskill writes in his study of British vernacular domestic buildings:

> Although there are sufficient similarities in the domestic architecture of England and Wales for the two to be considered as one group, the domestic buildings of Scotland are sufficiently different for them to be discussed separately. As elsewhere, the houses and cottages of Scotland are a product of geography and topography, history and economics; they reflect the culture of what was for long a separate country and one that retains its independence in important respects.[10]

This chapter will not so much challenge these views as argue that the similarities between Welsh and English country houses and the differences between Scottish and English ones resulted from the same cause: the failure to develop a British country-house style. The militarized frontiers between England and its western and northern neighbours ensured that the Welsh Marches and Scottish Borders retained distinctive regional identities which prevented the permeation of architectural fashions across them. On the European continent, bordering nations generally recognized their respective sovereignties and so did not fortify their borders against each other. England's imperial ambitions to rule all of the British Isles, however, did not allow a similar situation to prevail there.[11] The border zones therefore did not develop a hybrid architecture which would have encouraged the development of shared styles beyond them. Instead, both border zones were characterized by their fortified domestic buildings.

The early emergence of a powerful English state made these defensive borders necessary and ensured that a clear sense of difference persisted between England and its neighbours. Max Lieberman writes:

> By c. 1300 ... the Englishness of the English 'state' had reached new heights. In particular ... there were ever clearer signs that the English 'state' operated on the assumption that it existed only for Englishmen ... Thus, it retained the close association of English settlers and English institutions characteristic of the late Anglo-Saxon 'state', but lacked the latter's flexibility in incorporating territories not settled by Englishmen. The entrenchment

of the idea that the English kingdom was exclusively the 'state' of the English people was a many-faceted process bearing on the history of four countries.[12]

On the Anglo-Welsh border, the Marcher Lords were able to prevent the expansion of the English state into Wales, but they 'failed to integrate Welshmen and Englishmen within single administrative bodies'. Instead, the two ethnic groups were 'treated as distinct entities, each with their own place in the administrative framework'. Although the Marches were a 'region of multiple identities', the inhabitants 'developed no identity of their own to rival the options of being either Welsh or English'.[13] Similarly in Scotland, as Maureen Meikle writes, 'if any state building was being attempted on the Anglo-Scottish frontier prior to 1603, it was more from an English imperialist basis and not a truly British foundation.'[14] There the border remained a fortified zone for even longer than in Wales, as it did not become fully pacified – in the sense that defensible houses were no longer necessary – until the Act of Union in 1707. England's attitude towards its frontiers and the nations beyond them therefore played a significant role in the failure of a British country-house style to emerge.

Though the term 'Dark Ages' is for good reason out of fashion, the departure of the Romans from Britain brought major changes, which ultimately led to the division of the island into three nations.[15] As the Celtic Britons were pushed to the west, the leaders of Mercia, the early Saxon kingdom based in what is now the Midlands, made the first attempt to delineate a boundary between British and Saxon territory. Wat's Dyke, an earthen bank with a ditch on the western side, ran for forty miles along what is now the northern section of the Anglo-Welsh border. Its date is uncertain: it was long thought to have been built in the seventh or eighth century, but archaeological excavations since the 1990s have suggested that its origins lie in either the fifth or early ninth century.[16] More definite is the eighth-century date of Offa's Dyke, which placed a 150-mile barrier between Mercian and British territory. These two borders marked the beginning of a division in which the people to the east of the boundary spoke English and those to the west spoke Welsh. Once Offa's Dyke had been constructed, the numerous Welsh kingdoms began to merge; by 950 the number had been reduced from six to three. This consolidation 'deepened the self-awareness of the Welsh people', but at the same time, many continued to live to the east of the dyke.[17]

In Scotland the Picts had by the fifth century become the dominant kingdom north of the Forth. The Northumbrians tried to conquer them but were crushed at Dunnichen in 685. By preventing an early English conquest of Scotland, Dunnichen was in large measure responsible for Scotland's independence for the next thousand years. By AD 500, however, the Dál Riada had migrated from Ireland and established themselves in present-day Argyll. Over the next several centuries, the 'Dál Riada Scots' assimilated the Picts into their way of life, including the use of the Gaelic language. After 800 any lingering differences between the two peoples were eliminated by the need to unite against the Vikings, who raided Scotland for the next 250 years. In the mid-ninth century the Picts and the Dalriadans united under their first joint king, Kenneth MacAlpin. This unity would soon be needed not only against the Vikings but against England. By the late ninth century the kingdom of Wessex had grown strong enough to challenge the Scots, but Malcolm II's victory at Carham in 1018 led to the establishment of a stable frontier between England and Scotland along the River Tweed.

By the early eleventh century, then, British borders were roughly in the same place that they are today. These boundaries, however, were permeable. Trade and cultural interchange took place across them, and the Normans carried out military expeditions over them. After completing the conquest of England by 1070, William the Conqueror did not seek to annex Wales directly, but rather to secure the frontier and then compel the Welsh to accept his sovereignty. He created new earldoms of Chester, Shrewsbury and Hereford along the border, which was redefined as a special administrative zone called the 'Marches'. The Marches were not actually part of England and were therefore neither under the jurisdiction of the English king nor English Common Law. Instead, the Marcher Lords were granted sole authority in the region under the 'Law of the March'. They were chosen not only for their loyalty but for their aggressive and ruthless characters, and, just as William expected, they advanced into Wales. By 1100 they had built castles at Chepstow, Monmouth and Caerleon and planted towns around them which were soon settled by English tenants; the manors of Glamorgan were farmed mostly by men with English names.[18] The Welsh princes did not acquiesce passively to these Norman incursions. In 1194 Llywelyn the Great drove the Normans out of the northern part of the country, compelling William II and Henry I to dispatch royal armies into Wales. For two centuries after 1066 a precarious balance prevailed in which the

Normans were able to secure the border, but never managed to establish complete domination.

In Scotland, meanwhile, the chaos into which England had been plunged by the Norman Conquest provided King Malcolm III, later nicknamed 'Canmore', with an opportunity to press southwards into Northumbria in 1079, leading to an agreement that the border would be between the Solway and the Tyne, exactly where the Romans had placed it nine centuries earlier. In 1237 the Treaty of York confirmed that the border was located along the Tweed-Cheviot line, essentially where it is today. Its establishment, Alastair Moffat writes, must have thoroughly bemused the locals, as on both sides

> of the imaginary line everyone spoke English, lived in shires, revered the same saints, ploughed their furrows and pastured the stock in the same way. But even as early as the twelfth century forces to the north and south had begun to pull them apart as they grew into two distinct communities of English and Scots ... By the time of Alexander III [1249–86] the idea of Scotland ended at the Tweed and the Cheviot tops, and beyond them the Englishness of the Haliwerfolc was clearly understood.[19]

These borders with Wales and Scotland would ultimately hold despite the efforts of English kings to conquer the nations on the other side. In 1272 Edward I embarked on a massive campaign of conquest in Wales which resulted in his famous 'Iron Ring' of castles. This meant the end of any possibility of even a semi-independent Wales, but at the same time Edward had given a major boost to a Welsh sense of proto-nationhood. Subordination, in other words, did not mean subjugation, as the Welsh continued to resist English domination, culminating in Owen Glyndŵr's rebellion in 1400. The English and Welsh retained distinct identities, separated by their different languages and customs. The Marches continued to exist as a quasi-independent zone for another 250 years, until Henry VIII imposed direct royal control on Wales in 1536. In the fourteenth century the most powerful Marcher lordships had upwards of fifty knights in their service, which meant that they possessed 'considerable military clout to back up their spirit of independence'.[20] This gave them the capacity not only to defend themselves, but to interfere in English affairs, although they were too fractious to unite and cause serious trouble for English kings.

Regarding Scotland, Henry III attempted to secure the border permanently by creating Scottish Marches to parallel their Welsh counterpart in 1249, but his successors failed to respect it. Alexander III's drunken tumble off a cliff on a stormy night in 1286 unleashed a brutal contest for power between Edward I and Robert the Bruce. Edward, acting with the same ruthless efficiency with which he had conquered Wales, brought his forces north every year from 1296 until his death in 1307. The conflict heightened the nascent sense of Scottish nationhood, famously expressed in the Declaration of Arbroath in 1320. Edward could invade and achieve temporary victories, but after expending vast resources in conquering Wales, he could not afford to garrison Scotland and build castles in which to house his troops. Robert the Bruce's stunning victory over Edward II at Bannockburn in 1314 gained him the Scottish throne, but the war continued for decades afterwards. The Scots fought ferociously, but in 1385 Richard II's invasion signalled that the English still regarded the Tweed and Teviot Valleys as theirs. They were finally forced to relinquish this claim in 1460, when James II of Scotland captured Roxburgh Castle and expelled the last English occupiers.

The effect on the Borders as army after army marched across them was catastrophic:

> Scotland was hammered into nationhood by the Wars of Independence, but the anvil of its forging was the Border countryside. And the Borders has never recovered from that historical curse. As the line drawn between Berwick in the east and the Solway mouth in the west hardened into a national frontier so the communities on either side suffered as national conflict rumbled across their fields and villages. This was warfare often directed from long distances, and carried on by people with no connections to the place where they fought, looted and burned.[21]

Incessant war also intensified a sense of difference between England and Scotland. The strong links which had existed between the two countries in the twelfth and thirteenth centuries were broken; cross-border landholding, their most obvious manifestation in the Borders, became untenable, forcing many landowners to forfeit their property on the other side. In England, Northumberland and Durham began to develop into more cohesive county communities which saw themselves as distinct from Scotland.[22]

The end of the Wars of Independence brought little relief, as the depredations of the two armies were succeeded by the depredations of the Border Reivers:

> Over a huge area of mainland Britain either side of the Cheviot Hills, perhaps a tenth of the landmass of Britain, there existed a society which lived entirely beyond the laws of England and Scotland, which successfully and persistently ignored royal or central government, kept its own ancient culture intact, gave familiar words and concepts to the language of crime, and created little except trouble and indelibly famous stories.[23]

The Reivers took advantage of the Law of the Marches, as the wardens were powerless to curb this general lawlessness. Justice was instead dispensed according to the Reivers' own codes. In this world, it mattered little on which side of the border one had been born; family ties were far more important, and intermarriage and cross-border alliances were common.[24] The age of the Reivers lasted into the early seventeenth century. The Borders also continued to fall victim to the whims of faraway kings. In the 1540s Henry VIII tried to intimidate the Scots into agreeing to a marriage between his son Edward and Mary, Queen of Scots, heir to the Scottish throne. When the Scots betrothed Mary to the Dauphin of France instead, Henry dispatched a force that besieged and destroyed Kelso Abbey and then carried out a destructive march through the Borders in which 287 towns, villages, farms and churches were attacked and burned.[25]

The Borders as Militarized Frontiers

Edward I's conquest of Wales marked the end of the existence of the Welsh Marches as a distinct political entity, but the frontier zone lived on as a distinct cultural space. Lieberman writes that by the thirteenth century, 'The age of large-scale population movements had passed, and the frontier of peoples on the ... borders had become fixed.'[26] This increasing similarity in patterns of settlement was not entirely the product of English colonization and increasing domination, as it was also the result of the eastward migration of Welsh settlers into the less-populated zones in between the castle-boroughs. Ewyas Lacey was a Welsh enclave in southwest Herefordshire, as was Archenfield near

Hay on Wye, while Herefordshire had a large and thriving Welsh community.[27]

The English border counties were shaped by their proximity to the Welsh border. Cheshire's importance in the centuries after the Norman Conquest was, for example, 'not so much in its being the gateway to the impoverished north-west but rather in being the entry to north Wales and Ireland':

> It was because Chester served as a base for the subjugation of the Welsh coastal strip that William I granted the area the privileged status of a palatinate. The crown took over control from the earls of Chester in 1237, extended its virtually independent administration and used Chester as the base for the Edwardian campaign of conquest ... Though modestly populated, Chester came into its own historically during the late thirteenth century through the provision of valued soldiers during the Welsh campaigns of Edward I. Their abilities were appreciated even more by the Black Prince and Richard II whose favour lifted the county and its families above that of its neighbours.[28]

The typical border settlement in the Middle Ages was a borough which had grown up next to a castle, the position of which had originally been chosen primarily for defensive reasons; examples include Ludlow, Oswestry, Caus and Clun on the English side of the border and Montgomery and Welshpool on the Welsh.[29] Functioning 'as military centres and as points of economic exchange', these settlements were frontier towns which were situated on top of hills or in the loops of rivers so as to take advantage of natural defences, as well as being protected by town walls and other fortifications.[30]

In these towns, the most important defensive structure was the castle; there were more Anglo-Norman castles along the border between England and Wales than in any other part of the two countries, with most concentrated on the English side in Shropshire and Herefordshire.[31] Marcher castles were not, to be sure, an entirely separate genre from their counterparts elsewhere, but they did feature some distinctive characteristics. The first generation, designed by William FitzOsbern and built immediately after the Norman Conquest, formed a line along the border and included Monmouth and Chepstow in Monmouthshire, Berkeley in Gloucestershire and Clifford and Wigmore in Herefordshire. Although little is known about their physical form, they were probably standard Norman motte-and-bailey castles built originally of timber and later rebuilt in stone. There is evidence to suggest that these castles shared key attributes with other 'frontier' castles built by the Normans elsewhere as they consolidated their conquest of England, in that they tried to avoid antagonizing the local population. When building his castles FitzOsbern did not destroy existing settlements: Clifford and Wigmore, for example, were described in the Domesday survey as standing on 'waste' land.[32]

The thirteenth century saw a 'concentrated effort at refortification' in which many new castles were built in the Marches. Although they stretched along the border from Whittington in the north to Clun in the south, they were not the result of any overall strategic plan for border defence or territorial expansion, but were rather built by individual lords to protect their lands.[33] In the southern Marches, the most important families were the de Clare earls of Gloucester, the de Valence earls of Pembroke and the Bigod earls of Norfolk. Their castles feature similar details, making it possible to consider them a 'regional group'. John Goodall argues that they 'constitute an architectural family' and were most likely 'designed by masons who shared a common training and access to an archive of architectural drawings', and probably related to 'the king's works ... in the south-east of England'.[34] They can therefore be seen as the product of a unique environment in which rival families imported the latest ideas from the royal court in England, in order to display their cultural erudition and knowledge of defensive architecture.

With 'one of the greatest castle densities in Europe' due to 'its character as a military borderland', the medieval Marches was a distinct cultural as well as political and legal zone, as was demonstrated by the continuing presence of fortified buildings long after they had disappeared from other parts of the country.[35] This was also the case along the border between England and Scotland, as well as in the Pale in Ireland. The border between England and Wales is often considered an exception, however, because early pacification meant that landowners there were able to move from castle to fortified manor house much earlier than their counterparts did along the border between England and Scotland. This transition is embodied by Stokesay Castle, a fortified house in Shropshire which was built by the wool merchant Laurence of Ludlow around 1290, immediately after Edward I's conquest. This is a very early date for a fortified house in a border region. Stokesay is, however, more castle-like in form than later fortified manor houses, even if its defences would only have repelled local raiders and not a serious attack by a Welsh rebel prince. Moreover, its relatively small size reflects Laurence's need to reassure the Marcher lords that he was in no way attempting to challenge their authority.[36] Stokesay was therefore a building which reflected its location in the unique environment of the Marches.

It is also misleading to assume that few other fortified houses besides Stokesay were built along the Anglo-Welsh border. Instead, the local elite continued to occupy defensible residences into the fifteenth century, after the Glyndŵr Rising of 1400–1415 unleashed a wave of destructive violence. Fortified houses were not evenly distributed as in the Scottish Borders, but rather were concentrated on the English side of the border, where 'wariness was maintained' long after Edward I had supposedly conquered Wales.[37] Although no new English castles appeared after the early fourteenth century, around 35 defensible houses date from Stokesay's time or after.[38] On the Welsh side, in contrast, very few fortified houses were built after 1250, and these were concentrated in the far south. Few were substantial purpose-built defensive buildings; the majority were simply older manorial complexes to which light fortifications were added.[39]

Dating from the late 13th century, Stokesay Castle in Shropshire embodies the unique architectural environment of the Anglo-Welsh border in the late Middle Ages.

The 14th-century tower house at Talgarth in Powys, an example of a fortified residence in the Welsh Borders in the late Middle Ages.

There were also some tower houses along the border between England and Wales, although they were much rarer than along the Scottish border and significantly less sophisticated in design.[40] The East Gate Tower of Powis Castle (fifteenth century) probably began as a tower house, and there were others at Scethrog and Talgarth in Brecknockshire (both fourteenth century), Bodidris in Denbighshire (late sixteenth century), Broncoed in Flintshire (*c.* 1440–50) and Langstone (fifteenth century), Coldbrook (sixteenth century) and Kemys (sixteenth century) in Monmouthshire.[41] Wattlesborough Castle in Shropshire is an example on the English side of the border, but is much earlier (thirteenth century) in date.[42] This chronology suggests that the situation on the Anglo-Welsh border was similar to that which occurred in the Scottish Borders at a later date: as direct military conflict between the two nations diminished, raiding in the border zone became increasingly prevalent, requiring the construction of new types of fortified residences. Anthony Emery observes that the towers at Scethrog and Talgarth were built by 'Englishmen to provide summary protection against Welsh maurauders'. He continues:

No tower houses were built in Wales before the late thirteenth century and therein lies the reason for their paucity compared with the considerable number in northern England. Between about 1300 and 1650, the frontier towards Scotland was in a constant state of unrest and sometimes anarchy, whereas Wales enjoyed relative peace after the final annexation of the country in 1284.[43]

In the late fifteenth century and the sixteenth, families on both sides of the border, particularly in its central and southern zones, surrounded their houses with walls entered through strong gatehouses. Examples on the Welsh side, which were concentrated in south Brecknockshire, include Tretower Court (*c.* 1480), Great Porth-aml (*c.* 1480–1500), Ty-Mawr (fifteenth century) and Porth Mawr (*c.* 1500).[44] On the English side, the gatehouses were built slightly later, and include Madley Court (*c.* 1560), Upton Cressett (*c.* 1580–1600), Orleton (1588) and Stokesay (1640).[45] Militarized architecture therefore continued to be found in the Marches into the seventeenth century. Emery attributes these later fortifications to two causes: 'local unrest stemming from political manoeuvrings' and a desire to display rising status.[46] In other words, they did not represent an attempt to prevent incursions from across the border, since the outcome of the political struggle between England and Wales had long been determined.

The picture along the Anglo-Welsh border therefore reveals four phases. First, a burst of Anglo-Norman castle-building associated with the conquest of Wales, culminating in Edward I's late thirteenth-century 'Iron Ring'. Second, in the wake of Owen Glyndŵr's rising from 1400 to 1415, a number of fortified houses were constructed on the English side of the border, demonstrating that the Welsh were still regarded as a threat. Third, a number of tower houses were built in the fifteenth and sixteenth centuries, often by English families on the Welsh side of the border, as a defence against raids. Fourth, defensive walls and gatehouses were added to some houses on both sides of the border from the late fifteenth to the early seventeenth centuries, to provide added protection from family feuds and to display the status of the owners. There were considerably fewer fortified buildings than along the Anglo-Scottish border, but this is a somewhat misleading comparison as the northern border was highly unusual in both the number and strength of its defensive structures. Although its smaller number of fortified houses suggests that it was more peaceful than its Anglo-Scottish counterpart, the Anglo-Welsh border remained partially militarized into the sixteenth century.

IN THE SCOTTISH BORDERS, first the Wars of Independence and then the Border Reivers had an enormous impact on the region's architecture, as 'the militaristic divide across the Tyne found expression in stone.'[47] Having expended prodigious sums on his 'Iron Ring' in Wales and on fighting the Scots, Edward I could not afford to build new castles in Scotland, but he probably carried out some building works, as James of St George, the master-mason responsible for his Welsh castles, appears to have been summoned north in 1303. A more enthusiastic builder in Scotland, Edward III executed improvements to a number of castles. These works were purely practical, however, as there was no attempt to build innovative castles like Caernarvon, Harlech or Beaumaris.[48] Such works were necessary because Scottish military leaders had quickly realized that it was necessary to destroy their own castles in order to prevent the English from occupying them.

The following decades saw a substantial wave of rebuilding as Border nobles sought to repair the damage caused by the war. Before the Wars of Independence they had often lived in unfortified hall houses and only retreated to castles in times of extremity. Now, however, they lived permanently in tower houses, or 'peel/pele' towers, from the Latin *palus*, meaning 'wooden stake', in a reference to the palisades which surrounded the early versions. As they were vulnerable not only to the Reivers but to sporadic English raids, the Borders saw the highest concentration of tower houses, which were 12–18 metres (39–59 ft) in height and had walls up to 3 metres (9¾ ft) thick. Although they could not have withstood a long siege, they presented formidable obstacles to Reiver raiders. Lacking artillery, the Reivers usually targeted the door, which was made of strong, thick wood backed by an iron gate or mini-portcullis called a 'yett'. If the attackers did manage to get inside, the staircase was a clockwise spiral so that the defenders could wield their swords right-handed while forcing the intruders to fight with their left as they climbed. Tower houses were surrounded by defensive walls called 'barmkins', which sometimes featured parapet walks. Over time, tower houses gained wings and became L- or occasionally Z-shaped, although this latter form was rare in the Borders.[49]

Lesser landowners, particularly in Tynedale and Redesdale, built less costly defensible residences called 'bastles'; the name possibly derives from *bastille*, French for 'fortified house'. Bastles were essentially fortified farmhouses or small manor houses. Their main defensive feature was their thick walls; if attacked, the livestock could be herded into the ground floor while the residents took refuge above. The ground floor had only a single door and narrow slits for ventilation rather than windows. An external staircase led to the door to the first floor, which was reinforced by a drawbar.[50] Mostly dating from around 1500, more than two hundred bastles have been identified within twenty miles of the border.[51]

In late medieval England the opposite was happening, as in most parts of the country houses no longer required defensive features. This development was later used to support views that the English country house symbolized England's uniquely peaceful political evolution. These same views claimed that Scottish tower houses were necessary because Scotland was riven by feuds among its warlike clans, who refused to accept a stable central government. In 1927 the architectural writer Sir Lawrence Weaver contrasted the 'subtle refinements' of Inigo Jones's Banqueting House, built in the early 1620s, with its near-contemporary Scotstarvit Tower in Fife, which he described as the 'lair of a robber chieftain, no more and no less'. Weaver summed up early-modern Scottish houses as the expressions of 'the long-continuing element of private warfare that seethed through Scottish life until a far later period'.[52]

Tower houses were not confined to the Scottish side of the border, however, but rather were part of the region's distinctive cross-border architectural ecosystem. In 1296 there were around twenty castles in Northumberland. In 1415 there were 37, along with 75 tower houses. A century later, the number of tower houses had doubled again.[53] Some of these English towers had Scottish characteristics. In Northumberland, Cockle Park near Morpeth (early sixteenth century) features corbelled-out bartizans, a typically Scottish feature, and Hetton Hall (fifteenth century), Coupland Castle (late sixteenth century) and the towers at Dilston (fifteenth century) and Duddo (sixteenth century) all have Scottish-style broad newel stairs leading to the first floor, with a narrower staircase in a corbelled-out circular turret with a conical roof (often called a 'pepper-pot' turret) providing access to the floors above.[54] In Cumbria, fifteenth-century Dalston Hall features a tall, thin tower, 'the details of which, such as the stone "gun barrel" water spouts, are more Scottish than English'.[55] Kirkandrews is a red sandstone tower house built in the 'Scottish tradition'; it closely resembles Gilnockie across the border in Dumfriesshire, which was built around the same time in the sixteenth century.[56] Another Cumbrian tower with Scottish attributes is Brackenhill (1586), with its corbelled-out battlements and crow-stepped gables.[57]

These houses all had real defensive capability, which remained essential along the Anglo-Scottish border. In the late 1550s Elizabeth I built a massive ring of fortifications around Berwick, costing a staggering £128,648, the largest expenditure on a single defensive project of her reign. Its arrowhead-shaped bastions, designed to be able to rake attackers with cannon-fire, pointed not towards the mouth of the Tweed but landward, because that was the direction from which the danger was most likely to come.[58] Beyond Berwick, the tower houses and bastles of the Borders retained formidable defensive features well after the Union of the Crowns in 1603.[59] In 1535 an Act of the Scottish Parliament ordered all men owning land worth more than £100 in the Borders to build a barmkin, with a tower 'if he thinks it expedient', and 'men of smaller

With its corbelled-out bartizans, one of which can be seen at the top left of this image, Cockle Park Tower in Northumberland is an example of how typically Scottish features were incorporated into tower houses on the English side of the border.

rent and revenue' to build a palisade 'for the safety of themselves, men, tenants and goods'.[60] Even churches in the Borders retained defensive features such as strong doors, thick walls, small windows and, in some cases, fortified towers.[61]

Long after the Wars of Independence had ended, the Anglo-Scottish border therefore remained a distinct political zone. On the English side in Northumberland:

> Years of Anglo-Scottish wars had resulted in the development of a distinct body of law and government which survived into the late sixteenth and early seventeenth centuries. Government and administration was dependent on march wardens, whose principal obligation was to keep their wardenry, or march, prepared against incursions from the Scots by maintaining fortifications and ensuring their tenants were sufficiently armed ... The area inevitably was more militarised than elsewhere in the kingdom.[62]

In the Tudor era, Steve Ellis writes, the *raison d'être* of the border between England and Scotland was 'still primarily a military one', as it continued to form a 'buffer zone between lowland England and the independent kingdom of the Scots to the north'.[63] In some of the more remote corners of the Borders, bastle houses were still being built at the time of the Act of Union in 1707.[64]

We should not, however, exaggerate the distinctiveness and lawlessness of the Borders in the early modern era. By the end of the sixteenth century some Border landowners felt sufficiently secure to build lightly fortified houses rather than towers. Examples include Huttonhall, built by Alexander Home in 1573, and Ferniehurst, built by Sir Andrew Ker in 1598. After 1603 the sense of security increased further, and many castles and tower houses were abandoned or demolished as their owners decided to live more comfortably. Some of them continued to complain about unrest, but this may have been an effort to retain the immunity from some forms of taxation which had been granted to them because of their defensive responsibilities. If the Union of Crowns did not entirely achieve James I's vision of the Anglo-Scottish border as a place of 'ease and happy quietness', it did make it possible for it to function in ways other than as an 'insecure frontier zone' or 'a bulwark against an actively hostile neighbour'.[65]

Charles McKean has argued forcefully against regarding pre-1707 Scotland as 'a country isolated from the mainstream European Renaissance, turned in on itself and continuing anachronistically to build castles when mansions, country houses and villas were being constructed elsewhere'.[66] McKean concedes that Scottish houses retained a castle-like appearance longer than their English counterparts, but he argues that any serious defensive capability had largely disappeared by the fifteenth century. Far from being war-torn, Scotland was in fact one of the most peaceful countries in Europe at this time, without any religious wars or massacres and only occasional civil strife. In most of the country, the houses of the Scottish elite were weakly protected in comparison to the fortified residences that were still necessary in many places on the European continent, where religious conflict and political and civil unrest remained rife.[67] The martial appearance of many Scottish houses was a stylistic choice, not a defensive necessity. Deborah Howard writes:

> Even new constructions ... were embellished with bartizans, gunloops, turret stairs and corner towers long after the introduction of gunpowder artillery had rendered their military functions obsolete. Their use was adapted to the new social rituals of the Renaissance: the bartizans became studies or closets, the turret stairs ensured the privacy of the lodgings above, gunloops simply provided basic domestic security against robbers, and the corner towers simply became bedrooms with dramatic views over the landscape.[68]

Whether symbolic or real, however, the military character of Scottish architecture emphasized that Scottish national identity was increasingly 'based on martial success in repelling a succession of attempted English conquests':

> The martial values which, it was claimed, had secured the country's independence were also reflected within architecture, in the emergence of an appropriately showy, military style – the castellated architecture that was employed for almost all secular buildings and even some churches. This trenchantly militarised protonationalism intentionally contrasted with the contemporary architecture of England.[69]

In other words, it was an indication that Scottish identity was increasingly defined against its English counterpart, which meant that English and Scottish architecture were, from both perspectives, increasingly distinct. As English identity became associated with stability and continuity and England's architecture became less militarized, Scotland's became more so, reflecting its fierce resistance to English political control and cultural dominance.

The Borders as Cultural Barriers

The militarized borders between England and Wales and England and Scotland intensified cultural differences. Cultural influences can – and did – cross physical boundaries, but the failure of the border regions to become places where national influences blended was a major factor in the failure to develop truly British architectural forms and styles. Although tower houses had previously shared some characteristics, as time went on the architecture of the Borders became less blended. A case in point is Stonegarthside Hall in Cumbria, only a mile from the Scottish border. In 1682 Henry Forster converted Stonegarthside from a medieval tower house into an H-plan manor. As it stands on the southern edge of what were known as the 'Debatable Lands', a piece of territory on the western Anglo-Scottish border which local families prevented from being claimed by either England or Scotland, had things evolved differently Stonegarthside might display hybrid English and Scottish characteristics. Instead, it is a Scottish house on the wrong side of the border. Nicholas Cooper writes:

> A number of features link it closely with Scottish houses: it has external details which include crow-stepped gables and decorated quoins like those to Heriot's Hospital in Edinburgh, the centre of the front range was originally flat roofed between flanking gables like Methven Castle of 1664 and Caroline Park, outside Edinburgh, of 1685, the stair position is identical with that of Methven, and the stair jambs have mouldings of a common Scottish form that occurs as late as 1697 at Melville House, Fife. Although in England, Stonegarthside is thoroughly Scottish, confirming a continuing regionalism and the part played in the adoption of new architectural forms by the connections of the builders themselves.[70]

Stonegarthside shows how even in the Borders country houses remained English or Scottish and were rarely influenced by both architectural traditions.

The same was true in Wales, but there Welsh forms and styles lost their distinctiveness and gave way to English ones after the union with England in 1536. That union is usually seen as having three architectural consequences, all of which increased English influence and reduced Welsh distinctiveness. First, it prevented the development of an independent Welsh architecture. John Hilling observes: 'The incorporation of Wales within a much larger state prevented the possibility of her developing further a national culture (including the arts and architecture) based on her own administrative, ecclesiastical and educational institutions, such as no doubt would have evolved if Glyndŵr's bid for independence had been successful.'[71] Second, it meant that Wales became sufficiently stable that even minimally defensible houses were no longer needed. In the sixteenth and seventeenth centuries a building boom occurred in which the 'living conditions of the gentry improved immensely', as their houses were 'rebuilt, extended or renovated':

> The delight in introducing newer methods of Renaissance architecture and establishing the country mansion on a more elevated plane as a symbol of the aesthetic tastes of the most opulent was becoming more apparent in different parts of the country. As military functions began to recede ... luxury and sophistication ... assumed greater prominence. The influence of Renaissance architecture gradually penetrated the most richly endowed areas of Wales, particularly the north and southeastern parts as well as the lowlands of Glamorgan and south Pembrokeshire.[72]

Stone and brick replaced timber as the preferred building materials; fireplaces with chimneys replaced open hearths; glass began to be used for windows; and upper floors were added to previously open-roofed halls: the greater the height, the more prestigious the occupant. Increasing their comfort and flaunting their owner's prestige, these houses were divided into more spaces and in some cases acquired cross-wings. Third, the wealthiest and most prominent Welshmen moved to England in order to be closer to the royal court and seat of government. Elizabeth I's leading advisor William Cecil spoke Welsh and proudly proclaimed his descent from the Welsh Marcher 'Seisyll' family, but he built his two great houses, Hatfield and Burghley, in Hertfordshire and Lincolnshire respectively. The Herberts, Dukes of Beaufort, moved their seat from Wales to Wiltshire after Raglan Castle was severely damaged in the Civil War. There was nothing Welsh about its replacement, Badminton House, one of the most important classical houses of the mid-seventeenth century.[73]

But if there was little Welsh influence in England, there was a great deal of English influence in Wales. The addition of cross-wings to the houses of the Welsh gentry, for example, reflected the geographical spread of a form common to central and southern England.[74] Dating from the early seventeenth century, the black-and-white timber-framed houses of Montgomeryshire 'in all essential respects' follow 'Shropshire techniques' in their building methods.[75] In the last quarter of the sixteenth century, Raglan, Powis and Carew Castles all acquired Elizabethan-style long galleries. The elaborate gatehouses which were a prominent feature of many contemporary English houses also appeared at Beaupré in the Vale of Glamorgan (1586) and Cefnamlwch (1607) and Cors-y-gedol (1630) in Gwynedd.[76] Trevalyn Hall (1576) in Flintshire featured pediments above the windows, a decorative element most frequently seen in East Anglia.[77] Another English influence was the position of the entrance in a side wall of a porch or gabled projection so that it was less visible, in order to conceal how it was off-centre due to the need to enter the great hall at one end, opposite the dais where the high table for the lord and his family stood. This occurred at Llanvihangel Court (expanded early seventeenth century) in Monmouthshire, following precedents at Burton Agnes (1601) in Yorkshire and Chastleton (1607) in Oxfordshire.[78]

Architectural influences in Wales were not exclusively English, however. Having lived in Antwerp from 1552 to 1565, the merchant Sir Richard Clough hired Flemish craftsmen and imported stone, wood panelling and stained glass from the Continent to build the first brick houses in Wales, the lodge Bach-y-Graig and the full-size house Plas Clough in Denbighshire, both built around 1567. They featured many design elements, such as crow-stepped gables and tiered dormer windows, derived from the buildings Clough had seen in Flanders, and they inspired a fashion for stepped gables in North Wales in the second half of the sixteenth century.[79]

Other Welsh houses were influenced by southern as well as northern Europe. Plas Teg in Flintshire (*c.* 1610) featured designs on the posts and newels of its main staircase that were taken from the engravings of

Trevalyn Hall (1576) near Wrexham displays English influence in the pediments over the windows, a feature imported from houses in East Anglia.

Vredeman de Vries, while its overall design embodied principles taken from Palladio, Serlio and other architects of the Italian Renaissance. Its builder, Sir John Trevor, had travelled to Spain as part of a diplomatic mission to conclude peace negotiations with Philip III. While there, he encountered the work of the court architect Juan de Herrera, in particular the monastery of El Escorial (1563) outside Madrid, one of the most important buildings of the Spanish Renaissance and one with which Plas Teg shares an 'austere classicism'.[80] Other Welsh houses which show clear evidence of Continental Renaissance influence include Brymbo Hall (c. 1625) in Wrexham and Edwinsford (c. 1635) in Carmarthenshire.[81] These houses show that Wales had its own cultural connections with the European continent independent of those which were filtered through England.

A third influence on Welsh houses was local building tradition. The Welsh gentry, while trying to be part of a British elite, remained aware of their Welsh nationality and their status in local society.'[82] Welsh country houses often evolved using what Mark Baker calls the 'unit system', in which self-contained blocks were added to existing buildings to accommodate extended family members. There were a few examples of the unit system in England and eastern Wales, but it was predominantly a phenomenon of western Wales.[83] The adoption of this practice for high-status houses such as Edwinsford and Llwynywormwood, both in Carmarthenshire, and Brynkir in Gwynedd, shows that it did not occur because Welsh owners lacked the financial resources to demolish and rebuild. Rather, it occurred because the heirs to Welsh estates tended to live in the same house as their fathers rather than in their own establishments.[84]

Just as there were in England, there were regional clusters of houses with similar architectural features in Wales, and for the same reason: the same craftsmen carried out work on them. Baker has identified such a group who worked in the Vale of Clwyd in northwest Wales in the 1620s and '30s. Their designs were characterized by fine ashlar stonework, deep mullioned windows, elaborate staircases and Renaissance detailing such as shaped or stepped gables and ball finials. The houses they may have worked on include Brymbo (1624) in Wrexham; Rhual (1634) and Nerquis (1638) in Mold; and Henblas (1645) in Llanasa.[85] In Flintshire, a group of houses featured 'mullioned and transomed windows and coped and finialed gables', along with asymmetrical H-plans.[86] In North Wales, seventeenth-century gentry houses tended to have their chimneys on the outside walls. In Brecknockshire, however, the main chimney was usually internal, with its back to the cross-passage linking the front and rear entrances, and in Montgomeryshire there were often two chimneys back-to-back in the middle of the cross passage, thereby creating an entrance lobby.[87]

Welsh houses of the sixteenth and early seventeenth centuries therefore display a complex mixture of influences. The main front and internal plan of St Fagan's Castle (1560) near Cardiff has Renaissance-style symmetry, but its steeply pitched roofs and tall gables are traditional Welsh characteristics.[88] Ruperra Castle (c. 1626) in Caerphilly is a symmetrical building with a round tower on each corner and classical detailing on its porch and doorways. Possibly its builder Sir Thomas Morgan gained his architectural expertise while serving as a volunteer in the Low Countries during the Thirty Years' War; Ruperra shows signs of being influenced by du Cerceau's pattern-books.[89] It also, however, closely resembles Lulworth Castle (1608) in Dorset, which Morgan may well have seen while serving as the Earl of Pembroke's steward at Wilton House in Wiltshire in the early 1620s. Finally, Ruperra derives some elements from local Welsh tradition. Its round towers echo those of Caerphilly Castle, built by the Marcher lord Gilbert de Clare in the late thirteenth century. Ruperra, Baker writes, 'represents an instant of archaism as a form of traditionalism yet also of radicalism, incorporating battlemented circular corner towers, which evoke medieval Wales, and originally gables, characteristic of vernacular houses of the area'.[90] Unlike Lulworth, which was built as a hunting lodge, Ruperra was built as the seat of its upwardly mobile owner. Its conscious archaism and references to much older local buildings were intended to suggest that Morgan had a longer pedigree than he actually had.

Welsh houses clearly felt the influence of English architectural developments, but they also reflected how Wales had its own links to the European continent through which Renaissance ideas were conveyed. In addition, Welsh landowners often wished to retain local building traditions so as to emphasize their own dynastic histories, leading to regionally distinctive clusters of houses. Such houses are sometimes seen as evidence of Wales's cultural isolation because their designs did not fully embrace Renaissance innovations. Hilling asserts that even in a region which was 'open to outside influence', such as the Wye Valley,

Ruperra Castle (c. 1626) in Caerphilly combines Renaissance, English and traditional Welsh elements.

houses such as Trefecca Fawr and Tredwstan Court, although they 'approach ... the image of a Renaissance house', were in fact built with L-shaped plans and did not achieve full symmetry until additional wings were added in the early eighteenth century.[91] Such houses would appear to support Iorwerth Peate's contention that 'a nation bereft of its sovereignty cannot promote the growth of fine arts except by indirect and generally innocuous means.'[92] But such a view is only correct if the standard of comparison is what was happening in England, and if architectural excellence is measured by the most rapid and thorough absorption of Continental Renaissance influences. Welsh architecture suffers when it is evaluated in this way, because it was slower to embrace such influences. If on the other hand the standard is the retention of independence and distinctiveness from England, then the picture looks different. Edward Hubbard notes that 'two conflicting trends' were seen in Welsh houses from the late sixteenth century onwards: 'the continuation of regional character and traditions, medieval in origin' and 'Renaissance movement for regularity and uniformity fused with classical discipline and detail'.[93] Wales, in other words, absorbed Renaissance influences in its own way, and at its own pace, in ways that made sense in a Welsh context.

AS IN WALES, Renaissance ideas from France and northern Europe flowed into Scotland not through England, but through direct contacts.[94] James III's rebuilding of the east facade of Linlithgow Palace in the late fifteenth century may have been inspired by the buildings which the palace's Flemish-born Keeper Anselm Adornes had seen on his visit to Rome in 1470.[95] James IV and James V spent extended periods in France. Around 1500 James IV added a new entrance to Stirling Castle, which copied its round towers from French military architecture and featured a central gateway flanked by small pedestrian entrances in the form of a Roman triumphal arch.[96] His new great hall at Edinburgh Castle (1511) featured a hammer-beam roof supported by heraldic and decorative stone corbels carved by an Italian sculptor.[97] After James V reached his maturity in the late 1520s, the chronicler Robert Lindsay recorded that he 'plenished the country with all kinds of craftsmen out of other countries, as, French-men, Spaniards, Dutch men and English-men, which were all cunning craftsmen, every man for his own hand ... His craftsmen apparel his palaces in all manner of operation and necessities.'[98] Renaissance influences are apparent in the west front of Holyrood

Palace (mid-1530s) in Edinburgh, and more fully in the rebuilding of the south and east ranges of Falkland Palace in Fife a few years later:

> The Falkland courtyard design divides the building into regular bays marked by Corinthian columns, inverted consoles and statuary. The large main windows are arranged symmetrically, and flanked by a sequence of medallion heads within foliage wreaths, carved in a mature classical style. Each head is individual and strongly characterized: there is a beautiful young lady, a soldier in Roman garb, a bearded man and a laughing woman. A marked French flavour is imparted by the conical-capped stair turrets, pedimented dormer windows and tall, slender chimneys ... James v clearly took inspiration for his Falkland scheme from the palaces and chateaux he had seen in the Loire and Paris regions during his visit to the court of Francis I in 1536–7.[99]

There are several possible specific antecedents for Falkland, including the chateaux of Villers-Cotterets, Fontainebleau, Amboise, Bury and de la Verraine.[100] But whatever their inspiration, the 'Falkland courtyard facades ... represent the earliest wholly Renaissance architectural scheme in the British Isles'.[101] After his embellishments to Falkland, James v added a Renaissance-inspired block to Stirling Castle between 1538 and 1541.[102]

The architectural Francophilia of these Scottish kings was not merely 'fashion'; it also served as a reminder to the English of their failure to conquer their northern neighbour. Miles Glendinning and Aonghus MacKechnie argue that the military and French character of Scottish architecture in the late fifteenth and early sixteenth centuries reflected the belief that Scotland's independence from England had been preserved by martial means. 'This trenchantly militarized proto-nationalism', they write, 'intentionally contrasted with the contemporary architecture of England, while making frequent reference to that of England's main enemy – France.'[103]

It did not take long for royal fashion to filter down to the Scottish nobility. McKean notes that by the mid-sixteenth century

> most people building or refashioning their country seats had travelled, fought or studied abroad. Not to have continental European experience ... was something of which to be ashamed

... Travellers, scholars, politicians and mercenaries returned to Scotland with ideas and, possibly, publications and engravings. The country was awash with current design information on symbols and motifs for interior paintwork, and there is little reason to believe that there was not comparable information about contemporary architecture.[104]

Sir James Hamilton of Finnart, who served as Master of Works during the alterations to Falkland Palace and Stirling Castle, built his own house at Craignethan around 1530. In 1517, while in the retinue of the Duke of Albany, Hamilton had visited the French court at Amboise and was introduced to Leonardo da Vinci, who had entered the service of Francis I the previous year. At the time, Leonardo was sketching a plan for a new palace at Romorantin. It is possible that he showed his designs to Hamilton, for the axial, double-pile plan of Craignethan bears a strong resemblance to them.[105]

By the mid-sixteenth century there were at least fifty Scottish examples of the French castle fashion of a rectangular main block with circular towers on the corners.[106] In the 1550s Archbishop John Hamilton rebuilt his castle at St Andrews with more sumptuous and comfortable accommodations. With its 'large, regularly spaced windows, arched entrance and elegant mouldings', the new wing displayed 'the cultivated tastes of a man who lived in France in the 1540s'. Mar's Walk in Stirling, built for the Earl of Mar in the early 1570s, imitated elements of Renaissance design from James V's works at both Falkland Palace and Stirling Castle. Drochil Castle in the Scottish Borders featured a distinctive double-pile plan that was 'almost certainly derived' from the publications of the French architect Jacques Androuet de Cerceau.[107]

French influence decreased after Mary, Queen of Scots, was deposed in 1567, and Scottish houses began to reflect a broader range of Renaissance influences.[108] In the 1580s the new north range of the Earl of Bothwell's Crichton Castle may have been inspired by the Palazzo dei Diamanti in Ferrera, with its arched loggia, symmetrical windows and diamond-studded wall.[109] Other Scottish houses that were influenced by the Italian Renaissance include Boyne Castle (1575) in Aberdeenshire; the new east wing of Castle Campbell (early 1590s) in Clackmannanshire; Craigston Castle (1604) in Aberdeenshire; and the new Nithsdale Lodging for Caerlaverock Castle (1636) in Dumfries and Galloway. Other influences came from the Low Countries: the King's Room of Pinkie

The diamond-studded wall and arched loggia in the courtyard
of the north range of Crichton Castle (*c.* 1580) in Midlothian
possibly derived from the Palazzo dei Diamanti in Ferrera, Italy.

House (*c.* 1613) in East Lothian featured a cupola derived from Vredeman de Vries's writings on perspective and emblems on the ceiling derived from Otto Vaenius's *Emblamata Horatiana* (1607). These houses also reflected up-to-date Continental principles of design such as state apartments, or antechamber, chamber and bedchamber arranged in a horizontal sequence.[110]

The Scots, like the English, wished to remain connected to their national past by retaining medieval forms as well as Renaissance influences, but in the Scottish case the particular gothic styles were the Romanesque and the Franco-Burgundian rather than the Perpendicular.[111] Ian Campbell writes that after 1500:

> The Scots no longer looked to contemporary English models as they had before [the Wars of Independence], but often looked back instead to their own Romanesque and early Gothic architecture. Late Gothic projects throughout Scotland, from St Andrews Cathedral in the east to Iona Abbey in the west, include features such as round-headed arches for arcades, triforia, windows and doorways, and cylindrical piers or columns. Similar, seemingly Romanesque features can be found elsewhere in contemporary European architecture, but they occur in such profusion in Scotland that some commentators have interpreted them as a conscious revival of other forms. Typically, however, these writers devalue the revivalist elements in relation to more conventional late Gothic architecture in northern Europe, equating backward-looking with being backward... Such judgments sit uneasily with the growing evidence that, besides seeking inspiration from their own past, Scottish patrons and masons were also importing architectural ideas from mainland Europe: often both Romanesque-looking elements and continental ideas appear in the same buildings.[112]

The mixing of these Scottish gothic traditions with Renaissance classicism led to the emergence of the early Scottish Baronial style, which featured medieval components such as 'battlements, crow-stepped gables, machicolations, projecting towers, bartizans, conical turrets and gunholes', as well as classical elements such as symmetrically arranged windows, pediments, columns, pilasters and friezes. Surviving examples include a group of Aberdeenshire castles: Midmar (1565), Crathes (c. 1596), Fyvie (1598), Huntly (c. 1602), Fraser (1617) and Craigievar (1626), along with Glamis (1606) in Angus.[113] After 1550, then, 'the adaptation of foreign and native' – but not English – styles became 'a conspicuous feature' of Scottish architecture.[114] In 1632 Robert Kerr, Earl of Ancrum, cautioned his son William, Earl of Lothian, not to imitate English models, and to build his new house, Newbattle Abbey, 'either in the fashion of this country or France'.[115]

The merging of monarchies in 1603 resulted in closer cultural ties between Scotland and England. James VI/I wished to dissolve the border as not only a political and military boundary but as a cultural barrier; he even proposed moving his capital to York and began referring to the border region as the 'Middle Shires' in order to alter perceptions of centre and periphery in geographical conceptions of Britain.[116] 'Almost overnight political and cultural trends in England became the chief points of reference in Scotland,' and a new architectural unionism began to evolve as the dominant 'court style', which echoed English architecture with squared-off rooflines, mullioned-and-transomed windows, and Anglo-Dutch style ornament.[117] The new palace block at Edinburgh Castle, built from 1615 onwards, closely resembled the 'Little Castle' that Sir Charles Cavendish had begun building at Bolsover in Derbyshire three years earlier.[118] The chapel at Holyrood was rebuilt in an English Episcopalian style for the coronation of Charles I in 1633.[119] In the houses of the Scottish elite, this trend produced some blatantly unionist propaganda, in the form of the alternating thistles and roses which began to adorn contemporary plasterwork ceilings, such as at Winton House (1620) in East Lothian, Baberton House (1622) in Edinburgh, Craigievar Castle (1626) in Aberdeenshire, and the House of the Binns in West Lothian, which was specially commissioned for Charles I's visit to Scotland in 1633.

There were limits, however, to this blurring of architectural boundaries. 'The idea mooted after 1603 by King James VI and I', Meikle writes, 'that there was one British monarch and nation, rather than a united sovereignty of independent states, was overwhelmingly rejected by both Scots and English.'[120] Many members of the Scottish elite maintained their cultural independence from English influence, and beyond court circles castellated houses remained common until the end of the seventeenth century.[121] Even houses which were symmetrical in plan, such as Castle Stuart (1619) on the Moray Firth, were given 'intentionally different superstructures' and 'asymmetrical fenestration' in order to maintain their martial appearance.[122] When Sir Robert Kerr contemplated rebuilding his tower house at Ancrum in the Borders in 1632, he resisted the entreaties of his son William, Lord Kerr of Newbattle and Earl of Lothian, to transform it into a modern house: 'By any meanes, do not take away the battelments, as some [advised] ... me ... to do, ... for that is the grace of the house, and makes it looke lyk a castle, and hence so nobleste.'[123]

After the Restoration, however, Scottish houses such as Thirlstane Castle (1670) in the Borders and Drumlanrig Castle (1679) in Dumfries and Galloway began to display symmetrical exteriors, as classicism began to dominate.[124] In 1661 Sir John Gilmour reduced the original structure of Craigmillar Castle, his tower house near Edinburgh, to a picturesque historical relic, and built an adjoining wing without castellations as his new residence.[125] Even so, Scottish houses retained distinct features. France remained the principal source of inspiration, embodied by dramatic rooflines studded with towers and pavilions, in contrast to the flat roofs and pediments of their Italian-inspired English counterparts.[126]

Inigo Jones had introduced a more coherent Italian Renaissance classicism to England with his adaptations of the architecture of Andrea Palladio. At the end of the seventeenth century Sir William Bruce did the same in Scotland. 'Where I make any designe', he wrote, 'I have no regard to irregular planning, ... or any other old matter wch are oblique & not agreeable to a modish & regular designe.'[127] A high-church Episcopalian, Bruce had escaped from the puritanism of Cromwell's Commonwealth to La Rochelle and Rotterdam, where he had worked as a merchant. After the Restoration he was awarded a series of lucrative

The symmetrical facade of Drumlanrig Castle (1679) in Dumfries and Galloway shows the increasing importance of classical ideas in Scotland.

posts in the Scottish government, culminating in his appointment as Surveyor General of the King's Works in 1671. Although he was dismissed in 1678, he maintained a prominent public profile, but after the Glorious Revolution his allegiance to the Jacobite cause damaged his chances of being awarded architectural commissions.

While at the peak of his career in the 1660s and '70s, Bruce was the first Scottish architect to 'work in a concerted way to make architectural classicism a norm for Scottish builders'.[128] Bruce's own Kinross House (*c.* 1685), overlooking Loch Leven in Kinross-shire, had English predecessors such as Sir Roger Pratt's Coleshill (*c.* 1660) in Berkshire, but it also retained Scotland's cultural links with France through its resemblance to the mid-seventeenth-century royal pavilions at Vincennes.[129] Other houses designed by Bruce, meanwhile, displayed a greater allegiance to the Scottish castle tradition. Leslie House (1667) in Fife had 'dormer heads reaching through the eaves and cornice in a traditional "castle-like" manner', while Panmure House (*c.* 1666) in Angus had 'square angle pavilions overlaying the outer gables as on a castle'.[130] Bruce's reconstruction of Holyrood Palace (1671) used classicist symmetry, but rather than demolishing James V's castellated tower from the 1520s, he balanced it with a copy. Between 1674 and 1684, Bruce rebuilt the Marquess of Atholl's castle at Dunkeld in Perthshire. He designed a classical square block, but also installed a parapet and corner bartizans, indicating 'the value of tradition'.[131]

After the Glorious Revolution, however, 'everything associated' with traditional Scottish castellated architecture was 'rejected by the new ascendancy as being tainted with the values of the outgoing "Jacobite" dynastic succession'.[132] This change is seen in Bruce's design for Hopetoun House (1699) near Edinburgh.[133] A number of Continental inspirations for Hopetoun have been suggested, including Italian Palladian buildings; French models such as the Hotel Tambonneau (1642) in Paris or the Château de Marly (1679); and Dutch models such as the palace of Het Loo (1684).[134] But there are also possible English precedents, including Eaton Hall (1675) in Cheshire and Belton House (1685) in Lincolnshire.[135] Hopetoun shows that both English and Scottish architecture in the late seventeenth century were influenced by Continental ideas, by each other and by a shared commitment to classicism. It also shows that Scottish architecture was not subservient to its English counterpart. Bruce was not immune to English influence, but neither was he enslaved by it.

William Bruce's Kinross House (c. 1685) in Fife shows the French influence on contemporary Scottish classicism.

The Act of Union of 1707 and the Hanoverian Succession of 1714 brought Scottish and English architecture closer together. Bruce's successors James Smith and William Adam followed English classicism more closely than he had done. Adam, in particular, 'built for a pro-union landed clientele who wanted houses that looked less Scottish and more classically mainstream'; his houses closely resembled those that his fellow Scot James Gibbs was building in England.[136] The most talented Scottish architects – among them Gibbs, Robert Mylne and Colen Campbell – migrated to England, further blurring the division between 'Scottish' and 'English' country houses. Campbell's *Vitruvius Britannicus* (1715) 'advocated a "neo-Palladianism" as a national style' not just for England but 'for the new "Great Britain"'.[137]

By the middle decades of the eighteenth century, Palladianism had become the accepted style in Scotland, reflecting an era in which most Scots 'regarded themselves both Scottish and British'.[138] This new sense of Britishness, however, did not mean that Scottish architecture was completely subordinated to its English counterpart. Instead, a degree of cultural independence was maintained, as houses such as Kelburn Castle (1692) in Ayrshire and Craighall Castle (1697) in Fife remained rooted in the Scottish castle tradition. Traquair House in the Borders was perhaps the best example of this nationalist spirit. It was rebuilt by Smith between 1700 and 1705 and again by John Douglas around 1740; although both schemes classicized the interior, the house's external traditional martial character was left largely untouched, presumably in accordance with the wishes of Traquair's staunchly Jacobite laird, Charles Stewart, 4th Earl of Traquair.[139] The 6th Earl of Mar, later one of the military leaders of the Jacobite rebellion of 1715, took a similar approach with his remodelling of Alloa Tower in Clackmannanshire in 1706: he kept the castellated exterior of the fourteenth-century tower house but classicized the interior. So although some examples of Scottish domestic architecture embraced the new 'British' fashion for classicism, others maintained their independence.[140]

Traquair and Alloa were old houses rather than newly built counterblasts to the prevailing political winds, however. The continuing threat posed by Jacobitism made such expressions of Scottish nationalism fraught, so that in the first half of the eighteenth century castellated houses were rare. This era marked 'the lowest point in the fortunes of castellated architecture in Scotland, and also the dominance of the

Despite being rebuilt twice in the first half of the eighteenth century,
Traquair House in the Borders maintained its martial appearance
on the exterior, in keeping with Scottish tradition.

fashion for a purer classicism in both Scotland and England'.[141] In 1720, however, John Campbell, 2nd Duke of Argyll, decided to rebuild Inveraray Castle in Argyll and commissioned a sketch from Sir John Vanbrugh which featured a quadrangular design with a round tower on each corner.[142] When his younger brother Archibald succeeded to the dukedom in 1743, he began to translate this sketch into reality by consulting with some of Scotland's leading architects, including William Adam and Robert Mylne. He ultimately, however, chose the Englishman Roger Morris, who closely followed Vanbrugh's concept for the house. Why did the 2nd Duke of Argyll choose to build a castle at a time when such a design was politically problematic because of its association with Jacobitism? It was not because of any Jacobite leanings: he was a staunch unionist who had served as one of Queen Anne's commissioners in 1707 and was wounded fighting for the government at Sheriffmuir during the 1715 rising. It was rather due to the changing landscape of Scottish nationalism, which was beginning to shift away from politically oriented Jacobitism to cultural forms of expression. Together with the poems of Ossian and the cult of Mary, Queen of Scots, castles helped to 'highlight Scotland as the archetypical land of romanticism'.[143] Murray Pittock writes that 'the consciously outdated model of a Highland fastness at Inveraray told ... a story of Protestant and Hanoverian victory.'[144]

Inveraray was the first of these romantic castles, but many followed. We think of the Adam brothers as the leading architects of mid-eighteenth-century classicism, but in Scotland they designed a number of castellated houses, including John and James Adam's Douglas Castle (partially built, 1757) and Robert Adam's Wedderburn Castle (1771), Caldwell House (1773), Culzean Castle (1777), Oxenfoord Castle (1780), possibly Pitfour Castle (1785), Seton House (1789), Dalquharran Castle (1789), Airthrey Castle (1791), Stobs Castle (1792), Mauldslie Castle (1792) and Barnton Castle (1794), as well as his hybrid Mellerstain House (1770), into which he inserted a castellated central tower between two classical wings designed by his father. James Playfair, another Scottish architect associated with Neoclassicism, built Melville Castle (1786) for Henry Dundas, 1st Viscount Melville. So many imitators followed over the next century that Glendinning and MacKechnie refer to a 'Second Castle Age'.[145]

As in England, the era of the Revolutionary and Napoleonic Wars saw an upsurge in the construction of castellated houses in Scotland, with thirty built between 1800 and 1810 alone.[146] These houses were

Shown here in a photographic print from 1905, Inveraray Castle (1743) in Argyll was a rare example of a Scottish castellated house built while Jacobitism was still an active threat, but after 1745 many imitators would follow.

certainly not nationalist statements; they were instead the architectural expressions of 'a Scottish elite uncertain about its competing national identities'.[147] In addition, they embodied a British revival of interest in national history and cultural traditions as the basis for nationhood. The disappearance of Jacobitism as a serious threat after 1745 made this revival politically possible in Scotland.

The Scottish castellated houses of the late eighteenth and early nineteenth centuries did not differ significantly from their English counterparts. In the middle decades of the nineteenth century, however, the differences between English and Scottish architecture re-emerged. This change related to evolving attitudes towards Scotland's traditional culture and natural environment. Before the late eighteenth century, visitors from England frequently highlighted the poverty of the Scottish people and the desolation of the landscape. At century's end, however, the rise of Romanticism transformed the Scottish Highlands from barren wasteland to a celebrated embodiment of the picturesque, and the region's culture from primitive to quaint. The tourists and sportsmen who poured into the region pointed to clear distinctions from the gentler English countryside. After Napoleon's defeat in 1815 removed the French threat, there was less need to assert a unified British identity. The incorporation of Ireland into the Union in 1801 also required a greater recognition of cultural and religious diversity. The United Kingdom's four component nations retained a considerable degree of religious, legal and educational autonomy. Lawrence Brockliss and David Eastwood write:

> Perhaps the most striking characteristic of the United Kingdom, as established in 1800, was the space it allowed to different identities. Every Briton in 1800 possessed a composite identity. Certainly the British state embodied something approaching the political and cultural primacy of the English, but here primacy should not be equated with hegemony. Other identities persisted, and were even rediscovered, in the nineteenth century. There was nothing peculiar about the fact that British people at the turn of the nineteenth century were an amalgam of identities. This was equally true of the inhabitants of other European states. However, what was more extraordinary in the British case was the extent to which a particularly pervasive spatial identity was seen in national terms.[148]

Dunrobin Castle (1845) in Sutherland, which maintains an exterior commitment to Scottish tradition even though the function of the house and its estate had changed.

The desire to retain a sense of difference between Scottish and English culture was not only the product of Scottish resistance to English encroachment, but of an English desire to romanticize Scotland now that it no longer posed a threat to the political stability of the United Kingdom. Both sides therefore contributed to the development of the architectural style known as the Scottish Baronial, which employed typically Scottish architectural features such as crow-stepped gables, round towers with conical roofs and machicolations; interiors were filled with weapons, tartan and taxidermy.[149] The first Baronial house was Sir Walter Scott's Abbotsford (1817), and the most famous was Balmoral Castle, the retreat in Royal Deeside acquired by Prince Albert in 1852 and rebuilt to designs by the Aberdeen architect William Smith a few years later. Balmoral was decorated in a Scottish style that bordered on kitsch. 'Thistles', wrote the 4th Earl of Clarendon, 'are in such abundance that they would rejoice the heart of a donkey.'[150] Scottish Baronial was the Scottish version of the English gothic and Jacobethan revivals: a style that was intended to invoke a past that had existed in an imprecisely defined era seen as essential to the development of a national culture.[151] It was uniform across the country, with no regional variation, as it was intended to serve as a national style in a manner which had little to do with any real historical precedent.[152]

Dunrobin Castle in Sutherland, the most northerly large country house in Britain, shows how Scottish Baronial served as a British means of conveying difference between England and Scotland. With its slim, round towers topped by tall conical roofs, Dunrobin maintains the Scottish tradition of French architectural influence; its mid-nineteenth-century renovation was modelled on the Château de Chenonceau in the Loire Valley. The machicolations just below the roofline, meanwhile, are taken from Scottish precedent. Dunrobin's history, however, is more complicated than a Highland landlord expressing his sense of Francophilia and national identity. When it was remodelled between 1845 and 1851, it was owned by George Granville Sutherland-Leveson-Gower, 2nd Duke of Sutherland. He was, thanks to his family's extensive property in Staffordshire, Shropshire and Yorkshire and the vast estates he inherited from his canal-building uncle, the 3rd Duke of Bridgewater, the richest man in England. This enormous English wealth was combined with the 750,000 acres in the Scottish Highlands, encompassing two-thirds of the county of Sutherland, which his mother Elizabeth Sutherland, 19th Countess of Sutherland, had inherited. An overgrown hunting box rather than the centre of an agricultural estate, Dunrobin was a monument to this immense cross-border wealth. Moreover, by the mid-nineteenth century the Sutherlands were the arch-villains of the Highland Clearances because of their ruthless replacement of tenants with more profitable sheep.[153] To top it all off, the new house was not even designed by a Scottish architect, but was Charles Barry's only Scottish country-house commission. Sutherland was therefore happy to display a romantic vision of his attempt to play the role of Scottish landlord, but in truth Dunrobin was an expression of superficial cultural difference without any real effort to comprehend or follow the traditional modes of Highland life. In fact, its owners had done much to undermine them.

In the second half of the nineteenth century the Scottish Baronial became a 'new money' style preferred by bankers, industrialists and businessmen from England, Lowland Scotland or, in a few cases, continental Europe or the United States as they attempted to 'join the ranks of upper-class society and embrace the fashionable sporting and social pursuits that came with a property in the Highlands'.[154] They used their Scottish estates not only for their own pleasure, but to entertain clients or host politicians whom they wished to influence. By the 1870s half a dozen architects had an office in Inverness, although the leading practitioners of the Scottish Baronial style, Burn and Bryce, worked in Edinburgh, and Burn moved to London in 1844.[155] As the decades passed and each newcomer to the Highlands attempted to surpass his predecessors, the Baronial style became increasingly flamboyant, as was exemplified by the swaggering Glenborrodale Castle (1902) in Argyll, built for Charles Dunell Rudd, one of Cecil Rhodes's partners in the De Beers Mining Company in South Africa.

Some commercial and industrial magnates fully embraced their new role as Highland landlords. Andrew Carnegie hired a personal piper from the legendary Macpherson piping clan. George Bullough's family fortune came from selling textile machinery to Lancashire's cotton mills. In 1897, he inherited the Isle of Rum, which his father had leased as a shooting reserve, and shipped in a vast quantity of Arran sandstone to build a pink fantasy house which he named Kinloch Castle. Bullough commissioned his own tartan and hired a full-time bagpiper so as to ensure that he felt like a true Scottish laird. When in the 1890s he visited Glen Tanar, the Aberdeenshire home of the Manchester-born barrister and banker Sir William Cunliffe Brooks, the garden designer Thomas

Hayton Mawson complained: 'Promptly at seven o'clock in the morning the piper's wail began, first indistinctly as he left his cottage, and then by degrees gathering power as he approached. At five minutes past he was going the rounds of the house, piping as if to wake the dead.'[156] In the 1930s the writer George Scott-Moncrieff coined the phrase 'Balmorality' to refer to the ludicrous antics of new arrivals playing the role of Highland chieftains.[157]

As a reaction to such excess, at the very end of the nineteenth century some Scottish architects began building in a style that paralleled the English vernacular which had emerged in Kent and Sussex slightly earlier, as seen in the buildings of George Devey and Richard Norman Shaw. The leading architects of this 'Old Scots' style included James MacLaren, whose career was cut short by tuberculosis, and Robert Lorimer, whose Ardkinglas (1906) in Argyll was one of its most outstanding examples. But today the best-known practitioner is undoubtedly Charles Rennie Mackintosh, who believed, as he wrote in 1892, that architecture should be 'less cosmopolitan and rather more national'.[158] Around the same time, a fashion developed for restoring genuine medieval castles and tower houses. The most ambitious result was Eilean Donan Castle (restored 1919–32) on Loch Duich, owned by Colonel John McRae-Gilstrap and paid for by his wife's pig-iron fortune.

Incongruously, the English vernacular style appeared in Scotland at the same time. Devey, pioneer of the style in Southeast England, was tasked in 1873 with rebuilding Macharioch Castle on the Kintyre peninsula for the Marquess of Lorne. The roughcast exterior with stone dressings was typically Scottish, but the gabled wing looked as if it had come straight from the Cotswolds.[159] With its half-timbered gables, Wyvis Lodge (1884) in Easter Ross, designed by an unknown architect for the London furniture manufacturer Walter Shoolbred, would have been far more at home in the Stockbroker Belt of Surrey.[160] Similar in style was Mar Lodge (1897) in Aberdeenshire, by Alexander Marshall Mackenzie for Princess Louise, the third child and eldest daughter of King Edward VII and Queen Alexandra, and her husband, the 1st Duke of Fife. These houses did feature some Scottish elements, as they were predominantly built of stone, which would have been unusual in an English vernacular house of the Norman Shaw type. But their half-timbering and red-tiled roofs were out of place in the Scottish Highlands. These houses cannot be described as a combination of English and Scottish architectural trends; although they featured elements of both, they did not combine them in any real sense. They were the product not of any architectural movement towards a hybrid 'British' style, but rather were built by transplanted Englishmen who wanted to bring a piece of England with them to Scotland.

There were also a few Scottish Baronial country houses in England, including Fonthill Abbey (1846) in Wiltshire, Killhow (1865) in Cumbria, Ringmore (1880) in Devon, Stone Cross (1874) in Cumbria, Elgin Tower (1887) in Somerset and Trefusis House (1891) in Cornwall.[161] Of the English houses, two of the six were in Cumbria and therefore close to the border, but the other four, somewhat oddly, were located far from Scotland in the Southwest. The reasons for the choice of style in those four cases seem random, and were certainly not the product of any attempt to blur the geographical boundaries of English and Scottish architecture. The Marquess of Westminster appears to have chosen William Burn as his architect for Fonthill because he was fashionable. The neighbours commented on the incongruity of a Scottish house in Wiltshire: W. Coxe Radcliffe, the rector of Fonthill Giffard, described it bemusedly as 'a mixture of the *light* French Castle with the Scotch'.[162] Elgin Tower was built for the Scottish confectioner J. B. Kennedy and so was the reverse of the English vernacular houses built by Englishmen in the Scottish Highlands. These were not hybrid or 'British' houses or houses intended to express a unionist form of British nationalism; they were

Robert Lorimer's Ardkinglas (1906) in Argyll,
an outstanding example of the Scottish vernacular revival.

No Such Thing as a British Country House

Mar Lodge (1897) in Aberdeenshire was an incongruous example of an English vernacular revival house built far north of the Anglo-Scottish border.

merely Scottish houses transplanted to England because their owners and architects liked the Baronial style.

IN CONTRAST WITH SCOTLAND, Wales did not produce a classical architect who was William Bruce's equal in talent and influence. Its houses of the late seventeenth century and the eighteenth are therefore often seen as derivative of England's. Hilling writes:

> Though there is little to compare with the palatial mansions of favoured English shires, Wales has a number of country mansions that were designed on a smaller scale in the fashionable style of the period. The architects employed were more often than not from England, for the gentry were becoming more and more estranged from their Welsh background and now organized their way of life on English patterns.[163]

Not all Welsh country houses from this period should be dismissed as mere imitations of English precedents, but even a house like Tredegar (1664) in Monmouthshire, which appears very different from the compact, double-pile houses that were prevalent in England at the time, thanks to its quadrangular plan and corner pavilions, had an English parallel, Ragley Hall (1678) in Warwickshire, and was probably built by the same master carpenters, the brothers Roger and William Hurlbutt of Warwick.[164] A typical interpretation of Welsh country-house architecture in this period is John Newman's assessment of Drybridge House (1671) in Monmouthshire: 'The builder, William Roberts, held a post in the Office of Works and later was Paymaster during Hugh May's remodelling of Windsor Castle. So here was a direct link with the metropolitan centre of architectural innovation.'[165]

Seen in another light, however, Tredegar could be seen as a specifically Welsh interpretation of the Baroque style: austere, stripped down and more determined to maintain an indigenous character. If the Baroque took hold only briefly and incompletely in England, then its influence in Wales was even less. Was this provincialism or Welsh resistance to the incursion of a Continental style, similar to but not driven by what occurred in England? Or was it merely relative poverty? Most Welsh landowners could not afford to build a house as lavish as Tredegar. Instead, they rebuilt their houses using as much of the existing fabric as possible and added superficial classical details such as porticos and pediments. To produce the designs, they commissioned provincial

One of the most impressive 17th-century Welsh houses, Tredegar House (1664) in Monmouthshire resembles and may have shared its master carpenters with the near-contemporary Ragley Hall in Warwickshire.

architects, often from border towns such as Bristol, Chester and Shrewsbury and with patronage networks that extended into Wales. In South Wales, for example, Anthony Keck from Gloucestershire was the leading architect of the late eighteenth century.[166] As in previous centuries this reliance on local architects produced clusters of related buildings. In Monmouthshire, for example, there was a group of houses in the late eighteenth and early nineteenth centuries which were 'tall and block-like', with 'full-height bows' projecting from their facades.[167]

At the century's end, increased industrialization brought new wealth and new wealthy families into Wales. The houses they built, which were larger in scale than anything that had existed in Wales since the great castles of the Middle Ages, followed national trends by adopting the gothic style. Early examples included Robert Adam's Glenvoe Castle and John Johnson's Gnoll Castle, both from the mid-1770s and both in Glamorgan. In the mid-1820s, Cyfarthfa Castle in Merthyr Tydfil was designed by Richard Lugar for the Crawshay family, whose fortune came from iron founding, and a few years later Thomas Hopper's Llanover House appeared in Monmouthshire. In 1826 the Myddleton-West family built a new gothic mansion inside the ruins of medieval Ruthin Castle in Clwyd; it was substantially enlarged between 1848 and 1853 by the architect Henry Clutton. In the 1860s and '70s the 3rd Marquess of Bute commissioned William Burges to transform Cardiff Castle and Castell Coch, just north of Cardiff, into exemplars of the Victorian gothic revival.

These houses did not, however, express Welsh nationalist sentiments, in contrast to the role that the Scottish Baronial played in Scotland. This was because the castle in Wales could never be anything other than a reminder of foreign conquest, so strongly associated was it with Edward I's 'Iron Ring'. A case in point was Penrhyn Castle in Gwynedd, built by the slate-mining magnate George Hay Dawkins-Pennant between 1820 and 1845. The Pennants were new to North Wales, and so Penrhyn was intended 'to suggest their permanence in a landscape that was being profoundly reshaped by their recent arrival'. But the castle 'occludes Wales', for 'to build a neo-Norman castle in a landscape where real castles built by the regal descendants of Norman conquerors flourished, and where such castles signified the colonial conquest of Wales by Edward I' had a very different meaning for the local population than it did for the non-Welsh Pennants. Penrhyn, writes Trevor Burnard, 'is a disturbing intrusion into a settled landscape of an alien form'.[168]

In late nineteenth-century Scotland, as we have seen, there were specifically national manifestations of the Arts and Crafts and vernacular revival movements. In Wales these movements were not as nationally distinctive. When the writer for *Country Life* H. Avray Tipping designed Mounton House (1912) in Chepstow, he used late medieval Markenfield Hall in Yorkshire and Edwin Lutyens's Marshcourt (1901) in Hampshire as his inspirations, and not local buildings.[169] This was typical of Arts and Crafts and neo-vernacular houses in Wales, which, apart from a tendency to replace brick with stone, were largely indistinguishable from their English counterparts. John Douglas worked extensively in Wales, but brought his preference for timber-framing from his native Cheshire. W. E. Nesfield's Plas Dinam (1873) in Powys recalls Leyswood, the Sussex house designed by Richard Norman Shaw in the late 1860s. A search for examples of a Welsh vernacular revival, then, will fail.

AFTER THE NEED FOR DEFENCE dissipated, the Anglo-Welsh and Anglo-Scottish border regions demarcated permanent political divisions between nations which continued to be defined as separate, with future consequences for their respective architectural development. There was constant pressure from England to conform to not only its political dictates but its cultural hegemony, with corresponding resistance from Wales and Scotland, both of which continued to emphasize their own indigenous architectural traditions and to import influences directly from the European continent. In England, meanwhile, there was almost no Welsh or Scottish influence on country-house architecture, underlining the fact that there was no such thing as a 'British' country house. There were, or would later be, English-influenced houses in Wales and, to a lesser extent, Scotland, but the absence of Welsh or Scottish influences in England shows that the cultural exchange was far from mutual.

In the eighteenth century, when the need to integrate Scotland into the Union produced a demand for 'British' architectural forms, there were as a result no shared traditions to draw upon. In Wales, Palladianism and Neoclassicism were applied to Welsh country houses with no particular 'Welsh' attributes. In Scotland, William Bruce ensured that there was, initially, a Scottish form of Palladianism, but there too the Neoclassical houses of the mid-eighteenth century were more English than Scottish. This moment was, however, brief, as castellated houses never fully disappeared north of the border. The Scottish gothic revival was a manifestation of the cultural nationalism that flowered after the threat of Jacobitism receded. By the early nineteenth century the Baronial style had emerged as a uniquely Scottish version of neo-gothicism. In Wales, however, the castle was associated with English conquest rather than resistance to English incursion, and so the gothic could not serve as an expression of cultural nationalism. The castellated Welsh houses of the nineteenth century were alien intruders and not embodiments of national identity.

All of this had important implications for English country houses, because they remained English rather than becoming British. English architectural styles were never combined with indigenous styles in Wales in a way that led to the creation of hybrid Anglo-Welsh country houses. They were instead *imports* reflecting England's political dominance over Wales, while the Welsh chose to display their cultural independence in other forms such as language and literature. In Scotland, meanwhile, the contrast between English and Scottish country-house styles remained. By the nineteenth century the Scottish Baronial was widely used by owners who wished to display their national identity in architectural form, or occasionally as an exotic curiosity by an English builder. But in whatever context it remained defiantly Scottish, while in none of the three nations did a British style of country house emerge.

5
The Empire Does Not Strike Back

From around 1600 the presence of the British Empire became increasingly significant in English society and culture. This meant that it left its mark on English country houses, both financially and on their architecture and decoration. I have written about the extent and nature of these forms of imperial influence elsewhere.[1] This chapter, however, examines how the display of empire in country houses reflected the changes in English identity which occurred as English people confronted what it meant to rule over colonial subjects. This was a long process. In the late sixteenth and early seventeenth centuries, the dominant mode of expression as manifested in country houses was enthusiasm for empire and curiosity about its strange and exotic inhabitants. In the eighteenth century, however, the need to emphasize the unity of the rapidly increasing settler population came to the fore, which meant that country house styles in the colonies paralleled those at home. In the nineteenth it became imperative to express difference between white Britons, both at home in the metropolis and in the colonies, and the largely non-white subjects over whom they ruled, and so the country house became a space in which Englishness was increasingly displayed in hierarchical and racial terms.

Indigenous Americans in Elizabethan Country Houses

On 2 July 1557 the wealthy lawyer Sir John Cope died, leaving behind a considerable estate which he bequeathed to his sons and grandsons. His will did not list any bequests to his daughter Elizabeth, but that was because she had already been given the Canons Ashby estate in Northamptonshire.[2] Six years earlier Elizabeth had married the Cumbrian schoolmaster John Dryden, great-grandfather of the famous poet. John and Elizabeth Dryden expanded it into an H-shaped Elizabethan manor.[3] In the 1590s their son Erasmus, a prosperous London grocer who later purchased a baronetcy, added an impressive Great Chamber to the first floor. In 1632 Canons Ashby passed to Erasmus's son John, who carried on his father's trade and who like him was a staunch Puritan and Parliamentarian who served as MP for Northamptonshire in the politically tumultuous 1640s and '50s. John Dryden carried out further improvements to the house, including the addition of an elaborate plasterwork ceiling – Simon Jenkins describes it as 'overpowering' – to the Great Chamber.[4]

The story so far is a conventional tale of a family whose wealth and social stature grew steadily between 1550 and 1650. Many middling families of the time took advantage of expanding commercial opportunities to claw their way into the gentry. Also conventional is the way in which the Copes and their in-laws, the Drydens, invested their new riches in land. What makes the story of Canons Ashby about something more than social climbing, however, are the decorative motifs featured on the ceiling of the Great Chamber, which was installed by John Dryden in the 1630s. In Elizabethan houses, such spaces functioned as places for the display of portraits of the family and elaborate plasterwork decorated with emblems and devices highlighting their lineage. The Great Chamber at Canons Ashby is no exception: the arms of John Dryden and his third wife Honor Bevill, whom he married the year he inherited the house, are over the fireplace. In addition to these dynastic displays, however, great chambers often featured decorative motifs reflecting the latest fashions. As newcomers to the upper ranks of society, the Drydens would have been particularly concerned to appear fashionable. The ceiling of Canons Ashby's Great Chamber reflects this, incorporating motifs, including thistles, greenery and pomegranates, which were probably copied from the books of Continental classical decoration which were appearing in England with increasing frequency.[5]

More unusual, however, are what appear to be female indigenous North Americans, which were possibly references to the visit of the Algonquian 'princess' Pocahontas to England in 1616–17. Canons Ashby's indigenous Americans are one of a number of examples of similar figures in English manor houses from the late sixteenth and early seventeenth centuries. They represent more than an interest in the strange and exotic, but also reflect contemporary social, economic and imperial developments. The contemporary commercial context, which allowed some members of the middling ranks to improve their material and social standing, has already been mentioned. One factor in producing this context was the expansion of investment opportunities provided by the establishment of colonies in North America. By the 1630s, when John Dryden installed the ceiling in the Great Chamber, the Virginia colony was beginning to produce substantial profits from the cultivation of tobacco. Dryden was not, so far as we know, directly involved in the Virginia enterprise, but as a member of a family whose wealth derived from trade, he would have been aware of the impact colonial commerce was having on his fellow merchants. By the 1630s the new foodstuffs which were being imported from North America were beginning to have an impact on the grocery trade. For example, although potatoes had been slow to gain popularity after they were first introduced in the 1580s, by the 1650s they were a common ingredient in recipes.[6] The Great Chamber may therefore have featured indigenous Americans in its plasterwork because John Dryden had a sense of the increasing impact of America on his livelihood.

Canons Ashby was only one of a number of examples of late sixteenth- and early seventeenth-century English houses which used indigenous Americans as a decorative motif, an indication that they were a significant presence in the imaginations of English people. One way in which they learned about America was through the printed word, as by the end of Elizabeth I's reign there were about five publications a year on the subject.[7] These publications could hope to reach a relatively wide audience, as literacy rates had significantly increased, particularly in large cities like London. The Virginia Company's frequent broadsides, meanwhile, were nailed to trees, church doors and other vertical surfaces; as Catherine Armstrong writes, they were 'designed to be seen by as many people as possible, with no limits placed on the social status of the reader they attracted'.[8]

But with 70 per cent of men and 90 per cent of women still unable to read, the printed word was not yet an effective way of disseminating information.[9] There were other ways, however, for English people to learn about America. Ballads about the colony were sung in inns and taverns; ministers preached sermons about the conversion of America's indigenous peoples to Christianity; and plays depicting encounters with this strange new world appeared on the stage.[10] Another source of information was indigenous Americans themselves. The 1580s and '90s saw at least twenty indigenous Americans come to England, and after 1600 visits occurred every few years, with the most famous example being the journey of Pocahontas and her entourage in 1616–17. During these visits, which lasted for months and sometimes years, there were many opportunities for the indigenous Americans to be seen by the English public. In 1603 several of them were paid nine shillings to offer a demonstration of canoe paddling on the Thames.[11] Seven years later, a Powhatan named Eiakintomino 'caused a sensation' when he appeared alongside a collection of American flora and fauna in St James's Park.[12] Pocahontas's party created a spectacle

> in the streets and markets of the capital, and they found themselves feted wherever they went. The great and the good were particularly excited at the prospect of being entertained by a group of genuine savages, and [Pocahontas's brother] Tomocomo proved a good sport when it came to delighting his hosts. His party turn was 'to sing and dance his diabolical measures' – something which never failed to impress his audience. His war dances were even more impressive – 'singing and clapping hands ... shooting, hollowing, stamping with antlike gesture, like to many devils'.[13]

Those English people who had no opportunity to meet visiting Americans themselves could still see visual images of them.[14] In order to garner favourable publicity for his expeditions, Sir Walter Ralegh dispatched the artist John White to his doomed colony at Roanoke. Transformed into copperplate engravings, White's work appeared in 1590 in the first volume ('America') of the German printer Theodore de Bry's *The Great Voyages*.[15] Artists who had not been to Virginia also painted indigenous Americans, using as inspiration visitors to England, previously published illustrations or their imaginations. An engraving of Pocahontas by Simon van de Passe, for example, was 'rushed out as a single sheet to exploit a short-lived market' at the time of her visit in 1617 and bound into a book of 'royal' portraits published the following year.[16] Londoners had a regular opportunity to see Pocahontas: the proprietor of the Belle Sauvage Inn on Ludgate Hill, where she had stayed during her visit, replaced his previous sign with her portrait.[17] Other images of indigenous Americans appeared in advertising material for the Virginia Company. In 1615, for example, the Company held a lottery to raise funds which was advertised by a broadside featuring two full-length drawings.[18]

Because these pictures were of peoples very different from themselves, they raised questions for English men and women about their own nation and identity. In 1580 or even 1620 it would certainly have been impossible to predict that the colony in Virginia would lead to the creation of an enormous empire which would transform Britain into the most powerful nation on earth, but even so there was a recognition that colonization could enhance England's global power, as it had already done for Spain. At the time, England was seen – by foreigners and by its own citizens – as a small, isolated country. Colonization offered a way for England to expand its prestige and wealth.

But if England's new American colonies offered an opportunity for national expression and fulfilment, then what of their inhabitants, who were decidedly un-English? Scholars once assumed that, before the development of more enlightened views in the second half of the twentieth century, most Europeans regarded indigenous Americans as primitive, bloodthirsty savages.[19] But although there were abundant examples of negative stereotypes, in this earliest period of contact there were more positive images, even if they were also distorted by cultural preconceptions and biases. Investors in the colonies needed to attract settlers and further investment, which meant that 'it was necessary to make the native a part of the attraction of the New World – to make sure that he was a propaganda asset rather than a liability.'[20] Further, the increased exposure of English people to Indians in various direct and indirect forms helped to make them appear less strange, exotic and threatening, and more human. Indigenous Americans turned out to be 'people quite similar to themselves in size and general physical appearance', not 'monsters or sharp-toothed cannibals'.[21]

This growing familiarity led to more nuanced views of indigenous Americans. Instead of being seen as permanently inferior and barbaric, they were regarded as less historically evolved, so that with proper instruction and guidance from Europeans they might advance. Karen Kupperman writes:

> Reflecting the doubleness of vision they brought to their task, writers assured their audiences that the American natives would benefit from exposure to the sophistication and learning that the English would bring them, especially knowledge of the Bible; only intermittently did they acknowledge that they also brought the corrupting influences they saw with dismay in their own world.[22]

Some commentators took these arguments one step further, by claiming that indigenous Americans resembled the English at an earlier, simpler and therefore *superior*, stage of evolution, before they were corrupted by material wealth and cosmopolitan values. It became commonplace to draw comparisons to ancient Britons or Germans, England's strong and virtuous forebears, who had resisted Roman oppression and therefore remained uncorrupted by the artifice and luxury of modern civilization:

> Every letter, broadside and book about America by a writer with transatlantic experience was steeped in ambivalence. England was proud of its accomplishments as a nation and looked forward to a greater role in the world, and the English people valued their civility and refinement in comparison to even the very recent past. They loved the magnificence of the court and demanded displays of sovereignty of their local rulers. Yet at the same time they felt profound unease over what they saw as the consequences of sophistication, luxury and commerce. They read all the signs of decline around them and feared that England had lost its special vigor and virtue forever.[23]

Seen from this perspective, the physical attributes of indigenous Americans confirmed their simplicity, and therefore their superiority. Some commentators praised them for the practicality of their minimal attire, which was perfectly suited to their environment without any unnecessary adornment.[24] It became fashionable in late sixteenth-century England for men to wear their hair in a cut similar to Powhatan warriors, longer on the left side than the right. Style-leaders such as the Earls of Southampton and Essex were early adopters of these so-called 'love-locks'; the irony of such foppish types imitating the supposedly unsophisticated indigenous Americans did not escape contemporary observers, who poked fun at the dandies.[25] English descriptions of indigenous systems of government, meanwhile, 'affirmed that the Americans lived in well-governed civil societies' which had many of the attributes of their English counterparts, including the orderly succession of power, restraint on tyranny and an unwritten system of laws based upon custom.[26] The English perspective, therefore, did not mean seeing them exclusively in a negative light. Nor was the appearance of indigenous Americans in English culture merely an expression of a proto-orientalist fetish for the strange and exotic. Instead, in the early stages of colonization in America, the English also 'looked for and invented points of similarity and contact'.[27]

It is in this context that we must consider representations of the American colonies and their indigenous peoples in late Elizabethan and early Jacobean country houses, which occurred in a variety of forms. American plants became common in many English gardens, both as exotic curiosities and as more practical sources of food and medicine.[28] Commodities such as sugar and tobacco, which had previously been enjoyed only by the upper classes, became available to a far wider range of people.

The consumption of these items did not require English men and women to think directly about America and its peoples, but what of the more direct domestic encounters? We have already seen evidence of the popularity of paintings and engravings of American subjects. In addition, indigenous American artefacts were frequently included in 'cabinets of curiosities', or collections of items from around the world, the precursors of modern museums. These cabinets developed from the *Kunst-* and *Wunderkammern* assembled by kings and scholars on the European continent during the first half of the sixteenth century, many of which had included American material.[29] In England, one of the most famous of these cabinets was 'The Ark', created by the royal gardener John Tradescant the Elder in the 1620s and '30s. Tradescant's collection, which became the basis of the Ashmolean Museum at the University of Oxford, contained at least 29 items from North America, including artefacts from Virginia, Canada and Greenland.[30] The highlight was 'Powhatan's Mantle', or 'the robe of the King of Virginia', which had entered the collection by 1638.[31] Accumulated by the antiquary Walter Cope, another prominent collection contained 'several crowns which the Queen of America has worn' and 'several Indian capes made of parrot feathers', as well as an Indian canoe which hung from the ceiling of Cope's London house.[32] The Royal Society's cabinet contained a kayak, wampum and birchbark containers, while in the 1660s the cabinet of John Bargrave, a canon of Canterbury Cathedral, featured a set of porcupine quill ornaments from New England.[33] The antiquary Ralph Thoresby accumulated around thirty Indian items in his collection, including artefacts associated with the 'Queen of Maryland', Anna Sonam.[34]

As Canons Ashby shows, another way in which English people brought Indians into their homes was through plaster or carved-wood representations which appeared on walls, ceilings and fireplaces. At least seven examples of this fashion remain extant:

HOUSE	COUNTY	DATE*
Canons Ashby	Northamptonshire	1630s
Dodington Hall	Somerset	1581
King's House	Wiltshire	Early 17th century
Levens Hall	Cumbria	1580s–90s
Red Lodge	Somerset	*c.* 1590
Westwood Manor	Wiltshire	Early 17th century
Wolfeton House	Dorset	1590s

*The date is that of the Indian representation, not of the house.

Looking at this list, two general conclusions may be drawn. First, with two exceptions (Canons Ashby and Levens Hall), the houses are all found in the Southwest of England, with two in Somerset (Dodington Hall, Red Lodge), two in Wiltshire (King's House, Westwood Manor) and one in Dorset (Wolfeton House). Second, these examples all date from the early period of North American colonization from the 1580s to the 1630s, when Jamestown and other colonial projects first excited the interest of people in England.

Neither of these observations is particularly surprising. The Southwest was the point of departure for many voyages to America in the late sixteenth and early seventeenth centuries. Located between two waterways, the Bristol and English Channels, the Southwest was the birthplace of the nation's most famous maritime adventurers, including Sir John Hawkins, Sir Richard Grenville, Sir Francis Drake and Sir Walter Ralegh. It was in the taverns of the Southwestern ports where the most ambitious plans for overseas commercial expansion were hatched. As the archaeologist Ivor Noël Hume has written:

> Any early sixteenth-century Englishman would have wagered his last groat that his country's future would continue to be shaped by the monarch and a circle of self-seeking advisers drawn from the church and from the great landowning families. Instead the impetus came from the courage and patriotism (leavened with no little greed) of a handful of outsiders – West Countrymen with tar in their nostrils and salt in their beards. They were the

ones who forged the Elizabethan spirit that was to steel Britain's empire-building backbone through three hundred years.[35]

The dates of these representations of indigenous Americans also make sense. The final decades of the sixteenth century and the first decades of the seventeenth saw an enthusiasm for anything related to American exploration and colonization, which as we have already seen manifested itself in books, plays, visual images, hairstyles and a fashion for tobacco-smoking. The carved and plasterwork Indians which adorned late Elizabethan and Jacobean homes are further iterations of this phenomenon. By the 1630s the novelty of America and its inhabitants had worn off, and interior decoration schemes favoured different motifs.

These houses share another characteristic: they were all built or owned by members of the Elizabethan or Jacobean 'middling gentry', the key players in the significant social changes that were happening in England at the time. The ever-rising middle class in English history has long provided a fruitful source of scholarly debate. Though some historians claim that it was not until the first half of the eighteenth century that the middle class was fully formed, others locate the origins of that emergence in the decades around 1600.[36] Certainly, this period saw economic developments which increased the prosperity of the middling ranks.

Their rise in the late Elizabethan and Jacobean eras was accompanied by a change in the strict hierarchy that governed English social relations. On the one hand, contemporary English men and women accepted that their social universe was both stratified and inequitable, with the upper ranks sharply divided from the mass of common people below. But on the other, there was increased fluidity, with advancement made possible by both achievement and accumulated wealth. Climbs from the very bottom to the very top of the social ladder were rare, but the ascension of a step or two was more common. The 'line dividing gentlemen from the rest', Keith Wrightson notes, was a 'permeable membrane': 'Whatever the definitions of gentility itself and of different degrees of gentility, the very complexity of the criteria which, in practice, established a man's rank meant that there was always room for movement both into and within the ranks of the gentry.'[37]

There were a variety of ways in which aspiring men from the middling orders could rise through the ranks. Merchants and lawyers might accumulate sufficient wealth to buy a landed estate, or yeomen farmers could increase their landholdings until they met the standard for membership in the gentry. A mercantile path offered another route of entry, as the practice of primogeniture meant that many younger sons of landed gentlemen were forced into commercial careers, creating blood ties between the upper and merchant classes. Moreover, this was an era in which a successful merchant could amass a significant fortune, in some cases greater than that of many gentlemen. In spite of the traditional disdain for hands-dirtying, money-grubbing trade displayed by the upper echelons of English society, they sometimes found themselves welcoming men from the merchant classes into their ranks.[38]

In many ways, the realization of the social aspirations of the middling ranks was made possible by the development of opportunities to participate in global commercial activity. Men like Walter Ralegh and Francis Drake were not born to wealth, status and power, but rather amassed them through the shrewd manipulation of a commercial world that was expanding both economically and geographically. Born to humble Devonshire yeoman stock, Drake was a particularly spectacular example of the kind of rise that might now take place. He made an enormous fortune and earned a knighthood through a career that encompassed slaving voyages to Africa, pirate raids in the West Indies and South America, military expeditions to Ireland and a voyage around the world – all by the time he was forty.

Drake may have been exceptional, but plenty of others took advantage of the opportunities presented by overseas ventures. Middling people invested in the joint-stock companies that funded colonial forays, and they profited once the money from the tobacco trade began to arrive. The late sixteenth and early seventeenth centuries saw both increased prosperity and social mobility for the middling ranks, much of which was fuelled by expanding opportunities to invest in colonial projects. Kupperman writes:

> European life was transformed by its contacts with America. The flooding in of products and information forced the creation of structures to organize and establish them. The flow of people out of Europe into the newly revealed lands also changed Old World life. These indirect effects worked in many directions, but they all had one impact in common: unevenly but inexorably they jolted Europe's society and economy in the direction of influence by people farther down the social scale. Cracks in the aristocratic

mold would certainly have appeared without America, but the timing and the fault lines were affected by transatlantic enterprises that allowed, even encouraged, assumption of initiative by the excluded. America helped open up Europe.[39]

Ascension to the uppermost rungs of the social ladder required not only wealth but the purchase of a landed estate. This reflected the security of land as a long-term investment, but it also shows that, as Wrightson argues, 'whatever a man's urban riches, the idea of rural gentility retained its superior prestige and cultural force': 'In the final analysis the establishment and maintenance of gentility depended upon the acquisition and retention of landed wealth. Birth, a genteel life-style and activity in places of authority were secondary criteria, buttressing the fact of substantial landownership.'[40] The houses which these upwardly mobile men acquired sometimes became sites for the display of images of the new world of global and colonial commerce that had generated the wealth which had paid for them, in the form of plasterwork on the ceilings and walls or wood-carvings on the fireplaces and panelling. This is not to suggest that there was always a literal relationship between the estate owner's source of wealth and investment in trade and colonization in America. So far as we know, none of the houses listed above had an owner who was directly involved in American enterprises in any significant way. Instead, the display of images of indigenous peoples and other American motifs reflects a broader interest in America by a social group that was excited by the possibilities offered by colonization and who may have profited from the enhanced investment opportunities they provided.

Westwood Manor in Wiltshire was originally a modest two-storey dwelling dating from around 1400. In 1435 it was bought by Henry Culverhouse, whose son Thomas built much of the house that exists today. In 1492 it was acquired by Thomas Bailey, a member of a prominent family of clothiers from nearby Stowford. Bailey's purchase inaugurated a long link between Westwood and the clothing trade. In 1518 the lease was acquired by Thomas Horton, the son of a clothier from Lullington, just across the border in Somerset. Thomas Horton developed his father's business so successfully that he was able to buy a number of landed estates in the area, as well as an impressive house in Bradford-on-Avon. Horton died childless in 1530, and the Westwood estate passed through various members of his family until 1616, when Toby Horton fell into debt, forcing him to sell Westwood Manor to his brother-in-law John Farewell. Farewell does not seem to have been involved in the clothing trade, but rather exemplifies the move from merchant to genteel status that had become possible for families at the time.

Farewell made several alterations to Westwood, including the demolition of the north, west rear and southeast wings and the construction of a new wing to the east. His most significant changes, however, were to the interior, and included the addition of a turret staircase and a porch on the south front. It was also during Farewell's time that much of the plasterwork was executed, including the chimneypiece in the King's Room, which features a representation of an indigenous American along with double-tailed mermaids, two geese hanging a fox and a rose and thistle growing out of a grotesque face, which probably alluded to the Union of the Crowns of England and Scotland in 1603.[41] Farewell had no direct involvement with North American trade that might have

The chimneypiece (*c.* 1620) in the King's Room at Westwood Manor in Wiltshire, with its images of North American Indians.

inspired him to install a representation of an indigenous American over his fireplace. Instead, he probably wanted to ensure that his house conformed to the fashions of the day, which as we have seen reflected excitement about the colonization of North America.

Just outside Dorchester, Wolfeton House is an exception to the usual pattern of indigenous American decorative motifs in late sixteenth- and early seventeenth-century English houses. Wolfeton's sheep-farming owners never relied upon trade for their income, and so its Americans did not derive from a commercial interest in the colonies. In the second half of the fifteenth century, Wolfeton passed through marriage to Sir John Trenchard, from a prominent Hampshire family. The Trenchards carried out a number of improvements to the house in the last two decades of the sixteenth century, including the installation of a plasterwork ceiling in the downstairs parlour which features exotic, Aztec-like faces with grotesquely oversized lips and sunburst headdresses, surrounded by maize-like plants and reliefs of animals, including bulls, stallions, rams and stags. Upstairs, the Great Chamber, a masterpiece of Elizabethan classicism which was probably executed by craftsmen who had also worked on the Marquess of Bath's much grander house at Longleat, features a stone fireplace extending from floor to ceiling, on which are carved what appear to be Asiatic figures and, above them, indigenous Americans with feathers in their hair.

So why, in this corner of rural Dorset, in a house owned by a family whose income derived from agriculture rather than trade, are there two rooms featuring indigenous Americans? The houses with similar decorative motifs were owned by families not far removed from the middling ranks of society, with business interests that may have caused them to pay at least some attention to the developments taking place across the Atlantic, but Wolfeton does not fit that model. Instead, its Americans probably relate to the visits of Sir Walter Ralegh during the period when the alterations to the house were being made. Ralegh lived only seventeen miles from Wolfeton at Sherborne Castle. In 1594, when Sir George Trenchard was serving as a local Justice of the Peace, an Irish Catholic priest named Cornelius was held at Wolfeton while awaiting his trial for treason. Ralegh grew to admire the priest and visited Wolfeton several times to see him, although he did not intervene to prevent his execution. It is possible that during these visits Ralegh discussed his ventures in America with the craftsmen responsible for the plasterwork and stone carvings, and they incorporated his descriptions of the indigenous peoples into their designs. Ralegh first travelled to South America in 1595, a year after his first visit to Wolfeton, and so he may have described the peoples whom he had encountered after his return. Ralegh never travelled to Virginia himself, but he was close to men who had, which would have enabled him to supply an accurate picture of its indigenous peoples as well. The depictions of indigenous Americans at Wolfeton are therefore possibly the product of the link with Ralegh.

Trans-Imperial Identities in the Eighteenth Century

The purpose of imperial display in English country houses changed in the late seventeenth century and the eighteenth. Instead of exhibiting curiosity about the colonies and enthusiasm about their commercial potential, the display of empire was now used to express a common sense of identity that bound metropole and colony together. This change in emphasis was reflected in the growth of the colonial settler population, which reached 260,000 in 1700 and surged to over 2.5 million by 1770. Richard Olwell and Alan Tully write:

> The growth of the colonies dramatically altered their relative importance within the larger British Atlantic world. In the seventeenth century, when the number of colonists was small (in 1660, for example the total colonial population was only a third of that of the city of London alone), the primitive, simplified and subordinate nature of colonial society was self-evident. By 1710, however, the half-million inhabitants of British America were nearly equal to that of [London]. By 1760, Britain's two million colonists formed a population treble London's and larger than that of Scotland.[42]

Although the population of British North America would plunge to less than 500,000 after the loss of the American colonies, in 1815 there remained 85,000 Britons in India and the rest of Asia; 65,000 in the West Indies; 35,000 in Australia; and 20,000 in Africa. These colonists were no longer unsophisticated bumpkins scraping out a spartan existence on the fringes of the known world. Olwell and Tully continue:

> In the fashion of their homes, furnishings and clothes, as well as in their choice of reading matter (in fact, most of these things

were either imported from England, or copied from English models), colonial elites in the third quarter of the eighteenth century lived in a style and manner very like that of the provincial gentry of England.[43]

There were clear differences, however, between colonial and metropolitan societies, because 'the cultures of the British colonies ... each adapted to suit the limitations and possibilities of their own local situation'. Encompassing food, accents and other customs, these differences made the colonists 'something less than truly British' and therefore potentially destabilizing to the Empire, as the Americans would show after the Seven Years' War.[44] There was therefore a need for cultural displays which could bind the Empire together and elide the increasing distinctions between metropolitan and colonial peoples.

This imperative was clearly seen in architecture. From the second half of the seventeenth century onwards, architectural fashion in Britain's colonies tended to follow metropolitan models at a delayed pace. Houses such as Drax Hall (c. 1650) and St Nicholas Abbey (1658) in Barbados and Bacon's Castle (1665) in Virginia were smaller copies of early Jacobean mansions. Several decades later, the plain, compact houses that were popular in Restoration Britain were echoed by the Governor's Palace (1705) in Williamsburg, Virginia; Stenton House (1723) in Philadelphia; the plantation houses along the James River in Virginia such as Westover (1730), Ampthill (1732) and Shirley (1735); and the Brick House (c. 1725) on Edisto Island and Fenwick Hall (1730) on Johns Island in South Carolina.[45]

In the mid-eighteenth century, however, Palladian architecture in the colonies became more than mere imitation; instead it was used to embody a common imperial identity at a time when empire was becoming central to Britain's view of itself. The earliest example was Drayton Hall (c. 1738) outside Charleston, South Carolina, with its 'clear transatlantic effect expressed in architecture and design'.[46] Drayton Hall inspired local imitations such as the Charles Pinckney House (1746), and others further afield, including the Governor's House (c. 1744) in Annapolis, Maryland, and Shirley-Eustis House (1747) in Boston.[47] The design of Mount Airy (1764) in Virginia was copied almost exactly from a drawing in James Gibbs's *Book of Architecture* (1728), while Miles Brewton House (1769) in Charleston was based on Palladio's Villa Pisani.[48] In the 1750s the merchant Phillip Pinnock built a house

Drayton Hall (c. 1738), a Palladian house in South Carolina and an example of how houses were coming to express the desire for shared imperial identities between the metropole and the colonies.

imitating Palladio's Villa Valmarana outside Kingston, Jamaica.[49] The King's House in Spanish Town, built as a residence for the Governor in 1762, was 'a replica of a Palladian pile in England'.[50] Colen Campbell's *Vitruvius Britannicus* was a key source of ideas in the Presidency towns of India, and James Paine's Palladian design for Kedleston Hall in Derbyshire (1759–65) served as the model for Government House (1803) in Calcutta.[51] And in Singapore, 'the early style for everything', including the Raffles Institution (1836–41), was 'a skillful adaptation of Palladianism to suit the tropics'.[52]

This is not to suggest that the very different geographical settings of the British Empire in the eighteenth century had no influence on colonial buildings.[53] As Swati Chattopadhyay notes in describing eighteenth-century Calcutta, there were 'critical points of difference' between English antecedents and colonial buildings, and the same was true in North America, the West Indies and elsewhere.[54] But the commitment to Palladianism across the Empire reflected a growing need for a common approach which would link metropole and colony together. This applied principally to British settler communities, but also to indigenous peoples, at least in theory. In the eighteenth century the differences between European and non-European peoples were regarded as evolutionary rather than biological, products of their respective stages of historical development. Classical architecture therefore represented an aspiration for a future in which the colonies would follow British patterns of political, economic and cultural evolution. Daniel Maudlin and Bernard L. Herman write of the colonial architecture of the Atlantic world, but with its applicability to other colonial settings:

> For both colonists and the colonized, for good or ill, British-looking buildings were clear signs of a British presence across many different landscapes and climates. Abstracted from the local environment, carefully constructed, decorated and furnished interior spaces provided the dressed stage for the repeated performance of British Atlantic society's rituals – from the extraordinary (such as court appearances) to the everyday (such as afternoon tea) – where consistency of design, dominated by neoclassicism, provided a consistent social space.[55]

Classical buildings in the colonies therefore showed that differences between metropole and colony could be erased over time and that an imperial community based on free trade and political liberty could be created.[56]

Cultural forms which did not invoke specifically English, British or colonial historical references were essential to the creation of these identities, and so models were sought that were appropriate to a geographically and ethnically diverse empire. This led to a strong interest in Roman antiquity: numerous treatises on Roman buildings and art were published in Britain from the 1720s onwards, and there was increasingly keen interest in Britain's Roman ruins among British antiquaries.[57] Country houses began to incorporate 'Roman' architectural elements.[58] Holkham Hall (1734–59), the Earl of Leicester's Palladian house in Norfolk, was based on the buildings described in Daniele Barbaro's sixteenth-century translation of Vitruvius, and even included a hypocaust-type heating system beneath the floor of the Great Hall. Other country-house builders used local Roman archaeological sites as a source of inspiration. Sir Thomas Robinson's Rokeby Park estate in Durham, for example, included the ruins of a Roman fort. When he began building a new house in 1725, Robinson deliberately imitated the twin towers of a Tuscan villa which Pliny had described in his letters from the first century AD.[59]

This fascination with ancient Rome grew in the middle decades of the eighteenth century as Palladianism, in which classical influence was filtered through Renaissance interventions by Palladio and others, gave way to Neoclassicism, in which Roman models served more directly as the inspiration. The most influential Neoclassicist was Robert Adam, who visited the continent in the 1750s to study Roman buildings in Italy and Croatia. Adam played a key role in mid-eighteenth-century efforts to evolve an architecture suited for what was now a self-consciously imperial British nation. In 1759 he was commissioned to produce interior designs for Hatchlands Park in Surrey, home of Admiral Edward Boscawen, whose victories during the Seven Years' War contributed to the expansion of Britain's maritime and imperial power. Celebrating Boscawen's exploits, Adam incorporated dolphins and figures of Neptune, Justice, Fame and Victory into the ceiling of the library. Kedleston Hall was intended to have a Palladian design by James Paine and Matthew Brettingham until Adam took over in 1759 and gave the south front a Neoclassical facade based on the Arch of Constantine in Rome. His designs for the drawing room featured seahorses and mermaids in the ceiling plasterwork, while blue damask upholstery and wall coverings completed the maritime effect.[60]

Adam was working in an environment in which it was a priority to develop an imperial architecture. Some historians have argued that the debate over the appropriate style of architecture for the British Empire did not reach its height until 1850. But that debate, as we will see, was over the suitability of various styles for different colonial contexts. In the mid-eighteenth century the question was a very different one: how to produce an imperial architecture which would be appropriate in both the British metropolis and a wide variety of colonial contexts, at a time when the Empire was inhabited predominantly by white settlers, and before India became a zone of conquest and political control rather than trade. Adam's approach was to use Roman-inspired architectural forms as a triumphalist celebration of Britain's growing power, which was particularly appropriate after the victory in the Seven Years' War in 1763.

There were other possibilities, however. Increased British engagement with India, as the subcontinent replaced America as Britain's most important colonial possession, led to experimentation with Indian architectural styles. George Dance installed Indian-influenced turret-caps on a number of his buildings, including the Guildhall (1788) in London, a

Part of Robert Adam's first country-house commission in England, the figure of Neptune (left) on the ceiling of the library at Hatchlands Park in Surrey is an example of the room's maritime theming, in honour of its owner Admiral Edward Boscawen.

gateway to Stratton Park (1803) in Hampshire and houses at Cole Orton (1804) in Leicestershire and Ashburnham (1807) in Sussex; he also used them in his unexecuted plans for Norman Court (1810) in Hampshire.[61] Dance's designs show how in the decades around 1800 there was a minor 'imperial moment' in country-house architecture. This was the period in which more houses were built or purchased from imperial profits than at any other point. Between 1760 and 1810 more than one hundred such purchases occurred every decade, in contrast to fewer than forty per decade in the periods before and after.[62] To be sure, the majority of the returning nabobs and planters who made these acquisitions chose conventional Palladian or Neoclassical styles for their country houses, because they wanted to blend in with their neighbours rather than openly display the origins of their wealth. Basildon Park in Berkshire was built in the early 1770s by Sir Francis Sykes, who had accumulated a fortune of £250,000 in India. He concealed the source of his wealth beneath a Palladian veneer; Edith Hall writes that he 'lived amongst innumerable Greek-inspired decorations, from the spectacular classical-themed internal plasterwork to the plant containers between the arches under his Grecian portico'.[63] The only possible references to India in

The Empire Does Not Strike Back

the house were the plasterwork griffins in the entrance hall and on the frieze and door surrounds of the library. They may have alluded to the source of Sykes's wealth, as griffins were the mythical guardians of India's gold; moreover, a 'griffin' was also a slang term for a newly arrived European in India.[64] But griffins were also common motifs in Neoclassical decoration in the second half of the eighteenth century, and so if Sykes was using them to refer to his time in India, he did so in a covert way which was in line with contemporary classical taste.

In a few houses, however, the Indian backgrounds of the owners were displayed more openly.[65] James Forbes returned to England in 1784 after serving the East India Company for more than twenty years. He acquired Great Stanmore in Middlesex and filled it with Indian art, and then in 1793 built an octagonal Indian-style temple in his garden in order to house statues which had been given to him 'by the Brahmins of Hindoostan as a grateful acknowledgement of benevolent attention to their happiness during a long residence among them'.[66] After purchasing Daylesford in Gloucestershire in 1788, the former Governor-General of Bengal Warren Hastings added a Mughal-style dome and had its

Plasterwork griffins in the ceiling of Basildon Park (1776) in Berkshire, a possible reference to the Indian career of its owner Sir Francis Sykes.

interior painted to resemble the blue skies he had seen in India. The house was a veritable museum of Indian artefacts:

> Among the first collectors of Mughal drawings and art objects, he and his wife filled Daylesford with Indian treasures – ivories, silks, silver filigree ornaments, fly flaps set with rubies and emeralds, an agate jewel casket with single-stone diamond spring to lock, Persian weaponry, and chain mail. These 'Oriental' antiques vied with Indian-inspired, Western art, such as the fireplace frescos by Thomas Banks, the scenes of William Hodges and the portraits of Johan Zoffany which, along with Hastings' extensive library on Indian subjects (the former Governor-General had commissioned the first translations of the *Bhagavad-Gita* and *The Hedaya*), intimated that Daylesford was the home of a true connoisseur.[67]

There was a defiant note to Hastings's ostentatious display. At the time he purchased Daylesford, he was being tried before the House of Commons on charges of corruption and mismanagement.[68] Ostensibly over Hastings's conduct, the trial expanded into a debate over the present and future of Britain's colonial rule in India. Hastings defended his actions by arguing that colonial sovereignty was 'based on absolute power and national interests'. He asserted that colonial subjects could only be ruled by force; without it, 'chaos and anarchy would ensue and the very existence of the colonial state would be at risk.' His fierce critic Edmund Burke, however, argued that the British should practise a 'deterritorialized juridical-imperial sovereignty that would be exercised not in the pursuit of the exclusive interest of the colonizing nation but, rather, in ensuring that colonial administration in India remained firmly grounded in "native" society and prevented from exercising absolute and arbitrary power over it'.[69] Burke, in other words, was proposing that the relationship between the metropole and its empire should not simply be that of conqueror over the conquered. Instead, 'the sovereignty of empire was different from national sovereignty and had to be founded on juridical principles of universality and extraterritoriality that transcended the discourse of national interests and the simple domination and subjugation of one nation by another.'[70] Given its timing, Hastings's ostentatious display of his Indian experience at Daylesford can be interpreted as an extension of his defence and a counterblast to Burke's call for a trans-imperial community based upon shared ideas of subjecthood, citizenship and equal justice.

In 1800 the artist Thomas Daniell, who worked extensively in India, designed an Indian-style temple for the garden of Melchet Park in Wiltshire, the estate of Major Sir John Osborne, who had been a soldier in India. The temple was intended as a declaration of support for Hastings, who had been acquitted of all charges five years earlier. Its interior contained a bust of Hastings, under which was the inscription: 'Sacred to the Genii of India, who, from time to time, assume material forms to protect its nations and its laws, particularly to the immortal Hastings, who, in these days, has appeared the saviour of those regions of the British Empire.'[71] Daylesford's dome and Melchet's temple were complex buildings. On the one hand, they expressed a clear awareness of and interest in Indian architectural forms, and sought to recreate them in reasonably accurate ways. On the other, however, the owners of the estates on which they were situated advocated authoritarian structures of rule over colonized peoples. They reflected the knowledge of India that Hastings and Osborne had gained, but used it in a manner not to display their admiration of Indian culture but to confirm Britain's right to rule.

The only fully Indian-style country house ever built in Britain was Sezincote in Gloucestershire, which was designed by Pepys Cockerell, the same architect who was responsible for Daylesford's dome. Although Cockerell never visited India, his father John enjoyed a distinguished career in the East India Company's army, and his brother Charles became Postmaster General of Calcutta in 1784, accumulating a large fortune in the process. On his retirement from military service in 1795, John Cockerell acquired the Sezincote estate and began discussing the renovation of the run-down Jacobean manor house with his architect son, but he died in 1798 before any major works could be carried out. Charles Cockerell then bought out his siblings' shares of the estate and began planning to rebuild the house. He commissioned an Indian-inspired design from Samuel, with a main block topped by an onion dome, a *chhatri* (an elevated and domed pavilion) on each corner and a *chhajja* (projecting cornice) surrounding the facade on three sides. Cockerell's bedroom took the form of a tented pavilion linked to the main block by a colonnade.

Sezincote resulted from a moment when some English connoisseurs sought to engage with Indian culture in a sincere and thorough way. In late eighteenth- and early nineteenth-century England, a brief flurry of interest in Indian architecture was sparked by the paintings of artists

Sezincote House in Gloucestershire (1800), from F. O. Morris, ed., *A Series of Picturesque Views of Seats of the Noblemen and Gentlemen of Great Britain and Ireland* (1880). The tent-like wing in which Charles Cockerell's bedroom was located is on the left.

working in India, including most prominently William Hodges, Thomas Daniell and his nephew William Daniell.[72] Charles Cockerell owned works of art by Hodges and the Daniells, and he consulted Thomas Daniell about some of Sezincote's architectural details as he tried to ensure that it would be an authentic representation of Indian culture.[73] In 1811 Daniell advised Cockerell not to move two statues of Brahmin bulls that had been installed on an Indian-style bridge because 'could Viswakarma, the Artist of the Gods, of Hindoos take a peek at Sezincote, he would say let the bulls remain where they are.'[74] Perhaps these efforts were intellectually naive and can be criticized for their contribution to the cultural appropriation that inevitably accompanied imperial conquest, but even so the Cockerell brothers had a genuine interest in and respect for Indian culture. It is tempting to see Sezincote as a riposte to Daylesford in its support for Burke's vision of empire.

But if this was the case, it was not a moment which lasted for long, as the tentative steps towards an Anglo-Indian cultural hybridity that were made in the late eighteenth century were soon reversed by an aggressive drive for conquest in the early nineteenth.[75] For all of its hybridity, Sezincote reminds us of how the ideal vision of an empire of liberty, trade and cultural enlightenment became in reality an empire of conquest, subjugation and rapaciousness. The tent-like wing in which Charles Cockerell slept hints at his father's career in the military, and also at a later history in which captured campaign tents became prized loot from imperial conquest, with the most famous example that which belonged to Tipu Sultan at Seringapatam, now displayed at Powis Castle in Wales.[76]

After 1800: Race and Hierarchy

Daylesford and Sezincote show how the nature of the British Empire changed in the late eighteenth and early nineteenth centuries. The loss of the American colonies disrupted the settler colonialism that had predominated in the Empire's first two centuries. Though it would continue in Australia, New Zealand and southern Africa, it was a century before the combined British populations of those colonies surpassed the number of white American colonists who were lost through independence in 1783. Previously the most lucrative part of the Empire, the West Indies diminished in profitability after the abolition of the slave trade in 1807 and of slavery in 1834. India then became the most important part of the Empire, as British power expanded steadily through treaties with local rulers and the conquest of those who refused to cooperate. After victory over the Marathas in 1818, Britain dominated the subcontinent, which meant that it was now ruling an empire with a vast non-white population.

In the nineteenth century the Empire became so large – at its peak containing 415 million people (a quarter of the earth's population) and 14 million square miles (a quarter of the earth's surface) – that it threatened to destabilize the nation that ruled it. There was no longer any pretence that the Victorian Empire was an extension of that nation in the way that Burke had advocated; the colossal scale of Britain's global territories made it impossible to act as if they were a homogeneous realm. Governing India, with a population numbering in the hundreds of millions and, according to the census of 1861, only 125,000 British inhabitants, was very different from governing Australia, with a white settler population that increased from 400,000 to 4 million between 1800 and 1900 and an aboriginal population that plummeted from 750,000 to 100,000.

In any event, with the Empire now based on white minority rule, the existence of a common identity among its peoples became significantly less important than the establishment and maintenance of a clear sense of authority of ruler over subject. Charlotte Sussman writes that from the late 1830s onwards,

> appeals to a universal sensibility – mutual emotions discovered in sympathy and tears across vast distances – began to disappear from British conceptions of cultural difference, to be replaced by a more essentialist and 'scientific' understanding of 'race'... By the mid-nineteenth century, these views had given way to a more pessimistic, deterministic belief in the ineradicable savagery of inferior nations.[77]

In the early nineteenth century many British people believed that non-white colonial subjects were capable of being transformed into people like themselves, but by mid-century more rigid racial attitudes had formed which drew clear biological distinctions between the British and their colonial subjects.[78]

How did these changing attitudes influence architectural developments? There was no single 'imperial' style in this period, in the way that classicism had been in the eighteenth century. To be sure, classical buildings continued to appear. Thomas Metcalf argues that classical architecture in nineteenth-century India

> marked out the limits, or one might say the incomplete nature, of Britain's empire ... The British had conquered the land by virtue of their superior military force, and so subordinated the Indian people to their rule; but they had developed no conception of their Raj as an imperial Indian state, nor had they as a government penetrated Indian society at all deeply. They did not indeed yet possess knowledge of India and its peoples sufficient to permit them to do so effectively ... Hence, not surprisingly, British building in India inevitably and of necessity remained confined within a European, and largely classical, idiom.[79]

The meaning of classical buildings in the colonies therefore shifted. They now served as evidence of belonging to a superior race which was capable of understanding sophisticated architectural concepts, in contrast to Britain's biologically inferior and benighted colonial subjects.

The Roman precedent was still, however, useful for the comprehension and governance of such a large and diverse entity. Krishan Kumar writes:

> With the increasing importance of India, with the 'scramble for Africa' in the 1880s and 1890s, the British Empire was ever more multinational and multicultural, ever more in need of guidance as to how to manage such a diverse entity. That had been Rome's challenge too; and for many British thinkers of the nineteenth century, schooled as they were in the classics, it was natural to draw upon the experience of Rome for possible lessons that could be applied to the British Empire.[80]

The Roman experience was seen as useful for the difficult task of unifying the disparate parts of the Empire. In the second half of the nineteenth century comparisons between the Roman and British empires were common, so much so that the study of ancient Rome as an academic subject was significantly shaped by the contemporary imperial context in obvious and specific ways.[81] In particular, the Roman Empire provided an example of how a superior civilization could improve an inferior one. In his oft-quoted lectures of 1881–2, the historian J. R. Seeley declared:

> If the English conquest of India is to be classed along with the Greek conquest of the East and the Roman conquest of Gaul and Spain, we shall be prepared to place it among the transcendent events of the world, those events which rise as high above the average of civilised history as an ordinary Oriental conquest falls below it.[82]

This was not, to be sure, the imperial classicism of the eighteenth century. Classicism was no longer seen as a universal style which could transcend the differences between metropole and colony and so produce a common sense of identity across the Empire. That view was only valid when the peoples of both were white. Now, classicism was regarded as evidence of the superiority of white European culture. If Indian and other non-white imperial subjects accepted this and absorbed its lessons, then they might perhaps advance to a European level of civilization at some point in the future. When used for important late nineteenth-century imperial building projects such as the Victoria Memorial in Calcutta, classical architecture in the Empire was therefore increasingly rooted in European conceptions of the superiority of Western civilization, even if it allowed for the possibility of advancement by colonial subjects.

Increasing resistance to colonial authority, however, forced the British to confront the fact that Indians and other non-white colonial subjects might not be, as Rama Sundari Mantena writes, 'transformable after all'. Instead, imperial ideology increasingly espoused 'the idea that native cultures and colonial subjects [were] intransigent, and an emphasis on colonial reform gave way to the management of cultural intransigence'.[83] But there was no consensus about what this meant for building styles. Instead, there was a debate in which one side argued that colonial buildings should be built in European styles, in order to demonstrate the superiority of Western culture, while the other contended that the British should adopt indigenous styles of building, in order to show their understanding of the peoples over whom they ruled. Both sides, though, agreed that colonial buildings should help to increase British power over colonial peoples.

The obvious alternative architectural style to classical was gothic. The prevalence of the gothic in colonial contexts has been downplayed because it was principally used for religious buildings, which have received less attention from architectural historians than their secular counterparts. Gothic churches and cathedrals, however, played a vital role in the articulation of difference between metropole and colony, because in colonial contexts they could both invoke the long history which had led Britain to its current imperial might and demonstrate the superiority of its particular form of Christianity in colonial contexts. The earliest cathedrals in the Empire were St Andrew's (1837) in Sydney and St Paul's (1839) in Calcutta, both built in what was seen as the most English gothic style, the Perpendicular. They were copied all over the Empire.

These buildings had to be adapted to colonial climates, many of which were considerably warmer – and in the Canadian case colder – than Britain's. G. A. Bremner writes:

> It was apparent to all concerned that simply transposing English Middle-Pointed Gothic to these regions, unaltered in any way

from its original context, would not work. It was recognised that the English Gothic was itself an environmentally determined species of Christian architecture and that a similar process of adaptation was to be expected when it came to developing an appropriate ecclesiology for the colonies.[84]

Architects who designed churches for colonial climates tried to find ways to keep buildings warm or cool. They also used local materials creatively – rimu pine in New Zealand, iron bark in Australia, elephant grass in Africa, balean ('iron wood') in Malaysia – and allocated interior spaces to suit local circumstances. Religious buildings in colonies with large Muslim populations, for example, required separate worship spaces for men and women.

Even so, the desire to imitate English precedent remained strong. When building churches in Queensland, the architect R. G. Suter used exposed framing in a way that was intended to achieve a 'half-timbered effect' in imitation of traditional English buildings.[85] Gothic buildings in colonial settings therefore functioned in the same way as their classical counterparts: to show the superiority of European culture. But they differed by invoking the national rather than the universal: they were buildings taken from *English* history, and therefore were intended to convey how that history had led England to its colonial mastery. There was no possibility that a colony could share that history, and therefore no possibility for Burke's vision of a colonial community to be achieved.

A third possibility for colonial architecture in the second half of the nineteenth century was the adaptation of indigenous styles. This strategy was most obviously pursued in India, where the 1857 rebellion rattled Britain's confidence in its authority. The Indo-Saracenic style, which drew inspiration from Mughal and, to a lesser extent, Hindu buildings, was the result. It is tempting to see the Indo-Saracenic as evidence that cultural contact between colonial rulers and subjects will over time lead to hybridity as they begin to influence one another. But in reality the Indo-Saracenic shared more with the gothic in India than initially appears, as it also invoked a specific history in order to legitimize and enhance British colonial authority, in this case that of the Mughal dynasty, which had ruled India before the British. It was not in any way an indigenous style, but rather a British interpretation of one. Michael Mann writes that Indo-Saracenic architecture

> resembles the then British-Victorian romantic-picturesque imagination of an Indian past encapsulated within the Britishers' own buildings ... To judge and select, to merge and fuse particular Arabic, Saracenic, Mughal and Rajput components, crowned by a few gothic elements into a modern and representative 'national' architecture demonstrated the colonial regime's ability to contribute to India's aesthetic improvement ... In this way the architecture of 'rude and cruel nations' like the Saracens and Arabs as well as Rajput-Muslim Indians, which stood for the despotic character of their political rulers, was civilized through aesthetic refinement into a 'benevolent paternalism', as colonial rule was commonly characterized by the British.[86]

The underlying assumption was that the British were the natural successors to the Mughals, and therefore 'not mere foreign conquerors', but 'legitimate, almost indigenous rulers' who were 'linked directly ... to India's own past'.[87]

In the second half of the nineteenth century, then, whether it was classical, gothic or an imitation of an indigenous style, colonial architecture was seen as separate from indigenous culture and society and as a tool for demonstrating Britain's authority over colonial populations. Mann writes that in India:

> Architecture ... remained the sole domain of the British ... Indians were excluded from the highly political debate on the question of a representative imperial style in terms of architecture which was also to epitomise a kind of 'colonial national style', a question which became increasingly important particularly in the second half of the nineteenth century.[88]

As a representative non-white colonial society, India was regarded as incapable of producing high art. Instead, it was relegated to the status of a 'traditional' (that is, a small step up from 'primitive') culture which could only produce crude vernacular buildings and handicrafts.

Before returning to imperial influence on architecture in England, a brief diversion is necessary to consider the effect of this increasingly hierarchical relationship between metropole and colony in Ireland. Like Scotland, Ireland has often been seen as architecturally 'backward' because fortified buildings continued to appear after they had become obsolete in England.[89] Eric Klingelhofer writes, 'Where the [English] Tudors may have retained crenellation as a decoration for high status buildings, in defence-conscious Ireland both crenellation and machicolation appear regularly on residences. These were fortified manor houses, not quite castles, but not English manor houses either.'[90] Also as in Scotland, however, the 'militaristic atmosphere' created by tower houses was in some ways 'deceptive, the *show* of defence being as relevant as defence *per se*'.[91] Like Scotland, Ireland was receptive to classical ideas. Plantation was one channel through which these ideas reached Ireland, but they also arrived independently of England, as numerous Irish people travelled to the European continent to acquire a cosmopolitan education, to join Catholic religious orders or to serve as mercenaries in foreign armies.[92] At Moore Abbey in County Kildare, a window surround decorated with *putti* and Roman armour may have reflected the term of its owner Lord Audley as Governor of Utrecht in the late sixteenth century.[93] Around 1635 the Earl of Hamilton built a new residence within the walls of medieval Dunluce Castle in County Antrim, featuring a symmetrical front, large windows and a 'little portico more suited to the Mediterranean than the North Atlantic'.[94]

In the second half of the seventeenth century, however, English influence increased rapidly, as the rebellion of 1641 and the subsequent Cromwellian conquest led to the large-scale transfer of land from Catholic and Gaelic owners to Protestant English and Scottish settlers. Giles Worsley writes that the situation in Ireland differed significantly from that in Scotland: 'Instead of an impoverished native aristocracy proud of their ancestral tower houses, Ireland saw a new class of owners . . . owing no loyalty to earlier building forms and happy to make a statement of their power and their English origins in the houses that they built.'[95] Portumna Castle (*c.* 1610–17) in County Galway, Oldbawn (*c.* 1635) in County Dublin and Finnebrogue (*c.* 1660) in County Down were similar to late Elizabethan and Jacobean English H-plan houses. Several Irish houses – including Jigginstown Castle in Kildare, Portmore and Joymount in Antrim and the portico of Lismore Castle in Waterford – have been attributed to Inigo Jones for stylistic reasons (even though none of them has ever been proved to have been designed by him), another indication that English influence was on the rise. The Earl of Orrery acquired Castlemartyr Castle in Cork in the 1650s and began making it more 'English-like'.[96] In the 1660s, when the 3rd Viscount Conway decided to remodel his house at Lisburn in County

Antrim, the builder, Thomas Abbott, was dispatched to London 'to inform himself of the new fashion worke' in architecture. He returned with drawings 'of stately buildings going up' there, in particular Clarendon House, which was being built by Roger Pratt in Piccadilly for the Lord Chancellor Edward Hyde.[97]

English influence continued to grow after 1688, as William of Orange's victory led to the creation of a newly secure and confident Protestant Ascendancy, which built in the latest fashions imported from England. In the early 1720s Castletown House in County Kildare marked the first appearance of Irish Palladianism, which was derived from English models, with an interior plan taken from Pratt's Coleshill and colonnaded wings from Campbell's *Vitruvius Britannicus*. Mount Ievers in County Clare was similarly influenced by English Palladianism. After 1730 economic growth bolstered by international trade led to a fresh wave of building: the best examples were Castletown, Bellamont Forest (1729) in Cavan, Summerhill House (1731) in Meath (in collaboration with the German-born architect Richard Cassels) and possibly Desart Court (c. 1733) in Kilkenny by Edward Lovett Pearce. Pearce looked to English sources for inspiration, but also studied Continental buildings and architectural treatises. He was a major influence on Cassels, who succeeded him as the leading architect of Irish Palladianism, as shown by his designs for Powerscourt House (1741) and Russborough House (c. 1741) in Wicklow and Bellinter House (1750) in Meath. Together, Pearce and Cassels 'established a particular interpretation of Palladianism in Ireland' which 'followed Palladio's example more faithfully than did the English themselves'.[98] After 1750 Irish architectural independence increased further, as Anglo-Irish Protestants increasingly emphasized their Irish over their British identity. Irish Palladianism therefore developed along its own path, 'at one remove from the English example'.[99] Around the same time, Irish country houses began to feature distinctive Rococo-style plasterwork, with the best examples by the three Lafranchini brothers from Bironico, an Italian-speaking cantonment in Switzerland.[100]

This moment of architectural independence proved fleeting, however. In nineteenth-century Ireland, Unionism became the dominant political influence on country-house architecture, as was shown by the gothic-style houses of the time.[101] Geoffrey Tyack writes that 'for the Protestant ascendancy in Ireland, following the convulsions of the 1790s and the Union of 1801, castles acquired further resonance as symbols of authority and security among a potentially hostile population.'[102]

Charleville Castle (1801) in County Offaly featured distinctively Irish elements such as two-stepped crenellations and the tall tower which adorned one corner, an echo of the round towers of medieval Irish monasteries, but at the same time its imposing castle-like form embodied 'British authority'.[103] The house's owner, Charles William Bury, was a committed Unionist who was elevated to his titles – Viscount Charleville in 1801 and 1st Earl of Charleville in 1806 – as a reward for his loyalty.

Charleville was one of a number of castellated Irish houses that were built or rebuilt around the time of the Act of Union, including Kilwaughter (1803) in Antrim, Tullynally (1803) in Westmeath, Freke (1807) and Bernard (1815) in Cork, Duckett's Grove (1818) in Carlow and Gosford Castle (1819) in Armagh. Valentine Richard Quin, 1st Earl of Dunraven, had entered the Irish Parliament in 1800 solely to vote for the Act of Union. The decision of his son Windham Henry, the 2nd Earl, to build Adare Manor (1832) in Limerick in an Elizabethan style was not politically neutral, as in Ireland the reign of Elizabeth I was still associated with the plantations of English settlers in Munster and Leinster. Judith Hill describes how, in the perception of the Ascendancy, 'the survival of Ireland within the Union relied on the landed families that had dedicated their lives to its leadership. For such families, notwithstanding their English or mixed roots, their self-assertion through English-inspired design in an Irish context could comfortably be construed as a statement of ascendancy Irishness.'[104] Ireland did not, therefore, evolve a nationally distinctive style of architecture as a corollary

Although Charleville Castle (1801) in County Offaly had distinctly Irish features, such as the round tower which can be seen on the left side of the image, its gothic architecture was imitative of English fashion and expressed the Unionism of its owner Viscount Charleville.

to the Scottish Baronial. Instead, nineteenth-century Irish country houses imitated English fashion in their preference for gothic and Jacobethan styles.

WHAT, THEN, DID ALL OF THIS mean for country houses in England? After the very early nineteenth century, Metcalf writes, imperial-influenced designs in Britain 'abandoned Sezincote's careful attention to detail in favour of a more extravagant notion of Oriental "exoticism"', as embodied by John Nash's Brighton Royal Pavilion (1815), with its incongruous quasi-Indian exterior and Chinese interior.[105] 'Neither Nash nor the Prince Regent', Metcalf continues, 'had any commitment to Indian design other than as a way of representing the fantasy world of a pleasure dome.'[106] Although it was used for piers, theatres and other leisure sites, the Royal Pavilion's new style of Empire-inspired architecture had little influence on the English country house. The sisters Marianne and Eliza Constable visited the Royal Pavilion in the late 1820s and installed a room in Burton Constable Hall in Yorkshire which imitated its flamboyant chinoiserie interior, but it is a unique example. More to the point, there was not a single country house in nineteenth-century Britain that was designed in a style imported from one of the colonies. Sezincote proved a dead end, not a sign of things to come, because colonial cultures were no longer seen as having anything to offer to the British metropolitan world.

How, then, *did* the Empire manifest itself in nineteenth-century country houses? There were two ways in particular. First, there was what I have described in my previous work on this subject as a 'discourse of conquest', which first appeared during the Seven Years' War but after 1800 came to focus specifically on colonial rather than European enemies.[107] Tipu Sultan, ruler of the Indian state of Mysore, became what C. A. Bayly describes as the first 'black bogeyman' to strike fear into the hearts of metropolitan Britons.[108] After he was defeated and killed at the Battle of Seringapatam in 1799, his vast treasure was plundered by British troops and much of it was taken to Britain for sale.[109] For country-house owners, the looted objects became highly desirable relics of a great victory which had secured British control of southern India. George Harris, the commanding general at Seringapatam, displayed many items at Belmont House in Kent. Others ended up in the hands of the 1st Marquess of Cornwallis, who had previously fought against Tipu Sultan in the Third

Mysore War from 1789 to 1792, and were later taken to Audley End in Essex, after his daughter Jane married the 3rd Baron Braybrooke.[110] The majority of Seringapatam souvenirs, however, were given as gifts or sold at auction. The Marchioness of Salisbury acquired a sword to display at Hatfield House in Hertfordshire; William Beckford purchased a hookah for his collection at Fonthill Abbey in Wiltshire; and a gold chain made its way to Puslinch in Devon.[111] Objects associated with Tipu continued to attract interest well into the nineteenth century: the 4th Marquess of Hertford purchased a Pathan knife at a Paris sale in 1850, and the 1st Marquess of Curzon, who served as Viceroy of India from 1899 to 1905, acquired a set of ivory furniture that had purportedly belonged to Tipu, although the provenance was dubious.[112]

Trophies from other imperial victories also made their way into country houses. Arthur Herbert Cocks, General Sir Hugh Gough's political officer during the First Sikh War (1845–6), displayed Sikh weapons and armour at Eastnor Castle in Herefordshire which had been given to him after he saved Gough's life in the Battle of Gujrat. A Sikh cannon known as the 'Sutlej Gun', which had been captured in the same war, guarded Belvoir Castle in Lincolnshire after it was given to the 5th Duke of Rutland by the 1st Viscount Hardinge, who was Governor-General of India from 1844 to 1848.[113] Bernard Cohn writes that after the Indian Rebellion of 1857, 'loot poured into England to be treasured as memorabilia of families, symbolising the ... sense of triumph generated by the war.'[114] When British and French troops sacked the Summer Palace in Peking during the First Opium War in 1860, the spoils were distributed among the troops according to rank. Many soldiers sold their plunder at auction. A set of iron gates ended up at Dewlish House in Dorset; a 'travelling watch' that had belonged to the Chinese Emperor at Anglesey Abbey in Cambridgeshire; and brass and gilt-enamel jardinières at Shugborough House in Staffordshire.[115] Spoils from later imperial wars in Africa were also brought back to England and displayed in country houses.

The second way in which imperial objects made their way into English country houses was through the display of exotic artefacts. Colonial administrators, soldiers and civil servants often collected objects while they were serving overseas, and they sent or brought back items for their families and friends as well. Some country-house owners eagerly sought exotic plants for their landscape gardens, while others proudly displayed the animals, now stuffed, which they had slaughtered on big-game hunts.

Even today, a number of animals roam England which were imported from the colonies and later escaped from the parks of landed estates. These include Sika and Chinese water deer, muntjac and, perhaps most incongruously, Tasmanian wallabies.[116] To be sure, the accumulation of artefacts from Britain's colonies had been going on for centuries, but in the nineteenth century they were frequently displayed in purpose-built 'museums' which were separate from the rest of the house, therefore presenting the colonies as something alien and 'other'. A prime example, dating from the 1890s, still exists at Claydon House in Buckinghamshire. These collections 'were premised upon the drawing of clear distinctions between European and non-European cultures'.[117] Nicholas Thomas writes that after 1800 the idea of a 'curiosity', or an object from an unfamiliar place, shifted from simply being a source of pleasure and interest for the collector to the embodiment of a 'savage condition'.[118] In this way, 'curiosity about other cultures was converted ... into a desire to possess and control.'[119] The same process occurred in Ireland, where the Ascendancy moved away from the Irish identities they had prioritized in the late eighteenth century. Their houses began to convey a difference from, and superiority over, their Irish setting, as Irishness, like other indigenous colonial identities, came to be seen as something exotic, primitive and inferior. There was virtually no architectural exchange between England and Ireland in the nineteenth century, beyond the imposition of English country-house styles on Irish estates.

THE TRANSFORMATION of the appearances of the British Empire in English country houses from the eighteenth to the nineteenth century reflects changes in English national identity over the same period. Ian Baucom describes how earlier ideas of Englishness were rooted in insular and romanticized ideals of the landscape, but in the nineteenth century these were replaced by the outward-facing national identity demanded by imperialism, which entailed racialized ideas of human hierarchy.[120] Similarly, Simon Gikandi sees Englishness as shaped by consciousness of empire, which made it prone to moral panics about race and later about immigration.[121] These views of the development of English national identity in the nineteenth century argue that the sense of difference between England and the Empire increased, as did that between English people and colonial subjects. English identity was, in other words, increasingly defined against a colonial 'other'.

This sharpening of English identity in the nineteenth century was reflected in contemporary country houses. In the Elizabethan era, country houses expressed a curiosity about and enthusiasm for empire through the depiction of indigenous Americans in woodcarvings and plasterwork. As the British population of the colonies grew, there was a need for a sense of identity that could transcend the physical distance between colony and metropole, and so country houses in both places featured the Palladian and Neoclassical styles. But in the nineteenth century, country houses became sites for the display of the spoils of conquests or for collected objects and animals which were used to highlight the exoticism and difference of the colonies. This reflected the increasing perception of a clear racial difference between metropole and colony. It meant that the emphasis in a country-house context was no longer on the equality of elite Britons across various colonial contexts, but rather on the expression of the hierarchy of the colonizer over the colonized.

6
Fog in Channel

Kingston Lacy in Dorset was originally built between 1663 and 1667 by the courtier Sir Ralph Bankes, son of Charles 1's Attorney General John Bankes. Flush with optimism after the Restoration, the staunchly royalist Bankes harboured grandiose architectural ambitions. He commissioned Sir Roger Pratt to design his new house in the style of Inigo Jones, and was rewarded with a fashionable compact brick block, its hipped roof topped by a cupola. Over the course of the eighteenth century Kingston Lacy was altered several times, but by the time it was inherited by Sir Ralph's great-great-grandson William John Bankes in 1834, its style was no longer in fashion, and so he decided to remodel it. The commission went to Charles Barry, later the architect of the new Houses of Parliament, who had already acquired a solid reputation for his work in designing churches and country houses such as Trentham Hall in Staffordshire and Bowood House in Wiltshire.

Barry's design for Kingston Lacy was more restoration than innovation, as his design remained true to Pratt's original vision. He stripped off the eighteenth-century accretions and reinstalled the original hipped roof, and clad its brick facades in cream-coloured Chilmark stone. This work was done in close consultation with William John Bankes. On the one hand, Bankes was a thorough Italophile, and his ideas for Kingston Lacy, recorded in a notebook that he kept from 1836 onwards, abound with references to Italian buildings.[1] One example among many is Bankes's thoughts about the north front of the house:

> I have not observed that in the principle [*sic*] examples of the Florentine manner there is any diminution in the scale of the upper range of windows, as compared with those of the *piano nobile*, but this practice was universal with Bramante in his domestic

elevations (see the Cancellerie & the Palazzo Giraud at Rome &c.) and the effect is so satisfactory, and it seems based upon such good common sense that, where the rooms are smaller & inferior, they should have a less portion of light assigned them, & display less external ostentation, that I do not hesitate to adopt it.[2]

But on the other hand, Bankes wanted the house to reflect English tradition, and in particular its origin as an example of Inigo-Jones-style Palladianism. He visited many of the houses that had been designed by Jones and his disciples, including Amesbury Abbey and Wilton House in Wiltshire, Lees Court in Kent and Coleshill in Berkshire. Moreover, he was conscious of adapting Italian modes of building to the English climate:

> A solid oblong-square structure, in which ranges of apartments can circulate compactly all round, and reciprocally communicate and retain warmth, thus precluding the risk of draught penetrating quite through, or of damp and cold air being pent up and confined within ... seems to be the plan best adapted for a comfortable English country-house, but this form, if character be not given to it, will inevitably appear as a mere box with windows.[3]

Sadly, Bankes would never get to live in his finished house. In 1841 he was caught committing an 'indecent act' with another man. It was his second offence, as he had been arrested for a similar act eight years earlier, and only his social status and the influence of powerful friends kept him from a severe punishment at a time when homosexuality was still a capital offence in England. This time there was no escape. Bankes went into exile in Italy and signed Kingston Lacy over to his brother in order to avoid its seizure by the authorities. He did not, however, abandon his plans for the house, but rather continued to manage its decoration from abroad, through a constant stream of letters full of suggestions and advice.

One of these letters, dating from sometime in the 1840s, concerns the panelling for the doors of the Spanish Picture Room, so named because it was intended to display the paintings by Spanish artists that Bankes had acquired while serving as aide-de-camp to the Duke of Wellington during the Peninsular War. The room's tooled leather panelling came

Detail of 'June' panel on the door of the Spanish Picture Room, Kingston Lacy, mid-19th century.

from several Venetian palazzos, while the grotesque foliage panels on the ceiling had originally been in the Palazzo Contrari degli Scrigni on the Grand Canal.[4] But the panelling on the doors, which was specially commissioned by Bankes, had a very different source of inspiration. For them, Bankes called for zodiac designs featuring a variety of English pastoral motifs. April (Taurus), for example, displayed a

> rainbow, umbrella with drops at the points, boy catching rainwater, another catching the sun with a looking glass, swallows, primrose, violets, wild hyacinth, daffodil, olyanthus, narcissus, anemone, scarlet ranunculus, cowslip, early tulips, pyrus japonica, Judas tree, wallflower, bees out of hive, snail crawling, periwinkle, lady smocks, crown imperial, April fool, hod, trowel, St George's Day, mare & foal, drops of rain over the whole.

June (Cancer) depicted a

> boy shearing a lamb, opposite one shearing a poodle dog, haymaking, roses, pinks, carnations, sweetpeas, columbine, larkspur, strawberries in pottles, ditto with flower, currants, raspberries, Duke of Wellington's head in a medallion with the date of Waterloo round it & laurel, rakes &c for haymaking, shorn sheep, yellow jasmine.[5]

Bankes's ideas for Kingston Lacy therefore combined his admiration for Italy, his respect for the house's seventeenth-century history and his love of the English pastoral tradition. Despite his experience of exile, he did not entirely turn his back upon his house's English setting.

Kingston Lacy raises an important question about English culture: must Englishness be expressed in cultural form as 'pure' and untainted by continental European influence, or can it be a transformation of continental influences into something locally distinct? What, in other words, makes a building 'English': its resistance to continental influences or its transformation of them into something unique to the national context? Must it rely for its Englishness upon the development of a style of architecture entirely unique to England? Or can that Englishness stem from the adoption and adaptation of European continental styles? These questions are the catalysts for this chapter.

The Tudor Engagement with Renaissance Classicism

In the 1570s the architect Robert Smythson remodelled Wardour Castle in Wiltshire for Sir Matthew Arundell. It is usually assumed that – at a moment when classical designs were becoming an indication of sophistication and erudition – Arundell wanted to make his late fourteenth-century castle more fashionable, and so commissioned Smythson to add classical detailing to the stairways, chimneypieces and doorcases, as well as a classical gateway to the entrance front. The relationship between the gothic and the classical at Wardour, however, is more complicated than the replacement of the former by the latter. Arundell chose to update Wardour when he could easily have afforded to build an entirely new house. Presumably at his request, Smythson preserved the traceried windows in the great hall and used gothic-style arched lights rather than 'modern' square-headed ones for the new windows he inserted in the rest of the castle.[6] Arundell therefore did not view the classical as superior to the gothic. Rather, the mix of new and old was the result of a deliberate choice to introduce the former while preserving some of the latter, with no attempt to elevate one or downgrade the other. Alice Friedman writes:

> No attempt was made to fit all the detailing at the castle into a consistently modern, that is consistently Italianate, scheme. On the contrary, the authenticity of the medieval building seems to have added to its value ... By sacrificing neither the evocative pointed arches of the original gothic building nor the monumental solemnity of the Doric order, Smythson was able to feature both and to communicate a more complicated message about the oldness and newness of Elizabethan culture. The resulting image ... drew its power from this conflation of meanings.[7]

Wardour shows that the Elizabethans saw the relationship between the gothic and the classical differently from how it would come to be seen later. In modern eyes, as Maurice Howard writes, 'classicism's stylistic authority appears to possess a natural and aesthetic inevitability. This is largely due to classicism's manifest success throughout Europe following its revival in the buildings of fifteenth- and sixteenth-century Italy.' But Howard reminds us that the 'authority' of the classical 'is not intrinsic'; rather, it depends upon the beholder of a building ... finding the style persuasive and having the ability to read its language. Four hundred years ago the English were not in a position to find it persuasive as we do: the very idea of choosing the classical style needed a social and economic rationale that took time to emerge.[8]

The alterations to Wardour show how the classical did not sweep all before it in early modern England. Its amalgamation of architectural styles resulted in part from the social position of Wardour's owner, as Arundell was a relatively 'new man' with a somewhat chequered lineage. His father had elevated the family from minor Cornish gentry to prominent players on the national political scene, but had then been attainted and stripped of his estates after he supported the Duke of Somerset's plot to usurp the throne in 1551. This somewhat precarious status may have influenced the particular form of his alterations to Wardour Castle. On the one hand, he wanted to stress his ancient lineage by preserving its gothic character, but on the other, he wanted to prove his intellectual worth and cultural sophistication through his display of the latest architectural fashions.

Wardour serves as an example of how many Elizabethan houses combined older English traditions with innovations from the European continent. By fostering military conflict with Catholic Europe, the Protestant Reformation heightened English insularity and xenophobia, as did Elizabeth I's resistance to marriage with a continental royal. At the same time, however, events across the Channel could not be ignored entirely. The journeys of Henry VIII's emissaries to Rome to negotiate his divorce brought them into close contact with the leading scholars at Italian universities.[9] During the reign of Mary I, many English Protestants fled to the Low Countries, where the Northern Renaissance was in full bloom. There were diplomatic contacts as well: the French King Henry IV found a receptive audience when he approached Elizabeth I about the possibility of a European Christian confederation, although these plans crumbled when he renounced Protestantism in 1593. The English economy increasingly relied on Continental trade, with Antwerp the main entrepôt for English cloth exports while Baltic and Iberian networks were growing in importance.[10] Continental craftsmen settled in England in rising numbers, while continental universities remained popular with English students. Padua, whose Venetian rulers protected Protestants, was a particular draw, as were Basel and Heidelberg.

The complexities of England's relationship with the continent carried over into country-house architecture. As the cultural movement conventionally labelled the 'Renaissance' gradually spread westward and northward from Italy, it carried with it an admiration for the symmetry and mathematical proportions of classical architecture. The English, however, resisted the increasing incursion of continental influence.[11] Although they were 'indebted to European art and architecture for particular features of design or solutions to problems', early Tudor buildings such as Hampton Court (1515–35) and Nonsuch Palace (1538–41) remained committed to 'native traditions' and maintained a fundamental loyalty to the English Perpendicular style.[12]

Even as it made some inroads, then, Renaissance classicism continued to be seen as an exotic import. This had advantages and disadvantages for its acceptance in England. Some observers saw classicism as embodying erudition and sophistication, but others criticized what they saw as an English tendency to embrace foreign cultural influences to the detriment of their own. Both of these views are found in the writings of the early seventeenth-century scholar-poet Henry Peacham. In his *The Compleat Gentleman* (1622), Peacham listed a number of Renaissance authors and artists with whom a young man should be familiar if he wanted to be considered well educated. In *The Truth of Our Times* (1638), however, Peacham derided his countrymen's fascination with the latest continental fashion:

> I have much wondered why our English above other nations should so much dote upon new fashions, but I more wonder at our want of wit that we cannot invent them ourselves, but when one is grown stale, run presently over to France to seek a new, making that noble and flourishing kingdom the magazine of our fooleries.[13]

As Peacham suggests, some elite Englishmen were keen to include continental innovations in their country houses. The lawyer and MP Edward Hall complained in 1542 that when Englishmen returned from across the Channel, 'nothing by them was praised, but it was after the French form.'[14] By the middle decades of the sixteenth century it was essential in court circles to be familiar with continental fashion, and over the next half-century that attitude spread to the provinces. Even in distant corners of England, symmetry became more prevalent; the classical orders were used more frequently; and important rooms were moved from the ground to the first floor in imitation of Italian fashion. Over time the number of houses with such 'Renaissance' characteristics increased steadily beginning in the 1540s, followed by a sharp rise in the number between 1590 and 1610.

Even at its peak in the decades around 1600, however, there were limits to the influence of the Renaissance in England. The Elizabethans saw nothing wrong with combining the gothic and the classical; it was not until later that they came to be seen as antithetical.[15] There was a curiosity about, and often enthusiasm for, foreign ideas and concepts, but when pushed too far it could provoke a backlash and a retreat to more 'national' styles. It would be easy to dismiss Elizabethan architecture as unorthodox and at times inappropriate in its application of classical orders and ornament. As Alice Friedman notes, it seemed to ignore 'the conceptual framework of classicizing humanist culture' and so existed 'without rules, without a sense of decorum'. But, Friedman continues, it is wrong to see it as 'a garbled version of a stylistic language misunderstood by provincial patrons and artists'; rather, it was a uniquely English version of a Renaissance style.[16]

IN THE 1560s ROBERT DUDLEY, 1st Earl of Leicester, began making changes to Kenilworth Castle in Warwickshire. For inspiration, Leicester looked to Italy: a classically arched loggia in a new forebuilding to the

NUMBER OF RENAISSANCE CLASSICAL HOUSES

keep was an example of an Italian fashion that swept across England in the mid-sixteenth century.[17] English builders saw illustrations of loggias in the architectural treatises that arrived from the continent in the second half of the sixteenth century, although they referred to them not by their Italian name but as 'cloisters', 'galleries' or 'terraces'. The earliest known English example was a detached outbuilding at Horton Court in Gloucestershire by William Knight, Prothonotary to the Holy See and later Bishop of Bath and Wells. Knight probably saw loggias when he was dispatched to Rome in 1527 to help press the case for Henry VIII's divorce.[18] Loggias open to the elements were not particularly suited to the English climate, however, and so they were typically incorporated into the physical fabric of buildings, as was the case at Kenilworth.[19] After installing the loggia, Leicester continued to make Renaissance-influenced additions to the castle. In the early 1570s, he built splendid new accommodations for Elizabeth I known as 'Leicester's Building', and also made alterations to the upper floor of the keep and converted the Swan Tower to a banqueting house.

At the same time, however, Leicester preserved the castle's medieval fabric. Leicester's Building was the same height and built of the same colour stone as the keep, with an austere, boxy design that echoed its mass.[20] He repeated this juxtaposition of old and new over the entrance to the loggia by retaining a Perpendicular gothic window.[21] This was

The building on the left is the 'ambulatory' (c. 1530) at Horton Court in Gloucestershire, the earliest Italian-style loggia in England.

The late 12th-century keep of Kenilworth Castle (right) looms in the background, with the 1st Earl of Leicester's building from the early 1570s in the foreground. The juxtaposition of the two structures makes clear that Leicester imitated the stone and massing of the keep in his design for the newer building.

not done to reduce costs by recycling some of the castle's existing fabric, but rather to enhance Kenilworth's primary role as a theatrical set for an audience of one, Elizabeth I, as he sought to convince her that he was a worthy suitor. He emphasized Kenilworth's roots in English history in order to highlight England's growing political, military and cultural ambitions, while adding elements to the castle that would have been perceived as 'modern' and 'foreign' by his contemporaries. It was no accident that he decided to build the new quarters for the queen in the latest Continental style, as he wanted to assert his equality, in taste if not in rank, to the European royal suitors who were seeking Elizabeth's hand.[22] He was making a very modern argument: that cultivation and merit should matter more in determining suitability for a royal marriage than birth and blood. By displaying his erudition, his use of classical architecture was part of that claim, but it would not have been as effective a message had it not been set against the backdrop of the castle's medieval fabric, which allowed him to keep his argument grounded firmly in national soil.

Although Leicester's new building at Kenilworth was a major step forward, it was not the first English country house to embrace fully the architectural ideas of the Italian Renaissance. That distinction belongs to Longleat in Wiltshire. In 1540 the former Augustinian priory of Longleat was acquired for £53 by Sir John Thynne, an ambitious 25-year-old steward in the household of Edward Seymour, at the time Earl of Hertford and later 1st Duke of Somerset. As part of his duties, Thynne supervised the construction of Somerset House in London, as well as of two of Somerset's other building projects, Syon House on the western outskirts of London and Bedwyn in Wiltshire. He developed an enthusiasm for architecture; in a satire written by his neighbour William Darrell in 1575 he was accused of 'infesting his Master's head with plattes and forms and many a subtle thing'.[23]

Over the next two decades, as Thynne accumulated wealth, land and a knighthood, he planned a grand new house at Longleat. He began making improvements as early as 1546, but his initial plans merely added Renaissance flourishes to the existing monastic buildings.[24] In April 1567, however, a fire gutted the house. No longer constrained by what previously existed, Thynne hired a 31-year-old master-mason named Robert Smythson to supervise the conversion of Longleat into the most architecturally advanced house in England.[25] After consulting with Thynne, Smythson designed a new set of facades that wrapped around the house on all four sides, thereby transforming Longleat into a compact, outward-looking block that imitated Palladio's Villa Rotunda (*c.* 1552). The classical orders were used correctly on the pilasters flanking the bay windows, with Doric on the ground floor, Ionic on the first and Corinthian on the second.[26] Classical friezes surrounded the house, and classical busts in roundels filled the space beneath the windows. External symmetry was made possible by adopting the French idea of putting the service rooms under the house rather than in a separate wing. One traditional English element survived, however: the gothic great hall with its hammer-beam roof, because purely classical houses were ill-suited to the traditional hospitality which an English lord was expected to provide.[27]

Similar influences were at work at Burghley House in Lincolnshire, which was built between 1555 and 1587 for Sir William Cecil, 1st Baron Burghley. Like John Thynne, Cecil began his career in the service of Edward Seymour in the 1540s, and he too was significantly influenced by Seymour's advanced ideas about architecture. Burghley House contains a number of Renaissance features, including loggias which overlook the gardens on the south front and line the inner courtyard on all four sides; a 'Roman' staircase with a coffered stone vault leading from the kitchen into the main house; and classical busts in roundels on the facade. The house also incorporates the latest ideas from France, such as the loggia-pavilions in the courtyard, which were probably based on those from the chateau at Écouen. The loggia overlooking the south garden, meanwhile, was in place by 1562, making it the earliest example to be fully integrated into an Elizabethan house, rather than a later addition.[28]

But even with this embrace of the Renaissance, a great deal of English gothic tradition remained. Burghley's kitchen was probably based on the fourteenth-century example at Ely Cathedral, and Cecil retained the feudal tradition of making the great hall visible from the exterior, highlighting its importance for lordly hospitality. The hall's gothic interior, meanwhile, was not a survival as at Longleat, but part of the new design. On the exterior, the massive, pseudo-medieval gatehouse dates from the late 1570s, making it later than the Roman staircase.[29] Adding to the gothic feel, the spiky silhouette of Burghley House resembles the outline of a castle. Jill Husselby notes:

> The militaristic overtones of a castle have been deconstructed: the ramparts converted to roof walks, turret and towers to banqueting houses and prospect rooms, the portcullis replaced by

Longleat (1568) in Wiltshire, often characterized as the first true Renaissance house in England.

Burghley House (1555) in Lincolnshire, with its combination of Renaissance and English gothic architectural elements.

a classical triumphal arch ... The aspect of defence was transformed into a celebration of the arrival of the honoured guest who came to enjoy a place designed [in Edmund Spenser's words] 'rather for pleasure than for battery for fight'... At the same time these innovations were subsumed within a familiar framework suggesting not a radical departure but continuity with the past and locality.[30]

Also weaving together classical innovation and gothic tradition was Smythson's first entirely new house, Wollaton Hall (1580) near Nottingham, which was owned by Sir Francis Willoughby. By starting fresh rather than having to adapt an existing building, Smythson was able to make Wollaton perfectly symmetrical: the house is an elongated H-shape with a recessed square block over the centre bar. He replaced the internal courtyard with a great hall aligned with the entrance, in keeping with the economy and symmetry of Palladio's villas. He repeated a number of motifs that he had used at Longleat: a classical frieze separates the ground and first floors; classical pilasters – again in correct order as they ascend – flank the large windows and serve as grid-lines on the facades; and classical busts decorate the entrance front. As at Longleat, the house stands on a semi-basement, with its entrance above ground level.

Wollaton shows the arrival in England of classical influences from northern as well as southern Europe. In Flanders, Renaissance ideas imported through trading contacts spread rapidly in the densely populated port cities and towns, where they took on a specifically northern cast involving exaggerated forms, flamboyant ornamentation and bright colours.[31] An example of how northern European fashion spread to the far reaches of England was Trerice (1572–3) in Cornwall, which boasted curved 'Dutch' gables on its entrance front. Within a decade, English houses all over the country featured similarly elaborate gables, along with the riotous profusions of scrolls and the ribbon-like forms known as 'strapwork' which were popular in Flanders. Wollaton followed this fashion: its four corner towers were crowned by curved gables.

But Wollaton was inspired by English as well as foreign models. It features a great hall with a hammer-beam roof as at Longleat and Burghley, although the beams provide no actual support and are there only to supply gothic character. The house's plan, meanwhile, was English medieval rather than classical. Friedman writes:

> The traditional castle type called for a carefully monitored approach via a series of checkpoints, turnings and open spaces: the main gatehouse gave access to a courtyard surrounded by high walls; opposite, the entrance porch protecting the front door led past a porters' lodge and into a narrow hallway; inside, the screens passage and screen created a series of ninety-degree turnings which eventually opened onto the great hall ... [These elements] disrupted the orderly Palladianism of the plan but could not be omitted if the chivalric imagery and ceremonial traditions of the English countryside were to be maintained.[32]

Gothic influence is even more apparent on the exterior.[33] Wollaton's most striking feature is the height of its central block, which is created by the fourth-storey 'prospect room' with castle-like turrets corbelled out from its corners. These turrets may have been inspired by French precedents – the chateaux at Chenonceau and Anet both feature them – but it is equally possible that they were derived from Prior Overton's Tower (*c.* 1438) and Mackworth Castle (*c.* 1495), both in nearby Derbyshire.

In contrast with the rest of the house, which has rectangular mullioned windows, the windows in the prospect room feature gothic tracery derived from Chenonceau and Challuau, another chateau in the Loire Valley.

Wollaton showed that the castle form did not disappear from English architecture despite the rise of the classical style. Nor did the form of another type of English medieval building, the cathedral. Mark Girouard notes that 'much of the inspiration of ... later Elizabethan architecture seems to have come from the last, the Perpendicular, period of medieval architecture, with its squareness and high proportion of window to wall.'[34] In the first half of the sixteenth century Renaissance ornament was grafted on to English gothic tradition. In the century's final decades, however, a more thorough synthesis occurred. In particular, the vertical, airy grace of the Perpendicular cathedral helped to inspire a new mode of country-house design, as English houses came to feature walls of glass derived from the Perpendicular style.[35] Among the ranks of these Elizabethan 'lantern houses', one example stands supreme:

Wollaton House (1580) in Nottinghamshire,
a combination of English castle and Renaissance palazzo.

Famously 'more glass than wall', Hardwick Hall (1590) in Derbyshire echoed the design principles of an English Perpendicular cathedral.

Hardwick Hall in Derbyshire, created by its owner, Bess of Hardwick, and Smythson, between 1590 and 1597.

Hardwick's interior features a symmetrical plan and a great hall aligned directly with the front door, in accordance with Palladio's principles. The exterior, however, could never be confused with an Italian villa. Famously described as 'more glass than wall', Hardwick was a secular cathedral, a domestic parallel to King's College Chapel, Cambridge (1446–1515), one of the most admired English buildings during the Tudor era. Girouard writes:

> The native Perpendicular gothic tradition was too strong to succumb to the new style; ... for thirty years or so in the middle of the century the two joined battle and classical architecture, having influential backers, nearly won the day; but in the end the victory went to the native style. The gothic element in Elizabethan architecture has of course always been recognized, but it has tended to be regarded as something conservative and reactionary, whereas it seems to me that it was responsible for nearly everything that is most interesting and alive about Elizabethan architecture. It is far more illuminating to regard the Elizabethans as working out and improving ideas inherited from their own gothic tradition,

rather than as bungling ideas which they had borrowed from the continent.[36]

Hardwick is an example of how the Elizabethans embraced the ideas of the Renaissance without regarding them as superior to indigenous tradition.

Elizabethan country houses therefore demand a reassessment of what is typically assumed to be the hierarchical relationship between gothic and classical architecture. Later, classicism became what Lucy Gent terms 'a powerfully normalizing mode' representing the most perfect aesthetic form, as 'art history ... marginalized or depreciated what could not be met on the terms of the classical canon'. As a result, Elizabethan and Jacobean architecture was 'regarded as destined to move from benighted ignorance towards continental adulthood'.[37] The gothic, however, was 'a continuous undercurrent in English architecture' which was not a 'regression but ... a conscious stylistic choice'.[38] Elizabethan houses did not welcome the replacement of the 'barbarous' gothic by the 'superior' classical, but rather assimilated both. Catherine Belsey writes:

> The introduction of antique statuary in portraiture or a new symmetry in building, like the addition of a stone portico to an Elizabethan country house, does not necessarily effect a transformation from vernacular to classical. On occasions, in other words, a classical allusion in art or architecture is no more than an idiosyncratic element in a native whole ... But at other times the introduction of classicism into the Elizabethan world marks a radical shift of meanings and aspirations and the erasure, for better or worse, of a previous culture.[39]

It is tempting to assume, for example, that square (that is, classical) windows were newer than arched (gothic) ones, but this was not always the case, as the gothic continued to be used well after 1600. The response of Elizabethan architecture to continental Renaissance influences was both receptive and hostile, simultaneously welcoming its artistic innovations and fiercely defending English tradition.

Inigo Jones and the Early Palladian

Inigo Jones's emergence as the leading architect in England in the first half of the seventeenth century is often regarded as marking a greater commitment to classicism, with a corresponding increase in continental influence. Although Smythson and other Elizabethan architects incorporated elements from it in order to improve the English Perpendicular gothic, they did not deny the essential foreign-ness of the classical style. Jones, in contrast, loathed the eclectic nature of Elizabethan architecture, which he described as 'the monstrous Babels of our Moderne Barbarisme'.[40] Instead, he set out to establish not only the superiority of classicism, but to show that it was a native English style.

Only six of Jones's buildings survive, only two of which, Chevening House in Kent (1617, but much altered) and Stoke Park House in Northamptonshire (c. 1630, only two pavilions still standing), were country houses. There are other houses, however, to which Jones contributed his expertise. He added classical centrepieces to the facades of Houghton Conquest (c. 1615) in Bedfordshire and Byfleet House (1617) in Surrey, and was possibly involved in the design of Coleshill (1649) in Berkshire, but he may have merely provided advice to Roger Pratt.[41] Finally, there is Wilton House, the Earl of Pembroke's seat in Wiltshire. In 1633 Pembroke decided to build a new garden front, with, in the words of the antiquary John Aubrey, 'two stately pavilions at each end, all *al Italiano*'.[42] Pembroke wanted Jones to design it, but he was too busy with other projects, and so he recommended the French architect Isaac de Caus, who had assisted Jones with the design of St Paul's Church in Covent Garden. Jones, however, maintained a supervisory role and may have produced the 'grand design' for the house and garden.[43] In addition, a significant number of houses were influenced by Jones's ideas, although he did not design them himself. The chart overleaf shows that Jones-influenced houses began appearing in the 1620s and peaked in the 1650s.

Jones believed that classicism was an indigenous English style. To make his case, he looked to early medieval chroniclers like Geoffrey of Monmouth, who claimed that Britain had been founded by Brutus, grandson of Aeneas of Troy, thereby linking national history and classical antiquity.[44] Jones asserted that Stonehenge – because its geometry was based on four equilateral triangles – must be from the Roman era, and argued that it had been built as a model to demonstrate to ancient

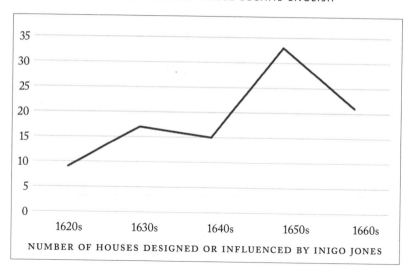

NUMBER OF HOUSES DESIGNED OR INFLUENCED BY INIGO JONES

Britons the superiority of Roman building methods. If Stonehenge was Roman, then classicism was as native to England as it was to Italy.[45]

If Jones had pursued his agenda in a different political environment, it might have succeeded, for an English classicism did emerge later in the form of the neo-Palladian style of the eighteenth century. But in the short term, political events intruded. From the 1640s onwards, Jones faced hostility from Puritans, who saw his work as tainted by popery and absolutism. After they removed the statues of James I and Charles I from the west front of St Paul's Cathedral, Puritans 'hewed and defaced' the Corinthian columns of Jones's classical portico from the 1630s.[46] In 1650 the regicide Colonel John Okey tore down the buildings that Jones had installed at Newmarket to accommodate the King and Prince of Wales during the racing season. The Queen's Chapel at St James's Palace and the chapel Jones had built at Somerset House in the early 1630s were also damaged, confirming that Jonesian classicism was viewed by many Puritans as foreign and popish.

In 1649 Charles I faced the executioner's axe on a scaffold erected outside the windows of the Banqueting House, an architectural irony that Jones doubtless noted. But by then he had plenty of troubles of his own: Parliament had dismissed him from his post as the King's Surveyor six years earlier, after he accompanied Charles I to Yorkshire to assist in building fortifications for the siege of Hull. In 1645 he was captured at the siege of Basing Castle; his captors sniggered that 'he was carried away in a blanket, having lost his cloaths'.[47] Unlike his king, Jones escaped with his life, but his estates were sequestered. (Parliament eventually settled for a £1,000 fine.) By the time of his death in 1652 his influence had waned.[48] Jones had, however, managed to introduce 'a normative idea of the classical against the more fluid use of the style by other English architects'.[49] For the first time since the Reformation, the emphasis was on similarity with and not difference from European culture. After Jones, the classical could no longer simply be rejected as 'foreign' or juxtaposed against a 'native' gothic. There would be no comprehensive return to the gothic as an indigenous English style while the rest of Europe continued to develop the classical; Christopher Wren, for example, denigrated the Goths as 'rather Destroyers than Builders'.[50]

This did not mean, however, that English classicism continued to imitate continental precedent. During the Interregnum and the Restoration, the Palladianism of the Stuart court was rejected in favour of a more minimalist and restrained style. The country houses that it produced were square blocks or shallow E-shapes, with regular fenestration, symmetrical fronts and limited ornamentation. These outwardly simple houses conveyed a powerful political message: they were the physical embodiments of a new English patriotism based on resistance to overmighty royal authority, reflected in an avoidance of ostentatious display. For the first time, English builders were attempting to create a classicism of their own instead of copying it from the continent.[51] These houses were the descendants of the simple double-pile houses such as Chevening and Coleshill which Jones and his followers had pioneered. They first appeared in the 1660s and then peaked in number between 1690 and

NUMBER OF COMPACT CLASSICAL RESTORATION HOUSES

Depicted in an 18th-century engraving, Coleshill House (1649) in Berkshire was the model for the type of compact classical house that became fashionable in England after the Restoration.

1710. Houses of this type show that continental classicism had become sufficiently established in England to produce a reaction against it, which allowed the possibility of an *English* classicism as an alternative.[52] Their simplicity and restraint differed greatly from what was happening on the continent. From this point onwards, although classicism became the dominant style, England's architectural path diverged from that of its European neighbours.

Vanbrugh and the Baroque

The arrival of the Baroque style in England has always seemed a brief interruption of the progression from Jonesian to eighteenth-century neo-Palladianism, as it appears antithetical to the cultural imperatives which led to the development of an English classical style. The Baroque's elevation of drama above restraint and of flamboyance above simplicity is a massive leap from the simple, compact classical houses of the late seventeenth century. It is therefore tempting to dismiss it as an 'un-English' diversion before the arrival of neo-Palladianism after 1720, but it is more accurate to view the Baroque as complementing the minimalist classicism which had evolved as a reaction to Stuart excess, and as another way in which English country-house owners attempted to display their political beliefs and social aspirations through architecture. With Stuart claimants still lurking and the balance of power between king and Parliament still being negotiated, the future of English governance was far from settled in the aftermath of the Glorious Revolution. It is therefore not surprising that country-house architecture wavered between different styles.

Given lingering discomfort with the more extravagant modes of Stuart classicism, it is also not surprising that the Baroque was first seen on the interior of English country houses. In the 1670s, beginning with Hugh May's redecoration of the state apartments at Windsor Castle (1674), elaborate Baroque paintings on the walls and ceilings of important rooms became fashionable, with the Italian painter Antonio Verrio, the Frenchman Louis Laguerre and the Englishman James Thornhill becoming the most sought-after artists.[53] In some ways, their works reveal a tepid English commitment to the Baroque, as their paintings were cheaper substitutes for three-dimensional decorative interiors.[54]

The Baroque was therefore seen as problematic in an English political and cultural context, and accordingly its moment in England would be short in duration and limited in scope.[55] Even so, it produced more than 330 country houses from the 1670s to the 1750s. Although we typically associate the Baroque with the decades immediately before and after 1700, in fact it peaked in the 1720s, but fell off sharply thereafter. Even Sir John Vanbrugh, the English architect most closely associated with the Baroque, ultimately found it too limiting. His first country house, Castle Howard (1699), was almost exclusively continental in inspiration, with references to French buildings such as Vaux-le-Vicomte (1658) and the Château de Marly (1679).[56]

Later, however, Vanbrugh began to draw inspiration from English medieval and Elizabethan buildings. He was fascinated by the 'form and massing' of Elizabethan buildings, in particular their dynamic skylines pierced by towers, domes and pinnacles, a far cry from the flat or hipped rooflines of classical houses.[57] To be sure, many of the design elements of Blenheim Palace (1705), such as the four open towers on the roof, were derived from continental classical sources, but its 55-metre-long (180 ft) 'great gallery' echoed an Elizabethan long gallery, while the bow windows

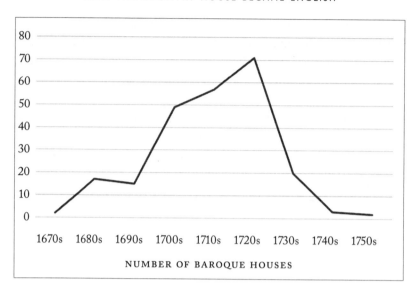

NUMBER OF BAROQUE HOUSES

on the east and west fronts resembled those of Burghley House.[58] Hardwick Hall may have inspired the square corner pavilions at Eastbury Park (1718) in Dorset, though it was Wollaton Hall, another Smythson house, which provided a prototype for the clerestory hall in Vanbrugh's original design.[59] Eastbury's clerestory was never built, but another of Vanbrugh's houses, Seaton Delaval (1718) in Northumberland, had one, and Blenheim's hall was lit by clerestory windows.[60]

Vanbrugh was fascinated by not only Elizabethan but medieval architecture. His houses frequently used medieval forms such as battlements, turrets and towers, and he liked to surround his landscape gardens with walls and bastions.[61] The house that Vanbrugh built for himself at Chargate (1708) in Surrey was castellated, and his later house in Greenwich (1718) was a compact brick imitation of a castle with two crenellated towers on the corners of the facade and a central round tower with a conical cap. King's Weston House (1712) in Somerset was classical in style, but it had an unusual castellated arcade on the roof that resembled a medieval fortification when seen from a distance. Though it too was outwardly classical, Grimsthorpe Castle (1723) in Lincolnshire copies in its basic form a late medieval quadrilateral castle, with Bolton or Wressle in nearby Yorkshire its possible inspirations.

Vanbrugh's approach to medieval architecture is best seen, however, at Kimbolton Castle in Cambridgeshire, which he redesigned for the Earl of Manchester between 1707 and 1710. There he juxtaposed a plain classical facade against an embattled parapet. In a letter to Manchester

Sir John Vanbrugh's Castle Howard, North Yorkshire (1699); and Vaux-le-Vicomte (1658) in the Seine-et-Marne, probably one of Vanbrugh's models.

in July 1707, he acknowledged the tension between the two styles, and gave his reasons for combining them:

> As to the Outside, I thought 'twas absolutely best, to give it Something of a Castle Air, tho' at the Same time to make it regular ... So I hope your L^{d}ship won't be discourag'd, if any Italians you may Shew it to, shou'd find fault that 'tis not Roman, for to have built a Front with Pillasters, and what the Orders require cou'd never have been born with the Rest of the Castle: I'm sure this will make a very Noble and Masculine Shew; and is of as Warrantable a kind of building as Any.[62]

Vanbrugh took a similar approach to his alterations to Lumley Castle in County Durham for his friend Richard Lumley, Earl of Scarborough, in the early 1720s. He preserved the late fourteenth-century castle's outline and crenellated corner towers, but the south elevation was brought up-to-date with sash windows, and the interior was fitted with grand living spaces divided by *serliana* (or 'Venetian screens') inspired by Palladio.[63]

At the end of his career Vanbrugh combined classical, medieval and Elizabethan elements in his ambitious design for Seaton Delaval Hall.

Kimbolton Castle (1707) in Cambridgeshire, an example of Vanbrugh's use of medieval forms and design elements, from W. H. Bernard Saunders, *Legends and Traditions of Huntingdonshire* (1888).

The house's plan was derived from Palladio, but its massing evokes a late medieval castle or an Elizabethan house. Jeremy Musson writes:

> Though on first glance one sees it as a classical villa between symmetrically disposed long wings, its composition and particularly the effect of the stair turrets at either side and the half-octagonal bays have long inspired architectural historians to read references to medieval, Tudor and Jacobean [buildings], such as Wollaton or Bolsover Castle.[64]

Why did Vanbrugh combine these references in this way? Giles Worsley argues that it was because he was

> making a deliberate attempt to create a national style, a new self-consciously English architecture ... This ambition was to be achieved by marrying the forms of the last great period of English architecture, the prodigy houses of the Elizabethans and the Jacobeans, with their overtones of Elizabethan greatness, with up-to-date classical detail.[65]

With his references to medieval and Elizabethan precedent, Vanbrugh sought particularity of time and place, thereby making the case that the Baroque needed to be 'nationalized' by incorporating elements from England's past. English architecture could now move into its next phase, during which the classical would be developed into a national style.

Neo-Palladianism and Neoclassicism

The emergence of neo-Palladianism is often interpreted as a Whig response to the 3rd Earl of Shaftesbury's call for an English national style in his *Letter concerning the Art or Science of Design* (1712). Shaftesbury's essay, however, reached only a small audience before the mid-1730s, and so was unlikely to have been the impetus behind an architectural style which had appeared more than a decade earlier.[66] An alternative explanation, put forward by Barbara Arciszewska, is that Palladianism was brought to England by King George I, who, while in Hanover, had sought an alternative to the Baroque because it was favoured by German Catholic princes and the French. After the Glorious Revolution, 'the House of Hanover needed to present itself publicly as a champion of the Protestant cause' in order to ensure its accession to the English throne.[67] Although their views regarding the origin of English Palladianism differ, both these interpretations endorse the idea that Palladianism emerged from a political context in which England was attempting to present itself as a rising Protestant power in the early eighteenth century.

Houghton Hall (1722) in Norfolk fits this image. It was built by Sir Robert Walpole, who had consolidated so much political power in his hands that he is now regarded as England's first Prime Minister. In the early 1720s Walpole commissioned first James Gibbs and then Colen Campbell to design his new house, and entrusted the interiors to William Kent. The result was a celebration of England's growing power and Walpole's position as its leader. On the east front the sculptor John Michael Rysbrack installed figures of Britannia and Neptune, symbolizing the nation's expanding maritime reach. On the west front, figures of Demosthenes, the defender of liberty; Minerva, the goddess of wisdom; and Justice topped the pediment, proclaiming that England was in good political hands. Inside, the Stone Hall reiterated this point: over the chimneypiece was a bust of Walpole himself, again by Rysbrack and depicting him in a toga and wearing the star of the Order of the Garter. These features combined to make a national, and nationalist, argument which was intended to emphasize England's distinctiveness from and superiority over its European rivals. By pointing to England's maritime prowess, Houghton drew a contrast with France's land-based power, while also highlighting England's balanced political system in which Parliament and Cabinet government superseded royal authority, in contrast to France's absolute monarchy. This message culminated in the ceiling of the saloon, where a painting of Apollo driving his chariot across the sky referred to how England had surpassed the 'Sun King' Louis XIV's France in the years since his death in 1715.

The fact that Walpole felt a need to stake his claim in relative rather than absolute terms, however, shows that the European standard remained essential for the measurement of England's power. Elizabeth Angelicoussis writes that 'Walpole was anxious to present himself as a discriminating connoisseur with classically-orientated cultural values – the sort of gentleman who had benefited from a Grand Tour ... in spite of the fact he entered into political life so early that he never had an opportunity to venture abroad.'[68] It was possibly *because* of this perceived self-deficiency that Walpole was so eager to display his collection of Continental art. With its busts of figures from Roman antiquity, the Stone Hall was

Houghton Hall (1722) in Norfolk, the most famous example of Whig Palladianism.

intended to serve as 'a Vitruvian atrium, echoing the domestic ancestor shrines where ancient Romans exhibited wax images to illustrate their families' distinguished history'.[69] Walpole brazenly placed his own image among them, sending a message few contemporaries would have missed:

> The classical mien of Walpole's portrait and its deliberate juxtaposition with the wise and heroic visages of the ancients are a statement of doctrine: that Sir Robert has inherited and maintains the ancient values of political liberty and civic virtue here and now in the 'New Rome' of England's realm. Walpole boldly proclaims that, during his leadership, he had acted according to ancient, honourable political and civic codes whose validity sprang from antiquity and would last for all time ... For Walpole it was not enough merely to be compared with the best thinkers and heroes of classical times. By taking centre stage on the mantelpiece and literally rising above the level of the 'ancient worthies' on their consoles and terms, Sir Robert takes command of the Roman host.[70]

Outside, Campbell's plans had called for four square, pedimented pavilion towers on the corners, in accordance with Palladian convention, but Gibbs's idea of having four domes instead prevailed. The domes were a

Baroque feature, and so echoed the interior in placing Houghton more in a European context.[71] Walpole intended not to make a statement that England's greatness depended upon its separation and distinctiveness from continental Europe, but rather that its power was in relation to, and over, its European rivals.

AS ENGLAND EVOLVED into the dominant European power, it came to see itself as sharing a European heritage which included classical culture. Not being part of this heritage would mean that England was culturally inferior; the absence of a classical patrimony was, as Christy Anderson writes, an 'essential cultural failing, as if English art had to make up for, or catch up with, the development of art on the continent'.[72] As Houghton shows, the English elite was now sufficiently confident to mould continental models into forms which they could claim as their own, rather than needing to emphasize their distinctiveness. Neo-Palladianism fulfilled this purpose, by presenting a Protestant vision of national glory based on constitutional monarchy, global commerce and naval might, and culturally on a sense of restraint which contrasted with the grandiosity of Catholic cultures.[73]

The publication of the first volume of Colen Campbell's *Vitruvius Britannicus* in 1715 is generally seen as marking the return of Palladian influence to England, even though Campbell was a Scot. He expressed frustration with the readiness to accept the superiority of European continental architecture:

> The general Esteem that Travellers have for things that are Foreign, is in nothing more conspicuous than with Regard to Building. We travel, for the most part, at an Age more apt to be imposed upon by Ignorance or Partiality of others, than to judge truly of the Merit of Things by the Strength of Reason. It's owing to this Mistake in Education, that so many of the British Quality have so mean an Opinion of what is performed in our own Country; tho', perhaps, in most we equal, and in some Things we surpass, our Neighbours.

This was a tricky way to make a case for the classical style, but Campbell squared the circle by insisting that, although classicism had been worthy of great admiration from ancient times to the Renaissance, it had become 'affected and licentious' in the hands of seventeenth-century Italian artists like Bernini and Boromini. Inigo Jones, however, had saved it by combining the order and regularity of Palladio with 'an Addition of Beauty and Majesty'.[74] Present-day English classicism had therefore not originated from continental Europe, but rather had been invented by Jones a century earlier.[75]

In this context, neo-Palladianism became, in the words of Robert Fermor-Hesketh, 'England's answer to the architecture of Catholic Europe – and Baroque Catholic Europe in particular. It makes statements about prosperity, self-confidence and fundamental beliefs that transcend mere architectural detail.'[76] The English advocates of the neo-Palladian were conscious of a need to produce architecture which could be seen as national rather than a slavish imitation of foreign models.[77] Chiswick House (1729), Lord Burlington's villa in southwest London, was 'far removed from anything Italian', altered 'almost beyond recognition' from Palladio's Villa Rotonda, its supposed inspiration.[78]

By 1730 neo-Palladianism was the dominant architectural style in England, and there was a rapid increase in the number of neo-Palladian houses until the 1750s. Landowners felt pressure to convert their houses to the new style. When the 2nd Earl of Strafford died without direct heir in 1695, he left his estates, including Wentworth Woodhouse in South Yorkshire, to his wife's nephew Thomas Watson. This set off a race between rival branches of the family to build the most splendid house. Embittered by being denied what he felt was his rightful inheritance, Thomas Wentworth, Baron Raby, whose paternal grandfather had been the 1st Earl of Strafford, acquired nearby Stainborough House in 1708 and began rebuilding it three years later. His purpose, as Raby wrote to his brother, was to 'make his Great Honour [Watson] burst with envy'.[79]

Not to be outdone, Watson's son Thomas Watson-Wentworth, later Baron Malton and 1st Marquess of Rockingham, embarked upon the building of a new house at Wentworth Woodhouse in 1725. The west front, probably designed by the York architect William Thornton, copied Stainborough's Baroque style.[80] By the mid-1730s, however, the Baroque had come to be associated with Toryism and was declining in popularity. As a Whig with political ambitions, Watson-Wentworth commissioned Henry Flitcroft to design a massive new neo-Palladian east front stretching 185 metres (606 ft) from one wing to the other, the longest facade in England. 'The contrasting styles of Wentworth Woodhouse...', writes Dylan Wayne Spivey, 'reflect not only the rising tide of Palladianism in

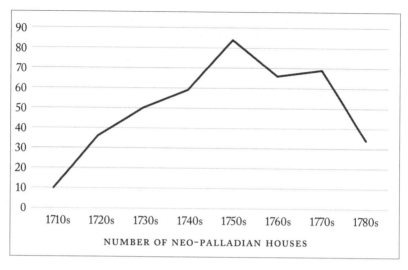

NUMBER OF NEO-PALLADIAN HOUSES

England but echo the shifting motivations of its construction, from the personal to the political.'[81]

Another example of the transition from Baroque to neo-Palladian is Shardeloes in Buckinghamshire. In the 1720s Montague Garrard Drake commissioned Giacomo Leoni to rebuild the undistinguished manor house, presumably in Leoni's preferred Baroque style. The plans were sufficiently advanced that in March 1728 Leoni submitted a bill for £45 – a not insubstantial sum at the time – 'for going to Shardeloes to directe the workmen for to begin to build the new house'.[82] A month later, however, Drake died of gout at the age of thirty-six, leaving his five-year-old son William as his heir. In the 1740s William Drake, fancying himself an amateur architect, revived his father's plan to rebuild and produced sketches of more than thirty different floor plans.[83] In 1748 he estimated that the new house would cost £2,919.[84] It was another ten years, however, before the project started, by which time the cost had escalated significantly. In 1758 the architect Stiff Leadbetter was commissioned to design an 'Additional Building' at Shardeloes, at a cost of £4,300. The Baroque was by now out of fashion, and so Leadbetter's design was in the neo-Palladian style.[85] Robert Adam, newly arrived from Edinburgh and so unknown in England that Leadbetter referred to him as 'Mr Adams', was hired to decorate the interiors.[86] The work dragged on: in February 1761, Leadbetter wrote to Drake that

> it gives me great concern that the multiplicity of my engagements (which now draw to a conclusion) has given you reason

to complain of my neglecting your business, but beg leave to assure you that every thing in my power shall be done to expedite your works pursuant to your desires; I hope when completed I shall have the honor of giving you satisfaction.[87]

Despite these reassurances, Shardeloes was still unfinished at the time of Leadbetter's death in 1766. And the cost continued to rise: Leadbetter's final bill, which was submitted to Drake by his executors in 1768, totalled £22,767.[88] By that point William Drake had spent almost ten times the original estimate in order to ensure that his house was in the fashionable neo-Palladian style.

Although Palladianism pointed towards a nationalist future for English country-house architecture, admiration for and exchange with continental culture persisted, as the Grand Tour continued to be seen as essential to a young upper-class man's education.[89] There were three ways in which country houses felt the Grand Tour's impact. First, they served as places where the art and artefacts their owners acquired could be displayed. This category was so broad that most country houses in the eighteenth century could be included within it. Second, houses were altered or expanded in order to house Grand Tour treasures. William Holbech of Farnborough Hall in Warwickshire travelled extensively in Italy in the 1730s and acquired a number of works of art, including three paintings by Panini and two by Canaletto, as well as a number of antique and contemporary busts.[90] After returning home in the 1740s, Holbech installed ornate Rococo plasterwork in the hall and drawing room and on the staircase, in order to transform Farnborough into a copy of 'the houses he had seen and loved in Italy'.[91]

William Windham II of Felbrigg House in Norfolk went on his Grand Tour from 1738 to 1741. In Geneva he joined a group of English tourists who called themselves the 'Common Room'; they spent their days climbing glaciers near Chamonix and their nights performing amateur theatricals. In Italy he commissioned a series of views of Roman ruins and bought French and Italian Old Master paintings. He must have stopped in Vienna as well, because a full-length portrait of him in the uniform of a Hungarian hussar now hangs in Felbrigg's stair hall. Upon his return, he turned to James Paine to improve Felbrigg with the addition of a bay window to a room at the north end of the west wing, in order to create a 'cabinet' where he could display his smaller Grand Tour treasures, including 26 gouache views of Rome by Giovanni Battista Busiri. His larger acquisitions were displayed in the drawing room.[92]

Petworth House in Sussex was altered several times to accommodate Grand Tour treasures. In the 1750s the 2nd Earl of Egremont transformed an external cloister into a corridor in order to display the collection of antique statuary he had acquired on his Grand Tour three decades earlier. His son, the 3rd Earl, added a second corridor and then built the North Gallery in order to display his own collection of Neoclassical sculpture.[93] Sir Matthew Fetherstonhaugh had already commissioned James Paine to make alterations to Uppark in Sussex when in 1748 he departed on a two-year trip to Italy, where he acquired paintings by Pompeo Batoni, Joseph Vernet and Antonio Canaletto. On his return, he directed Paine to incorporate his acquisitions into his designs. In the saloon, fixed plaster frames were installed to hold two paintings illustrating the biblical story of the Prodigal Son by Luca Giordano.[94] In 1769, at the same time as he was making alterations to Burton Constable in Yorkshire, William Constable travelled to Italy, where he acquired objects and ideas for the house. Once he was back home, he commissioned copies of paintings by Guido Reni and Titian which still hang at the bottom of the staircase.[95]

The third way in which the Grand Tour influenced country houses was when the house itself was built or rebuilt to reflect the knowledge

Farnborough Hall (1745) in Warwickshire, where William Holbech displayed his Grand Tour treasures.

The Grand Tour 'Cabinet' installed by William Windham II at Felbrigg Hall in Norfolk. Windham commissioned James Paine to design the room after his return from the Continent in 1741.

that the owner had gleaned on his travels. Thomas Coke embarked on the Grand Tour when he was fifteen and spent six years on the continent, most of it in Italy. He decided to rebuild his house at Holkham on the north Norfolk coast according to Palladio's principles. William Kent, whom Coke had met while he was in Italy, produced drawings for the new house and Lord Burlington was consulted as well, but the commission ultimately went to Matthew Brettingham, perhaps because he was from nearby Norwich. Coke lost large sums in the South Sea Bubble of 1720, however, and so work did not begin until 1734. Kent's design was based on Palladio's unbuilt Villa Mocenigo, while the interior contained elements from buildings that Coke had seen on his Grand Tour. The domed Marble Hall into which guests entered was modelled on a Roman basilica, with a coffered ceiling copied from the Pantheon and a colonnade copied from the Temple of Fortuna Virilis.[96] The Statue Gallery housed Coke's vast collection of Roman statuary, while Roman busts were scattered throughout the house. Twenty-two Old Master paintings were displayed in the Landscape Room specially created to house them.

Holkham is exceptional in the size and quality of its collection and the splendour of the interiors created to house it, but it is far from the only house whose design was influenced by the Grand Tour. When Sir Andrew Fountaine, a member of Lord Burlington's circle, returned from the Grand Tour in 1716, he remodelled a courtyard of Narford Hall in Norfolk in imitation of Colen Campbell's Wanstead House, one of the first neo-Palladian houses in England.[97] The 2nd Duke of Richmond went on the Grand Tour from 1719 to 1722. When he inherited the Goodwood estate in Sussex the year after his return, he was eager to put what he had seen into practice. He commissioned Colen Campbell to design a new Palladian house, but the plans, apart from a detached kitchen, were never executed, probably because Richmond had also inherited a substantial debt. He was forced to be content with acquiring paintings by Italian artists such as Canaletto and Antonio Joli instead.[98]

Between 1726 and 1741 Sir Francis Dashwood took several trips to the continent including, unusually, visits to the Ottoman Empire, and behaved so badly that he was banned from the Papal States. In 1732 he founded the Society of Dilettanti, a group of around fifty young men who had recently gone on the Grand Tour. Horace Walpole described the Dilettanti in 1743 as 'a club, for which the nominal qualification is having been in Italy, and the real one being drunk'.[99] But Dashwood had a more serious side, and his estate at West Wycombe in Buckinghamshire became, as Jason Kelly writes, 'a laboratory to experiment with constantly evolving aesthetic ideas'.[100] Beginning in the 1730s, the exterior of the house became a catalogue of references to buildings he had seen on his travels: the ruined Temple of Dionysos at Teos in Turkey, conjecturally reconstructed by Dilettanti members Richard Chandler and Nicholas Revett in *Antiquities of Ionia* (1769), was the source for the west end of the house, and Palladio's Villa Rotunda for the east. The principal (south) facade was based on the Church of St Sulpice in Paris and Palladio's Palazzo Chiericati, Vicenza. Over the next half-century he filled the house 'with references to the classical and Renaissance worlds, ensuring that the interior was richly infused with quotations, references to and representations of the Grand Tour'.[101] In 1766 William Weddell brought back nineteen chests of classical statues from Italy and commissioned John Carr to add two wings to Newby Hall in Yorkshire to make room for them. Later, Robert Adam was retained to insert a statue gallery into the south wing; the design, which featured a central rotunda flanked by two square rooms, was inspired by Hadrian's Villa at Tivoli.[102]

Some ambitious plans for Grand Tour houses were never completed. After inheriting Garendon in Leicestershire in 1729, Ambrose Phillipps set off on a Grand Tour of France and Italy. After joining the Society of Dilettanti on his return, he designed a Neoclassical arch, temple and obelisk for Garendon's park and drew up a neo-Palladian plan to rebuild the house. Phillipps died in 1737 before the plan could be executed, however, and his brother William built only the south range.[103] Another planned Grand Tour house that was reduced in size because of the early death of its owner was Mersham Hatch in Kent. In the early 1760s Sir Wyndham Knatchbull Wyndham commissioned Robert Adam to design a neo-Palladian house inspired by his travels on the continent, but it was unfinished at the time of his death in 1763. His uncle Edward Wyndham completed it, but its simplicity suggests that he ordered Adam to reduce costs.[104]

The most dramatic example of the influence of the Grand Tour upon an English country house was at Ickworth in Suffolk, designed by the Italian architect Antonio Asprucci for Frederick Augustus Hervey, 4th Earl of Bristol, in 1795.[105] The design was strikingly original, if impractical, comprising a domed central rotunda housing the living quarters and curving wings on each side for the large collection of paintings and sculpture he had acquired on his Grand Tour and on several other visits to Italy, which occupied eighteen years of his life in total. Bristol had

Ickworth (1795) in Suffolk was designed to be more Grand Tour gallery than home.

earlier built a smaller version of the house, which drew inspiration from the Pantheon in Rome and Palladio's Villa Rotonda, on his Ballyscullion estate on the north Antrim coast of Ireland.[106] Neither Ballyscullion nor Ickworth ever fulfilled their purpose, however, because Bristol's collection was seized by the French revolutionary army before it could leave Italy and sold at auction. His son, the 5th Earl, finished Ickworth in 1829, but he converted the space in the rotunda to rooms for entertaining guests and moved the living space to the east wing. The west wing, which was not built until the mid-1840s, was an unfinished shell which existed only to balance the composition.[107] More than any other English country house, Ickworth was intended to show off its owner's knowledge and appreciation of continental art and architecture and not to serve as a comfortable home.

The Search for an English (Historical) Style

The prominence of the Grand Tour in country houses showed that the debate between English and continental influences that had been ongoing since the second half of the sixteenth century continued well into the eighteenth. In the late eighteenth and early nineteenth centuries, the debate between classicism and the gothic continued as well. After the reaction to the French Revolution accelerated the revival of gothic architecture, it entered a new phase which moved away from precise historical points of reference. It now looked to an idealized English past, which William Hazlitt in a popular essay of 1819 called 'Merry England', and which has been labelled more recently by Peter Mandler the 'Olden Time':

> the Olden Time became the Victorians' common heritage, the past in which the whole nation saw itself. The appeal of the Olden Time was various and complex. It benefited from being neither medieval nor modern, neither barbaric nor over-refined, neither too distant nor too recent. Victorian popular writers were very clear about the Olden Time's positive qualities. Prominent among them was the vision of social connection, of nascent nationhood, that it conveyed.[108]

A key text was Joseph Nash's *Mansions of England in the Olden Time* (1839), which presented houses from the Middle Ages to the seventeenth century as Nash imagined them to have been in their own time, 'enlivened with the presence of their inmates and guests, enjoying the recreations and pastimes, or celebrating the festivals, of our ancestors'.[109]

The influence of the 'Olden Time' was also apparent in new country houses, with some of the earliest examples of the Jacobethan revival represented by Barningham Hall (1805) in Norfolk and Endsleigh House (1810) in Devon. At the same time, survivals such as Little Moreton Hall (mid-sixteenth century) in Cheshire and Haddon Hall (oldest parts eleventh century) in Derbyshire were transformed from decrepit relics to national treasures. The subject of romantic veneration in the mid-nineteenth century, Little Moreton would serve by century's end as the inspiration for vernacular revival houses such as Hill Bark on the Wirral and Wightwick Manor in Staffordshire. Haddon was the medieval home of the Manners family, but after the 9th Earl of Rutland was elevated to a dukedom in 1703, he moved his seat to Belvoir Castle in Leicestershire. By the nineteenth century Haddon was a rare surviving example of a medieval manor house. In 1846 the socialite and author Catherine Ball, who adopted the title 'Baroness de Calabrella' after acquiring property in southern Italy, edited a collection of stories entitled *Evenings at Haddon Hall*, which began:

An illustration of the Great Hall of Littlecote House (1590) in Wiltshire from Joseph Nash's *Mansions of England in the Olden Time* (1839).

In the most singular and romantic, and withal the most beautiful, of the divisions of our all-beautiful England – the district of the Peak – is situated one of the noblest of the architectural relics of the times of Chivalry and Romance, which any country, even England itself, can boast – a relic that is preserved by its owners with as pious care, and made the object of as many pilgrimages of admiring interest, as the shrines of saints are wont to be, in countries where saints were needed to supply the place of those social virtues of which the 'merry England' of the olden time was the chosen home.[110]

As this passage suggests, Haddon became a favourite subject of Victorian artists, novelists and even of comic opera, when Arthur Sullivan and Sydney Grundy dramatized in *Haddon Hall* (1892) the house's most famous legend, the sixteenth-century elopement of Dorothy Vernon with John Manners, son of the 1st Earl of Rutland.[111]

Some houses were subjected to aggressive and often anachronistic campaigns to strip out later accretions and return them to their 'original' state so as to fit romantic ideals of the 'Olden Time'. Montacute House (1598) in Somerset is often regarded as one of the finest surviving examples of an Elizabethan prodigy house, but in fact it was continually remade to fit the contemporary vision of late Tudor architecture. Dating from half a century earlier than Montacute, the west front was moved from Clifton Maybank in Dorset in 1786. The Victorians were even more aggressive in their ideas of what Montacute should look like. In the mid-nineteenth century Sir William Phelips 'commissioned an ambitious architectural scheme which would have made Montacute into a wild Victorian parody of an Elizabethan house', though fortunately his gambling debts prevented him from realizing it. Similarly, Charlecote Park in Warwickshire seems little changed from when it was built in the 1550s, but in fact:

> George Hammond Lucy and his wife Mary Elizabeth had a romantic vision of Merrie England in the reign of 'Good Queen Bess', and they wanted to make Charlecote conform to it. So between 1829 and 1865 they refitted the main rooms in the Elizabethan Revival style ... They filled their new rooms with heraldic stained glass, early editions of Shakespeare and ebony furniture (which was then thought to be Tudor).[112]

Not every landowner, however, had an old house suitable for restoration, leaving a choice of converting the existing house to the gothic or 'Jacobethan' style or building an entirely new one. Or the owner could

This mid-19th-century aquatint of Haddon Hall shows how its medieval character was romanticized in the Victorian era.

This watercolour by John Buckler from 1811 shows the west front of Montacute House in Somerset, which was moved from Clifton Maybank in Dorset in 1786.

do both, as was the case with Huntsham Court in Devon. In 1852 Huntsham's owner, the Reverend Edward Troyte, died childless, but instead of leaving his estate to another member of his family, he left it in trust for Arthur Henry Dyke Acland, a relative of his mother Lady Cecily Acland, whose wealth had been used to purchase Huntsham. As a condition of his inheritance, Arthur Acland was required to take the surname 'Troyte' and to reside at Huntsham for six months a year. When he first saw his new estate, he was appalled: the land was boggy and overgrown, and the Elizabethan house was crumbling. There was little money to carry out improvements because the Reverend Troyte had left the bulk of his fortune to other relatives. In February 1857 Arthur wrote to his father Sir Thomas Dyke Acland to report that he and his wife Frances had 'prayed together' for the 'right judgment'. At first they decided to carry out repairs which would 'cost about ¼ of a new house'. Arthur told Sir Thomas that 'I have but one anxiety which is to do the least possible and do that little so as to take away the necessity of our children being [saddled with] an expenditure of which they might not see the end.'[113]

Arthur's biggest fear was that he would start a major rebuilding project and then die before it was complete, leaving his eldest son Charles with a massive financial burden. The letter to his father is full of premonitions of his death; he says at one point that the repair plans have been 'all on paper for 2 or 3 years ... though I may not live to do it'.[114] He was right to worry: four months later he died of diphtheria at the age of forty-six, leaving Huntsham to his son Charles, then aged fifteen. In 1863 Charles married Katherine Walrond, whose family demanded that the still-decrepit house be pulled down and rebuilt. Before construction could begin, an Act of Parliament was required to obtain permission from the trustees for the new house to be built. Passed in 1866, the Act described the existing house as 'an old Structure', which was 'originally ill and inconveniently constructed, and the Back Part thereof ... now unfit for Habitation, and the Front and habitable Portion ... insufficient for the Requirements of the Family of the resident Owner of the said Estates'.[115] It permitted a maximum expenditure of £10,000, but the following year the tenders from contractors put the price of the new house at between £10,764 and £13,000.[116] The architect, Benjamin Ferrey, acknowledged that they would need to 'modify the plans a little in order to bring the work within the prescribed amounts'. Even so, after building had started costs soon exceeded the original estimates and further reductions were required, including 'the abandonment of the Entrance Tower', which Ferrey deeply regretted, 'as that *really* forms a conspicuous feature of the house, as it wants some large object towering a little above the rest of the building'.[117] The reduced version of Huntsham was completed in 1870.

Huntsham was far from a solitary example. Between 1820 and 1920, more than three hundred gothic-style houses were built in England and

Huntsham Court, Devon, an Elizabethan house which was rebuilt by Benjamin Ferrey in the late 1860s.

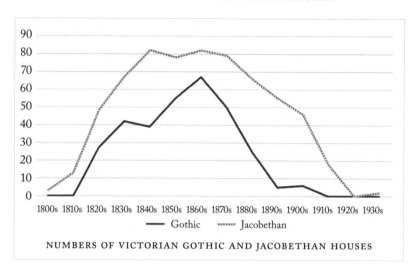

NUMBERS OF VICTORIAN GOTHIC AND JACOBETHAN HOUSES

over 670 Jacobethan ones.[118] The desire to incorporate 'authentic' medieval or Elizabethan architectural details could produce comical moments. In 1856, while he was rebuilding Taplow Court in Buckinghamshire in the Tudor style, William Burn wrote to the house's owner, the railway magnate Charles Pascoe Grenfell:

> I am quite aware of the character of the intended griffins, and that they might look like something else, but the fact is, it is impossible to make them simply heraldic, and secure them on the pinnacles of the gables, where strength as well as a solid mass of material is required ... On the pinnacles they can only be regarded as architectural decorations, or a sort of conventional animal, approximately as nearly as possible to the real one (if there has been such a beast).[119]

To be sure, many Victorian country houses continued to be built in the classical style or in its updated form, the Italianate. Italian influence had been felt in England for so long by this point that it was not truly considered a foreign intrusion. But the growing rejection of styles that *were* perceived as foreign can be seen in the reaction to the brief fashion for French-inspired houses in the middle decades of the nineteenth century. Between the 1840s and 1880s more than fifty houses were built in French styles from various eras, with a peak in the 1870s. There was reluctance, however, to describe such buildings as 'French'. The Second-Empire house depicted in Robert Kerr's influential *The Gentleman's*

House (1864), for example, was captioned 'English Renaissance'.[120] Such evasions were not only the result of Francophobia, but of snobbery stemming from the fact that the French style was favoured by parvenu owners rather than traditional landed magnates.[121]

These negative attitudes were clearly seen in the response to the three French-style houses – Tring, Waddesdon and Halton – built or redecorated by the Rothschild family in the Vale of Aylesbury in Buckinghamshire in the late nineteenth century. Waddesdon (1874) imitated the French chateaux of the Loire Valley: the round corner tower was copied from the Château de Maintenon and the staircase tower from the Château de Chambord. For the interior, Baron Ferdinand de Rothschild imported 385 *boiseries* (wood panels) and other furnishings from town houses (*hôtels particuliers*) demolished during Baron Haussmann's rebuilding of Paris between 1853 and 1870.[122] The result was not to everyone's taste: the phrase '*le goût Rothschild*', which came to be used after 1900, was not a compliment. After visiting Waddesdon in 1885, William Gladstone's daughter Mary complained that she 'felt much oppressed with the extreme gorgeousness and luxury': 'The pictures in [the Baron's] sitting room are too beautiful, but there is not a book in the house save twenty improper French novels.'[123] Sir Edward Hamilton grumbled about Alfred Freiherr de Rothschild's Halton that 'the decorations are sadly overdone and one's eye longs to rest on something which is not all gilt and gold.'[124] The socialite Lady Frances Balfour, daughter of the Duke of Argyll, felt much the same: 'I have never seen anything more terribly vulgar ... Oh

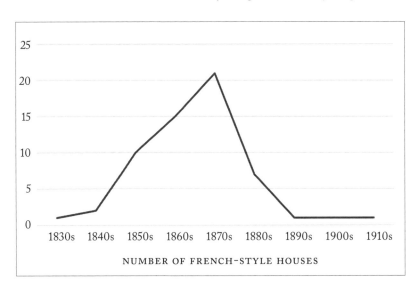

NUMBER OF FRENCH-STYLE HOUSES

Waddeson Manor (1874), one of the French-style houses
built by the Rothschild family in the Vale of Aylesbury.

but the hideousness of the thing, the showiness! The sense of lavish wealth, thrust up your nose! ... Eye hath not seen nor pen can write the ghastly coarseness of the sight.'[125]

These reactions show that cosmopolitanism in some eyes had come to have negative connotations in late Victorian and Edwardian England, as it related to 'the social impact of capitalist mobility and, by extension, for the shadowy attributes of Jews and other perceived *arrivistes*'.[126] There is no doubt that some of the negative comments about the Rothschild houses were motivated by antisemitism.[127] Earlier in the nineteenth century there had been no real concept of a 'Jewish' country house, but after 1870 attitudes changed.[128] When the MP David Lindsay, Lord Balcarres, visited Halton in 1898, he complained that 'the number of Jews in the place was past belief. I have studied the anti-semite question with some attention always hoping to stem an ignoble movement [but] feel some sympathy with [others who say] the Jew is the tapeworm of civilisation.'[129]

As a result of such attitudes, some Jewish country-house owners eschewed Rothschild-style flamboyance. Ludwig Messel, from a German banking family and founder of the London stockbroking firm L. Messel & Co., purchased the Nymans estate in Sussex in 1890. The house was a dull Regency box, and so Messel asked his brother Alfred, a noted architect in Germany, to design an overgrown Bavarian chalet with a tall tower in the middle, suggesting that Messel initially had no wish to hide his heritage. Over the next quarter-century, however, two things intervened to change his attitude. First, the Second Anglo-Boer War introduced what Claire Hirshfield refers to as 'a Jewish question' into British society in which some commentators claimed that 'the British government had been tricked into war by the machinations of shady Jewish capitalists and that the public had been intentionally misled by omnipotent Jewish presslords.'[130]

Second, the First World War led to a surge of Germanophobia in Britain.[131] As Messel was both Jewish and German he came under extra suspicion, and rumours spread that the tower at Nymans was being used as a spy post. After Messel died in 1915, the house was inherited by his son Leonard, whose wife Maud refused to move into the house unless its Teutonic appearance was altered. She produced sketches of her ideas for the house; John Hilary writes that she

> looked to the fifteenth century and drew her inspiration from West Country houses such as Great Chalfield Manor in Wiltshire, as well as nearer models such as Brede Place in East Sussex. Yet the point of the Old English style that Maud favoured was not to attempt the slavish reconstruction of any single moment in architectural time but, rather, to suggest the organic development of a manor house over centuries of accretion. In this way the new Nymans would stand as a realistic monument to a history that never existed.[132]

Norman Evill, a protégé of Sir Edwin Lutyens, designed the western section of the house but then fell out with the Messels. They turned to Sir Walter Tapper, who sourced masonry, doors, fireplaces and beams from medieval buildings all over England. Writing in *Country Life* in 1932, Christopher Hussey described Nymans as 'an exquisite example of pastiche' and proclaimed that 'some future antiquary might be deceived by it.'[133] In 1911 Leonard Messel had obtained an official coat of arms from the College of Arms featuring a fir tree, and it was carved in stone in various places on the new house, including over the gateway in front of the main entrance. But Leonard Messel did not entirely forget or disguise his heritage: a small star of David was carved into the stonework of the entrance courtyard.[134]

The more insular and xenophobic attitudes that compelled Leonard Messel to rebuild Nymans also contributed to the emergence of the vernacular revival style in the final decades of the nineteenth century. The vernacular revival produced more than 130 houses. The movement began in the 1850s, with one of its earliest manifestations a group of cottages by George Devey near the entrance gate to the late medieval Penshurst Place. Devey based his designs, which featured timber-framing, steeply pitched roofs and tall chimneys, on his close study of the vernacular buildings of the Sussex Weald. Over the next three decades he continued to use the vernacular style of Southeastern England for his country houses, including Betteshanger House (1856), Hall Place (1870), Denne Hill (1871), Nonington (1874) and St Alban's Court (1875) in Kent; Goldings (1871–4) in Hertfordshire; Akeley Wood (1866) and Ascott House (1874) in Buckinghamshire; and Adderley Hall (1877) in Shropshire.[135]

Devey's work inspired other architects to study and copy the vernacular buildings of Kent and Sussex. In 1862 and 1863 William Eden Nesfield and Richard Norman Shaw, friends and later partners in an architectural practice, toured Sussex in order to study the 'Wealden' style. Shaw's first two country houses – Glen Andred (1865) and Leyswood (1868) – 'welded and tested the elements' of his vernacular style.[136] As Charles Eastlake wrote in his *History of the Gothic Revival* (1872), Shaw's aim was 'to revive ... the distinctive traditions of style which in former days belonged to certain districts of England'. Referring specifically to Leyswood, Eastlake continued, 'Mr Shaw has done his best to introduce in his design the elements of old Sussex architecture. The half-timber construction, the tile-weathered walls, lofty chimney shafts, steep roofs and overhanging gables of this building reflect not only national but local peculiarities.'[137] Shaw later adapted this vernacular style to a variety of English contexts, while Nesfield also produced vernacular-inspired country houses all over the country from the 1860s onwards. Half of all vernacular revival houses were located in the Southeast of England, with Surrey (19) and Sussex (29) leading the way, but half were located elsewhere. Those in the latter half were for the most part not built in the vernacular of their region, but rather represented the diffusion of the Southeastern English vernacular throughout the country.

Why was the vernacular revival so concentrated in and on the Southeast of England? Starting in the mid-nineteenth century, concerns grew in England that living conditions in London and other large cities were

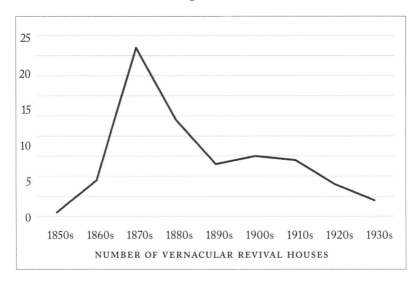

NUMBER OF VERNACULAR REVIVAL HOUSES

leading to the physical degradation of the population.[138] This led to what Alun Howkins describes as a 'discovery of rural England', as a return to rural life was advocated to restore the health of the nation's genetic stock. At the same time, authors such as Thomas Hardy and artists such as John Constable, who featured idyllic rural settings in their works, became very popular.[139] By the 1890s travellers could visit 'Constable Country' in Suffolk on tours organized by Thomas Cook or the Great Eastern Railway.[140] The increasing prominence of places like Hardy's Wessex (that is, his native Dorset) and Constable's Suffolk reflected a shift in the primary geographical location of Englishness from the industrial North to the pastoral South. Howkins attributes this shift to the relative decline of industry in the face of competition from other countries, which meant that England was no longer envisioned first and foremost as an industrial nation. This decline caused 'the perceived centre of its economy' to shift from north to south which, in the words of Stephen Daniels, caused 'the displacement of a "north country" metaphor of England as the workshop of the world' and replaced it with an emphasis on the 'South Country' as England's most important region.[141] These cultural forces helped to produce what Sheila Kirk terms a 'national vernacular approach' to architecture, in which the Southeast came to represent the entire nation.[142] In the late nineteenth and early twentieth centuries, the Southeastern vernacular appeared in distant parts of the country. Oakleigh (1893), one of M. H. Baillie Scott's houses on the Isle of Man, for example, featured 'the front entry porch and hanging tiles common in many parts of the

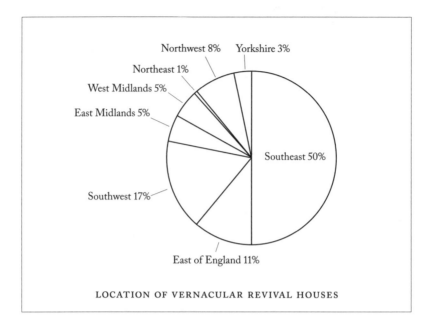

LOCATION OF VERNACULAR REVIVAL HOUSES

south', while 'the half-timbering and carved bargeboards on the front pay homage to the Tudor houses from the south of England that so obviously influenced the architect.'[143]

At the same time, another cultural movement was emerging in response to the same cultural forces. From the 1860s onwards, the Arts and Crafts movement sought to alter the priorities in the manufacture of goods from speed and efficiency to quality and the welfare of the worker. There were around a hundred English Arts and Crafts country houses in total, with the numbers peaking around the turn of the century. The leading architectural practitioner of Arts and Crafts was Philip Webb, who produced eight houses: Church Hill House (1868) in Hertfordshire; Joldwynds (1870), Willinghurst (1886) and Hurlands (1897) in Surrey; Rounton Grange (1871) and Smeaton Manor (1876) in Yorkshire; Clouds (1877) in Wiltshire and Standen (1891) in Sussex. Much like the practitioners of the vernacular revival style, Webb's priorities as a designer were nationally – and often regionally – specific, and were informed by 'his great love for the English landscape and its old buildings'; 'his wide knowledge of ... traditional buildings and their materials'; 'his appreciation of the beauty of simple vernacular buildings'; and 'his understanding of English architecture as a common tradition of good building'.[144]

Underlying Webb's conception of the relationship between a nation and its architecture was his love of the English countryside, which he described as 'full of exquisite beauty and thousands of lovely beasts'.[145] Like the vernacular revival, the Arts and Crafts movement celebrated England's rural heritage, albeit with less of a regional emphasis. A number of preservation societies, most notably the National Trust, were founded in the decades around 1900. At the same time, publishers such as Methuen and Ward Lock began producing travel guidebooks to rural England, while holiday resorts adopted consciously historicist architectural styles, with Thorpeness in Suffolk a prime example, and even bucket-and-spade seaside resorts like Great Yarmouth, Lowestoft and Hunstanton sported new half-timbered buildings.[146] These cultural productions were, as Paul Readman writes, 'conceptualised as distinctively English'.[147]

As summarized by Peter Mandler, in late Victorian culture:

> a historical construct ... was developed towards the end of the nineteenth century by the 'dominant classes' in British society in order to tame or thwart the tendencies of their day towards modernism, urbanism and democracy that might otherwise have overwhelmed elite culture. These aspirations for social control determined the lineaments of the new 'Englishness'. Nostalgic, deferential and rural, 'Englishness' identified the squirearchical village of Southern or 'Deep' England as the template on which the national character had been formed and thus the ideal towards which it must inevitably return.[148]

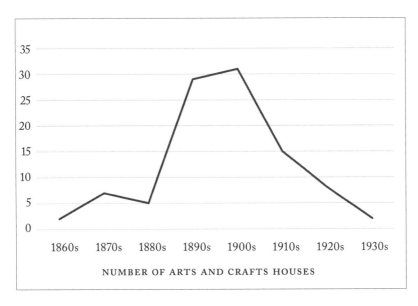

NUMBER OF ARTS AND CRAFTS HOUSES

Country houses had to conform to this culture, by being seen as 'English'. Reginald Blomfield captured this attitude when he described Christopher Wren as 'not only the greatest but the most English of all English architects. He went to see Bernini in France and talked with Mansard and Perrault, yet their influence on him was merely superficial. It spoilt his ornament, but left his essential faculty untouched.'[149] In this interpretation, Wren was a great architect because he had resisted French and Italian influence. But what did it mean to describe architecture as 'English'? Blomfield wrote in his essay 'The English Tradition' (1893) that it must display 'steadfastness of purpose, reserve in design and thorough workmanship'. Blomfield was public school- and Oxford-educated, but the views of his working-class, socialist contemporary William Lethaby did not much differ. To him 'English' meant 'simple, well-off housekeeping, with tea in the garden. Boy-scouting, and tennis in flannels.'[150]

Such statements encapsulated English identity in the late Victorian era, which was, as Paul Readman writes, 'distinctive, largely inward-looking and importantly localised' and included an 'engagement with the past' which was 'pervasive among all social groups' and which 'reflected a widely felt desire to sustain a sense of continuity at a time of change'.[151] These two themes – insularity and continuity – came to define the idealized version of the country house in the late nineteenth and early twentieth centuries. In 1922 Vita Sackville-West wrote of Knole, her family's home in Kent, that it was no 'mere excrescence, no alien fabrication, no startling stranger set between the beeches and the oaks. No other country but England could have produced it, and into no other country would it settle with such harmony and quiet.'[152] New houses, too, were expected not to be 'startling strangers'. Clive Aslet observes that Leonard Stokes's Minterne Magna (1903) 'does not hint at one historical period but many': 'It is as though an actor had gone to the property shop and picked out parts of a costume at random, and gone on the stage in doublet and hose, a frogged coat and top hat.' Stokes was trying to convey an organic evolution which would make a new house appear as if it had evolved over centuries. The tapestry room was therefore 'practically a duplicate' of the one in the old house.[153] Aslet continues:

> This was typical of the era, when owners and architects sought to reproduce the exact appearance of an old – preferably half-timbered – building, so that it genuinely did look like the real

Standen (1891) in Sussex, by Philip Webb, the leading architectural practitioner of the Arts and Crafts style.

thing, down to the last wobbly beam and lichen-covered tile. Not only were new country houses constructed out of old building materials, which had already become gnarled with age; but whole buildings were transported entire and tacked on to new ones to ensure that verisimilitude was absolute.[154]

Edwin Lutyens was a champion of the latter practice: he moved late medieval and Tudor buildings and attached them to newly designed companions at Ashby St Ledgers (1904) in Northamptonshire and Great Dixter (1909) in Sussex. Similarly, Bailiffscourt (1931) in Sussex, which was designed by the antiques dealer Amyas Phillips, was expanded from a thirteenth-century chapel and constructed of stones and fixtures taken from various old buildings, including an archway from Holditch Priory and an oak door from the parish church in South Wanborough; Phillips also hauled in a fifteenth-century brick and half-timbered gatehouse from nearby Loxwood. Other architects sought to reproduce traditional Englishness by creating village-like settings. Philip Webb positioned Standen next to a cluster of outbuildings surrounding a lawn, like a village green in miniature. After he purchased Hever Castle in Kent in 1903, the American plutocrat William Waldorf Astor added a guest wing that was supposed to look like the village that would have surrounded the castle when it was first built in the thirteenth century.

AND SO BY THE TWENTIETH CENTURY the country house was established as distinctively 'English'. But, in the end, was this the winning argument? In other words, is this what saved them? Yes and no. The 'nationalization' of the country house undeniably contributed to its reinvention as a heritage site in the second half of the twentieth century. The idea, or ideal, of the country house as the embodiment of vernacular, rural Englishness represented the beginning of its transition from a real-life centre of wealth, status and power to a vehicle for nostalgic views of English society and culture. But this came at a price: the country house was frozen in amber, a part of the nation's past but no longer of its present. To be sure, it remained a home for old money and an aspiration for new, as rock stars, corporate CEOs and footballers moved in. But the architectural evolution of the country house essentially ceased in the early twentieth century. Arts and Crafts was followed by the Queen Anne and neo-Georgian, two more styles that found their inspiration in the past. The international modern style made little impression in England, and the few new houses that were built after 1920 were generally small in scale.

Medieval Hever Castle, with the new guest wing built by
William Waldorf Astor in the early 20th century in the background.

Moreover, it took some time for the power of the Englishness of the English country house to be felt. Arguing that Englishness was not nearly as potent a force in the late Victorian and Edwardian eras as has been claimed, Peter Mandler claims that England was no more, and probably less, backward-looking than other European nations at the time. He reminds us that the National Trust in its early years was not the national-heritage juggernaut that it is today, but rather minuscule in membership and 'distrusted by government as wet and faddish' and 'by most landlords as a threat to private property'. 'The fact is', Mandler concludes, 'that before the First World War English culture was aggressively urban and materialist, and the rural-nostalgic vision of "Englishness" remained the province of impassioned and highly articulate but fairly marginal artistic groups.'[155]

For much of the twentieth century, as well, the preservation of country houses was motivated by desperate owners rather than a public outcry to preserve them as national treasures. But in the 1970s and '80s, when the state of the British economy made the recognition of national decline unavoidable, nostalgia rose to the fore and country houses became the subjects of more widespread admiration, as their owners, promoters and visitors looked back wistfully to the late nineteenth and early twentieth centuries, when Britain was still a great power, with England at the centre of it.

But as profitable as it has been for some houses – *Downton Abbey* has transformed Highclere Castle from a cash-haemorrhaging white elephant to a cash-register-ringing profit machine – the nostalgic view of the country house has its limits. The National Trust has discovered to its peril in recent years that ignoring the complexities of its houses' histories leads to trouble, as historians demand a fuller picture and its traditional clientele resents what they see as excessive concessions to 'wokeness'.[156] The expectation that a visit to a country house should present no challenge to a comfortable view of history – an expectation largely created by the Trust itself in recent years – will not be easy to overturn.

This book argues that such expectations are the result of the invention of the 'English' country house in the nineteenth century. After the French Revolution contributed to the elevation of political stability and cultural continuity as key components of English identity, English country-house architecture became more isolated from the continent and more referential to national history. Castellated houses served as reminders that England had supposedly passed from the Middle Ages to the present without the violent upheaval that had taken place in France, even if their real sixteenth- and seventeenth-century histories belied this claim. Over the next hundred years, the definition of English identity narrowed and became more distinct from the identities of the other nations of the British Isles, the British Empire and continental Europe. By century's end it contained a prominent strain of nostalgia for a pastoral, preindustrial England, which was represented in the vernacular revival and Arts and Crafts country houses of the era.

Conclusion

In his essay 'Building with Wit', published in the *Architectural Review* in 1951, Nikolaus Pevsner dismissed Edwin Lutyens as 'a layman's architect'. Pevsner claimed that Lutyens's 'importance in the development of European architecture seems to me without any doubt less than, amongst his British contemporaries, Voysey's, and his originality less than Mackintosh's'.[1] Seven months later, the famous American architect Frank Lloyd Wright, then aged 84, offered a spirited defence of Lutyens, who he declared 'so thoroughly expressed the cultural feeling of the English of his day, that a new-world reaction like mine could not be trusted to do more than voice admiration of the love, loyalty and art with which this cultured Architect, in love with Architecture, shaped his buildings'.[2]

Here we have two very different views of not only Lutyens but of the place of architecture in English culture in the mid-twentieth century. Making the case that 'modernism and Englishness were entirely compatible', Pevsner saw Lutyens as anti-modern and old-fashioned. In contrast, Lloyd Wright presented a more conventional view of English architecture in which modernism was a 'continental invasion'.[3] This was a new iteration of a debate that had been present in English architecture for centuries over two issues. First, could 'English' buildings adopt new styles, given that continuity had come to be a mainstay of English national identity? Second, must they reflect purely native influences, or was it possible for them to absorb external influences and transform them into something nationally distinctive?

Lutyens's career raised both of these questions. In its early years he designed houses almost exclusively in Surrey in his interpretation of that county's vernacular style.[4] His houses were also closely tied to the English landscape through his collaboration with the garden designer

Gertrude Jekyll, which began in 1889. In this phase, then, Lutyens belonged with those contemporary architects who advocated a close adherence to national and regional traditions, in keeping with the idea that English identity was rooted in the rural and pastoral. In the last years of the nineteenth century, however, Lutyens began to move 'towards the greater formality and order of both the classical and the Tudor manners'.[5] This transition was apparent in the increased symmetry of his houses and in the shift of classical elements from the interiors to the exteriors. Later still, Lutyens moved from the free Tudor of Marshcourt (1901) in Hampshire and Little Thakeham (1902) in Sussex towards the classically inspired 'grand manner' of Nashdom (1905) in Buckinghamshire and Heathcote (1906) in Yorkshire. For the rest of his career, Lutyens maintained his commitment to the classical, as one of his last houses, Gledstone Hall (1925) in Yorkshire, attests.

This is the standard account of the evolution of Lutyens's career, but in reality the progression of his architectural style was considerably less straightforward than this orderly sequence suggests. Elizabeth Wilhide writes: 'Just as classicism never entirely supplanted Lutyens's more "romantic" and poetic vision, evidence of classical inspiration can be seen quite early on in his career.'[6] Examples include Folly Farm (1905) in Berkshire, which combines a vernacular block with a Queen Anne wing. One would assume that the block came first, but in fact it was added to the house seven years later, after a new owner decided that he wanted additional space for guests. Similarly, when Lutyens altered his first country house, Crooksbury (1889) in Surrey, in 1914, he 'converted the neo-Georgian wing of 1898 into streamlined-roughcast-Tudor'.[7] He also often combined vernacular and classical elements in the same design. Gavin Stamp describes Overstrand Hall (1899) in Norfolk as 'mixing the Tudor and the classical and combining symmetrical elevations in a picturesque manner'; and Homewood (1900) in Hertfordshire as a 'highly sophisticated design in which vernacular forms are combined with classical formality'.[8]

The complex mix of styles in Lutyens's work is worth highlighting because he has for so long been considered, as Sir William Rothenstein described him in his collection of biographical sketches *Twenty-Four Portraits* (1923), 'the most English of architects'.[9] This description of Lutyens appeared at a time – the interwar period – when, according to Stamp, 'the insular conservatism of English domestic architecture became even more entrenched' and 'innovation and foreign influences were not welcomed.'[10] As evidence, Stamp cites this quotation from Lawrence Weaver, from the second volume of his *Small Country Houses of To-Day* (1919): 'A new method of design is incredible, simply because it is not feasible. We had our misfortunes a few years ago in that pursuit, but even before the war the "New Art" which pleased Germany and Austria so vastly was "dead and damned" in Great Britain.' This can certainly be regarded as a rejection of modern continental styles such as Art Nouveau, but crucially Stamp does not quote the sentences that follow:

> It is far more likely that we shall signify our essential sympathy with Latin culture by developing a national school of design inspired by a classical spirit. If its quality is akin to austerity, that will only be in accord with the sacrifices we made in the war and the burdens we shall long bear.[11]

Weaver was thus not rejecting all continental influences, only modern ones; he saw the classical style as entirely compatible with the sombre and restrained mood that prevailed after the Great War. Lutyens's contemporaries therefore did not see him as shifting from a more 'English' to a more 'continental' style. Instead, they saw classicism as appropriate to the cultural needs of interwar England.

The height of Lutyens's career is usually seen as the Viceroy's House, the centrepiece of New Delhi, the new capital of British India which was designed and built by Lutyens and Herbert Baker between 1911 and 1931. That building was the result of yet another debate over the most appropriate style of architecture for an imperial context, in this case the most important architectural project ever undertaken in the British Empire. This particular debate is often seen as being between Lutyens, who dismissed Indian architecture as 'just spurts by various mushroom dynasties' and insisted on the classical style, and the Viceroy Lord Hardinge, who declared his preference for a more 'Oriental' style to the Imperial Legislative Council in 1911. In reality, both Lutyens and Hardinge envisioned a hybrid style combining elements of the Eastern and Western architectural traditions. Robert Grant Irving writes that by the summer of 1912:

> Hardinge acknowledged a strong sentiment against Indian architecture among the Europeans in India, an attitude Lutyens evidently encouraged... Pure western or pure oriental architecture

both had their detractors. The solution, therefore, ... lay in the integration of Palladian and Pathan principles. Lutyens's British School at Rome, which Hardinge had studied in photographs, could be 'most successfully orientalized' with elements from the period preceding the Mughals, although doubtless some persons would call the result 'a bastard form of architecture'. But the Viceroy felt confident that the Pathan style 'with its rectangular or hexagonal columns, its breadth of treatment with big walls, buttresses, flat domes and few windows would lend itself to a composition with Italian architecture that would inspire beauty, solidity and originality.'[12]

Lutyens's assistant Herbert Baker agreed: even before he was appointed to the project, he called for a new architectural style that would be 'a blend of the best elements of East and West'.[13]

And, despite Lutyens's derogatory remarks about Indian architecture, he had no intention of ignoring it completely.[14] Instead, he 'adapted his personal classicism to local conditions', just as he had done with his country houses in England:

> Instead of the cornice, he adapted the thin, wide overhanging *chujja* to cast deep shadows, and on the parapet he placed the little pavilions, or *chattris*, which also appear on Moghul buildings [such] as those at Fatephur Sikri. And then there is the astonishing tall, imperious dome – placed at the very centre of the building and city – partly inspired by the Buddhist Great Stupa at Sanchi.[15]

'Thus was the fusion,' wrote Robert Byron in *Country Life*, 'so earnestly desired by political sentimentalists, accomplished. It was a fusion, not of historical reminiscences, but of two schools of architectural thought. The outcome of it is monumental.'[16]

During the two decades in which Lutyens was building New Delhi, he was also immersed in the design and construction of Castle Drogo (1911–30) in Devon, one of his last country houses to be completed. Its owner, Julius Drewe, a founding partner of Home and Colonial Stores, had accumulated a sufficient fortune to retire at 33 and take up life as a landed gentleman. He added an 'e' to his surname and convinced himself that he was descended from a twelfth-century knight named Drogo

Conclusion

(or 'Dru') de Teigne, who had supposedly held land on the edge of Dartmoor and for whom the manor of Drewsteignton was named. As Drogo must have lived in a castle, Drewe decided that he must have one too, and so he bought 450 acres high on the edge of the Teign Gorge and commissioned Lutyens to design a 'Commemorative Tower or Keep'.[17]

Castle Drogo is usually treated as an anomaly within Lutyens's oeuvre. Lutyens aficionados often express frustration that it is the only one of his houses that is owned by the National Trust, because it is considered to be so 'untypical'. But Castle Drogo is unmistakably a Lutyens building, and not just any Lutyens building, but the pinnacle of his career.[18] It combines the classical severity and mathematics of his later work with the medieval gothic, reducing both to their essence in a manner similar to his combination of classical and Indian styles in the Viceroy's House. It was not, to be sure, his first exercise in castle-building. He had previously restored two 'real' (albeit sixteenth-century) castles: Lindisfarne (1901) on Holy Island, off Northumberland, and Lambay (1905) on an island off the east coast of Ireland. Nor was Castle Drogo a singular

Castle Drogo, Devon (1911–30).

example of an entirely new castle: he would also use its 'abstracted castle' style on Abbey House (1914) in Lancashire and Penheale Manor (1920) in Cornwall.[19]

Castle Drogo was conceived and for the most part designed before the Great War, but finished over a decade later. That context directly and powerfully affected its final form. Work on the massive building slowed as many of the workers volunteered for service and horses and materials became scarce, and so by 1917 construction had virtually stopped. Then, in July of that year, Drewe's eldest son Adrian, who was 26, was killed at Ypres.[20] Drewe in his grief lost his enthusiasm for the project and the house, already reduced by half from the original plans in 1912, shrunk even further in consequence. Lutyens tried to convince him to keep building by erecting timber mock-ups of various features, such as a barbican, but without success. The biggest loss was the great hall planned for the south end, while even some partially completed elements were demolished.[21] After the Drewes took up residence in 1928, Julius's wife Frances transferred the 'Memorial Room' in Adrian's honour from their previous house, Wadhurst Hall in Sussex, to their new home. The wooden cross which originally marked Adrian's grave before his body was moved to Vlamertinghe Military Cemetery still hangs on the wall of Castle Drogo's chapel.[22]

Castle Drogo was therefore a war memorial as well as a country house, its truncated final form symbolizing the abrupt end of Adrian Drewe's life.[23] This draws us into the debate over whether the First World War caused a cultural break from the modes of representation that had been used in the past or whether older forms of commemoration persisted after the war.[24] A part of this debate concerns the place of classicism in British culture after that war. On the one hand, some observers have pointed to a 'complete hiatus' of British classicism, as there was 'a violent rejection of the Greek ideal of classical beauty in favour of the modern'.[25] But on the other, Ana Carden-Coyne writes:

> In the aftermath of the First World War, a classical imaginary was rehabilitated, not just as a familiar cultural vocabulary or retreat to a safe past, but as a relevant set of values regarding beauty, symmetry and gothicism. Since classicism was a universal aesthetic aimed at resolving paradoxes harmoniously, it offered a special understanding of the world in violent conflict.[26]

Lutyens resolved the debate by designing war memorials that were simultaneously both modern and classical. His Cenotaph (1919) 'immediately caught the public mood', with its 'apparent simplicity... based on a direct refinement of classical principles'.[27] His memorial to the missing at Thiepval (1928), meanwhile, was in Jay Winter's words 'not a cry against war, but an extraordinary statement in abstract language about mass death and the impossibility of triumphalism. In Thiepval Lutyens diminished the arch of triumph of Roman or French art... literally to the vanishing point.'[28]

Castle Drogo reflects a similar approach to the medieval castle, simultaneously traditional in form, but, as Jeremy Gould writes, 'essentially modern' in every other aspect. Even more than his classical houses or the Viceroy's House, it is all line and simple linear geometry; its elevations are 'abstract and scaleless'.[29] Peter Inskip writes:

> While Drogo was under construction Lutyens's architecture developed a ruthless elementalism as exemplified by the arch at Thiepval and the Viceroy's House at New Delhi. At Castle Drogo this progress can be traced from the rugged stonework of the north tower to the brilliant treatment of the knife-sharp edges of the granite planes rising from the moor on the south front.[30]

In this sense, it is a classical house in medieval guise; Lutyens hints at this with the Doric-columned bathroom he built for Drewe's use and the vaulted kitchen in the basement of the north wing, with its 'un-moulded dome and glazed rotundo strongly reminiscent' of Sir John Soane's Bank of England (1788).[31]

But Castle Drogo is also a fundamentally English house; Lutyens acknowledged that the modern, on its own, could not be truly English, and so required grounding in a sense of national history and the English rural landscape. By the 1920s modernism was seen as 'foreign'; although this did not necessarily entail hostility to or a rejection of it, it did lead to concerns that it needed to be balanced with a commitment to national forms of cultural expression. The painter Paul Nash wrote in 1932 that

> we are invaded by very strong foreign influences, we possess certain solid traditions. Once more we find ourselves conscious of a renaissance abroad, and are curious and rather embarrassed by the event; at once anxious to participate and afraid to commit

Castle Drogo combined an abstracted gothicism and classicism with a thorough grounding in English tradition, and included imperial elements carried over from Lutyens's contemporary work in New Delhi. The domed kitchen was copied from Sir John Soane's Bank of England; the Georgian drawing room was intended to make the house look as if it evolved over time; and the drawing-room corridor was patterned after the interior of the Viceroy's House.

ourselves, wishing to be modern, but uncertain whether that can be consistent with being British.[32]

Nash and Lutyens share this fundamental dilemma of trying to create art that is both modern and founded in English tradition and the English landscape. Alastair Curtis writes of Nash, but could have been writing of Lutyens: 'Critics often reduce his work to its essential Englishness. But while he took inspiration from mythic Albion, Nash was anything but parochial ... [He was] an artist working within the flourishing international modernist movement, trading techniques with those on the continent.'[33]

Like Nash's paintings, Castle Drogo, for all its superficial modernity, was rooted in English architectural tradition and English soil. Its granite came from two Dartmoor quarries located within twenty miles of the house. Its severe vertical lines resemble a Perpendicular gothic cathedral. The mullioned windows are taken from Tudor houses, and its interior styles vary so as to convey the organic evolution of a house over the centuries: there is a Jacobean dining room, a Georgian drawing room and modern bathrooms. The massive arch separating the library from the billiard room was deliberately truncated to suggest the later insertion of a window.[34] The entrance hall was designed to be similar to the great hall of a castle or late medieval country house, recalling traditional English notions of lordly hospitality. But at the same time, Lutyens incorporated a more outward-looking vision of Englishness as well: the domes in the drawing-room corridor resemble those on the interior of the Viceroy's House in New Delhi. Drewe tolerated the inclusion of such 'Eastern' influence because Drogo de Teigne had supposedly fought in the Crusades.

Castle Drogo therefore embodies the debate between continuity and disruption and between native and foreign which this book has found in English country-house architecture for centuries. Containing an element of virtually every important architectural movement in England since 1300, it is the perfect English house: at once old and new, traditional and modern, stable and disrupted, local and continental, vernacular and cosmopolitan, metropolitan and imperial, gothic and classical.

THIS BOOK HAS EXAMINED the complex nature of English national identity, and the ways in which country houses like Castle Drogo have reflected it. Defined neither by romantic dreams of a once-and-future nationhood – as it has been for the other nations of the British Isles – nor by 'blood and soil' notions of ethnic purity and territorial rootedness, English nationalism is perhaps best characterized by its contradictions. It may revere continuity, but it has frequently been characterized by disruption and violence. It may embrace the exclusive and insular, but it has often been inclusive and cosmopolitan.

Edwin Lutyens, the dominant country-house architect of the early twentieth century, freely combined vernacular and classical elements in his work, seeing them as complementary, not contradictory. At the end of his career he reconciled the gothic and the classical in his designs for Castle Drogo, a house which is often treated as an anomaly or a relic – England's 'last castle' – but which was in fact the logical conclusion of not only his development as an architect but of centuries of English country-house design. Castle Drogo is a house which can only exist in England, because it is the product of tensions which had long been defining features of English architecture: between adherence to tradition and new fashions and between domestic inspirations on the one hand and foreign ones on the other. And it is impossible to say – in that particular building or more generally in English country-house architecture over the centuries – which of these characteristics prevails, just as it is impossible to say which version of English national identity has been dominant. Instead, English country houses, like the country in which they reside, have been many different things at different times.

APPENDICES

APPENDIX 1: Extant Country Houses with Priest Holes

Abbey House	Yorkshire
Abbot's Salford Hall	Warwickshire
Albourne Place	Sussex
Angram Grange	Yorkshire
Ash Manor	Kent
Astley Hall	Lancashire
Athelhampton House	Dorset
Baddesley Clinton	Warwickshire
Baughton Court	Worcestershire
Bear Park	Yorkshire
Bell Hall	Yorkshire
Benthall Hall	Shropshire
Billesley Manor	Warwickshire
Birchley Hall	Lancashire
Borwick Hall	Lancashire
Bourton-on-the-Water Manor	Gloucestershire
Bovey House	Devon
Braddocks	Essex
Breckles Hall	Norfolk
Brockbury Hall	Herefordshire
Brockworth Court	Gloucesterhire
Brough Hall	Yorkshire
Buckland Old House	Berkshire
Carlton Towers	Yorkshire
Chambercombe Manor	Devon
Chastleton House	Oxfordshire
Chenies Manor	Buckinghamshire
Chideock Castle	Dorset
Clarke Hall	Yorkshire
Claydon House	Buckinghamshire
Cleeve Prior Manor	Worcestershire
Clopton Hall	Warwickshire
Coldham Hall	Suffolk
Compton Wynyates	Warwickshire
Costessey Hall	Norfolk
Coughton Court	Warwickshire
Cowick Barton	Devon
Crosby Hall	Lancashire
Denham Place	Buckinghamshire

Drayton House	Northamptonshire
Duckworth Hall	Lancashire
Edge Barton Manor	Devon
Esh Hall	Durham
Etwall Hall	Derbyshire
Feering House	Essex
Gawsworth Old Hall	Cheshire
Gayhurst	Buckinghamshire
Gosfield Hall	Essex
Greasby Old Hall	Cheshire
Grosmont Priory	Yorkshire
Hardwick Manor	Oxfordshire
Hardwicke Hall	Durham
Harrowden Hall	Northamptonshire
Harvington Hall	Worcestershire
Hawksworth Hall	Yorkshire
Heale House	Wiltshire
Hendred House	Berkshire
Hindlip Hall	Worcestershire
Holywell Manor	Oxfordshire
Huddington Court	Worcestershire
Ingatestone Hall	Essex
Irnham Hall	Lincolnshire
Kirby Hall	Northamptonshire
Lanherne House	Cornwall
Lawkland Hall	Yorkshire
Lea Hall	Derbyshire
Lowick Hall	Cumbria
Lydiate Hall	Lancashire
Lyford Grange	Berkshire
Madeley Court	Shropshire
Manor House (Moulton)	Yorkshire
Manor House (Stanton Woodhouse)	Derbyshire
Manor House (Uttoxeter)	Staffordshire
Mapledurham House	Oxfordshire
Middle House, West Wing	Sussex
Moat House (Charing)	Kent
Moseley Old Hall	Staffordshire
Myddleton Lodge	Yorkshire
Naworth Castle	Cumbria
Netherwitton Hall	Northumberland
Newbuildings Place	Sussex
Old Hall (Poolside)	Staffordshire
Old Manor House (Bracknell)	Berkshire
Oxburgh Hall	Norfolk
Packington Old Hall	Warwickshire
Parham	Sussex
Park Hall	Shropshire
Paxhill	Sussex

Paynsley Hall	Staffordshire
Pickersleigh Court	Worcestershire
Pitchford Hall	Shropshire
Plowden Hall	Shropshire
Reynolds Place	Kent
Ripley Castle	Yorkshire
Roche Court	Hampshire
Rufford Old Hall	Lancashire
Rushton Hall	Northamptonshire
Salford Prior Hall	Warwickshire
Samlesbury Hall	Lancashire
Sawston Hall	Cambridgeshire
Scotney Castle	Kent
Sheat Manor	Isle of Wight
Sledwick Court	Durham
Slindon House	Sussex
Snore Hall	Norfolk
Southrop Manor	Gloucestershire
Speke Hall	Lancashire
Stonor	Oxfordshire
Stonyhurst Hall	Lancashire
Thornley Hall	Durham
Thorpe Hall	Norfolk
Thurnham Hall	Lancashire
Todd Hall	Lancashire
Towneley Park	Lancashire
Treago	Herefordshire
Trent House	Somerset
Tudhoe Hall	Durham
Tusmore	Oxfordshire
Ufton Court	Berkshire
Upper House (Madeley)	Shropshire
Uxendon Hall	Middlesex
Vicarage (Uttoxeter)	Staffordshire
Weston Underwood	Buckinghamshire
Wollas Hall	Worcestershire
Wood Hall	Lancashire
Wroxton Abbey	Oxfordshire
Wymering Manor	Hampshire
Yew Tree House	Staffordshire

APPENDIX 2: Monastic Sites Converted to or Used to Supply Materials for Country Houses

RELIGIOUS FOUNDATION	COUNTY	COUNTRY HOUSE	USE
Abbotsbury Abbey	DORSET	Abbey House	Converted
Alcester Abbey	WARWICKSHIRE	Beauchamp Court	Materials
Alvecote Priory	WARWICKSHIRE	Alvecote Priory House	Converted
Amesbury Abbey	WILTSHIRE	Amesbury Abbey	Converted
Angelsey Priory	CAMBRIDGESHIRE	Angelsey Priory and Madingley Hall	Converted Materials
Appuldurcombe Priory	ISLE OF WIGHT	Appuldurcombe House	Converted
Arbury Priory	WARWICKSHIRE	Arbury Hall	Converted
Arthington Nunnery	YORKSHIRE	The Nunnery	Converted
Axholme Priory	LINCOLNSHIRE	Axholme Manor	Converted
Aylesford Priory	KENT	The Friars	Converted
Bailiffscourt	SUSSEX	Bailiffscourt	Converted
Bardney Abbey	LINCOLNSHIRE	Bardney Abbey	Converted
Barlings Abbey	LINCOLNSHIRE	Barlings Abbey	Converted
Barrow Gurney Nunnery	SOMERSET	Barrow Court	Converted
Battle Abbey	SUSSEX	Battle Abbey	Converted
Bayham Old Abbey	SUSSEX	Bayham Hall	Garden
Beaulieu Abbey	HAMPSHIRE	Beaulieu Palace House	Converted
Beeleigh Abbey	ESSEX	Beeleigh Abbey House	Converted
Bermondsey Abbey	LONDON	Bermondsey House	Converted
Biddlesden Abbey	BUCKINGHAMSHIRE	Biddlesden Park House	Converted
Bindon Abbey	DORSET	Bindon Abbey and Lulworth Castle	Materials
Bisham Abbey	BERKSHIRE	Bisham Abbey	Converted
Blanchland Abbey	NORTHUMBERLAND	Blanchland Manor	Converted
Blyth Priory	NOTTINGHAMSHIRE	Blyth Hall	Converted
Bottesford Preceptory	LINCOLNSHIRE	Bottesford Manor	Converted
Boxley Abbey	KENT	Boxley Abbey House	Converted
Breadsall Priory	DERBYSHIRE	Breadsall Priory	Converted
Brinkburn Priory	NORTHUMBERLAND	Brinkburn Manor	Converted
Bromfield Priory	SHROPSHIRE	Bromfield Priory	Converted
Bruisyard Abbey	SUFFOLK	Bruisyard Hall	Converted
Bruton Abbey	SOMERSET	Bruton Abbey	Converted
Buckland Abbey	DEVON	Buckland Abbey	Converted
Buildwas Abbey	SHROPSHIRE	Abbey House	Converted
Burford Priory	OXFORDSHIRE	Burford Priory	Converted
Burnham Priory	BUCKINGHAMSHIRE	Burnham Abbey	Converted
Burton Abbey	STAFFORDSHIRE	The Abbey and Newton Park	Converted, Materials
Bury St Edmunds Abbey	SUFFOLK	Bury St Edmunds Abbey	Converted
Bushmead Priory	BEDFORDSHIRE	Bushmead Priory House	Converted
Butley Priory	SUFFOLK	Butley Priory	Converted
Calder Abbey	CUMBRIA	Calder Abbey House	Converted
Calke Abbey	DERBYSHIRE	Calke Abbey	Converted
Calwich Abbey	STAFFORDSHIRE	Calwich Abbey	Converted

Appendices

Cammeringham Priory	LINCOLNSHIRE	Cammeringham Manor House	Converted
Cannington Priory	SOMERSET	Cannington Court	Converted
Canons Ashby	NORTHAMPTONSHIRE	Canons Ashby	Converted
Canterbury Greyfriars	KENT	Greyfriars Monastery	Converted
Castle Acre Priory	NORFOLK	Castle Acre Priory	Converted
Catesby Priory	NORTHAMPTONSHIRE	Catesby Abbey	Converted
Cawston Grange	WARWICKSHIRE	Cawston Grange	Converted
Cerne Abbey	DORSET	Abbey House	Converted
Chacombe Priory	NORTHAMPTONSHIRE	Chacombe Priory	Converted
Chatteris Abbey	CAMBRIDGESHIRE	Park House	Converted
Chester Priory	CHESHIRE	The Nunnes	Converted
Chicksands Priory	BEDFORDSHIRE	Chicksands Priory	Converted
Chirbury Abbey	SHROPSHIRE	Chirbury Hall	Materials
Church Gresley Priory	DERBYSHIRE	Gresley Hall	Materials
Clare Priory	SUFFOLK	Clare Priory	Converted
Cleeve Abbey	SOMERSET	Cleeve Abbey	Converted
Coggeshall Abbey	ESSEX	Coggeshall Abbey	Converted
Colne Priory	ESSEX	Colne Manor	Converted
Combermere Abbey	CHESHIRE	Combermere Abbey	Converted
Combwell Priory	KENT	Combwell Priory	Converted
Conishead Priory	CUMBRIA	Conishead Priory	Materials
Coombe Abbey	WARWICKSHIRE	Coombe Abbey	Converted
Coverham Abbey	YORKSHIRE	Coverham Abbey	Converted
Cowick Priory	DEVON	Cowick Barton	Materials
Delapre Abbey	NORTHAMPTONSHIRE	Delapre Abbey	Converted
Dinmore Preceptory	HEREFORDSHIRE	Dinmore Manor House	Converted
Donnington Priory	BERKSHIRE	The Priory	Converted
Dudley Priory	STAFFORDSHIRE	Priory Hall	Garden
Easebourne Priory	SUSSEX	The Priory	Converted
Ecclesfield Priory	YORKSHIRE	Ecclesfield Old Hall	Converted
Egglestone Abbey	DURHAM	Egglestone Abbey	Converted
Elstow Abbey	BEDFORDSHIRE	Elstow Abbey	Converted
Felley Priory	NOTTINGHAMSHIRE	Felley Priory	Converted
Fineshade Priory	NORTHAMPTONSHIRE	Fineshade Priory	Converted
Flaxley Abbey	GLOUCESTERSHIRE	Flaxley Manor	Converted
Flitcham Priory	NORFOLK	Flitcham Priory	Converted
Forde Abbey	DORSET	Forde Abbey	Converted
Fountains Abbey	YORKSHIRE	Fountains Hall and Studley Royal Park	Materials, Garden
Furness Abbey	CUMBRIA	Furness Manor	Converted
Garendon Abbey	LEICESTERSHIRE	Garendon Hall	Converted
Gisborough Priory	YORKSHIRE	Gisborough Hall	Garden
Godstow Abbey	OXFORDSHIRE	Godstow House	Converted
Grace Dieu Priory	LEICESTERSHIRE	Grace Dieu Priory	Converted
Great Limber Preceptory	LINCOLNSHIRE	Great Limber Preceptory	Converted
Hailes Abbey	GLOUCESTERSHIRE	Hailes Abbey	Converted
Hartland Abbey	DEVON	Hartland Abbey	Converted
Haughmond Abbey	SHROPSHIRE	Haughmond Abbey	Converted
Hawkshead Grange	CUMBRIA	Hawkshead Old Hall	Converted

Healaugh Priory	YORKSHIRE	Healaugh Priory	Converted
Hinchinbrook Priory	CAMBRIDGESHIRE	Hinchingbrooke House	Converted
Hinton Priory	SOMERSET	Hinton Priory	Converted
Hitchin Priory	HERTFORDSHIRE	Hitchin Priory	Converted
Holditch Priory	DORSET	Bailiffscourt	Materials
Horton Priory	KENT	Horton Priory	Converted
Hulne Friary	NORTHUMBERLAND	Hulne Friary	Converted
Hurley Priory	BERKSHIRE	Ladye Place Mansion	Converted
Ixworth Priory	SUFFOLK	Ixworth Priory	Converted
Jervaulx Abbey	NORTH YORKSHIRE	Jervaulx Abbey	Converted, Garden
Kenilworth Abbey	WARWICKSHIRE	Kenilworth Castle	Materials
Kingswood Abbey	GLOUCESTERSHIRE	Newark Park	Materials
Kington Nunnery	WILTSHIRE	Kington Priory	Converted
Kirklees Priory	YORKSHIRE	Low Hall	Materials
Kirkstead Abbey	LINCOLNSHIRE	Kirkstead Abbey	Converted
Lacock Abbey	WILTSHIRE	Lacock Abbey	Converted
Lanercost Priory	CUMBRIA	Dacre Hall	Converted
Langley Priory	LEICESTERSHIRE	Langley Priory	Converted
Launde Abbey	LEICESTERSHIRE	Launde Abbey	Converted
Lavendon Abbey	BUCKINGHAMSHIRE	Lavendon Grange	Converted
Lavenham Priory	SUFFOLK	Lavenham Priory	Converted
Leez Priory	ESSEX	Leez Priory	Converted
Leicester Abbey	LEICESTERSHIRE	Leicester Abbey	Converted
Lewes Priory	SUSSEX	Lord's Place, Kingston Manor, Hangleton Manor, Southover Grange, Broyle Place, Clayhill House	Converted, Materials
Lilleshall Abbey	SHROPSHIRE	Lilleshall Abbey	Converted
Lindisfarne Priory	NORTHUMBERLAND	Lindisfarne Castle	Materials
Little Malvern Priory	WORCESTERSHIRE	Little Malvern Court	Converted
Maldon Whitefriars	ESSEX	The Friars	Converted
Malton Priory	YORKSHIRE	Abbey House	Converted
Markyate Cell	HERTFORDSHIRE	Markyate House	Converted
Medmenham Abbey	BUCKINGHAMSHIRE	Medmenham Manor	Converted
Michelham Priory	SUSSEX	Michelham Priory	Converted
Milton Abbey	DORSET	Milton Abbey	Converted
Missenden Abbey	BUCKINGHAMSHIRE	Missenden Abbey	Converted
Monk Bretton Priory	SOUTH YORKSHIRE	Monk Bretton Priory	Converted
Monkton Farleigh Priory	WILTSHIRE	Monkton Farleigh Manor	Converted
Mottisfont Abbey	HAMPSHIRE	Mottisfont Abbey	Converted
Moxby Nunnery	YORKSHIRE	Moxby Priory	Converted
Muresley Priory	HERTFORDSHIRE	Muresley Manor	Converted
Netley Abbey	HAMPSHIRE	Netley Abbey	Converted
Newburgh Priory	YORKSHIRE	Newburgh Priory	Converted
Newnham Priory	BEDFORDSHIRE	Newnham Priory	Converted, Materials
Newstead Abbey	NOTTINGHAMSHIRE	Newstead Abbey	Converted
Nocton Priory	LINCOLNSHIRE	Nocton Priory	Converted

Appendices

North Ormsby Priory	LINCOLNSHIRE	North Ormsby Priory	Converted
Norton Priory	CHESHIRE	Norton Priory	Converted
Nostell Priory	YORKSHIRE	Nostell Priory	Converted
Notley Abbey	BUCKINGHAMSHIRE	Notley Abbey	Converted
Nun Cotham Priory	LINCOLNSHIRE	Nun Cotham Priory	Converted
Otham Abbey	SUSSEX	Otteham Court	Converted
Otterton Priory	DEVON	Otterton Manor	Converted
Pipewell Abbey	NORTHAMPTONSHIRE	Pipewell Hall	Materials
Polesworth Priory	WARWICKSHIRE	Polesworth Hall	Materials
Polsloe Priory	DEVON	Polsloe Priory	Converted
Prittlewell Priory	ESSEX	Prittlewell Priory	Converted
Ramsey Abbey	CAMBRIDGESHIRE	Ramsey Abbey and Hinchingbrooke House	Converted, Materials
Ranton Abbey	STAFFORDSHIRE	Ranton Abbey	Converted
Reigate Priory	SURREY	Reigate Priory	Converted
Ribston Preceptory	YORKSHIRE	Ribston Hall	Converted
Rievaulx Abbey	NORTH YORKSHIRE	Duncombe Park	Garden
Robertsbridge Abbey	SUSSEX	Abbey House	Converted
Roche Abbey	YORKSHIRE	Sandbeck Park	Garden
Rufford Abbey	NOTTINGHAMSHIRE	Rufford Abbey	Converted
Sandwell Priory	STAFFORDSHIRE	Priory House	Converted
Seaton Priory	CUMBRIA	Seaton Priory	Converted
Sempringham Priory	LINCOLNSHIRE	Sempringham Priory	Converted
Shelford Priory	NOTTINGHAMSHIRE	Shelford House	Converted
Shingay Preceptory	CAMBRIDGESHIRE	Shingay Hall	Converted
Shrewsbury Abbey	SHROPSHIRE	Whitehall	Materials
Shulbrede Priory	SUSSEX	Shulbrede Priory	Converted
Sixhills Priory	LINCOLNSHIRE	Sixhills Grange	Converted
Snelshall Priory	BUCKINGHAMSHIRE	Snelshall Priory	Converted
Sopwell Priory	HERTFORDSHIRE	Sopwell Priory	Converted
Southwick Priory	HAMPSHIRE	Southwick Park	Converted
St Andrews Priory	YORKSHIRE	Arden Hall	Converted
St Augustine's Abbey	KENT	St Augustine's Abbey, Hales Park	Converted, Materials
St German's Priory	CORNWALL	Port Eliot House	Converted
St Giles Almshouse	SHROPSHIRE	Ludford House	Converted
St John's Abbey (Colchester)	ESSEX	St John's Abbey	Converted
St Olave's Priory	SUFFOLK	St Olave's Priory	Converted
St Osyth's Abbey	ESSEX	St Osyth's Abbey	Converted
St Sepulchre's Priory	WARWICKSHIRE	St Sepulchre's Priory	Converted
Stanley Abbey	WILTSHIRE	Old Bromham Hall	Materials
Stavordale Priory	SOMERSET	Stavordale Priory	Converted
Stoneleigh Abbey	WARWICKSHIRE	Stoneleigh Abbey	Converted
Studley Priory	OXFORDSHIRE	Studley Priory	Converted
Syon Nunnery	LONDON	Syon House	Converted
Takeley Priory	ESSEX	Warish Hall	Converted
Tarrant Abbey	DORSET	Tarrant Abbey House	Converted
Taunton Priory	SOMERSET	Poundisford Park	Materials

Templecombe Preceptory	SOMERSET	Templecombe Manor	Materials
Thame Abbey	OXFORDSHIRE	Thame Abbey	Converted
Thelsford Priory	WARWICKSHIRE	Wasperton Manor	Materials
Thornton Abbey	LINCOLNSHIRE	Thornton Abbey	Converted
Thurgarton Priory	NOTTINGHAMSHIRE	Thurgarton Priory	Converted
Tilty Abbey	ESSEX	Tilty Abbey	Garden
Tiptree Priory	ESSEX	Tiptree Priory	Converted
Titchfield Abbey	HAMPSHIRE	Palace House	Converted
Torre Abbey	DEVON	Torre Abbey	Converted
Tortington Priory	SUSSEX	Tortington Priory House, Tortington Place	Converted, Materials
Trentham Priory	STAFFORDSHIRE	Trentham Hall	Converted
Tupholme Abbey	LINCOLNSHIRE	Tupholme Abbey	Converted
Tutbury Priory	STAFFORDSHIRE	Tutbury Priory	Materials
Vale Royal Abbey	CHESHIRE	Vale Royal Abbey	Converted
Vaudey Abbey	LINCOLNSHIRE	Vaudey Abbey	Materials
Walden Abbey	ESSEX	Audley End	Converted
Wallingwells Priory	NOTTINGHAMSHIRE	Wallingwells Hall	Converted
Waltham Abbey	ESSEX	Abbey House	Materials
Warden Abbey	BEDFORDSHIRE	Warden Abbey	Converted
Ware Friary	HERTFORDSHIRE	Ware Friary	Converted
Watton Abbey	WORCESTERSHIRE	Watton Abbey	Converted
Waverley Abbey	SURREY	Loseley Park and Waverley Abbey House	Materials
Wearmouth Abbey	TYNE AND WEAR	Wearmouth Abbey	Converted
Welbeck Abbey	NOTTINGHAMSHIRE	Welbeck Abbey	Converted
Wenlock Priory	SHROPSHIRE	Abbey House	Converted
West Dereham Abbey	NORFOLK	West Dereham Abbey	Converted
Whalley Abbey	LANCASHIRE	Whalley Abbey and Samlesbury Hall	Converted, Materials
White Ladies Priory	SHROPSHIRE	White Ladies Priory	Converted
Whitefriars (Bristol)	GLOUCESTERSHIRE	Red Lodge	Converted
Wilton Nunnery	WILTSHIRE	Wilton House	Converted
Winchcombe Abbey	GLOUCESTERSHIRE	Sudeley Castle	Materials
Woburn Abbey	BEDFORDSHIRE	Woburn Abbey	Converted
Wombridge Priory	SHROPSHIRE	Wombridge Hall	Converted
Wroxall Priory	WARWICKSHIRE	Wroxall Abbey	Converted, Garden
Wroxton Abbey	OXFORDSHIRE	Wroxton Abbey	Converted
Wymondley Priory	HERTFORDSHIRE	Wymondley Priory	Converted
Yarm Blackfriars	YORKSHIRE	The Friarage	Converted

APPENDIX 3: Country Houses Damaged or Destroyed in the Civil War

Abbotsbury House	DORSET	Parliament
Affeton Castle	DEVON	Parliament
Apley House	SHROPSHIRE	Both
Arwenack House	CORNWALL	Parliament
Ascott House	BUCKINGHAMSHIRE	Parliament
Ashridge House	HERTFORDSHIRE	Parliament
Aston Hall	WARWICKSHIRE	Parliament
Aynho Manor	OXFORDSHIRE	Royalists
Bache Hall	CHESHIRE	Parliament
Baddesley Clinton	WARWICKSHIRE	Parliament
Bagworth Manor	LEICESTERSHIRE	Parliament
Barham Court	KENT	Parliament
Barton Court	BERKSHIRE	Parliament
Barton Hall	DERBYSHIRE	Royalists
Basing House	HAMPSHIRE	Parliament
Beckett House	BERKSHIRE	Royalists
Belvoir Castle	LINCOLNSHIRE	Parliament
Benthall Hall	SHROPSHIRE	Royalists
Beoley Hall	WORCESTERSHIRE	Royalists
Berechurch Manor	ESSEX	Parliament
Bickleigh Castle	DEVON	Parliament
Biddlesden Park	BUCKINGHAMSHIRE	Royalists
Biddulph Old Hall	STAFFORDSHIRE	Parliament
Bindon House	DORSET	Parliament
Bockmer House	BUCKINGHAMSHIRE	Parliament
Boddington Manor	GLOUCESTERSHIRE	Royalists
Bolsover Castle	DERBYSHIRE	Parliament
Bourton Manor	BUCKINGHAMSHIRE	Parliament
Bradgate House	LEICESTERSHIRE	Royalists
Brambletye House	SUSSEX	Parliament
Bretby Hall	DERBYSHIRE	Parliament
Broad Hinton	WILTSHIRE	Royalists
Bromham House	WILTSHIRE	Royalists
Broughton Castle	OXFORDSHIRE	Royalists
Burley House	RUTLAND	Parliament
Burton Constable Hall	YORKSHIRE	Parliament
Caldecote Hall	WARWICKSHIRE	Royalists
Campden House	GLOUCESTERSHIRE	Royalists
Canon Frome House	HEREFORDSHIRE	Royalists
Canonteign Barton	DEVON	Parliament
Castle Ashby	NORTHAMPTONSHIRE	Parliament
Cavendish House	LEICESTERSHIRE	Parliament
Caversham Park	BERKSHIRE	Parliament
Charborough Park	DORSET	Royalists
Chatsworth	DERBYSHIRE	Both
Chicheley Hall	BUCKINGHAMSHIRE	Parliament

Chideock Manor	DORSET	Parliament
Chillington Hall	STAFFORDSHIRE	Parliament
Chilton House	BUCKINGHAMSHIRE	Royalists
Claverton Manor	SOMERSET	Parliament
Combe Sydenham	SOMERSET	Parliament
Compton Wynyates	WARWICKSHIRE	Parliament
Cothelstone Manor	SOMERSET	Parliament
Coughton Court	WARWICKSHIRE	Parliament
Court House	GLOUCESTERSHIRE	Royalists
Cranborne Manor	DORSET	Royalists
Creech Grange	DORSET	Parliament
Cuddesdon Manor	OXFORDSHIRE	Parliament
Diglis House	WORCESTERSHIRE	Parliament
Dunsby St Andrew Manor	LINCOLNSHIRE	Parliament
Dunster Castle	SOMERSET	Both
Eastwood Hall	DERBYSHIRE	Parliament
Faringdon House	BERKSHIRE	Parliament
Fawley Court	BUCKINGHAMSHIRE	Parliament
Fawns Manor	MIDDLESEX	Unknown
Frankley Hall	WORCESTERSHIRE	Royalists
Gaunt House	OXFORDSHIRE	Parliament
Great Houghton Old Hall	YORKSHIRE	Royalists
Great Marlow Manor	BUCKINGHAMSHIRE	Unknown
Greenlands House	BUCKINGHAMSHIRE	Parliament
Hampton Lovett Manor	WORCESTERSHIRE	Parliament
Hardwick House	OXFORDSHIRE	Parliament
Harvington Hall	WORCESTERSHIRE	Parliament
Hawkesley Hall	WORCESTERSHIRE	Royalists
Hawton Manor	NOTTINGHAMSHIRE	Unknown
Hayton Castle	CUMBRIA	Parliament
Helmsley Castle	YORKSHIRE	Parliament
High Ercall Hall	SHROPSHIRE	Parliament
Highnam House	GLOUCESTERSHIRE	Parliament
Hillesden House	BUCKINGHAMSHIRE	Parliament
Hinton on the Green Manor	WORCESTERSHIRE	Royalists
Hooke Court	DORSET	Parliament
Hothfield House	KENT	Both
Howley Hall	YORKSHIRE	Royalists
Hunsingore Manor	YORKSHIRE	Parliament
Kenilworth Castle	WARWICKSHIRE	Parliament
Knole	KENT	Parliament
Ladye Place	BERKSHIRE	Parliament
Lanhydrock	CORNWALL	Royalists
Lark Stoke House	WARWICKSHIRE	Parliament
Lathom House	LANCASHIRE	Parliament
Lea Head Manor	STAFFORDSHIRE	Unknown
Lilleshall Abbey	SHROPSHIRE	Parliament
Longford Castle	WILTSHIRE	Parliament
Lulworth Castle	DORSET	Parliament

Lypiatt Park House	GLOUCESTERSHIRE	Parliament
Mapledurham House	OXFORDSHIRE	Parliament
Melford Hall	SUFFOLK	Parliament
Menabilly	CORNWALL	Parliament
Milcote Hall	WARWICKSHIRE	Parliament
Monkwick Manor	ESSEX	Unknown
Moreton Corbet Castle	SHROPSHIRE	Parliament
Nunney Castle	SOMERSET	Parliament
Old Court	SOMERSET	Unknown
Oxburgh Hall	NORFOLK	Parliament
Packington Park	WARWICKSHIRE	Parliament
Pates Manor	MIDDLESEX	Both
Phyllis Court	OXFORDSHIRE	Royalists
Pinhills House	WILTSHIRE	Royalists
Place Barton	DEVON	Parliament
Poole Hall	CHESHIRE	Parliament
Prior's Court	BERKSHIRE	Parliament
Ridge Hall	CHESHIRE	Unknown
Rockingham Castle	NORTHAMPTONSHIRE	Both
Rowden Manor	WILTSHIRE	Royalists
Rushall Hall	STAFFORDSHIRE	Royalists
Shallcross Hall	DERBYSHIRE	Parliament
Shardeloes	BUCKINGHAMSHIRE	Parliament
Shaw House	BERKSHIRE	Parliament
Shelford Manor	NOTTINGHAMSHIRE	Parliament
Sodington Hall	SHROPSHIRE	Parliament
Somerleyton House	SUFFOLK	Parliament
South Kelsey Hall	LINCOLNSHIRE	Royalists
St Osyth Priory	ESSEX	Parliament
Stansted Park	HAMPSHIRE	Parliament
Stokesay Castle	SHROPSHIRE	Parliament
Stourhead House	WILTSHIRE	Parliament
Sudeley Castle	GLOUCESTERSHIRE	Parliament
Swarkestone Old Hall	DERBYSHIRE	Parliament
Tattershall Castle	LINCOLNSHIRE	Royalists
Tilstone Hall	CHESHIRE	Parliament
Torksey Castle	LINCOLNSHIRE	Royalists
Tregothnan	CORNWALL	Royalists
Warblington Castle	HAMPSHIRE	Parliament
Wellington Manor	SOMERSET	Royalists
West Hall	DORSET	Parliament
Weston Manor	SOMERSET	Unknown
White Cross Manor	GLOUCESTERSHIRE	Royalists
Wingfield Manor	DERBYSHIRE	Parliament
Wiston House	SUSSEX	Both
Wiverton Hall	NOTTINGHAMSHIRE	Parliament
Woodhouse Castle	WILTSHIRE	Royalists
Wootton Lodge	STAFFORDSHIRE	Parliament
Wormleighton Manor	WARWICKSHIRE	Royalists

Wressle Castle	YORKSHIRE	Parliament
Yate Court	GLOUCESTERSHIRE	Parliament

REFERENCES

Introduction: Englishness and the Country House

1 Stephanie Barczewski, *Country Houses and the British Empire, 1700–1930* (Manchester, 2014).
2 The debate between a 'minimalist' and 'maximalist' impact of empire on metropolitan Britain was most famously contested by John MacKenzie and Bernard Porter. See John M. MacKenzie, *Propaganda and Empire: The Manipulation of British Public Opinion, 1880–1960* (Manchester, 1984); John M. MacKenzie, ed., *Imperialism and Popular Culture* (Manchester, 1986); John M. MacKenzie, 'The Persistence of Empire in Metropolitan Culture', in *British Culture and the End of Empire*, ed. Stuart Ward (Manchester, 2001), pp. 21–56; Bernard Porter, 'Further Thoughts on Imperial Absent-Mindedness', *Journal of Imperial and Commonwealth History*, 36 (2008), pp. 101–17; and John M. MacKenzie, '"Comfort" and Conviction: A Response to Bernard Porter', *Journal of Imperial and Commonwealth History*, 36 (2008), pp. 659–68. See also Andrew Thompson, *The Empire Strikes Back?: The Impact of Imperialism on Britain from the Mid-Nineteenth Century* (London, 2005); and Stuart Ward, 'The MacKenzian Moment in Retrospect (or How One Hundred Volumes Bloomed)', in *Writing Imperial Histories*, ed. Andrew Thompson (Manchester, 2013), pp. 29–48.
3 For a discussion of the 'imperial turn', see Richard Price, 'One Big Thing: Britain, Its Empire, and Their Imperial Culture', *Journal of British Studies*, 45 (2006), pp. 602–27.
4 Antoinette Burton, 'Who Needs the Nation?: Interrogating "British" History', *Journal of Historical Sociology*, 10 (1997), p. 231.
5 Ibid., p. 236. For an older account seeing English state-formation as a culturally contingent rather than political process, see Philip Corrigan and Derek Sayer, *The Great Arch: English State Formation as Cultural Revolution* (London, 1985).
6 Andrew Mackillop, 'What Has the Four Nations and Empire Model Achieved?', in *The MacKenzie Moment and Imperial History: Essays in Honour of John M. MacKenzie*, ed. Stephanie Barczewski and Martin Farr (Basingstoke, 2020), p. 274.
7 Ibid., pp. 279–80.
8 Ibid., p. 279.
9 Christopher Hussey, 'Syon House, Middlesex', *Country Life*, CVIII (1 December 1950), p. 1873.
10 Giles Worsley, *England's Lost Houses* (London, 2002), p. 7.
11 The National Trust currently cares for approximately two hundred country houses.
12 Catherine Palmer writes that the discourse of heritage tourism is 'a hegemonic discourse of nationhood reflecting the values and agenda of those organizations that own and manage the

sites. It is a discourse where nationness is presented as unifying and where tourists are invited to celebrate and commune with the core characteristics of Englishness.' Catherine Palmer, 'An Ethnography of Englishness: Experiencing Identity through Tourism', *Annals of Tourism Research*, 32 (2005), p. 8.
13. Patrick Wright, *On Living in an Old Country: The National Past in Contemporary Britain*, new edn (Oxford, 2009), p. 44.
14. Ibid., p. xii.
15. Ibid., p. 51.
16. Andrew Marr, *The Day Britain Died* (London, 2000), p. 108.
17. Roger Scruton, *England: An Elegy* (London, 2000), pp. 240–42.
18. Sam Jacob, 'Opinion', *De Zeen*, 21 June 2016, www.dezeen.com.
19. Edoardo Campanella and Marta Dassù, *Anglo Nostalgia: The Politics of Emotion in a Fractured West* (Oxford, 2019), pp. 61–2.
20. Simon Schama, 'Why Americans Have Fallen for Snobby *Downton Abbey*', *Newsweek*, 16 January 2012, www.newsweek.com.
21. Quoted in Campanella and Dassù, *Anglo Nostalgia*, p. 69.
22. See the essays in Christopher Shaw and Malcolm Chase, eds, *The Imagined Past: History and Nostalgia* (Manchester, 1989).
23. James Raven, 'Introduction', in *Lost Mansions: Essays on the Destruction of the Country House*, ed. James Raven (Basingstoke, 2015), p. 13.
24. Raphael Samuel points out that 'the notion that nostalgia is a peculiarly British disease, and that the rise of "heritage" in the late 1970s and 1980s represented a recrudescence of "Little Englandism" is not one which could survive comparative analysis intact.' Raphael Samuel, *Theatres of Memory: Past and Present in Contemporary Culture*, new edn (London, 2012), p. 307.
25. Campanella and Dassù, *Anglo Nostalgia*, p. x.
26. I am grateful to John Moisson for this insight.
27. Michael Kenny, 'English Nationalism in Historical Perspective', in *Governing England: English Identity and Institutions in a Changing United Kingdom*, ed. Michael Kenny, Iain McLean and Akash Paun (Oxford, 2018), p. 277.
28. Camilla Schofield, *Enoch Powell and the Making of Postcolonial Britain* (Cambridge, 2013).
29. Enoch Powell, speech to the Royal Society of St George, London, 23 April 1961, available at www.whatenglandmeanstome.co.uk, accessed 12 October 2021.
30. Scruton, *England*, p. 240.
31. On the one hand, 'Englishness ... has a distinctive nostalgic feature that sets it apart from any other national identity', as 'yearning for the past is somewhat intrinsic to the English way of being.' But on the other, in England 'nostalgia is an emotion that is both inward and outward looking, generating conflicting worldviews: that of Global Britain and that of Little England.' Campanella and Dassù, *Anglo Nostalgia*, pp. 9–10. There has been, post-Brexit, considerable scholarly discussion of the role of nostalgia for empire in determining the outcome of the vote. See Danny Dorling and Sally Tomlinson, *Rule Britannia: Brexit and the End of Empire* (London, 2019); Robert Gildea, *Empires of Mind: The Colonial Past and the Politics of the Present* (Cambridge, 2019); Michael Kenny and Nick Pearce, *Shadows of Empire: The Anglosphere in British Politics* (Cambridge, 2018); and Stuart Ward and Astrid Rasch, *Embers of Empire in Brexit Britain* (London, 2019).
32. Michael Kenny, *The Politics of English Nationhood* (Oxford, 2014), p. 57. For an argument that English nationalism can be leftist and radical in its political orientation, see Billy Bragg, *The Progressive Patriot: A Search for Belonging* (New York, 2006).
33. E. P. Thompson, *The Making of the English Working Class* (New York, 1963), Chapter 4.

34 Conceptions of the polity in the pre-modern era were frequently based upon royal ideals of an ever-expanding empire, and thus did not need to invoke specific territorial boundaries. Modern nationalisms, however, rely upon popular support, which in turn necessitates the concept of a 'homeland' worthy of allegiance and defence. As Lloyd Kramer writes in his analysis of European and American nationalisms since 1775, 'Nationhood can scarcely be imagined without reference to specific lands.' Lloyd Kramer, *Nationalism in Europe and America: Politics, Cultures, and Identities since 1775* (Chapel Hill, NC, 2011), p. 57.

35 Paul Readman writes, 'Across the world in the modern period, landscapes ... have functioned as powerful symbols of national identity. The American "Wild West", the Swiss Alps and the Norwegian fjords are obvious examples here.' Paul Readman, *Storied Ground: Landscape and the Shaping of English National Identity* (Cambridge, 2018), p. 5. See also Kenneth R. Olwig, 'Natural Landscapes in the Representation of National Identity', in *The Ashgate Research Companion to Heritage and Identity*, ed. Brian Graham and Peter Howard (Aldershot, 2008), pp. 73–88.

36 David Lowenthal, 'British National Identity and the English Landscape', *Rural History*, 2 (1991), p. 213. Peter Ackroyd writes that 'English writers and artists, English composers and folk-singers, have been haunted by this sense of place in which the echoic simplicities of past traditions sanctify a certain spot of ground.' Peter Ackroyd, *Albion: The Origins of the English Imagination* (London, 2002), p. 449.

37 Raymond Williams, *The Country and the City*, new edn (London, 2016), p. 248.

38 Peter Parker, *Housman Country: Into the Heart of England* (New York, 2016), p. 18.

39 See Amanda Gilroy, ed., *Green and Pleasant Land: English Culture and the Romantic Countryside* (Leuven, 2004).

Prior to the eighteenth century, the cultural values that people associated with the English landscape were tied up with their religious beliefs, not their national identity. See Alexandra Walsham, *The Reformation of the Landscape: Religion, Identity and Memory in Early Modern Britain and Ireland* (Oxford, 2011).

40 Quoted in David Howe, *Rocks and Rain, Reason and Romance: The Landscape, History and People of the Lake District* (Salford, 2019), pp. 19–20.

41 Jane Bingham, *The Cotswolds: A Cultural History* (Oxford, 2009), p. xix.

42 Ibid., p. xviii.

43 Catherine Brace writes, 'In the representation of the Cotswolds the buildings could provide a reference to a distant but enduring past and censure inappropriate building styles and materials that were seen to disrupt the harmony between place, dwelling and society that characterized rural England.' Catherine Brace, 'Looking Back: The Cotswolds and English National Identity, c. 1890–1950', *Journal of Historical Geography*, 25 (1999), p. 506.

44 John James Tissey, *Through Ten English Counties* (London, 1894), p. 197.

45 Spencer Edge, 'The Cotswolds', *English Illustrated Magazine* (November 1909), p. 160.

46 Martin Wiener, *English Culture and the Decline of the Industrial Spirit, 1850–1980*, 2nd edn (Cambridge, 2004). Similarly, Robert Hewison has argued that Britain's increasing obsession with historic preservation and 'national heritage' was responsible for inhibiting economic innovation in his *The Heritage Industry: Britain in a Climate of Decline* (London, 1987).

47 See Robert Colls, 'The Making of Rural England', in *Englishness: Politics and Culture, 1880–1920*, ed. Robert Colls and Philip Dodd, 2nd edn (London, 2014), pp. 85–112. See also Georgina Boyes, *The Imagined Village: Culture, Ideology and the English Folk Revival* (Manchester,

1993); Michael Bunce, *The Countryside Ideal: Anglo-American Images of Landscape* (London, 1994); Stephen Daniels, *Fields of Vision: Landscape Imagery and National Identity in England and the United States* (Cambridge, 1993); and John Taylor, *A Dream of England: Landscape, Photography and the Tourist's Imagination* (Manchester, 1994). For a critique of Wiener, see W. D. Rubenstein, *Capitalism, Culture and Decline in Britain, 1750–1990* (London, 1993).

48 Simon Featherstone writes, 'The act of travelling in England during the first half of the twentieth century provided a means of describing the nation to itself in a popular literary genre that emphasized haphazard revelation and identity defined through rural, southern landscapes and communities.' Simon Featherstone, *Englishness: Twentieth-Century Popular Culture and the Formation of English Identity* (Edinburgh, 2009), p. 82.

49 Catherine Brace writes that Batsford was 'partially responsible for the popularization of a particular version of England and Englishness'. Catherine Brace, 'Publishing and Publishers: Towards an Historical Geography of Countryside Writing, c. 1930–c. 1950', *Area*, 33 (2001), p. 287.

50 Stanley Baldwin, *On England* (London, 1926), p. 16.

51 Marc Brodie, 'The Politics of Rural Nostalgia between the Wars', in *Struggle Country: The Rural Ideal in Twentieth-Century Australia*, ed. Graeme Davison and Marc Brodie (Clayton, Vic., 2005). See also Sian Nicholas, 'The Construction of a National Identity: Stanley Baldwin, "Englishness" and the Mass Media in Interwar Britain', in *The Conservatives and British Society, 1880–1990*, ed. Martin Francis and Ina Zweiniger-Bargielowska (Cardiff, 1996), pp. 127–46.

52 'Images of the countryside enjoyed the success they did because they could accommodate a variety of different responses, not just celebratory notions of an ideal England purged of social and political tensions.' Alex Potts, '"Constable Country" between the Wars', in *Patriotism: The Making and Unmaking of British National Identity*, ed. Raphael Samuel (London, 1989), vol. III, p. 163.

53 Elizabeth K. Helsinger, *Rural Scenes and National Representation: Britain, 1815–1850* (Princeton, NJ, 1997), p. 7.

54 See Peter Mandler, 'Against "Englishness": English Culture and the Limits to Rural Nostalgia, 1850–1940', *Transactions of the Royal Historical Society*, 6th series, 7 (1997), pp. 155–75.

55 David Matless, *Landscape and Englishness* (London, 1998), pp. 14 and 16–17.

56 Readman, *Storied Ground*, p. 15.

57 James Lees-Milne, *Caves of Ice* (London, 1983), p. 172.

58 Jon Stobart, 'Lost Aspects of the Country Estate', in *Lost Mansions: Essays on the Destruction of the Country House*, ed. James Raven (Basingstoke, 2015), p. 25.

59 Libby Purves, 'Dreaming the Land', in *Being British: The Search for the Values That Bind the Nation*, ed. Matthew d'Ancona (Edinburgh, 2009), pp. 76–7.

60 Allan Vorda and Kim Herzinger, 'An Interview with Kazuo Ishiguro', *Mississippi Review*, 20 (1991), p. 139.

61 Peter Mandler, *The Fall and Rise of the Stately Home* (New Haven, CT, 1997), p. 3.

62 I am indebted to John Moisson for the observation about *Pride and Prejudice*.

63 Mandler, *Fall and Rise of the Stately Home*, p. 4. For the history of country-house tourism, see Ian Ousby, *The Englishman's England: Taste, Travel and the Rise of Tourism* (Cambridge, 1990); and Adrian Tinniswood, *The Polite Tourist: Country House Visiting through the Centuries* (London, 1989).

64 See David Cannadine, *The Decline and Fall of the British Aristocracy* (New Haven, CT, 1990).

65 Mandler, *Fall and Rise of the Stately Home*, p. 252.

66 Peter Kalliney, *Cities of Affluence and Anger: A Literary Geography of Modern*

Englishness (Charlottesville, VA, 2006), p. 28.
67 Ibid., p. 28.
68 Ibid., p. 42.
69 Evelyn Waugh, *Brideshead Revisited: The Sacred and Profane Memories of Captain Charles Ryder* (1945) (London, 2000), p. 8.
70 Standish Meacham, *Regaining Paradise: Englishness and the Early Garden City Movement* (New Haven, CT, 1999), p. 10.
71 Samuel, *Theatres of Memory*, p. 295.
72 Mandler, *Fall and Rise of the Stately Home*, p. 173.
73 Samuel, *Theatres of Memory*, p. 297.
74 Quoted in Mandler, *Fall and Rise of the Stately Home*, p. 290.
75 Mandler, *Fall and Rise of the Stately Home*, p. 320.
76 Adrian Tinniswood, *Noble Ambitions: The Fall and Rise of the Country House* (London, 2021), p. 35.
77 Mandler, *Fall and Rise of the Stately Home*, pp. 335 and 340.
78 See P. W. Rickwood, 'The National Land Fund, 1946–80: A Study in Failure', *Leisure Studies*, 6 (1987), pp. 15–23.
79 Quoted in Tinniswood, *Noble Ambitions*, p. 42.
80 Mandler, *Fall and Rise of the Stately Home*, p. 373.
81 The V&A's new director Roy Strong admitted that one of the 'burning reasons' behind his decision to take the job the previous year was to combat what he saw as 'a huge threat' to 'everything that we now categorise as "heritage"'. Roy Strong, *The Roy Strong Diaries: 1967–1987* (London, 1998), p. 121.
82 James Lees-Milne, 'The Country House in Our Heritage', in *The Destruction of the Country House*, ed. Roy Strong, Marcus Binney and John Harris (London, 1974), pp. 13–14.
83 John Harris, 'Gone to Ground', ibid., p. 15. Ruth Adams observes that 'the exhibition promoted the idea that not only were England's great country houses under threat, but that if these richly symbolic buildings were lost, so too would be important aspects of English national history, culture and identity.' Ruth Adams, 'The V&A, the Destruction of the Country House and the Creation of "English Heritage"', *Museum and Society*, 11 (2013), p. 1.
84 Raven, 'Introduction', *Lost Mansions*, p. 10. Not everyone, to be sure, was convinced: the cultural historian Robert Hewison has described the exhibition as 'a covert piece of propaganda against the wealth tax and a lament for the disappearance of a genteel way of life'. Robert Hewison, *Culture and Consensus: England, Art and Politics since 1940* (London, 1997), p. 193.
85 Ruth Adams writes, since the 1970s the country house has come to be surrounded by 'an effective if not always coherent discourse, fashioned from an emotive combination of nostalgia, English nationalism and a (to some extent manufactured) sense of urgency'. Adams, 'The V&A', p. 13.
86 'National Trust Responds to Record Visitor Numbers with Ambitious Plans to Improve Visitor Experience', www.nationaltrust.org.uk, 7 September 2018.
87 Samuel, *Theatres of Memory*, p. 163.
88 Owen Hatherley, *The Ministry of Nostalgia* (London, 2016), p. 8.
89 Nityanand Deckha writes, 'The English country house becomes an auratic object at the level of the nation only when it loses its function as the seat of a landed gentry family.' Nityanand Deckha, 'Beyond the Country House: Historic Conservation as Aesthetic Politics', *European Journal of Cultural Studies*, 7 (2004), p. 413.
90 Laurajane Smith defines heritage as 'a constitutive cultural process that identifies those things and places that can be given meaning and value as "heritage", reflecting contemporary cultural and social values, debates and aspirations'. Laurajane Smith, *The Uses of Heritage* (London, 2006), p. 3.
91 Walker Connor, 'Beyond Reason: The Nature of the Ethnonational Bond', *Ethnic and Racial Studies*, 16 (1993), p. 382.

92 'Ethnography of Englishness', pp. 9–10. For a study of how a specific heritage site can become the subject of contested interpretations, see Tim Edensor, *Tourists at the Taj: Performance and Meaning at a Symbolic Site* (Abingdon, 1998).
93 Catherine Hall, *White, Male and Middle Class: Explorations in Feminism and History* (Cambridge, 1992), p. 205.
94 Timothy Garton Ash, 'Is Britain European?', *International Affairs*, 77 (2001), p. 6.
95 Krishan Kumar, 'English and French National Identity: Comparisons and Contrasts', *Nations and Nationalisms*, 12 (2006), p. 414.
96 G. E. Aylmer, 'The Peculiarities of the English State', *Journal of Historical Sociology*, 3 (1990), p. 92.
97 J. R. Maddicott, *The Origins of the English Parliament, 924–1327* (Oxford, 2010), Chapter 7.
98 G. R. Elton, *The Tudor Revolution in Government* (Cambridge, 1953).
99 Catherine Palmer, 'Touring Churchill's England: Rituals of Kinship and Belonging', *Annals of Tourism Research*, 30 (2003), p. 442. Similarly, Peter Mandler writes that 'the stately homes of England, it is now often claimed, are that country's greatest contribution to western civilization. They are the quintessence of Englishness: they epitomize the English love of domesticity, of the countryside, of hierarchy, continuity and tradition.' Mandler, *Fall and Rise of the Stately Home*, p. 1.
100 Jeremy Black writes that the British have 'a genius for the appearance of continuity', but notes that 'the manufacture of traditions often masks shifts in the character of power' and that 'change is readily apparent both in the landscape and in the experience of the people.' Jeremy Black, *A History of the British Isles* (London, 1997), p. 325.
101 Peter Marshall, 'Henry VIII's Savage Reformation', *History Extra*, 19 May 2017, www.historyextra.com.
102 Steven Pincus, *1688: The First Modern Revolution* (New Haven, CT, 2011), p. 223.
103 See Mandler, *Fall and Rise of the Stately Home*; and Tinniswood, *Noble Ambitions*.

1 Violence and the Country House, I: The Reformation

1 Yuval Levin, *The Great Debate: Edmund Burke, Thomas Paine and the Birth of Right and Left* (New York, 2014), p. 77.
2 Jonny Yarker, 'Continuity and the Country House: Preservation as a Strategy of Display from 1688 to 1950', *Art and the Country House*, www.artandthecountryhouse.com, accessed 15 May 2021.
3 Clare Jackson, *Devil-Land: England under Siege, 1588–1688* (London, 2021), pp. 1–2.
4 Jeremy Musson, *The English Manor House: From the Archives of Country Life* (London, 1999), p. 7.
5 Ibid., pp. 7–8.
6 Quoted in Musson, *English Manor House*, p. 7.
7 P. H. Ditchfield, *The Manor-Houses of England* (London, 1910), pp. 28–30.
8 Krishan Kumar, 'English and French National Identity: Comparisons and Contrasts', *Nations and Nationalisms*, 12 (2006), p. 425.
9 H. G. Wells, *Tono-Bungay* [1909] (London, 2005), p. 100.
10 Quoted in Charles McKean, *The Scottish Chateau: The Country House of Renaissance Scotland* (Stroud, Gloucestershire, 2001), p. 39.
11 G. R. Elton, *Reform and Reformation: England, 1509–1558* (Cambridge, MA, 1977), p. 371. See also Peter Clark, *English Provincial Society from the Reformation to the Revolution: Religion, Politics and Society in Kent, 1500–1600* (Cranbury, NJ, 1977).
12 See A. G. Dickens, *The English Reformation* (New York, 1964); and Claire Cross, *Church and People, 1450–1660: The Triumph of the Laity of the English Church* (Atlantic Highlands, NJ, 1976).

13 For the leading advocates of the revisionist view, see Eamon Duffy, *The Stripping of the Altars: Religion in England, 1400–1580* (New Haven, CT, 1992); Christopher Haigh, *English Reformations: Religion, Politics and Society under the Tudors* (Oxford, 1993) and J. J. Scarisbrick, *The Reformation and the English People* (New York, 1984).

14 Nicholas Tyacke, 'Introduction: Rethinking the "English Reformation"', in *England's Long Reformation, 1500–1800*, ed. Nicholas Tyacke (London, 1988), p. 2.

15 Peter Marshall, '(Re)defining the English Reformation', *Journal of British Studies*, 48 (2009), p. 565. See also Ethan Shagan, *Popular Politics and the English Reformation* (Cambridge, 2003).

16 Christopher Haigh, 'The Recent Historiography of the English Reformation', *Historical Journal*, 25 (1982), pp. 1004–5.

17 Ibid., p. 1005.

18 See Peter Marshall, *Heretics and Believers: A History of the English Reformation* (New Haven, CT, 2017).

19 Peter Marshall, 'Henry VIII's Savage Reformation', *History Extra*, 19 May 2017, www.historyextra.com.

20 See Philip Jenkins, 'From Gallows to Prison?: The Execution Rate in Early Modern England', *Criminal Justice History*, 7 (1986), pp. 51–72. For the most prominent assessment of capital punishment in the eighteenth century, see E. P. Thompson, Douglas Hay, Peter Linebaugh, John G. Rule and Cal Winslow, *Albion's Fatal Tree: Crime and Society in Eighteenth-Century England* (New York, 1975).

21 Alexandra Walsham, *The Reformation of the Landscape: Religion, Identity and Memory in Early Modern Britain and Ireland* (Oxford, 2011), p. 10.

22 Michael Hodgetts, 'Elizabethan Priest Holes I: Dating and Chronology', *Recusant History*, 11 (1972), p. 280. Granville Squires identified 350 priest holes or other hiding places in his *Secret Hiding-Places* (London, 1933), but many of these are questionable. Michael Hodgetts lists 393 examples, but not all of these are in country houses, not all of them are extant and not all of them are from the time of the Reformation. See Michael Hodgetts, 'A Topographical Index of Hiding-Places', *Recusant History*, 16 (1982), pp. 146–216; Michael Hodgetts, 'A Topographical Index of Hiding-Places II', *Recusant History*, 24 (1998), pp. 1–54; and Michael Hodgetts, 'A Topographical Index of Hiding-Places III', *Recusant History*, 27 (2005), pp. 473–520. For the difficulties of identifying and verifying priest holes in houses today, see Michael Hodgetts, '*Mille Maeandris*: Nicholas Owen, 1606–2006', *Recusant History*, 28 (2006), pp. 180–82.

23 For local studies of elite Catholic communities in post-Reformation England, see Christopher Haigh, *Reformation and Resistance in Tudor Lancashire* (Cambridge, 1975); Peter Marshall and Geoffrey Scott, eds, *Catholic Gentry in English Society: The Throckmortons of Coughton from Reformation to Emancipation* (London, 2009); and Michael C. Questier, *Catholicism and Community in Early Modern England: Politics, Aristocratic Patronage and Religion, c. 1550–1640* (Cambridge, 2006).

24 Christopher Haigh, 'The Continuity of Catholicism in the English Reformation', *Past and Present*, 93 (1981), p. 42. Looking at the 1640s, John Bossy found the highest concentrations of recusants in Lancashire, Durham, Herefordshire, Warwickshire, Sussex, Yorkshire, Northumberland, Hampshire, Staffordshire, Worcestershire, Shropshire and Oxfordshire. John Bossy, *The English Catholic Community, 1570–1850* (Oxford, 1976), pp. 404–5.

25 Peter Marshall and Geoffrey Scott, 'Introduction: The Catholic Gentry in English Society', in *Catholic Gentry in English Society: The Throckmortons of Coughton from Reformation to*

26 *Emancipation*, ed. Peter Marshall and Geoffrey Scott (London, 2009), pp. 1–2.
26 See Alexandra Walsham, *Church Papists: Catholicism, Conformity and Confessional Polemic in Early Modern England* (Woodbridge, 1993).
27 Adam Morton and Nadine Lewycky, 'Introduction', in *Getting Along?: Religious Identities and Confessional Relations in Early Modern England. Essays in Honour of Professor W. J. Shiels*, ed. Adam Morton and Nadine Lewycky (Farnham, 2012), p. 1. See also W. J. Shiels, '"Getting On" and "Getting Along" in Parish and Town: Catholics and Their Neighbours in England', in *Catholic Communities in Protestant States: Britain and the Netherlands, c. 1570–1720*, ed. Benjamin Kaplan, Bob Moore, Henk F. K. Van Nierop and Judith Pollman (Manchester, 2009), pp. 67–83.
28 Jessie Childs, 'Elizabeth's War with England's Catholics', *History Extra*, 1 May 2014, www.historyextra.com.
29 John Bossy, 'The Character of Elizabethan Catholicism', *Past and Present*, 21 (1962), pp. 40–42.
30 Hodgetts, 'Elizabethan Priest Holes I', pp. 279–80.
31 Ibid.
32 The hall fell into disrepair after the Fitzherberts, impoverished due to their recusancy, were forced to sell it in 1649; two barns which remain on the site were constructed from the ruins. The gatehouse, which was also used as a farm building, was converted to a Catholic chapel in 1933 in honour of the martyred priests. Every year in July a pilgrimage takes place from Grindleford railway station to the chapel in their memory. 'Padley Hall: A Medieval Great House', *Historic England*, https://historicengland.org.uk, accessed 30 March 2019.
33 For the Vaux family, see Jessie Childs, *God's Traitors: Terror and Faith in Elizabethan England* (Oxford, 2014).
34 Hodgetts, 'Topographical Index of Hiding Places', p. 157.
35 Quoted in Michael Hodgetts, 'Elizabethan Priest Holes III: East Anglia, Baddesley Clinton, Hindlip', *Recusant History*, 12 (1974), p. 187.
36 Christopher Rowell, *Petworth House* (London, 1997), pp. 58–9.
37 Ibid., p. 60.
38 R. Rapple, 'Writing about Violence in the Tudor Kingdoms', *Historical Journal*, 54 (2011), p. 831.
39 Brendan Kane, 'Ordinary Violence? Ireland as Emergency in the Tudor State', *History*, 99 (2014), pp. 444–5.
40 Malcolm Smuts, 'Organized Violence in the Elizabethan Monarchical Republic', *History*, 99 (2014), pp. 420–21.
41 Kane, 'Ordinary Violence?', p. 458.
42 P. R. Cavill, 'Heresy and Forfeiture in Marian England', *Historical Journal*, 56 (2013), pp. 883–4.
43 Diarmaid McCulloch, *Tudor Rebellions*, 7th edn (London, 2020), p. 44.
44 For the former view, see G. R. Elton, 'Politics and the Pilgrimage of Grace', in *After the Reformation*, ed. Barbara C. Malament (Manchester, 1980), pp. 25–56; for the latter, see R. W. Hoyle, *The Pilgrimage of Grace and the Politics of the 1530s* (Oxford, 2001). Hoyle concludes that 'there was no conspiracy among the gentry in October 1536, not even the passive conspiracy of allowing a conflagration – which they could tame and control – to take hold.' Instead, 'once the rebellion had started, there were a number of individuals who, for their own reasons – self-advancement, principle, fear – dabbled in treason.' Hoyle, *Pilgrimage of Grace*, p. 420.
45 McCulloch, *Tudor Rebellions*, p. 49.
46 Hoyle, *Pilgrimage of Grace*, p. 405.
47 Kathleen Kinder, 'North Craven and the Pilgrimage of Grace' and Karen and Francis Shaw, 'Hellifield Peel', North Craven Heritage Trust, www.northcravenheritage.org.uk, accessed 19 September 2019.
48 Hoyle, *Pilgrimage of Grace*, p. 399; Christine M. Newman, 'Sir Robert

Constable', *Oxford Dictionary of National Biography*, 23 September 2004, www.oxforddnb.com; and 'Flamborough Castle: A Fortified Manor House', Historic England, https://historicengland.org.uk, accessed 3 February 2020.

49 'Sir John and Lady Margaret Bulmer', Cleveland and Teeside Local History Society, http://ctlhs.co.uk, accessed 16 June 2019.

50 'Bolton Castle', Historic England, https://historicengland.org.uk, accessed 12 December 2019.

51 Michael Hicks, 'Sir Francis Bigod', *Oxford Dictionary of National Biography*, 23 September 2004, www.oxforddnb.com; and Alan Davidson and A.D.K. Hawkyard, 'Sir Francis Bigod [Bigot]', History of Parliament, 1982, www.histparl.ac.uk; and 'Settrington House: A Brief History', Orangery Settrington, https://orangerysettrington.co.uk, accessed 14 October 2019.

52 R. W. Hoyle, 'Darcy, Thomas, Baron Darcy of Darcy', *Oxford Dictionary of National Biography*, 23 September 2004, www.oxforddnb.com. In 1544 Henry VIII gave Temple Newsam to his niece Lady Margaret Douglas, Countess of Lennox. This led to the house playing one last role in the political and religious upheaval of the sixteenth century, as the son who was born there to Margaret and her husband Matthew Stewart, 4th Earl of Lennox, in 1545 was Robert Stuart, Lord Darnley. After Darnley's marriage to Mary, Queen of Scots in 1565, Temple Newsam was seized by the Crown for a second time. For Thomas Darcy's role in the Pilgrimage of Grace, see Hoyle, *Pilgrimage of Grace*, pp. 414–18.

53 R. W. Hoyle, 'John Hussey, Baron Hussey', *Oxford Dictionary of National Biography*, 23 September 2004, www.oxforddnb.com; and 'Hussey Tower', Historic England, https://historicengland.org.uk, accessed 6 October 2019.

54 J.P.D. Cooper, 'Henry Courtenay, Marquess of Exeter', *Oxford Dictionary of National Biography*, 23 September 2004, www.oxforddnb.com.

55 'Parishes: Ellesborough' and 'Parishes: Medmenham', *Victoria County History: Buckinghamshire*, vol. II, pp. 84–9 and pp. 331–8, available at www.british-history.ac.uk.

56 Stanford Lehmberg, 'Sir Nicholas Carew', *Oxford Dictionary of National Biography*, 23 September 2004, www.oxforddnb.com.

57 'Allington Castle', Historic England, https://historicengland.org.uk, accessed 19 December 2019.

58 'Inner Ward of Cooling Castle' and 'Cobham Hall', Historic England, https://historic england.org.uk, accessed 15 December 2020.

59 McCulloch, *Tudor Rebellions*, p. 73.

60 Andy Wood, *The 1549 Rebellions and the Making of Early Modern England* (Cambridge, 2007), pp. 61 and 63. The rebels were generally not, however, seeking a restoration of Catholicism. If anything, they adopted an evangelical Protestantism which aligned with their political radicalism. McCulloch, *Tudor Rebellions*, pp. 91–3.

61 K. J. Kesselring, *The Northern Rebellion of 1569: Faith, Politics and Protest in Elizabethan England* (Basingstoke, 2007), p. 119.

62 Krista Kesselring, 'Mercy and Liberty: The Aftermath of the 1569 Northern Rebellion', *History*, 90 (2005), p. 214.

63 Ibid., pp. 222–3.

64 Kesselring, *Northern Rebellion*, p. 137.

65 'Greatford Hall', Historic England, https://historicengland.org.uk, accessed 17 June 2020; and T. M. Hofmann, 'Edmund Hall', History of Parliament, 1982, www.histparl.ac.uk.

66 Kesselring, *Northern Rebellion*, p. 132.

67 Ibid., p. 133.

68 Paul Everson and David Stocker, 'The Archaeology of Viceregality: Charles Brandon's Brief Rule in Lincolnshire', in *The Archaeology of Reformation, 1480–1580*,

ed. David Gaimster and Roberta Gilchrist (Abingdon, 2003), p. 148.
69 Ibid., p. 153.
70 Hugh Willmott, *The Dissolution of the Monasteries in England and Wales* (Sheffield, 2021), p. 142.
71 James G. Clark, *The Dissolution of the Monasteries: A New History* (New Haven, CT, 2021), p. 3.
72 Ibid., p. 8.
73 Ibid., p. 296.
74 Willmott, *Dissolution of the Monasteries*, p. 21.
75 Alison Weir, *Henry VIII: The King and His Court* (New York, 2007), p. 64.
76 Clark, *Dissolution of the Monasteries*, pp. 425–6.
77 Quoted in Jane Whitaker, *Raised from the Ruins: Monastic Houses after the Dissolution* (London, 2021), p. 245.
78 Maurice Howard, *The Building of Elizabethan and Jacobean England* (New Haven, CT, 2007), p. 25.
79 Margaret Aston, 'Public Worship and Iconoclasm', in *The Archaeology of Reformation, 1480–1580*, ed. David Gaimster and Roberta Gilchrist (Abingdon, 2003), p. 25.
80 Clark, *Dissolution of the Monasteries*, p. 409.
81 Willmott, *Dissolution of the Monasteries*, pp. 47 and 52.
82 Clark, *Dissolution of the Monasteries*, p. 415.
83 Willmott, *Dissolution of the Monasteries*, p. 50.
84 Whitaker, *Raised from the Ruins*, p. 13.
85 Willmott, *Dissolution of the Monasteries*, p. 47.
86 Ibid., p. 41.
87 There are 217 religious foundations listed in Appendix 2 because nine additional ones were converted to landscape gardens in the late seventeenth and eighteenth centuries, as is discussed in Chapter Three.
88 Maurice Howard, 'Recycling the Monastic Fabric: Beyond the Dissolution', in *The Archaeology of Reformation, 1480–1580*, ed. Gaimster and Gilchrist, p. 226.

89 In absolute terms, if not as a proportion, this is probably an undercount. Hugh Willmott claims that 'there is good archaeological or historical evidence for at least 250 [monastic sites] having been converted to domestic use in the period 1536–1600, and this is likely a vast underestimate of the actual total. Indeed, it would probably be safe to say that only a minority of houses did not experience some form of secular occupation during the 16th century, even if only temporarily.' Willmott, *Dissolution of the Monasteries*, p. 99.
90 Ibid.
91 Anthony Masinton, 'The Destruction of the Monasteries: Dissolution and Continuity of Sacred Space in Yorkshire', in *The Archaeology of Destruction*, ed. Lila Rakoczy (Newcastle, 2008), p. 245.
92 Willmott, *Dissolution of the Monasteries*, p. 54.
93 Clark, *Dissolution of the Monasteries*, p. 483.
94 Whitaker, *Raised from the Ruins*, p. 105.
95 A digital map of monastic sites before the Dissolution can be found at 'Discover the Dissolution', National Archives Education Service, 15 August 2022, https://storymaps.arcgis.com.
96 See T. H. Swales, 'The Redistribution of the Monastic Lands at the Dissolution', *Norfolk Archaeology*, 34 (1966), pp. 14–44.
97 Graham Haslam, 'An Administrative Study of the Duchy of Cornwall, 1500–1650', PhD diss., Louisiana State University (1980), p. xviii.
98 Howard, *Building of Elizabethan and Jacobean England*, p. 23.
99 Willmott, *Dissolution of the Monasteries*, pp. 116–17.
100 Masinton, 'Destruction of the Monasteries', p. 246. For the origin of long galleries in England, see Rosalys Coope, 'The "Long Gallery": Its Origins, Development, Use and Decoration', *Architectural History*, 29 (1986), pp. 43–84.
101 Howard, *Building of Elizabethan and Jacobean England*, p. 37. Monastic conversions may have influenced other

aspects of country-house design, such as the moving of important domestic spaces to the first floor and the use of central staircases leading up from the great hall to reach them. Howard, *Building of Elizabethan and Jacobean England*, pp. 38–9.
102   Whitaker, *Raised from the Ruins*, p. 17.
103   Howard, 'Recycling the Monastic Fabric', p. 223.
104   Whitaker, *Raised from the Ruins*, p. 163.
105   Willmott, *Dissolution of the Monasteries*, p. 115.
106   Ibid., pp. 127–8.
107   'Mottisfont Abbey', Historic England, https://historicengland.org.uk, accessed 19 July 2020.
108   Willmott, *Dissolution of the Monasteries*, pp. 100–101 and 128. Willmott mentions Calwich Abbey in Staffordshire and Canons Ashby in Northamptonshire as other potential conversions of churches to domestic use. Howard suggests that these buildings 'can be said to foreshadow the more compact, high houses of the late Elizabethan age' such as Robert Smythson's Hardwick and Wollaton Halls, another way in which the Dissolution-influenced country-house design. Howard, *Building of Elizabethan and Jacobean England*, p. 43. For Audley End, see P. J. Drury and S. Welch, 'Walden Abbey into Audley End', *Saffron Walden: Excavations and Research, 1972–80*, ed. S. R. Bassett, CBA Research Report 45 (London, 1982), pp. 94–105, available at https://archaeologydataservice.ac.uk, accessed 14 October 2022.
109   Whitaker, *Raised from the Ruins*, p. 371. See also John Heward, 'The Restoration of the South Front of Wilton House: The Development of the House Reconsidered', *Architectural History*, 35 (1992), pp. 78–117.
110   'No. 17 and Adjacent Building to West, Now a Wing of the Lord Crewe Arms', 'Wroxton Abbey' and 'Forde Abbey', Historic England, https://historicengland.org.uk, accessed 19 August 2018; and 'Country Houses for Sale', *Country Life*, 3 July 2021, www.countrylife.co.uk.
111   'Thame Park', Historic England, https://historicengland.org.uk, accessed 19 August 2018.
112   W. Heneage Legge, 'Ancient Stones Found in Ringmer', *Sussex Archaeological Collections Relating to the History and Antiquities of the County* (Lewes, 1902), vol. XLV, p. 38; 'Uckfield Road: Clayhill', Oakley Property, https://oakleyproperty.com, accessed 30 May 2020; 'Hangleton Manor', Heritage Gateway, www.heritagegateway.org.uk, accessed 14 April 2020; 'Kingston Manor' and 'Southover Grange', Historic England, https://historicengland.org.uk, accessed 3 May 2020.
113   'Gresley Old Hall', Historic England, https://historicengland.org.uk, accessed 15 April 2020; and 'Site of Medieval Manor House at Beauchamp Court, Alcester', Our Warwickshire, www.ourwarwickshire.org.uk, accessed 3 May 2020.
114   Donald Woodward, '"Swords into Ploughshares": Recycling in Pre-Industrial England', *Economic History Review*, 2nd series, 38 (1985), p. 180.
115   The combined number of monastic sites that were converted to houses (189) or used for their materials (32) is greater than the total of 208 because some sites were both converted and quarried for materials. In some cases this was because some of the buildings of the monastic complex were converted for use as a residence and others pillaged for their stone. This occurred at Angelsey Priory in Cambridgeshire, which was mostly demolished by Sir John Hynde and used to supply materials for Madingley Hall. At the end of the sixteenth century the surviving walls of the chapter house were used as the basis for a residence called Angelsey Abbey. In other cases, the buildings were initially converted to a house which was later demolished and quarried for materials. This occurred at

St Augustine's Abbey, Canterbury, which survived as a residential conversion into the seventeenth century before it was dismantled by Sir Edward Hales and used to build Hales Place.
116 'Newark Park', Historic England, https://historicengland.org.uk, accessed 2 February 2019; 'Cistercian Abbeys: Stanley', *The Cistercians in Yorkshire*, Digital Humanities Institute, University of Sheffield, www.dhi.ac.uk, accessed 15 January 2019; and 'History of Waverley Abbey', English Heritage, www.english-heritage.org.uk, accessed 22 January 2019.
117 Woodward, '"Swords into Ploughshares"', p. 180.
118 J. C. Dickinson, 'The Buildings of the English Austin Canons after the Dissolution of the Monasteries', *Journal of the British Archaeological Association*, 3rd series, 31 (1968), p. 62.
119 Willmott, *Dissolution of the Monasteries*, p. 32.
120 'History of Binham Priory', English Heritage, www.english-heritage.org.uk, accessed 17 January 2019.
121 Howard, *Building of Elizabethan and Jacobean England*, p. 24.
122 Walsham, *Reformation of the Landscape*, p. 81.
123 Clark, *Dissolution of the Monasteries*, p. 25.
124 Ibid., p. 101.
125 Ibid., p. 420. Willmott concurs: 'Despite the scale of destruction, we should not underestimate the extent to which aspects of the monastic world were saved and curated, at least in the short term.' Willmott, *Dissolution of the Monasteries*, p. 161.
126 Sarah Tarlow, 'Reformation and Transformation: What Happened to Catholic Things in a Protestant World?', in *The Archaeology of Reformation, 1480–1580*, ed. Gaimster and Gilchrist, p. 110.
127 There are 26 English cathedrals whose buildings pre-date the Reformation. Of these, eight were already cathedrals before the Reformation: Canterbury, Carlisle, Durham, Ely, Norwich, Rochester, Winchester and Worcester. Of all pre-Reformation cathedrals, only Bath and Coventry did not continue to function in the same role after the Reformation. Two more monastic cathedrals, St Albans (1877) and Southwark (1905), became Anglican cathedrals later. Five medieval abbey churches were converted to cathedrals by Henry VIII (Bristol, Chester, Gloucester, Oxford and Peterborough), and three more monastic churches (Manchester, Ripon and Southwell) were converted later.
128 David Stocker with Paul Everson, 'Rubbish Recycled: A Study of the Re-Use of Stone in Lincolnshire', in *Stone: Quarrying and Building in England AD 43–1525*, ed. David Parsons (Chichester, 1990), pp. 83–101. Similarly, Michael Heaton observes that 'salvaged architectural details and materials' were often used in ways in which they were 'not meaningless instances of rational economic utility', but rather 'emblems of cultural legitimacy, tokens of social cohesion and agents of knowledge exchange'. Michael Heaton, 'Spolia Britannica', *Construction History*, 34 (2019), p. 12.
129 Tarlow, 'Reformation and Transformation', p. 118.
130 Harriet Lyon, *Memory and the Dissolution of the Monasteries in Early Modern England* (Cambridge, 2022), p. 159.
131 Ibid., p. 163.
132 Howard, *Building of Elizabethan and Jacobean England*, p. 14.
133 Ibid., p. 15.
134 Ibid., p. 19.
135 Lyon, *Memory and the Dissolution of the Monasteries*, p. 130.
136 Walsham, *Reformation of the Landscape*, pp. 151–2. Lyon concurs, arguing that the significance of monastic ruins lay in 'the eye of the beholder', as their meaning 'could not be fixed'. Lyon,

Memory and the Dissolution of the Monasteries, p. 132.

137 'Puritan commitment to the eradication of idolatry ... reached a climax in the 1640s.' Margaret Aston, 'Puritans and Iconoclasm, 1560–1640', in *The Culture of English Puritanism, 1560–1700*, ed. Christopher Durston and Jacqueline Eales (New York, 1996), p. 121.

2 Violence and the Country House, II: The Civil War

1 Tim Goodwin, *Dorset in the Civil War, 1625–1665* (Tiverton, 1996), p. 45.
2 Quoted ibid., p. 86.
3 Jonathan Scott, 'England's Troubles, 1603–1702', in *The Stuart Court and Europe: Essays in Politics and Political Culture*, ed. R. Malcolm Smuts (Cambridge, 1996), p. 20.
4 The best estimate of the total number of deaths in the Civil War suggests that 84,830 people in England and Wales died in combat: 34,130 Parliamentarians and 50,700 Royalists. Charles Carlton proposes that another 127,000 perished in non-combat deaths due to disease or other effects of the war. Of these, he estimates that around 77,000 were soldiers and 40,000 were civilians. This total of 212,000 deaths is out of a total population of England and Wales of around 5.5 million in the mid-seventeenth century. Charles Carlton, 'Civilians', in *The Civil Wars: A Military History of England, Scotland and Ireland, 1638–1660*, ed. John Kenyon and Jane Ohlmeyer (Oxford, 1998), pp. 273–7.
5 Peter Marshall, '(Re)defining the English Reformation', *Journal of British Studies*, 48 (2009), p. 567.
6 See Muriel C. McClendon, Joseph P. Ward and Michael MacDonald, eds, *Protestant Identities: Religion, Society and Self-Fashioning in Post-Reformation England* (Stanford, CA, 1999); and Nicholas Tyacke, ed., *England's Long Reformation* (London, 1998).
7 Marshall, '(Re)defining the English Reformation', p. 568.
8 'Cobham Hall: Historic House Overview', Cobham Hall, www.cobhamhall.com, accessed 17 July 2018; and P. W. Hasler, 'Henry Brooke II, alias Cobham', History of Parliament, 1981, www.histparl.ac.uk.
9 Mark Nicholls and Penry Williams, 'Sir Walter Ralegh', *Oxford Dictionary of National Biography*, 23 September 2004, www.oxforddnb.com.
10 Mark Nicholls, 'Treason's Reward: The Punishment of Conspirators in the Bye Plot of 1603', *Historical Journal*, 38 (1995), pp. 830 and 837.
11 'The History of Grafton Manor', Grafton Manor Hotel, www.graftonmanorhotel.co.uk, accessed 5 September 2019.
12 See Hilary L. Turner, 'Walter Jones of Witney, Worcester and Chastleton: Rewriting the Past', *Oxoniensia*, 73 (2008), pp. 33–44.
13 See Michael Hodgetts, 'Coughton and the Gunpowder Plot', in *Catholic Gentry in English Society: The Throckmortons of Coughton from Reformation to Emancipation*, ed. Peter Marshall and Geoffrey Scott (Farnham, 2009), pp. 93–121.
14 Christopher Clay, 'Chapter 14: Landlords and Estate Management in England', in *The Agrarian History of England and Wales*, ed. Joan Thirsk (Cambridge, 1985), vol. v/2, p. 119.
15 See Mark Stoyle, '"Whole Streets Converted to Ashes": Property Destruction in Exeter during the English Civil War', *Southern History*, 16 (1994), pp. 67–84.
16 See Margaret Aston, *England's Iconoclasts*, vol. I: *Laws against Images* (Oxford, 1988); Patrick Collinson, *From Iconoclasm to Iconophobia: The Cultural Impact of the Second English Reformation* (Reading, 1986); John Phillips, *The Reformation of Images: Destruction of Art in England, 1535–1660* (Berkeley, CA, 1973); and Julie Spraggon, *Puritan Iconoclasm during the English Civil War* (Woodbridge, 2003).

17 John Walter notes, 'That disorder was the work of "outsiders" was a useful claim.' John Walter, 'Popular Iconoclasm and the Politics of the Parish in Eastern England, 1640–1642', *Historical Journal*, 47 (2004), p. 279. For the religious motivations of seventeenth-century iconoclasts, see David Cressy, 'The Battle of the Altars: Turning the Tables and Breaking the Rails', in his *Travesties and Transgressions in Tudor and Stuart England* (Oxford, 2000), pp. 186–212; Jacqueline Eales, 'Iconoclasm, Iconography, and the Altar in the English Civil War', in *The Church and the Arts*, ed. Diana Wood, Studies in Church History 28 (Oxford, 1992), pp. 313–27; and John Walter, '"Abolishing Superstition with Sedition": The Politics of Popular Iconoclasm in England, 1640–1642', *Past and Present*, 183 (2004), pp. 79–123.

18 Rachel M. C. Askew, 'Political Iconoclasm: The Destruction of Eccleshall Castle during the English Civil Wars', *Post-Medieval Archaeology*, 50 (2016), p. 284.

19 David Appleby, 'Fleshing Out a Massacre: The Storming of Shelford House and Social Forgetting in Restoration England', *Historical Research*, 93 (2020), p. 286.

20 Ronald Hutton and Wylie Reeves, 'Sieges and Fortifications', in *The Civil Wars: A Military History of England, Scotland and Ireland, 1638–1660*, ed. John Kenyon and Jane Ohlmeyer (Oxford, 1998), p. 199.

21 Stephen Porter, *The Blast of War: Destruction in the English Civil Wars* (Cheltenham, 2011), p. 30.

22 Barbara Donagan, 'Atrocity, War Crime and Treason in the English Civil War', *American Historical Review*, 99 (1994), pp. 1149–50.

23 Imogen Peck, *Recollection in the Republics: Memories of the British Civil Wars in England, 1649–1659* (Oxford, 2021), p. 145.

24 Francis Young, *The Gages of Hengrave and Suffolk Catholicism, 1640–1767* (Woodbridge, 2015), p. 9.

25 John Barratt, *The Civil War in the South-West* (Barnsley, 2005), p. 87.

26 Quoted in Brian Stone, *Derbyshire in the Civil War* (Cromford, Derbyshire, 1992), p. 24.

27 Ian F. W. Beckett, *Wanton Troopers: Buckinghamshire in the Civil Wars, 1640–1660* (Barnsley, 2016), p. 61.

28 Young, *Gages of Hengrave*, p. 9.

29 Robert Sackville-West, *Inheritance: The Story of Knole and the Sackvilles* (New York, 2010), pp. 46–7.

30 Quoted in Beckett, *Wanton Troopers*, p. 63.

31 'Torksey Castle', Heritage Gateway, www.heritagegateway.org.uk, accessed 17 July 2020.

32 Appleby, 'Fleshing Out a Massacre', p. 288.

33 Beckett, *Wanton Troopers*, p. 76.

34 M. W. Thompson, *The Decline of the Castle* (Cambridge, 1987), Chapter 8 and pp. 179–85.

35 Matthew Johnson, *Behind the Castle Gate: From the Middle Ages to the Renaissance* (London, 2002), p. 173.

36 Stephen Porter, 'Property Destruction in the English Civil Wars', *History Today*, XXXVI/8 (August 1986), p. 38.

37 Johnson, *Behind the Castle Gate*, p. 173.

38 Ibid., p. 174.

39 Lila Rakoczy, 'Out of the Ashes: Destruction, Re-Use and Profiteering in the English Civil War', in *The Archaeology of Destruction*, ed. Lila Rakoczy (Newcastle, 2008), p. 283.

40 'Holdenby House', Heritage Gateway, www.heritagegateway.org.uk, accessed 12 December 2019.

41 Rachel Askew, 'Sheffield Castle and the Aftermath of the English Civil War', *Northern History*, 2 (2017), p. 204.

42 Clay, 'Landlords and Estate Management', pp. 133–4.

43 Anthony Fletcher, *A County Community in Peace and War: Sussex, 1600–1660* (London, 1975), p. 270.

44 Hutton and Reeves, 'Sieges and Fortifications', p. 228; and Jane Sterling, *The Civil War in Lancashire* (Lancaster, 1971), p. 17.

45 Quoted in David Cooke, *The Civil War in Yorkshire: Fairfax versus Newcastle* (Barnsley, 2004), pp. 110–11.
46 A tuck, from the French *estoc*, was a sword with a two-handed grip, cruciform hilt, and straight, edgeless blade with a sharp point. Stone, *Derbyshire in the Civil War*, pp. 95–6.
47 Ibid., p. 99.
48 Gareth Williams, *The Country Houses of Shropshire* (Woodbridge, 2021), p. 320.
49 'Civil War Petitions: Conflict, Welfare and Memory during the English Civil Wars, 1642–1710', *Civil War Petitions*, www.civilwarpetitions.ac.uk, accessed 3 July 2021. For an analysis of these petitions, see Mark Stoyle, '"Memories of the Maimed": The Testimony of Charles I's Former Soldiers, 1660–1730', *History*, 88 (2003), pp. 204–26.
50 Hutton and Reeves, 'Sieges and Fortifications', pp. 200–201.
51 Philip Tennant, *Edgehill and Beyond: The People's War in the South Midlands, 1642–1645* (Stroud, Gloucestershire, 1992), pp. 209–10.
52 Porter, *Blast of War*, p. 45.
53 Quoted in David Eddershaw, *The Civil War in Oxfordshire* (Stroud, Gloucestershire, 1995), p. 82.
54 Beckett, *Wanton Troopers*, p. 64.
55 Ben Coates, 'William Russell of Great Witley, Worcestershire', History of Parliament, www.histparl.ac.uk, 2010.
56 Malcolm Atkin, *Worcestershire under Arms: An English County during the Civil Wars* (Barnsley, 2004), pp. 116–17.
57 Quoted in Barratt, *Civil War in the Southwest*, p. 80.
58 Maxwell Craven and Michael Stanley, *The Derbyshire Country House* (Derby, 1982), vol. I, pp. 77–8.
59 'Boarstall Tower in Buckinghamshire', Benchmark House Histories, www.benchmarkhousehistories.com, accessed 5 July 2021.
60 Martin Baugh, 'The Final Battle of Basing House', Hampshire Cultural Trust, 14 October 2020, www.cultureoncall.com. For a more detailed account, see Tony MacLachlan, *The Civil War in Hampshire* (Salisbury, 2000), Chapters 8, 11, 15–18 and 20.
61 Quoted in S. R. Gardiner, *History of the Great Civil War, 1642–1649* (London, 1889), vol. II, p. 347.
62 Porter, *Blast of War*, pp. 59 and 63.
63 Ibid., p. 62.
64 Ibid., pp. 59–60.
65 Beckett, *Wanton Troopers*, p. 65.
66 Richard Ollard, *Dorset* (London, 1995), p. 5.
67 Desmond Seward, *Sussex* (London, 1995), p. 142. See also Mark Stoyle, *Loyalty and Locality: Popular Allegiance in Devon during the English Civil War* (Exeter, 1994).
68 Sterling, *Civil War in Lancashire*, pp. 3–4.
69 Jack Binns, 'Henry Constable, First Viscount Dunbar', *Oxford Dictionary of National Biography*, 23 September 2004, www.oxforddnb.com.
70 William Joseph Shiels, 'Bedingfield [Bedingfeld] Family', *Oxford Dictionary of National Biography*, 23 September 2004, www.oxforddnb.com.
71 Quoted in Tennant, *Edgehill and Beyond*, p. 136.
72 Beckett, *Wanton Troopers*, p. 67.
73 Thompson, *Decline of the Castle*, p. 138.
74 Malcolm Airs, *The Making of the English Country House, 1500–1640* (London, 1975), pp. 82–90.
75 Porter, *Blast of War*, p. 112.
76 Ibid., p. 114.
77 Stone, *Derbyshire in the Civil War*, pp. 48, 51–2 and 63–4.
78 Ibid., p. 42.
79 Eddershaw, *Civil War in Oxfordshire*, p. 77.
80 Atkin, *Worcestershire under Arms*, p. 109.
81 Porter, *Blast of War*, p. 2.
82 'Moated Site and Civil War Defences at Strensham Castle', Historic England, https://historicengland.org.uk, accessed 14 June 2020.
83 'Basing House and the Grange Field', Historic England, https://historicengland.org.uk, accessed 16 July 2020.

84 'Understanding Historic Parks and Gardens in Buckinghamshire: Horsenden Hall', Buckinghamshire Gardens Trust Research and Recording Project, http://bucksgardenstrust.org.uk, accessed 12 March 2019.
85 Williams, *Country Houses of Shropshire*, p. 32.
86 M. R. Toynbee, 'Historical Note', to B.H.St.J. O'Neil, 'A Civil War Battery at Cornbury, Oxfordshire', *Oxoniensia*, 10 (1945), pp. 77–8.
87 'Hound Hill', Heritage Gateway, www.heritagegateway.org.uk, accessed 19 September 2018.
88 'Rousham House', Historic England, https://historicengland.org.uk, accessed 2 October 2018.
89 M. W. Helms and Eveline Cruikshanks, 'Francis Godolphin', History of Parliament, www.histparl.ac.uk, 1983; and 'Godolphin', Heritage Gateway, www.heritagegateway.org.uk, accessed 5 May 2020.
90 Nicholas Cooper, *Houses of the Gentry, 1480–1680* (New Haven, CT, 1999), p. 238; and 'Family History', Hutton-in-the-Forest, https://hutton-in-the-forest.co.uk, accessed 19 June 2019.
91 'Rousham House', Historic England, https://historicengland.org.uk, accessed 4 November 2019.
92 Cooper, *Houses of the Gentry*, p. 158; and Penny Churchill, 'The Cornish Castle That Once Housed a Wife in Each Tower', *Country Life*, 21 April 2018, www.countrylife.co.uk.
93 R. G. Scriven, 'The History of Castle Ashby', *Archaeological Journal*, 35 (1878), pp. 360–71.
94 'Histories of Conservation Areas: Aston-on-Trent', South Derbyshire District Council, www.southderbyshire.gov.uk, accessed 11 November 2020.
95 'Baconsthorpe Castle', Baconsthorpe Village, https://baconsthorpe.org, accessed 6 April 2019; and 'History of Baconsthorpe Castle', English Heritage, www.english-heritage.org.uk, accessed 14 October 2019.
96 'About Us', Yarnton Manor, www.yarntonmanor.com, accessed 12 May 2020.
97 Susie Stubbs, *Little Moreton Hall* (Swindon, 2015), pp. 20–21.
98 Quoted in Michael Hall, *The English Country House: From the Archives of Country Life, 1897–1939* (London, 2001), p. 35.
99 Andy McSmith, 'Secateurs at Dawn at Sissinghurst', *The Independent*, 28 February 2009.
100 For a critique of 'the excessive amount of deferential attention and ahistorical celebration' which Sackville-West and Nicolson have received, see David Cannadine, 'Portrait of a Marriage: Harold Nicolson and Vita Sackville-West Revisited', in his *Aspects of Aristocracy: Grandeur and Decline in Modern Britain* (New Haven, CT, 1994), pp. 210–41. Cannadine writes that Sissinghurst's garden 'has been incorporated into that cult of snobbish nostalgia and conservationist escapism by which so much of post-war Britain has been blinded and blighted'. Cannadine, 'Portrait of a Marriage', p. 210.
101 Adam Nicolson, *Sissinghurst: An Unfinished History* (New York, 2009), pp. 210–11.
102 Ibid., p. 214.
103 Ibid.
104 Quoted ibid., p. 217.
105 'Sissinghurst Castle', National Trust Collections, www.nationaltrustcollections.org.uk, accessed 23 October 2020.
106 Clay, 'Landlords and Estate Management', pp. 120–21.
107 Christopher Clay observes that 'reductions in rent of one-third were nothing out of the ordinary'; ibid., p. 126.
108 Tennant, *Edgehill and Beyond*, p. 135.
109 'Gayhurst House', *DiCamillo*, www.thedicamillo.com, accessed 19 June 2020.
110 Stone, *Derbyshire in the Civil War*, p. 97.
111 Clay, 'Landlords and Estate Management', p. 128. For how sequestration affected Catholics, see

111 Eilish Gregory, *Catholics during the English Revolution, 1642–1660: Politics, Sequestration and Loyalty* (Woodbridge, 2021).
112 Clay, 'Landlords and Estate Management', p. 129; and John Morrill and John Walter, 'Order and Disorder in the English Revolution', in *The English Civil War*, ed. Richard Cust and Ann Hughes (London, 1997), p. 325.
113 Clay, 'Landlords and Estate Management', p. 131.
114 Beckett, *Wanton Troopers*, p. 66.
115 H. J. Habakkuk, 'Landowners and the Civil War', *Economic History Review*, new series, 18 (1965), p. 136.
116 Ibid., p. 139.
117 'A Brief History of Badsworth', Badsworth Village, www.badsworth-village.com, accessed 23 July 2020.
118 'Townships: Allerton', *Victoria County History: Lancashire*, vol. III, pp. 128–31, available at British History Online, www.british-history.ac.uk.
119 Joan Thirsk found that 126 of 130 estates in the Southeast of England were ultimately recovered, and P. G. Holiday traced a similar percentage in Yorkshire. Joan Thirsk, 'The Sales of Royalist Land during the Interregnum', *Economic History Review*, new series, 5 (1952), pp. 188–207; and P. G. Holiday, 'Land Sales and Repurchases in Yorkshire after the Civil Wars', *Northern History*, 5 (1970), pp. 67–92.
120 'Haines Hill', David Nash Ford's Royal Berkshire History, www.berkshirehistory.com, accessed 7 October 2020.
121 'The Lucy Family of Charlecote Park', National Trust, www.nationaltrust.org.uk, accessed 18 February 2019.
122 Clay, 'Landlords and Estate Management', p. 148.
123 'A Brief History of The Vyne', National Trust, www.nationaltrust.org.uk, accessed 12 December 2019.
124 'Clifford Manor', Historic England, https://historicengland.org.uk, accessed 19 May 2019.
125 'Farnborough Hall', Historic England, https://historicengland.org.uk, accessed 19 May 2019.
126 Richard Gough, *The Antiquities and Memoirs of the Parish of Myddle, County of Salop* (Cambridge, 2015), p. 46.
127 Onslow House had belonged to the Royalist Harries family at the time of the Civil War and was sold in 1658, probably because of the financial difficulties the war had caused.
128 Williams, *Country Houses of Shropshire*, pp. 539–40.
129 Christopher O'Riordan, 'Popular Exploitation of Enemy Estates in the English Revolution', *History*, 78 (1993), p. 183.
130 Quoted in Goodwin, *Dorset in the Civil War*, p. 48.
131 'Charborough Park', Historic England, https://historicengland.org.uk, accessed 30 March 2020; and Richard Cust, 'Sir Walter Erle [Earle]', *Oxford Dictionary of National Biography*, 23 September 2004, www.oxforddnb.com.
132 Michael Hill, *East Dorset Country Houses* (Reading, 2013), p. 231.
133 'Devizes Castle, Devizes, Wiltshire', Devizes Heritage, www.devizesheritage.co.uk, accessed 3 January 2020.
134 Williams, *Country Houses of Shropshire*, p. 669.
135 Mary Fielding, 'The History of Campden House', Chipping Campden History Society, www.chippingcampdenhistory.org.uk, accessed 19 March 2020.
136 See Madeline H. Caviness, 'Fifteenth-Century Stained Glass from the Chapel of Hampton Court, Herefordshire: The Apostles' Creed and Other Subjects', *Walpole Society*, 42 (1968–70), pp. 35–60.
137 Porter, *Blast of War*, p. 112.
138 'Old Sir John Spencer at Wormleighton', Our Warwickshire, www.ourwarwickshire.org.uk, accessed 16 August 2019.
139 Williams, *Country Houses of Shropshire*, pp. 443–4.
140 Porter, *Blast of War*, p. 113.
141 D. R. Hainsworth, *Stewards, Lords and People: The Estate Steward and His World*

142 Arthur Herbert Dodd, 'Somerset Family, of Raglan, Chepstow and Troy, Monmouth, Crickhowell, Brecknock, Badminton, Gloucestershire', *Dictionary of Welsh Biography*, 1959, https://biography.wales; and Ander Gomme, 'Badminton Revisited', *Architectural History*, 27 (1984), pp. 163–82.

143 'Ragley Hall', Historic England, https://historicengland.org.uk, accessed 30 March 2020.

144 Jacqueline Eales, *Puritans and Roundheads: The Harleys of Brampton Bryan and the Outbreak of the English Civil War* (Cambridge, 1990), pp. 165–89.

145 Habakkuk, 'Landowners and the Civil War', p. 148.

146 'Cadhay', Historic England, https://historicengland.org.uk, accessed 12 October 2020.

147 Paul Gladwish, 'The Sale of English Royalist Lands after the Civil War: Two Case Studies from the West Midlands', *Midland History*, 29 (2004), pp. 27–36.

148 'Site of Rotherwas House, Earthwork Remains of Formal Gardens and Rotherwas Chapel', Historic England, https://historicengland.org.uk, accessed 20 August 2019.

149 John Broad, 'Gentry Finances and the Civil War: The Case of the Buckinghamshire Verneys', *Economic History Review*, new series, 32 (1979), pp. 183–4.

150 Tim Knox, *Claydon House, Buckinghamshire* (Swindon, 1999), p. 41; and Beckett, *Wanton Troopers*, p. 67.

151 Porter, *Blast of War*, pp. 65–6.

152 Ibid., p. 123. Examples of ruins that were still standing long after the war include Milcote Manor (Warwickshire), White Cross Manor (Gloucestershire), Bagworth Park (Leicestershire), Wellington Manor (Somerset), Abbotsbury House (Dorset), Basing House (Hampshire), Moreton Corbet (Shropshire), Stepleton Castle (Herefordshire) and Torksey Castle (Lincolnshire).

153 Quoted in Peck, *Recollection in the Republics*, pp. 145 and 147.

154 See Lloyd Bowen and Mark Stoyle, eds, *Remembering the English Civil Wars* (London, 2022); Paulina Kewes, 'Acts of Remembrance, Acts of Oblivion: Rhetoric, Law and National Memory in Early Restoration England', in *Ritual, Routine and Regime: Repetition in Early Modern British and European Cultures*, ed. Lorna Clymer (Toronto, 2006), pp. 103–31; Edward Legon, *Revolution Remembered: Seditious Memories after the British Civil Wars* (Manchester, 2019); Matthew Neufeld, *The Civil Wars after 1660: Public Remembering in Late Stuart England* (Woodbridge, 2013); Peck, *Recollection in the Republics*; Erin Peters, *Commemoration and Oblivion in Royalist Print Culture, 1658–1667* (Cham, Switzerland, 2017); Mark Stoyle, 'Remembering the English Civil Wars', in *The Memory of Catastrophe*, ed. Peter Gray and Kendrick Oliver (Manchester, 2004), pp. 19–30; and Blair Worden, *Roundhead Reputations: The English Civil Wars and the Passions of Posterity* (London, 2001).

155 Ann Hughes, '"When the Scots Army Did March Thorow Our Country": Space, Place and Remembering in the English Civil War', in *Remembering the English Civil Wars*, ed. Bowen and Stoyle, pp. 49–50. Similar, Imogen Peck writes that after the Civil War 'place, and particularly places of war and wartime destruction, acted as sites of memory.' Peck, *Recollection in the Republics*, p. 129.

156 Imogen Peck, 'Civilian Memories of the British Civil Wars, 1642–1660', in *Remembering the English Civil Wars*, ed. Bowen and Stoyle, p. 26.

157 'Pike House', *DiCamillo*, www.thedicamillo.com, accessed 5 February 2019.

158 'The Royal Fort House – in the Place of the Old Fort', *Bristol Archaeology News*,

159 Peck, *Recollection in the Republics*, p. 151.
160 Ibid., p. 145.
161 Ibid., p. 134.
162 Eddershaw, *Civil War in Oxfordshire*, p. 154.
163 Beckett, *Wanton Troopers*, p. 65.
164 Neufeld, *Civil Wars after 1660*, p. 2.
165 Ibid., pp. 5 and 19.
166 Appleby, 'Fleshing Out a Massacre', p. 286.
167 Ibid., p. 297.
168 Ibid., p. 305.
169 Neufeld, *Civil Wars after 1660*, p. 93.

3 Reflections on the Non-Revolution in England

1 Francis Ingilby was beatified by Pope John Paul II in 1989.
2 John Izon, 'New Light on the Gunpowder Plot', *History Today*, IV/4 (April 1954), pp. 245–50.
3 Jenny Elliott, 'During the English Civil War, Women Fought, Spied and Defended Castles', *Atlas Obscura*, 30 July 2021, www.atlasobscura.com. See also Julian Humphrys, 'Did Women Fight in the British Civil Wars?', *History Extra*, 1 August 2016, www.historyextra.com; Mark Stoyle, 'The Women Who Swapped Dresses for Breeches', *History Extra*, 11 July 2019, www.historyextra.com; and Mark Stoyle, '"Give Mee a Souldier's Coat": Female Cross-Dressing during the English Civil War', *History*, 103 (2018), pp. 5–26.
4 Steve Pincus, *1688: The First Modern Revolution* (New Haven, CT, 2009), p. 254.
5 Ibid., pp. 256–7.
6 Ibid., p. 257.
7 Ibid., pp. 238–9.
8 The information in the preceding paragraphs is taken from Edward Corp, 'The Strickland Family', in *Sizergh Castle* (Swindon, 2001), pp. 44–50.
9 Hugh Dunthorne and David Onnekink, 'Bentinck, Hans Willem [William], First Earl of Portland', *Oxford Dictionary of National Biography*, 23 September 2004, www.oxforddnb.com.
10 Oliver Cox, 'Introduction: Political Positioning after the Glorious Revolution', in *Politics and the English Country House, 1688–1800*, ed. Joan Coutu, Jon Stobart and Peter N. Lindfield (Montreal and Kingston, ON, 2023).
11 'Gates and Gate Piers to Wilderness Garden at North End of Lime Avenue of Adlington Hall', Historic England, https://historicengland.org.uk, accessed 30 January 2020.
12 'Erle, Thomas', *Oxford Dictionary of National Biography*, 23 September 2004, www.oxforddnb.com; and 'Ice House in Charborough Park', Historic England, https://historicengland.org.uk, accessed 30 January 2020.
13 'Gayton Hall', Historic England, https://historicengland.org.uk, accessed 19 August 2019.
14 Rosemary Baird, *Goodwood: Art and Architecture, Sport and Family* (London, 2007), p. 9.
15 Ibid., p. 23.
16 See Lisa Jardine, *Going Dutch: How England Plundered Holland's Glory* (London, 2008); Wouter Kuyper, *Dutch Classicist Architecture: A Survey of Dutch Architecture, Gardens and Anglo-Dutch Architectural Relations from 1625 to 1700* (Delft, 1980); and Hentie Louw, 'Dutch Influence on British Architecture in the Late Stuart Period, c. 1660 – c. 1714', *Dutch Crossing: Journal of Low Countries Studies*, 33 (2009), pp. 83–120. For a cautionary note about the limits of Dutch influence on English houses before 1650, see Hentie Louw, 'Anglo-Netherlandish Architectural Interchange, c. 1600–c. 1660', *Architectural History*, 24 (1981), pp. 1–23.
17 Kuyper, *Dutch Classicist Architecture*, p. 121.
18 See ibid., pp. 45–56 and 121–3.
19 Anthony Mitchell, *Dyrham Park* (Swindon, 1999), pp. 5 and 39–40.

20 Garnett adds, 'Blathwayt furnished his new apartments primarily in the Dutch style, commissioning a vast state bed in the Anglo-Dutch manner of the King's favourite designer, Daniel Marot, and buying Dutch pictures, book and furniture from his uncle. During his continental travels he also picked up blue-and-white Delft china and Dutch leather hangings.' Oliver Garnett, *Dyrham Park* (Swindon, 2000), pp. 4 and 29.
21 Christopher Rowell, *Uppark* (Swindon, 1995), p. 10.
22 Ibid., pp. 12–13.
23 Laurel O. Peterson, 'A New Golden Age: Politics and Mural Painting at Chatsworth', *Journal 18*, 9 (2020), www.journal18.org.
24 See Catriona Murray, *Imaging Stuart Family Politics: Dynastic Crisis and Continuity* (Abingdon, 2016), pp. 130–33; and Lois G. Schwoerer, 'Images of Queen Mary II, 1689–95', *Renaissance Quarterly*, 42 (1989), pp. 717–48.
25 Peterson, 'A New Golden Age'.
26 Ibid. Richard Johns argues that James Thornhill's paintings for Chatsworth's Sabine Room (1707–8) continued the theme of celebrating Queen Mary, but it is equally possible that they were intended as an allegorical representation of the Act of Union with Scotland in 1707. Gervase Jackson-Stops writes, 'The intermarrying of two races and its peaceful result evidently counted for more than the initial scenes of violence.' Richard Johns, 'James Thornhill and Decorative History Painting in England after 1688', DPhil, University of York (2004), pp. 143–55; and Gervase Jackson-Stops, 'A British Parnassus: Mythology and the Country House', *Studies in the History of Art*, 25 (1989), p. 228.
27 Jackson-Stops, 'British Parnassus', p. 222.
28 Helen Jacobsen, *Luxury and Power: The Material World of the Stuart Diplomat, 1660–1714* (Oxford, 2012), p. 174.
29 Paul Monod, 'Painters and Party Politics in England, 1714–60', *Eighteenth-Century Studies*, 26 (1993), p. 377.
30 Jeffrey Haworth and Gervase Jackson-Stops, *Hanbury Hall* (Swindon, 1994), pp. 18–20.
31 'The Little Fort', Historic England, https://historicengland.org.uk, accessed 3 March 2018; and Charles Terrot, 'House of Jacobites and Red Indians: Westbrook Place, Godalming, Surrey', *Country Life*, CXXVII/3326 (1 December 1960), pp. 1348–9.
32 See Linda Colley, *In Defiance of Oligarchy: The Tory Party, 1715–60*, rev. edn (Cambridge, 1985).
33 John Addy and Peter McNiven, eds, *The Diary of Henry Prescott, LL.B., Deputy Registrar of Chester Diocese* (Liverpool, 1994), vol. II, p. 475.
34 'Leighton Hall', *DiCamillo*, www.thedicamillo.com, accessed 14 May 2019.
35 'History of Clifton Hall', English Heritage, www.english-heritage.org.uk, accessed 19 May 2019.
36 Daniel Szechi, *1715: The Great Jacobite Rebellion* (New Haven, CT, 2006), p. 199.
37 Margaret Sankey, *Jacobite Prisoners of the 1715 Jacobite Rebellion: Preventing and Punishing Insurrection in Early Hanoverian Britain* (Aldershot, 2005), p. ix.
38 Szechi, *1715*, pp. 199, 204–5 and 208.
39 'Dilston Castle', Historic England, https://historicengland.org.uk, accessed 10 October 2019; and 'Langley Castle', Historic England, https://historicengland.org.uk, accessed 15 August 2019.
40 Leo Gooch, *The Desperate Faction?: The Jacobites of North-East England, 1688–1745* (Hull, 1995), pp. 93 and 103.
41 Szechi, *1715*, p. 206.
42 Leo Gooch, 'Widdrington, William, fourth Baron Widdrington', *Oxford Dictionary of National Biography*, 23 September 2004, www.oxforddnb.com; and Sankey, *Jacobite Prisoners*, p. 137.
43 Gooch, *Desperate Faction*, p. 103.
44 Ibid., p. 104.
45 Sankey, *Jacobite Prisoners*, p. 130.
46 Gooch, *Desperate Faction*, pp. 54–5.

47 Szechi, *1715*, pp. 230–31.
48 By the mid-eighteenth century the house in Battersea was known as 'Bolingbroke House' due to its associations with its famous former resident. H. T. Dickinson, 'St John, Henry, styled first Viscount Bolingbroke', *Oxford Dictionary of National Biography*, 23 September 2004, www.oxforddnb.com.
49 Sankey, *Jacobite Prisoners*, pp. 133–4 and 137.
50 Szechi, *1715*, p. 231.
51 Ibid.
52 Quoted in Sankey, *Jacobite Prisoners*, p. 130.
53 'Leighton Hall', *DiCamillo*, www.thedicamillo.com, accessed 19 February 2020.
54 Gooch, *Desperate Faction*, p. 98.
55 Sankey, *Jacobite Prisoners*, p. 137.
56 Gooch, *Desperate Faction*, p. 101.
57 Szechi, *1715*, p. 231.
58 Sankey, *Jacobite Prisoners*, pp. 132 and 134; and Gooch, *Desperate Faction*, p. 125.
59 Sankey, *Jacobite Prisoners*, p. 149.
60 Neil Guthrie, *The Material Culture of the Jacobites* (Cambridge, 2013), p. 115.
61 See Jane Clark, 'The Mysterious Mr Buck', *Apollo*, CXXIX/327 (May 1989), pp. 317–22; Jane Clark, 'For Kings and Senates Fit', *Georgian Group Journal* (1989), pp. 55–63; Jane Clark, 'Lord Burlington Is Here', in *Lord Burlington: Art, Architecture and Life*, ed. Toby Barnard and Jane Clark (London, 1995), pp. 251–310; and Edward Corp, *Lord Burlington – The Man and His Politics: Questions of Loyalty* (Lewiston, NY, 1998).
62 Murray Pittock, *Material Culture and Sedition, 1688–1760: Treacherous Objects, Secret Places* (Basingstoke, 2013), pp. 4 and 20.
63 Ibid., p. 47.
64 Ibid., p. 135.
65 'The Jacobite Glass and the House of Stuart', National Trust, www.nationaltrust.org, accessed 19 July 2020.
66 Pittock, *Material Culture and Sedition*, p. 138.
67 Guthrie, *Material Culture of the Jacobites*, p. 130.
68 Pittock, *Material Culture and Sedition*, pp. 36–7.
69 Guthrie, *Material Culture of the Jacobites*, p. 111.
70 Elizabeth Williamson, Tim Hudson, Jeremy Musson and Ian Nairn, *Sussex: West* (New Haven, CT, 2019), p. 340.
71 Pittock, *Material Culture and Sedition*, p. 33.
72 Ibid., pp. 36–7; and Paul Kléber Monod, *Jacobitism and the English People, 1688–1788* (Cambridge, 1989), p. 289.
73 Pittock, *Material Culture and Sedition*, p. 37.
74 Monod, *Jacobitism and the English People*, p. 289.
75 Pittock, *Material Culture and Sedition*, p. 60.
76 'Queen Anne's Obelisk, off Rockley Lane, Wentworth Castle, South Yorkshire', Historic England, https://historicengland.org.uk, accessed 10 March 2019.
77 Pittock, *Material Culture and Sedition*, p. 37.
78 Ibid., p. 51.
79 For the legal dangers of expressing Jacobite sentiments, see Guthrie, *Material Culture of the Jacobites*, pp. 18–40.
80 See Katherine Clark, 'Getting Plastered: Ornamentation, Iconography and the "Desperate Faction"', in *Architectural Space in Eighteenth-Century Europe*, ed. Denise Amy Baxter and Meredith Martin (Aldershot, 2010), pp. 82–101.
81 'British classicism, positioned at the nexus of the indigenous and the foreign, was tied from the very beginning with the discourse of national identity.' Barbara Arciszewska, 'Classicism: Constructing the Paradigm in Continental Europe and Britain', in *Articulating British Classicism: New Approaches to Eighteenth-Century Architecture*, ed. Barbara Arciszewska and Elizabeth McKellar (Aldershot, 2004), p. 14.
82 Patrizia Granziera, 'Neo-Palladian Architecture and Its Political Association: The Contribution of Venice to Eighteenth-Century British Art', *Mediterranean Studies*, 13 (2004), p. 150.
83 Carole Fry, 'Spanning the Political Divide: Neo-Palladianism and the Early

Eighteenth-Century Landscape', *Garden History*, 31 (2003), p. 181. For Burlington's political views, see Clark, 'For Kings and Senates Fit', pp. 55–63; and Edward Corp, *Lord Burlington – The Man and His Politics: Questions of Loyalty* (Lewiston, NY, 1998).

84 There was a connection between this renewal of interest in the gothic and the emergence of the English landscape style. Kathleen Mahoney writes that as 'the mood shifted away from the reserved formality brought about by classical restraints toward a decidedly exuberant romanticism ... these new attitudes proved to be fertile soil for a style as eccentric as Gothick'. Kathleen Mahoney, *Gothic Style: Architecture and Interiors from the Eighteenth Century to the Present* (New York, 1995), pp. 19–20.

85 Megan Aldrich, *Gothic Revival* (London, 1994), pp. 44–6.

86 Christopher Christie, *The British Country House in the Eighteenth Century* (Manchester, 2000), pp. 131–2. Simon Keynes writes that in the first half of the eighteenth century, Alfred the Great served as not only a 'role-model' of kingship for George I and II, but also 'as an emblem of the kind of monarchy favoured by disaffected Whigs, and also by those of 'Tory' persuasion disappointed with the partisan tendencies of the reigning king'. Simon Keynes, 'The Cult of Alfred the Great', *Anglo-Saxon England*, 28 (1999), pp. 270–71.

87 For Hotman's influence in England, see Ethan Alexander-Davey, 'Restoring Lost Liberty', *Constitutional Studies*, 1 (2016), pp. 59–62.

88 Quoted in Chris Brooks, *The Gothic Revival* (London, 1999), p. 44. Brooks adds that 'architectural historians of the Gothic revival have consistently underestimated, sometimes ignored, the profound political significances that accrued to the notion of gothic during the seventeenth century'. Ibid., p. 46.

89 Quoted in David R. Coffin, *The English Garden: Meditation and Memorial* (Princeton, NJ, 1994), p. 114.

90 Michael Lewis, *The Gothic Revival* (London, 2002), pp. 17–18.

91 See Christine Gerrard, *The Patriot Opposition to Walpole: Politics, Poetry and National Myth, 1725–1742* (Oxford, 1994), pp. 108–49.

92 Michael McCarthy, *The Origins of the Gothic Revival* (New Haven, CT, 1987), pp. 30–31.

93 For a summary of views of medieval architecture in eighteenth-century England, see Peter N. Lindfield, *Georgian Gothic: Medievalist Architecture, Furniture and Interiors, 1730–1840* (Woodbridge, 2016), Chapter 1.

94 Quoted in Peter Lindfield, 'Serious Gothic and "Doing the Ancient Buildings": Batty Langley's "Ancient Architecture" and "Principal Geometric Elevations"', *Architectural History*, 57 (2014), p. 145.

95 Horace Walpole, *Anecdotes of Painting* (London, 1762), vol. I, pp. 18 and 107–8.

96 Lindfield notes that 'gothic was not understood and practised as a complete "system", unlike classicism with its rules, proportions and orders, but instead was interpreted as, and revived through, the deployment of motifs and surface ornament.' Lindfield, 'Serious Gothic', p. 150.

97 Christopher Hussey, 'Donnington Grove, Berkshire', *Country Life*, CXXIV/3218 (18 September 1958), p. 591.

98 Timothy Mowl, *Horace Walpole: The Great Outsider* (London, 1996), p. 6; and Matthew Reeve, 'Dickie Bateman and the Gothicization of Old Windsor: Architecture and Sexuality in the Circle of Horace Walpole', *Architectural History*, 56 (2013), pp. 121–2. Brooks writes, 'Though medieval religion drew gothicists aesthetically, as good Protestants they deplored its superstition and supposed sexual "unnaturalness", speculating voyeuristically on nunneries and convents, celibate priests, the secrets of the confessional and

the cult of the Virgin. Gothic fiction exploited such themes for prurient fantasies of sexual transgression.' Brooks, *Gothic Revival*, p. 114.
99 Matthew Reeve writes, 'Understood as a subversive "other" mode of spiritual and political allegiance within Protestant England that was anachronistic and/or decisively foreign, Catholicism and its perceived excesses were connected explicitly with sexual license. A rich satiric tradition across literature and prints in the eighteenth century puts lascivious monks and wayward nuns engaging in sexual acts in gothic monasteries and castles.' Matthew M. Reeve, 'Gothic Architecture, Sexuality and License at Horace Walpole's Strawberry Hill', *Art Bulletin*, 95 (2013), p. 419. See also George Haggerty, *Queer Gothic* (Champaign-Urbana, IL, 2006); and William Hughes and Andrew Smith, eds, *Queering the Gothic* (Manchester, 2009).
100 David Stewart, 'Political Ruins: Gothic Sham Ruins and the '45', *Journal of the Society of Architectural Historians*, 55 (1996), p. 400.
101 Brooks, *Gothic Revival*, p. 59. Cumberland, the younger son of George II, built his own gothic tower in Windsor Great Park, also to commemorate his victory at Culloden.
102 Stewart, 'Political Ruins', p. 403.
103 Alexandrina Buchanan, 'Interpretations of Medieval Architecture, *c.* 1550–*c.* 1750', in *Gothic Architecture and Its Meanings, 1550–1830*, ed. Michael Hall (Reading, 2002), p. 43.
104 Alexandra Walsham, *The Reformation of the Landscape: Religion, Identity and Memory in Early Modern Britain and Ireland* (Oxford, 2011), p. 311.
105 Jane Whitaker, *Raised from the Ruins: Monastic Houses after the Dissolution* (London, 2021), p. 129.
106 This perception of eighteenth-century landscape gardens as projectors of English national values has persisted to the present day. Their most famous designer, Lancelot 'Capability' Brown, has become a national hero and, as Oliver Cox writes, 'shorthand for a certain kind of Englishness': 'His tripartite concoction of trees, grass and water now represent a reassuring vision of Englishness: stable, secure, remote from the challenges of the twenty-first century and easily marketable to domestic and international tourists.' Oliver Cox, 'Why Celebrate Capability Brown?: Responses and Reactions to Lancelot "Capability" Brown, 1930–2016', *Garden History*, 44 (2016), p. 181.
107 Stephen Bending, 'A Natural Revolution?: Garden Politics in Eighteenth-Century England', in *Refiguring Revolutions: Aesthetics and Politics from the English Revolution to the Romantic Revolution*, ed. Kevin Sharpe and Steven N. Zwicker (Berkeley, CA, 1998), p. 243.
108 Hugh Willmott, *The Dissolution of the Monasteries in England and Wales* (Sheffield, 2021), p. 141.
109 See Keith Thomas, *The Perception of the Past in Early Modern England* (London, 1983).
110 'Priory Park, Dudley', Historic England, https://historicengland.org.uk, accessed 4 December 2019.
111 Diane Duggan, 'Woburn Abbey: The First Episode of a Great Country House', *Architectural History*, 46 (2003), p. 62.
112 Ibid., pp. 66–7.
113 Maurice Howard, *The Building of Elizabethan and Jacobean England* (New Haven, CT, 2007), p. 43.
114 Edward Legon, 'Heritage before Modernity: The Afterlife of a Dissolved Priory', *International Journal of Heritage Studies*, XXVIII/4 (2022), pp. 427–43.
115 See J. F. Merritt, 'Puritans, Laudians and the Phenomenon of Church-Building in Jacobean London', *Historical Journal*, 41 (1998), pp. 935–60.
116 Ian Atherton, *Ambition and Failure in Stuart England: The Career of John, First Viscount Scudamore* (Manchester, 1999), p. 59.
117 Ibid., p. 61.

118 Ibid., pp. 62–3.
119 Walsham, *Reformation of the Landscape*, p. 291.
120 Margaret Aston, 'English Ruins and English History: The Dissolution and the Sense of the Past', *Journal of the Warburg and Courtauld Institutes*, 36 (1973), p. 236.
121 Ibid., p. 254.
122 In 1767 Aislabie's son William purchased the abbey ruins and incorporated them into the estate.
123 'History of Guisborough Priory', English Heritage, www.english-heritage.org.uk, accessed 19 November 2018; and 'Rievaulx Terrace', Historic England, https://historicengland.org.uk, accessed 10 January 2019.
124 In 1805 Humphrey Repton recommended that the villa be demolished and replaced by a larger house on the other side of the valley, from which the ruins could be viewed at a greater distance. Repton's scheme was not adopted until the 1870s, and the existing villa was not demolished, but the ruins continued to serve as the garden's focal point. The architect William Wilkins was hired to carry out repairs and to render the ruins more picturesque, and soon thereafter they were opened to the public.
125 Quoted in Coffin, *English Garden*, p. 54.
126 'History of Bayham Abbey', English Heritage, www.english-heritage.org.uk, accessed 16 July 2018; 'History of Roche Abbey', English Heritage, www.english-heritage.org.uk, accessed 17 July 2018; and 'Priory Park, Dudley', Historic England, https://historicengland.org.uk, accessed 17 July 2018.
127 For the eighteenth-century 'cult of the ruin' and the rise of the picturesque, see Malcolm Andrews, *The Search for the Picturesque: Landscape Aesthetics and Tourism in Britain, 1760–1800* (Stanford, CA, 1989), pp. 41–50; and David Watkin, *The English Vision: The Picturesque in Architecture, Landscape and Garden Design* (London, 1982).

128 Horace Walpole, letter to George Montagu, 8 October 1751, in *The Letters of Horace Walpole, Fourth Earl of Oxford*, ed. Paget Toynbee (Oxford, 1903), vol. III, p. 70.
129 Whitaker, *Raised from the Ruins*, pp. 156–7.
130 See John Dixon Hunt, *Gardens and the Picturesque: Studies in the History of Landscape Architecture* (Cambridge, MA, 1992).
131 Quoted in Stuart Piggott, *Ruins in a Landscape: Essays in Antiquarianism* (Edinburgh, 1976), p. 120.
132 Both quoted in Coffin, *English Garden*, pp. 32 and 44–5.
133 Quoted ibid., p. 53. Maurice Howard writes that 'the loss of these buildings and the remains of so many within the landscape helped to shape attitudes towards the past, towards a growing English, anti-foreign nationalism.' Howard, *Building of Elizabethan and Jacobean England*, p. 44.
134 Whitaker, *Raised from the Ruins*, p. 135.
135 Coffin, *English Garden*, p. 53.
136 See Christopher Hill, 'The Norman Yoke', in *Democracy and the Labour Movement: Essays in Honour of Dona Torr*, ed. John Saville (London, 1954), pp. 11–67.
137 Richard Wilson and Alan Mackley, *Creating Paradise: The Building of the English Country House, 1660–1880* (London, 2000), p. 79.
138 The replacement of the Bastille by 'Temples of Reason', meanwhile, connected the French Revolution to classicism. In France, the Neoclassical maintained its position of dominance through the Napoleonic era. Brooks notes, 'France was not interested in reclaiming gothic: the style was tainted by its association with the *ancien régime*, and Napoleonic rule found its cultural and military forebears in imperial Rome – the ancient enemy of all gothic folk.' Brooks, *Gothic Revival*, p. 137.
139 Geoffrey Tyack writes, 'Houses in the medieval style could express a shared sense of indigenous cultural values

threatened, but not suppressed, by the might of Napoleonic France.' Tyack, 'Domestic Gothic', in *John Nash: Architect of the Picturesque*, ed. Geoffrey Tyack (Swindon, 2013), p. 40.
140 Ibid., p. 40.
141 Quoted in J. M. Frew, 'Gothic Is English: John Carter and the Revival of Gothic as England's National Style', *Art Bulletin*, 64 (1982), p. 317.
142 See Seamus Deane, *The French Revolution and Enlightenment in England, 1789–1832* (London, 1988), Chapter 2.
143 Quoted in Tyack, 'Domestic Gothic', p. 40.
144 Built on shoddy foundations – Wyatt was notorious for cutting corners – the tower collapsed in 1800, was hastily rebuilt, and then collapsed again in 1825. The spire was never built.
145 'Lowther', *Verse*, https://verse.press, accessed 10 December 2019.
146 For more on the specific context of the poem, see Tim Burke, 'Lord Lonsdale and His Protégés: William Wordsworth and John Hardie', *Criticism*, 47 (2005), pp. 515–29.
147 Lindy Woodhead, *Shopping, Seduction and Mr Selfridge* (New York, 2013), p. 148.
148 Michael Hill, *East Dorset Country Houses* (Reading, 2013), p. 212.
149 Charles Tracy, *Continental Church Furniture in England: A Traffic in Piety* (Woodbridge, 2001), p. 40.
150 John Harris, *Moving Rooms* (New Haven, CT, 2007), p. 38.
151 Quoted ibid., p. 63.
152 Ibid., pp. 38–41.
153 Ibid., p. 59. The 'Maintenon' *boiseries* may have come instead from the hôtel De Noailles in Paris, the home of Madame de Maintenon's niece. James Yorke, *Lancaster House: London's Greatest House* (New Haven, CT, 2001), p. 54, n.15.
154 David Lowenthal, *The Past Is a Foreign Country Revisited* (Cambridge, 2016), p. 415.
155 Quoted in Harris, *Moving Rooms*, p. 60.
156 Ibid., p. 60; and Lowenthal, *Past Is a Foreign Country*, p. 415.
157 Harris, *Moving Rooms*, p. 62; and Hill, *East Dorset Country Houses*, p. 213.
158 Francis Palgrave, 'Normandy: Architecture of the Middle Ages', in his *Collected Works* (Cambridge, 1922), vol. x, p. 402.
159 Particularly incensed by Wyatt's election to the London Society of Antiquaries in 1807, Carter wrote a series of letters protesting the free hand that Wyatt had used in his restoration – or 'devastation' as he termed it – of Canterbury Cathedral. Quoted in Frew, 'Gothic Is English', p. 316, n.26. For Wyatt's election, see J. M. Frew, 'Richard Gough, James Wyatt and Late Eighteenth-Century Preservation', *Journal of the Society of Architectural Historians*, 38 (1979), pp. 366–74.
160 Quoted in Frew, 'Gothic Is English', p. 317.
161 Brooks, *Gothic Revival*, p. 129.
162 Ibid., p. 137.
163 'Once applied to the gothic', writes Lewis, 'this patriotic vocabulary and the associations it aroused . . . would be difficult to extirpate.' Lewis, *Gothic Revival*, p. 49.
164 Bernard Porter, *The Battle of the Styles: Society, Culture and the Design of the New Foreign Office, 1855–1861* (London, 2011), p. 38.
165 Hanbury Tracy chaired the commission that selected the design to rebuild the Palace of Westminster after it was destroyed by fire in 1834, and Barry, who had not previously worked in the gothic style, may have consulted him. The Victoria Tower closely resembles the tower at Toddington. Aldrich, *Gothic Revival*, pp. 130–37.
166 David Cannadine, 'The Palace of Westminster as Palace of Varieties', in *The Houses of Parliament: History, Art, Architecture*, ed. Christine Riding and Jacqueline Riding (London, 2000), pp. 14–15.
167 Quoted in Dale Townshend, *Gothic Antiquity: History, Romance and the Architectural Imagination, 1760–1840* (Oxford, 2019), p. 326.

4 No Such Thing as a British Country House

1. Michael Hall, *The Victorian Country House* (London, 2009), p. 65.
2. Quoted in Paul Bradley, 'William Burn and the Design (and Re-Design) of Sandon Hall, Staffordshire', in *Studies in Victorian Architecture and Design: The 1840s*, ed. Rosemary Hill and Michael Hall (London, 2008), vol. I, p. 33.
3. Quoted ibid., p. 37.
4. Ibid., p. 39.
5. Jeremy Black writes, 'Nationalism, or at least a distinctive nationalism, has been precipitated, and, in part, forced upon England, by the development in the British Isles of strident nationalisms that have contested Britishness, and with much success. Irish nationalism was the first, but it was followed by those of Wales and, more prominently, Scotland.' Jeremy Black, *English Nationalism: A Short History* (London, 2018), p. 2. Certainly, English voters who felt unfairly disadvantaged by devolution were more likely to support Brexit. See 'May's "Precious Union" Has Little Support in Brexit Britain', Centre on Constitutional Change, 8 October 2018, www.centreonconstitutionalchange.ac.uk. See also Gavin Esler, *How Britain Ends: English Nationalism and the Rebirth of Four Nations* (London, 2021); Fintan O'Toole, *The Politics of Pain: Postwar England and the Rise of Nationalism* (London, 2019); and Mark Perryman, 'Becoming England', in *Imagined Nation: England after Britain*, ed. Mark Perryman (London, 2008), pp. 13–34.
6. Colin Kidd, 'It Took a Scot', *London Review of Books*, XXXVII/15 (30 July 2015).
7. For critiques of the idea of Welsh Anglicization, see Glanmor Williams, *Renewal and Reformation: Wales c. 1415–1642* (Oxford, 1993), p. 227; John Gwynfor Jones, *The Welsh Gentry, 1536–1640: Images of Status, Honour and Authority* (Cardiff, 1998), pp. 52–4; and Philip Jenkins, 'Seventeenth-Century Wales: Definition and Identity', in *British Consciousness and Identity: The Making of Britain, 1533–1707*, ed. Brendan Bradshaw and Peter Roberts (Cambridge, 1998), pp. 213–35.
8. Peter Smith, *Houses of the Welsh Countryside: A Study in Historical Geography* (London, 1975), p. 10.
9. Miles Wynn Cato, 'Nannau and Early Portraiture in Wales', *Journal of the Merioneth Historical and Record Society*, 11 (1990–93), p. 182.
10. R. W. Brunskill, *Houses and Cottages of Britain: Origins and Development of Traditional Buildings* (London, 2000), p. 223.
11. Steven G. Ellis, *Tudor Frontiers and Noble Power: The Making of the British State* (Oxford, 1995), p. 6.
12. Max Lieberman, *The March of Wales, 1067–1300: A Borderland of Medieval Britain* (Cardiff, 2008), p. 83. See also R. R. Davies, 'The English State and the "Celtic" Peoples', *Journal of Historical Sociology*, 6 (1993), pp. 1–14.
13. Lieberman, *March of Wales*, pp. 86 and 88.
14. Maureen M. Meikle, *A British Frontier?: Lairds and Gentlemen in the Eastern Borders, 1540–1603* (East Linton, East Lothian, 2004), p. 1.
15. John Davies writes, after the Roman era was when 'Britain came to be divided into a Brythonic west, a Teutonic east and a Gaelic north, and when the nations of the Welsh, the English and the Scots crystallized.' John Davies, *A History of Wales* (London, 2007), p. 45.
16. See Hugh R. Hannaford, 'An Excavation on Wat's Dyke at Mile Oak', *Transactions of the Shropshire Archaeological and Historical Society*, 73 (1999), pp. 1–7; and Tim Malim and Laurence Hayes, ' The Date and Nature of Wat's Dyke: A Reassessment in Light of Recent Investigations at Gobowen, Shropshire', in *Anglo-Saxon Studies in Archaeology and History* XV, ed. Sally Crawford and Helena Hamerow (Oxford, 2008), pp. 147–79.
17. Davies, *History of Wales*, p. 80.

18 Ibid., pp. 110 and 113.
19 Alistair Moffat, *The Borders: A History of the Borders from Earliest Times* (Edinburgh, 2018), pp. 247–8.
20 Lieberman, *March of Wales*, p. 5.
21 Moffat, *Borders*, p. 279.
22 Matthew Holford, Andy King and Christian D. Liddy, 'North-East England in the Late Middle Ages: Rivers, Boundaries and Identities', in *Regional Identities in North-East England, 1300–2000*, ed. Adrian Green and A. J. Pollard (Woodbridge, 2007), pp. 40–41.
23 Moffat, *Borders*, p. 315.
24 Ibid., p. 333.
25 Ibid., p. 343.
26 Max Lieberman, *The Medieval March of Wales: The Creation and Perception of a Frontier, 1066–1283* (Cambridge, 2010), p. 47.
27 Anthony Emery, *Greater Medieval Houses of England and Wales, 1300–1500* (Cambridge, 2000), vol. II, p. 474.
28 Ibid., p. 472.
29 Lieberman, *Medieval March of Wales*, pp. 38–9.
30 P. D. Wood, 'Frontier Relics in the Welsh Border Towns', *Geography*, 47 (1962), p. 54.
31 Emery, *Greater Medieval Houses*, vol. II, p. 476.
32 John Goodall, *The English Castle* (New Haven, CT, 2011), p. 62.
33 Eric Mercer, *English Architecture to 1900: The Shropshire Experience* (Logaston, Herefordshire, 2003), p. 92.
34 Goodall, *English Castle*, pp. 203 and 205.
35 Lieberman, *March of Wales*, p. 37.
36 'A History of Stokesay Castle', English Heritage, www.english-heritage.org.uk, accessed 31 July 2019.
37 Emery, *Greater Medieval Houses*, vol. II, p. 478.
38 Ibid.
39 Ibid., p. 653.
40 There were approximately thirty tower houses built in Wales, as compared to over 300 in the north of England and a similar number in Scotland. Ibid., p. 657.
41 Ibid., p. 654; and Smith, *Houses of the Welsh Countryside*, p. 339.
42 See J. J. West, 'Wattlesborough Tower, Shropshire', *Archaeological Journal*, 138 (1981), pp. 33–4.
43 Emery, *Greater Medieval Houses*, vol. II, p. 654.
44 Ibid., p. 653.
45 Ibid., p. 479.
46 Ibid., p. 654.
47 Holford, King and Liddy, 'North-East England in the Late Middle Ages', p. 43.
48 Michael Brown, *Scottish Baronial Castles, 1250–1450* (Oxford, 2009), p. 23.
49 Keith Durham, *Strongholds of the Border Reivers: Fortification of the Anglo-Scottish Border, 1296–1603* (Oxford, 2008), p. 21.
50 'History of Black Middens Bastle House', English Heritage, www.english-heritage.org.uk, accessed 2 February 2019.
51 Durham, *Strongholds of the Border Reivers*, p. 29.
52 Quoted in Charles McKean, *The Scottish Chateau: The Country House of Renaissance Scotland* (Stroud, Gloucestershire, 2001), pp. 41–2.
53 Adrian Pettifer, *English Castles: A Guide by Counties* (Woodbridge, 1995), p. 169; and Holford, King and Liddy, 'North-East England in the Late Middle Ages', p. 43.
54 Nikolaus Pevsner, John Grundy, Grace McCombie, Peter Ryder and Humphrey Welfare, *Northumberland*, The Buildings of England (New Haven, CT, 1992), p. 63.
55 John Martin Robinson, *A Guide to the Country Houses of the Northwest* (London, 1991), p. 902.
56 Nikolaus Pevsner and Matthew Hyde, *Cumbria: Cumberland, Westmorland and Furness*, The Buildings of England (New Haven, CT, 2010), p. 454.
57 Robinson, *Guide to the Country Houses of the Northwest*, p. 90.
58 Moffat, *Borders*, p. 350.
59 Geoffrey Snell, 'Foundations of a Castle Culture: Pre-1603', in *Scotland's Castle Culture*, ed. Audrey Dakin, Miles Glendinning and Aonghus MacKechnie (Edinburgh, 2011), pp. 30–31.

60 *Records of the Parliaments of Scotland to 1707*, www.rps.ac.uk, accessed 20 September 2018.
61 Durham, *Strongholds of the Border Reivers*, p. 35. Adrian Pettifer notes that 'even monasteries were fortified, notably Tynemouth Priory which became an important stronghold in its own right.' Pettifer, *English Castles*, p. 170.
62 Diana Newton, '"Dolefull Dumpes": Northumberland and the Borders, 1580–1625', in *Northumbria: History and Identity, 547–2000*, ed. Robert Colls (Chichester, 2007), p. 89.
63 Ellis, *Tudor Frontiers and Noble Power*, p. 4.
64 Durham, *Strongholds of the Border Reivers*, pp. 56–7. The Borders were not, it should be noted, uniformly barbarous and warlike. Meikle argues that the common perception of the Borders was more applicable in the west, while the Eastern Borders were 'neither a backwater, nor a constant war zone. Landed families here were no more violent than any other gentry community in Scotland and England ... The majority did not indulge in cross-border feuding and reiving activities, that were often linked more to poverty than malice. The Eastern Borderers were able to derive a sufficient living from their more fertile lands and thus did not raid unless it was part of an official Anglo-Scottish war.' Meikle, *A British Frontier?*, p. 4.
65 Keith Wrightson, 'Elements of Identity: The Re-Making of the North East, 1500–1760', in *Northumbria: History and Identity*, ed. Colls, p. 136.
66 McKean, *Scottish Chateau*, pp. 3 and 5.
67 Miles Glendinning and Aonghus MacKechnie agree, arguing that tower houses were in fact 'peacetime residences' reflecting 'the generally stable society of Scotland' after 1500. Miles Glendinning and Aonghus MacKechnie, *Scotch Baronial: Architecture and National Identity in Scotland* (London, 2019), p. 19.
68 Deborah Howard, 'Scotland's "Thrie Estates"', in *Albion's Classicism: The Visual Arts in Britain, 1550–1660*, ed. Lucy Gent (New Haven, CT, 1995), p. 57.
69 Glendinning and MacKechnie, *Scotch Baronial*, p. 9.
70 Nicholas Cooper, *Houses of the Gentry, 1480–1680* (New Haven, CT, 1999), p. 240.
71 John B. Hilling, *The Historic Architecture of Wales: An Introduction* (Cardiff, 1975), p. 105.
72 Gwynfor Jones, *Welsh Gentry*, p. 24.
73 Hilling, *Historic Architecture of Wales*, p. 116, n.11.
74 'Edward I's massive building operations necessarily demanded a large labour force and this was drawn from many parts of England. Furthermore, English people were encouraged to populate the newly founded royal boroughs in north Wales. The occurrence of a plan in particular parts of Wales, which was common in many areas of central and southern England, may be attributed to both these factors which encouraged people to take up residence across the border and helped to disseminate some of their cultural elements.' Emery, *Greater Medieval Houses of England and Wales*, vol. II, p. 668.
75 Robert Scourfield and Richard Haslam, *Powys: Montgomeryshire, Radnorshire and Breconshire*, The Buildings of Wales (New Haven, CT, 2013), p. 38.
76 Emery, *Greater Medieval Houses of England and Wales*, vol. II, p. 696.
77 Edward Hubbard, *Clwyd: Denbighshire and Flintshire*, The Buildings of Wales (Harmondsworth, 1986), p. 45.
78 John Newman, *Gwent/Monmouthshire*, The Buildings of Wales (London, 2000), p. 28.
79 Examples include Penissa Glasgoed (1570), Faenol Bach (1571), Llwyn-Ynn (c. 1590) and Faenol Fawr (c. 1597) in Denbighshire; Mertyn Abbot (1573), Llanasa (1578) and Golden Grove (1578) in Flintshire; Plas Mawr (1577–95) and Penrhyn Old Hall (1590) in Conwy; and Plas Coch (c. 1590) on the Isle of Anglesey.
80 Mark Baker, 'The Development of the Welsh Country House: *dy lŷs enaid y*

wlad/Your Court, the Soul of the Land', PhD diss., Cardiff University, 2015, pp. 155 and 169.
81 Both Ruperra and Plas Teg have been attributed to Inigo Jones, though it is unlikely he designed either.
82 Baker, 'Development of the Welsh Country House', p. 101.
83 Hubbard, *Clwyd*, p. 51.
84 Baker, 'Development of the Welsh Country House', pp. 102–5.
85 Ibid., pp. 137–41.
86 These houses included Gwysaney (1603), Pentrehobyn (1603), Ffferm (late sixteenth or early seventeenth century), Mostyn Hall (1631–2) and Henblas (1645). Hubbard, *Clwyd*, pp. 44–5.
87 Scourfield and Haslam, *Powys*, p. 37.
88 Hilling, *Historic Architecture of Wales*, pp. 106–7.
89 Baker, 'Development of the Welsh Country House', p. 101.
90 Ibid., p. 128.
91 Hilling, *Historic Architecture of Wales*, p. 110.
92 Iorwerth C. Peate, *The Welsh House: A Study in Folk Culture, Y Cymmrodor*, 47 (1940), p. 3.
93 Hubbard, *Clwyd*, p. 50.
94 Andrea Thomas, *Glory and Honour: The Renaissance in Scotland* (Edinburgh, 2013), p. 9. 'Culturally . . . there was no contest: Scotland leaned towards France, and the early French Renaissance architecture of the first thirty years of the century cast a spell upon Scotland until the end of the reign of Mary Queen of Scots in 1567.' McKean, *Scottish Chateau*, p. 101.
95 See Ian Campbell, 'A Romanesque Revival and the Early Renaissance in Scotland, c. 1380–1513', *Journal of the Society of Architectural Historians*, 54 (1995), pp. 302–25.
96 McKean, *Scottish Chateau*, p. 82; and Miles Glendinning, Ranald MacInnes and Aonghus MacKechnie, *A History of Scottish Architecture: From Renaissance to the Present Day* (Edinburgh, 1966), p. 14.
97 The corbels are, Andrea Thomas writes, 'probably the earliest sculptures in the British Isles in the classically inspired, Renaissance style'. Thomas, *Glory and Honour*, p. 18.
98 McKean, *Scottish Chateau*, pp. 86–7.
99 Thomas, *Glory and Honour*, p. 27.
100 Glendinning and MacKechnie describe James v's improvements to Falkand as 'derived straightforwardly from the Loire school': 'A French-looking castellated royal palace in Scotland underlined the alliance between the two kingdoms and hinted that France's military power might be available in defence of Scottish sovereignty if necessary.' Glendinning and MacKechnie, *Scotch Baronial*, p. 17.
101 Thomas, *Glory and Honour*, p. 28.
102 'The facades of the Palace of Stirling eschew all militaristic and heraldic overtones in favour of a paean to the ancients and to classical allusion.' McKean, *Scottish Chateau*, p. 89.
103 Glendinning and MacKechnie, *Scotch Baronial*, p. 10. This is not to say that Scottish architecture was indistinguishable from French in the sixteenth and seventeenth centuries. MacKechnie bristles at McKean's use of the term 'chateaux', which 'suggests that Scotland's castles were an offshoot of French architecture – which they were not. They remained unambiguously Scottish in character, with distinctive silhouettes and upper-level ornamentation contrasting with plainer mass walling below.' Aonghus MacKechnie, '1603–1746: Castles No More, or "the Honour and Pride of a Country"?', in *Scotland's Castle Culture*, ed. Audrey Dakin, Miles Glendinning and Aonghus MacKechnie (Edinburgh, 2011), p. 37.
104 McKean, *Scottish Chateau*, p. 64.
105 Ibid., p. 93.
106 Ibid., p. 114.
107 Snell, 'Foundations of a Castle Culture', p. 24.
108 'Towards the end of the sixteenth century, the Marian round-towered palaces were giving way to the return of the rectangular-towered formalisms of the Early Renaissance.' McKean, *Scottish Chateau*, p. 179.
109 Thomas, *Glory and Honour*, p. 36.

110 McKean, *Scottish Chateau*, p. 67.
111 Miles Glendinning and Aonghus MacKechnie write that 'early classicism during the "Scottish Renaissance" was inextricably intertwined with the castellated tradition.' Glendinning and MacKechnie, *Scotch Baronial*, p. 2. For the relationship between medieval chivalry and early modern Scottish nationalism, see Roger Mason, 'Chivalry and Citizenship: Aspects of National Identity in Renaissance Scotland', in *People and Power in Scotland: Essays in Honour of T. C. Smout*, ed. Roger Mason and Norman Macdougall (Edinburgh, 1992), pp. 50–73.
112 Campbell, 'Romanesque Revival', p. 302.
113 Thomas, *Glory and Honour*, pp. 38–9.
114 Snell, 'Foundations of a Castle Culture', p. 25.
115 Quoted in Howard, 'Scotland's "Thrie Estates"', p. 57.
116 Diana Newton, 'Borders and Bishopric: Regional Identities in the Pre-Modern North-East, 1559–1620', in *Regional Identities in North-East England, 1300–2000*, ed. Adrian Green and A. J. Pollard (Woodbridge, 2007), p. 64.
117 Glendinning and MacKechnie, *Scotch Baronial*, p. 25.
118 Ibid., p. 29.
119 'The experimental classicism of the 1580s–1600s was giving way to a more English-looking architecture, reflecting the new closeness with England. James' demand for conformity between his kingdoms in all things as part of his plan to create a Magna Britannia or Great Britain had architectural consequences.' MacKechnie, '1603–1746', p. 42.
120 Meikle, *A British Frontier?*, p. 3.
121 'Leading buildings of the previous century, such as Cawdor and Winton, had employed a distinctively Scottish design ethic, one outwith the mainstream of European architecture. The ensuing, evolutionary period looked rather to the comforts and grandeur of contemporary England, but still redolent of national style, as at Hatton castle (1664–75).' Alex Morrison, 'Housing 4: Country Seat, c. 1660–present', in *The Oxford Companion to Scottish History*, ed. Michael Lynch (Oxford, 2001), available at www.oxfordreference.com, accessed 23 May 2019.
122 Glendinning and MacKechnie, *Scotch Baronial*, p. 31. Other examples of these 'hybrid' houses (i.e., castles with classical attributes) were Hill House in Dunfermline (1621–3) and Innes House in Moray (1640–53).
123 Quoted in MacKechnie, '1603–1746', p. 52.
124 After 1660, MacKechnie writes, 'most new houses were classical and symmetrical, with crow-steps almost the only element of castellation's repertoire to remain in occasional use.' Ibid., p. 53.
125 Ibid.
126 See Charles Wemyss, 'Pavilion or Pediment? The Development of Scottish Country-House Architecture in the Post-Restoration Period', in *'The Mirror of Great Britain': National Identity in Seventeenth-Century British Architecture*, ed. Olivia Horsfall Turner (Reading, 2012), pp. 187–207.
127 Quoted in MacKechnie, '1603–1746', p. 58.
128 Aonghus MacKechnie, 'Introduction: Sir William Bruce and Early Modern Architecture in Scotland', *Architectural Heritage*, 23 (2012), p. 8. Bruce has long been interpreted as the progenitor of a new mode of Scottish architecture, as 'the stability of the Restoration' permitted the 'defensive tower-house' to be at long last superseded by 'the refinement of the classical country house'. Charles Wemyss, 'Image and Architecture: A Fresh Approach to Sir William Bruce and the Scottish Country House', *Architectural Heritage*, 23 (2012), p. 117.
129 Glendinning and MacKechnie, *Scotch Baronial*, p. 63.
130 Ibid. Panmure was probably designed by John Mylne rather than Bruce, but Bruce did give the Earl of Panmure architectural

advice after Mylne's death in 1667, and Bruce does seem to have designed the gates and gate piers.
131 MacKechnie, '1603–1746', p. 55. Other contemporary houses that retained bartizans include Gordonstoun in Moray and Granton near Edinburgh, both from around 1700.
132 Glendinning and MacKechnie, *Scotch Baronial*, p. 50.
133 MacKechnie writes, 'Hopetoun's centralized plan, channelled façade and colonnades made it the antithesis of the castle.' MacKechnie, '1603–1746', p. 61. The house was significantly altered by William Adam after 1721, so little of Bruce's work is visible today.
134 Alastair Rowan, 'The Building of Hopetoun', *Architectural History*, 10 (1984), p. 186; James Macaulay, *The Classical Country House in Scotland, 1660–1800* (London, 1987), p. 21; and Deborah Howard, 'Sir William Bruce's Design for Hopetoun House and Its Forerunners', in *Scottish Country Houses, 1600–1914*, ed. Ian Gow and Alastair Rowan (Edinburgh, 1998), pp. 61–3.
135 Konrad Ottenheym, 'Dutch Influences in William Bruce's Architecture', *Architectural Heritage*, 18 (2007), pp. 114–15.
136 Glendinning and MacKechnie, *Scotch Baronial*, p. 79. Smith's clients, MacKechnie has written elsewhere, 'wanted an architecture not resembling past Scottish ideals, but English or European paradigms'. MacKechnie, '1603–1746', p. 58.
137 Glendinning and MacKechnie, *Scotch Baronial*, p. 74. Worsley writes, 'It was to the court in London that Scottish aristocrats looked for political advancement, and this was inevitably the dominant cultural influence upon them.' Giles Worsley, *Classical Architecture in Britain: The Heroic Age* (New Haven, CT, 1995), p. 157.
138 Glendinning and MacKechnie, *Scotch Baronial*, p. 95.
139 Ibid., pp. 74–5.
140 Aonghus MacKechnie writes, 'Whilst one Scottish reaction was to celebrate the union as a demonstration of Scotland's modernizing achievement, another view grew stronger which held that Scotland's culture and commerce had suffered, its culture was being lost, and that something should be done about that.' MacKechnie, '1603–1746', p. 35.
141 Glendinning and MacKechnie, *Scotch Baronial*, p. 73.
142 'Elevation and Plan of the Ground Floor, Inveraray Castle, Argyll, Scotland', *From the Collections*, Victoria and Albert Museum, http://collections.vam.ac.uk, accessed 7 July 2019.
143 Glendinning and MacKechnie, *Scotch Baronial*, p. 112.
144 Murray Pittock, *Material Culture and Sedition, 1688–1760: Treacherous Objects, Secret Places* (Basingstoke, 2013), p. 39.
145 Glendinning and MacKechnie, *Scotch Baronial*, p. 91.
146 Ibid., p. 120.
147 Ibid., p. 112.
148 Lawrence Brockliss and David Eastwood, 'Introduction: A Union of Multiple Identities', in *A Union of Multiple Identities: The British Isles, c. 1750–c. 1850*, ed. Lawrence Brockliss and David Eastwood (Manchester, 1997), pp. 1–2.
149 For a similar use of romantic Scottish nationalism in a unionist context, see Graeme Morton, 'The Most Efficacious Patriot: The Heritage of William Wallace in Nineteenth-Century Scotland', *Scottish Historical Studies*, 77 (1998), pp. 224–51.
150 Mary Miers, *Highland Retreats: The Architecture and Interiors of Scotland's Romantic North* (New York, 2017), p. 110.
151 Alvin Jackson refers to the Scottish baronial as 'a Caledonian reading of the gothic'. Alvin Jackson, *The Two Unions: Ireland, Scotland, and the Survival of the United Kingdom, 1707–2007* (Oxford, 2011), p. 152.
152 Glendinning and MacKechnie, *Scotch Baronial*, p. 166.
153 Miers, *Highland Retreats*, p. 27.

154 Ibid., p. 127. Purchasers of Highland estates in the late nineteenth and early twentieth centuries included Baron Schröder from a German banking family (Attadale), the German-born South African mining magnate Sir Sigmund Neumann (Invercauld, Glenmuick), the Scottish-born American steel magnate and for a time world's richest man Andrew Carnegie (Cluny, Skibo) and the American railway tycoon William Winans, who rented nearly twenty sporting estates in Scotland in the 1880s, covering over 220,000 acres. Ian Gow writes, 'Those who were building in the Glens, and being advised professionally that Picturesque logic prescribed a Baronial interior as well as exterior, were either make-believe lairds or the international rich.' Ian Gow, 'Mary Queen of Scots Meets Charles Rennie Mackintosh: Some Problems in the Historiography of the Scottish Baronial Revival Interior', *Furniture History*, 32 (1996), p. 6.

155 Miers, *Highland Retreats*, p. 128.
156 Ibid., pp. 119, 127 and 210.
157 Ibid., p. 113.
158 Quoted in Glendinning and MacKechnie, *Scotch Baronial*, p. 216.
159 Ibid., p. 206.
160 Miers, *Highland Retreats*, p. 219.
161 There was a Scottish baronial house in Wales as well: T. H. Wyatt's Craig-y-nos (1843) in Powys.
162 Quoted in Caroline Dakers, *Fonthill Recovered: A Cultural History* (London, 2018), available at www.ucldigitalpress.co.uk, accessed 16 October 2022.
163 Hilling, *Historic Architecture of Wales*, p. 124.
164 Howard Colvin, 'An Architect for Tredegar House?', *Architectural History*, 25 (1982), pp. 6–7.
165 Newman, *Gwent/Monmouthshire*, p. 29.
166 Baker, 'Development of the Welsh Country House', p. 187.
167 This group included Ty Uchauf (*c.* 1792), Llanarth Court (1793), Bertholey House (*c.* 1795), Newton Court (*c.* 1799–1802) and Glen Usk (*c.* 1820). Newman, *Gwent/Monmouthshire*, p. 45.
168 Trevor Burnard, 'From Periphery to Periphery: The Pennants' Jamaican Plantations and Industrialisation in North Wales, 1771–1812', in *Wales and the British Overseas Empire: Interactions and Influences, 1650–1830*, ed. H. V. Bowen (Manchester, 2011), p. 135.
169 Newman, *Gwent/Monmouthshire*, pp. 412–14.

5 The Empire Does Not Strike Back

1 See Stephanie Barczewski, *Country Houses and the British Empire, 1700–1930* (Manchester, 2014).
2 Nicholas Harris Nicolas, *Testamenta Vetusta: Being Illustrations from Wills, of Manners, Customs, &c. as Well as of the Descents and Possessions of Many Distinguished Families. From the Reign of Henry the Second to the Accession of Queen Elizabeth* (London, 1826), p. 748.
3 For the history of Canons Ashby, see John Cornforth, 'Canons Ashby, Northamptonshire: A Property of the National Trust', *Country Life*, CLXIX/4364 (9 April 1981), pp. 930–33; and CLXIX/4365 (16 April 1981), pp. 1026–9.
4 Simon Jenkins, *England's Thousand Best Houses* (London, 2003), p. 540.
5 Amir Bassir, 'Historic Building Recording at Canons Ashby House, Northamptonshire, October–December 2017', MOLA Report, 18/82 (Northampton, 2018), pp. 143–4, available at https://heritagerecords.nationaltrust.org.uk, accessed 16 October 2022.
6 Joan Thirsk, *Food in Early Modern England: Phases, Fads and Fashions, 1500–1760* (London, 2007), p. 179.
7 Myron P. Gilmore, 'The New World in French and English Historians of the Sixteenth Century', in *First Images of America: The Impact of the New World on the Old*, ed. Fredi Chiappelli (Berkeley, CA, 1976), vol. II, p. 520.

8 Catherine Armstrong, *Writing North America in the Seventeenth Century: English Representations in Print and Manuscript* (Aldershot, 2007), p. 39.
9 Elizabethan and Jacobean literacy rates are extremely difficult to determine. See David Cressy, *Literacy and the Social Order* (Cambridge, 1980); and Margaret Spufford, *Small Books and Pleasant Histories: Popular Fiction and Its Readership in Seventeenth-Century England* (Cambridge, 1981).
10 For Jacobean and Caroline theatrical productions about America, see Philip L. Barbour, 'Captain John Smith and the London Theatre', *Virginia Magazine of History and Biography*, LXXXIII/2 (1975), pp. 277–9.
11 Ivor Noël Hume, *The Virginia Adventure: Roanoke to Jamestown, An Archaeological and Historical Odyssey* (Charlottesville, VA, 1994), p. 106. See also David Beers Quinn, *England and the Discovery of America, 1481–1620* (New York, 1974), pp. 419–31.
12 Benjamin Woolley, *Savage Kingdom: The True Story of Jamestown, 1607, and the Settlement of America* (New York, 2007), p. 332.
13 Giles Milton, *Big Chief Elizabeth: The Adventures and Fate of the First English Colonists in America* (New York, 2000), p. 322. For more on Indigenous American visitors to Britain, see Coll Thrush, *Indigenous London: Native Travelers at the Heart of Empire* (New Haven, CT, 2016); and Alden T. Vaughan, *Transatlantic Encounters: American Indians in Britain, 1500–1776* (New York, 2009).
14 For a survey of early visual representations of Indians, see William C. Sturtevant, 'First Visual Images of Native America', in Fredi Chiappelli, ed., *First Images of America: The Impact of the New World on the Old* (Berkeley, CA, 1976), vol. I, pp. 417–54.
15 David Beers Quinn writes that 'for generations engravers seeking illustrations for travel books about America, North or even South, lazily went to de Bry and copied and modified for their own purposes the engravings that came in the first place from Roanoke Island and its surrounding area.' David Beers Quinn, *Set Fair for Roanoke: Voyages and Colonies, 1584–1606* (Chapel Hill, NC, 1985), p. 418.
16 Hume, *Virginia Adventure*, pp. 345–6.
17 Milton, *Big Chief Elizabeth*, p. 321.
18 Alden T. Vaughan, 'Powhatans Abroad: Virginia Indians in England', in *Envisioning an English Empire: Jamestown and the Making of the North Atlantic World*, ed. Robert Appelbaum and John Wood Sweet (Philadelphia, PA, 2005), p. 57.
19 Bernard Bailyn and Philip D. Morgan assert that 'one pervasive trait' of English views of native peoples was their 'hostility to, or at least disdain for, the people they encountered and engendered'. Bernard Bailyn and Philip D. Morgan, 'Introduction', in *Strangers within the Realm: Cultural Margins of the First British Empire*, ed. Bernard Bailyn and Philip D. Morgan (Chapel Hill, NC, 1991), p. 18.
20 Loren E. Pennington, 'The Amerindian in English Promotional Literature, 1575–1625', in *The Westward Enterprise: English Activities in Ireland, the Atlantic and America*, ed. K. R. Andrews, N. P. Canny and P.E.H. Hair (Detroit, MI, 1979), p. 178.
21 Vaughan, 'Powhatans Abroad', p. 66.
22 Karen Ordahl Kupperman, *Indians and English: Facing Off in Early America* (Ithaca, NY, 2000), pp. 19–20.
23 Ibid., p. 30.
24 Ibid., pp. 51–3.
25 Ibid., p. 74.
26 Ibid., p. 91.
27 Linda Colley, *Captives: Britain, Empire and the World, 1600–1850* (London, 2002), p. 142.
28 Some scholars argue that the appearance in Europe of calorie-rich foods such as maize, sweet potatoes and beans contributed to the rapid growth of the European population in the late sixteenth and early seventeenth centuries. See Alfred W. Crosby Jr, *The Columbian Exchange:*

Biological and Cultural Consequences of 1492 (Westport, CT, 1972), Chapter 5.

29 See Christian F. Feest, 'North America in the European Wunderkammer', *Archiv für Völkerkunde*, 46 (1992), pp. 61–109; Detlef Heikamp, 'American Objects in Italian Collections of the Renaissance and Baroque: A Survey', in *First Images of America: The Impact of the New World on the Old*, ed. Fredi Chiappelli (Berkeley, CA, 1976), vol. I, pp. 455–82; and the essays in Oliver Impey and Arthur MacGregor, eds, *The Origins of Museums: The Cabinet of Curiosities in Sixteenth- and Seventeenth-Century Europe* (London, 2001).

30 J.C.H. King, 'North American Ethnography in the Collection of Sir Hans Sloane', in *The Origins of Museums: The Cabinet of Curiosities in Sixteenth- and Seventeenth-Century Europe*, ed. Oliver Impey and Arthur MacGregor (London, 2001), p. 319.

31 Alexander MacGregor, 'The Cabinet of Curiosities in Seventeenth-Century Britain', in *The Origins of Museums*, ed. Impey and MacGregor, p. 204.

32 The canoe was put to use in 1603 for the demonstration on the Thames described above. Christian F. Feest, 'The Collecting of American Indian Artifacts in Europe, 1493–1750', in *America in European Consciousness, 1493–1750*, ed. Karen Ordahl Kupperman (Chapel Hill, NC, 1995), p. 342.

33 King, 'North American Ethnography in the Collection of Sir Hans Sloane', p. 319; and MacGregor, 'The Cabinet of Curiosities in Seventeenth-Century Britain', p. 209.

34 King, 'North American Ethnography in the Collection of Sir Hans Sloane', pp. 319–20.

35 Hume, *Virginia Adventure*, p. 20.

36 See Peter Earle, *The Making of the English Middle Class: Business, Society and Family Life in London, 1660–1730* (Berkeley, CA, 1989).

37 Keith Wrightson, *English Society, 1580–1680* (New Brunswick, NJ, 1982), pp. 23 and 26.

38 Ibid., p. 28.

39 Karen Ordahl Kupperman, 'Introduction: The Changing Definition of America', in *America in European Consciousness*, ed. Kupperman, p. 15.

40 Wrightson, *English Society*, pp. 27 and 30.

41 The author of the National Trust guidebook claims that the pole on which the Indian is perched is a 'totem pole'. Denys Sutton, *Westwood Manor, Wiltshire* (London, 1999), p. 21. This is unlikely for two reasons. First, totem poles in their modern, monumental form probably did not exist until the nineteenth century. And second, even if they did, Europeans did not explore the Pacific Northwest, the only part of the North America region where totem poles form part of indigenous culture, until the second half of the eighteenth century, around 150 years after Westwood's plasterwork representation was created.

42 Richard Olwell and Alan Tully, 'Introduction', in *Cultures and Identities in Colonial British America*, ed. Richard Olwell and Alan Tully (Baltimore, MD, 2006), p. 2.

43 Ibid.

44 Ibid., pp. 2 and 5.

45 For Stenton House, see Stephen Hague, 'Building Status in the British Atlantic World: The Gentleman's House in the English West Country and Pennsylvania', in *Building the British Atlantic World: Spaces, Places and Material Culture, 1600–1850*, ed. Daniel Maudlin and Bernard L. Herman (Chapel Hill, NC, 2016), pp. 232–3.

46 Lee Morrissey, 'Palladianism and the Villa Ideal in South Carolina', ibid., p. 269.

47 Robert Fermor-Hesketh, 'Conclusion', in Jan Morris, Charles Allen, Gillian Tindall, Colin Amery and Gavin Stamp, *Architecture of the British Empire* (London, 1986), p. 215.

48 See Caroline Wyche Dixon, 'The Miles Brewton House: Ezra White's Architectural Books and Other Possible

Design Sources', *South Carolina Historical Magazine*, 82 (1981), pp. 118–42.
49 Louis P. Nelson, *Architecture and Empire in Jamaica* (New Haven, CT, 2016), p. 145.
50 Colin Amery, 'Public Buildings', in Morris et al., *Architecture of the British Empire*, p. 105.
51 In turn, Government House became the model for other buildings in colonial India, such as the residence of the Nawab of Bengal in Murshidabad (1825–6). Jan Morris, *Stones of Empire: The Buildings of the Raj* (Oxford, 1986), p. 20; and Sydney Ayers, 'An English Country House in Calcutta: Mapping Networks between Government House, the Statesman John Adam, and the Architect Robert Adam', *Architecture beyond Europe*, 14–15, 28 July 2019, available at https://journals.openedition.org, accessed 16 October 2022.
52 Amery, 'Public Buildings', p. 136.
53 The relationship between metropolitan and colonial architecture is more complex than mere imitation. Shelley E. Smith writes, 'Early historians naturally assumed a parallel significance with regards to English buildings and pattern books as direct sources for colonial architecture and decorative arts. However, a close reading of the buildings and documents reveals a more nuanced relationship to metropolitan models ... The design and construction process was one of selective adoption and modification guided by not only the particular conditions of time and place but also the irrepressible human urge to express a unique social and individual identity.' Shelley E. Smith, 'Architectural Design and Building Construction in the Provincial Setting: The Case of the Colonial South Carolina Plantation House', *South Carolina Historical Magazine*, 116 (2015), p. 4.
54 Swati Chattopadhyay, *Representing Calcutta: Modernity, Nationalism and the Colonial Uncanny* (London, 2005), p. 109.
55 Daniel Maudlin and Bernard L. Herman, 'Introduction', in *Building the British Atlantic World*, ed. Maudlin and Herman, pp. 2–3.
56 David Armitage, *The Ideological Origins of the British Empire* (Cambridge, 2000), Chapter 8.
57 'Since the death of Inigo Jones in 1652, Roman antiquity had never lost its fascination for British architects.' John Harris, *The Palladian Revival: Lord Burlington, His Villa and Garden at Chiswick* (New Haven, CT, 1994), p. 3.
58 Giles Worsley, *Classical Architecture in Britain: The Heroic Age* (New Haven, CT, 1995), pp. 134–5.
59 Ibid., pp. 138–40.
60 Eileen Harris, *The Country Houses of Robert Adam* (London, 2008), pp. 39–40.
61 Patrick Conner, *Oriental Architecture in the West* (London, 1979), pp. 116–17.
62 Barczewski, *Country Houses and the British Empire*, pp. 126–7.
63 Edith Hall, 'Mughal Princes or Greek Philosopher-Kings?: Neoclassical and Indian Architectural Styles in British Mansions Built by East Indiamen', in *India, Greece and Rome, 1757–2007*, ed. Edith Hall and Phiroze Vasunia (London, 2010), p. 13.
64 I am indebted to Michael Silvestri for the latter information.
65 Tillman Nechtman writes, 'While most nabobs purchased and lived in typical country homes, Georgian estates with neo-classical or Palladian facades, a select group of returning nabobs followed a different path, constructing homes using eastern architectural flourishes that quickly earned the appellation "the Indian style".' Tillman Nechtman, *Nabobs: Empire and Identity in Eighteenth-Century Britain* (Cambridge, 2010), p. 166.
66 Conner, *Oriental Architecture*, p. 119.
67 Elisabeth Lenckos, 'Daylesford', *East India Company at Home, 1757–1857*, August 2014, available at https://blogs.ucl.ac.uk, accessed 16 October 2022.
68 For the Hastings trial, see P. J. Marshall, *The Impeachment of Warren Hastings* (Oxford, 1965); and Geoffrey Carnall and

Colin Nicholson, eds, *The Impeachment of Warren Hastings: Papers from a Bicentennial Commemoration* (Edinburgh, 1989).
69 Mithi Mukherjee, 'Justice, War and the Imperium: India and Britain in Edmund Burke's Prosecutorial Speeches in the Impeachment Trial of Warren Hastings', *Law and History Review*, 23 (2010), p. 591.
70 Ibid., pp. 593 and 606.
71 Conner, *Oriental Architecture*, p. 117.
72 See Mildred Archer, 'The Daniells in India and Their Influence on British Architecture', *Journal of the Royal Institute of British Architects*, 67 (1960), pp. 439–44; and Giles Henry Rupert Tillotson, *The Artificial Empire: The Indian Landscapes of William Hodges* (Richmond, Surrey, 2000).
73 Jan Sibthorpe, 'Sezincote', *East India Company at Home, 1757–1857*, August 2014, available at https://blogs.ucl.ac.uk, accessed 16 October 2022.
74 Ibid.
75 For this transition, see William Dalrymple, *White Mughals: Love and Betrayal in Eighteenth-Century India* (New York, 2002); and Maya Jasanoff, *Edge of Empire: Lives, Culture and Conquest in the East, 1750–1850* (New York, 2005).
76 The National Trust is just beginning an effort to recontextualize the tent and its acquisition by the British. See 'Powis Castle and Colonialism: The Clive Museum', National Trust, www.nationaltrust.org.uk, accessed 12 May 2019.
77 Charlotte Sussman, *Consuming Anxieties: Consumer Protest, Gender and British Slavery, 1713–1833* (Stanford, CA, 2000), p. 193.
78 Catherine Hall, *Civilising Subjects: Metropole and Colony in the English Imagination, 1830–1867* (Chicago, IL, 2002). Peter Mandler has taken issue with Hall's argument, and asserted that, while the English clearly saw themselves as superior, the basis for this claim rested upon their institutions, values and Protestant religious beliefs, rather than any sense of racial difference. Peter Mandler, '"Race" and "Nation" in Mid-Victorian Thought', in *History, Religion and Culture: British Intellectual History, 1750–1950*, ed. Stefan Collini, Richard Whatmore and Brian Young (Cambridge, 2000), pp. 224–44.
79 Thomas Metcalf, *An Imperial Vision: Indian Architecture and Britain's Raj* (Oxford, 1989), p. 15.
80 Krishan Kumar, *Visions of Empire: How Five Imperial Regimes Shaped the World* (Princeton, NJ, 2017), p. 340. Rama Sundari Mantena argues that ancient Rome 'provided the imperial framework to imagine the meeting of different cultures within a single political unit'. Rama Sundari Mantena, 'Imperial Ideology and the Uses of Rome in Discourses on Britain's Indian Empire', in *Classics and Imperialism in the British Empire*, ed. Mark Bradley (Oxford, 2010), pp. 59–60. Norman Vance concurs: 'Rome ... supplied a vocabulary for coping with new peoples and new experiences. The increasingly familiar words "colony", "dominion" and "empire" all came from the Latin.' Norman Vance, *The Victorians and Ancient Rome* (Oxford, 1997), p. 222.
81 In analysing the works of writers on empire such as Charles Dilke and John Seeley, Phiroze Vasunia observes that their 'arguments about the Roman Empire are inseparable from their claims about the British Empire, and in fact reveal more about the latter than the former'. Phiroze Vasunia, *The Classics and Colonial India* (Oxford, 2013), p. 120.
82 Quoted in Emma Reisz, 'Classics, Race and Edwardian Anxieties about Empire', in *Classics and Imperialism in the British Empire*, ed. Mark Bradley (Oxford, 2010), p. 214.
83 Mantena, 'Imperial Ideology', pp. 67–8.
84 G. A. Bremner, *Imperial Gothic: Religious Architecture and High Anglican Culture in the British Empire, c. 1840–1870* (New Haven, CT, 2013), p. 127.
85 Bremner, *Imperial Gothic*, p. 163.
86 Michael Mann, 'Art, Artefacts and Architecture: Lord Curzon, the Delhi

References

Arts Exhibition of 1902–03 and the Improvement of India's Aesthetics', in *Civilizing Missions in Colonial and Postcolonial South Asia*, ed. Carey A. Watt and Michael Mann (London, 2011), p. 77.
87 Metcalf, *Imperial Vision*, p. 56.
88 Mann, 'Art, Artefacts and Architecture', p. 67.
89 'Ireland has no examples of the great palaces or "prodigy houses" associated with the Tudor magnates ... The fortified house continued to dominate the architectural landscape.' Roger Stalley, 'The End of the Middle Ages: Gothic Survival in Sixteenth-Century Connacht', *Journal of the Royal Society of Antiquaries of Ireland*, 133 (2003), p. 5.
90 Klingelhofer reminds us, however, that Irish houses only seem 'backward' from an English point of view, as 'it was not a peculiarity of circumstances in Ireland that led to this difference, but actually that of England, which alone among the northern European countries built undefended country houses in the sixteenth century.' Eric Klingelhofer, 'The Architecture of Empire: Elizabethan Country Houses in Ireland', in *Archaeologies of the British: Explorations of Identity in Great Britain and Its Colonies, 1600–1945*, ed. Susan Lawrence (London, 2003), p. 110.
91 Stalley, 'End of the Middle Ages', pp. 5–6.
92 Rolf Loeber, 'Early Classicism in Ireland: Architecture before the Georgian Era', *Architectural History*, 22 (1979), p. 50.
93 Ibid., p. 52.
94 Klingelhofer, 'Architecture of Empire', pp. 108–9.
95 Worsley, *Classical Architecture in Britain*, p. 160. In Ireland, the plantation of English settlers led to 'the building of houses, the design of gardens and the creation of orderly landscapes in styles already familiar to landlords in England'. Brenda Collins, 'The Conway Estate in County Antrim: An Example of Seventeenth-Century "English" Building Styles in Ireland', in *'The Mirror of Great Britain': National Identity in Seventeenth-Century British Architecture*, ed. Olivia Horsfall Turner (Reading, 2012), p. 165.
96 Worsley, *Classical Architecture in Britain*, p. 160.
97 Collins, 'Conway Estate', p. 175.
98 Worsley, *Classical Architecture in Britain*, p. 169.
99 Ibid., p. 273.
100 See Timothy Mowl and Brian Earnshaw, *An Insular Rococo: Architecture, Politics and Society in Ireland and England, 1710–1770* (London, 1999).
101 For the early gothic revival in Ireland, see Michael McCarthy and Karina O'Neill, eds, *Studies in the Gothic Revival* (Dublin, 2008); and Douglas Scott Richardson, *Gothic Revival Architecture in Ireland* (New York, 1983).
102 Geoffrey Tyack, 'Domestic Gothic', in *John Nash: Architect of the Picturesque*, ed. Geoffrey Tyack (Swindon, 2013), p. 40. They were certainly interpreted in this way in the early 1920s, when several of them, including Bernard Castle, were burnt down by Irish nationalists. For the post-independence fate of Irish country houses, see Emer Crooke, *White Elephants: The Country House and the State in Independent Ireland, 1922–73* (Dublin, 2018).
103 Miles Glendinning and Aonghus MacKechnie, *Scotch Baronial: Architecture and National Identity in Scotland* (London, 2019), p. 130.
104 Judith Hill, 'Gothic in Post-Union Ireland: The Uses of the Past in Adare, Co. Limerick', in *The Irish Country House: Its Past, Present and Future*, ed. Terence Dooley and Christopher Ridgway (Dublin, 2015), p. 72.
105 Metcalf, *Imperial Vision*, p. 20.
106 Ibid.
107 Barczewski, *Country Houses and the British Empire*, pp. 208–9.
108 C. A. Bayly, *Imperial Meridian: The British Empire and the World, 1780–1830* (London, 1989), p. 114.
109 Jasanoff, *Edge of Empire*, p. 176.

110 Denys Forrest, *Tiger of Mysore: The Life and Death of Tipu Sultan* (London, 1970), pp. 356 and 361.
111 Ibid., p. 356; Anne Buddle, *Tigers round the Throne: The Court of Tipu Sultan (1750–1799)*, exh. cat., Zamana Gallery, London (1990), pp. 10 and 14; and Eric R. Delderfield, *West Country Historic Houses and Their Families* (Newton Abbot, 1968), p. 127.
112 Mohammed Moienuddin, *Sunset at Seringapatam: After the Death of Tipu Sultan* (London, 2000), p. 85; and Amin Jaffer and Deborah Swallow, 'Curzon's Ivory Chairs at Kedleston', *Apollo*, CXLII/434 (1998), pp. 35–9.
113 Barczewski, *Country Houses and the British Empire*, p. 213.
114 Bernard S. Cohn, *Colonialism and Its Forms of Knowledge: The British in India* (Princeton, NJ, 1996), p. 105.
115 Barczewski, *Country Houses and the British Empire*, p. 213.
116 Wallabies have not been spotted in the Peak District since 2000; they may now exist only in Scotland and on the Isle of Man.
117 Barczewski, *Country Houses and the British Empire*, p. 229.
118 Nicholas Thomas, 'Licensed Curiosity: Cook's Pacific Voyages', in *The Cultures of Collecting*, ed. John Elsner and Roger Cardinal (London, 1994), p. 122.
119 Barczewski, *Country Houses and the British Empire*, p. 229.
120 See Ian Baucom, *Out of Place: Englishness, Empire and the Locations of Identity* (Princeton, NJ, 1999).
121 See Simon Gikandi, *Maps of Englishness: Writing Identity in the Culture of Colonialism* (New York, 1996).

6 Fog in Channel

1 William John Bankes, 'The Renovation of Kingston Lacy', Dorset Heritage Centre, D-BKL/H/J/2/1/228.
2 William John Bankes, 'The English Country House and Other Essays', Dorset Heritage Centre, D-BKL/H/J/3/1/1.
3 Ibid.
4 'The Spanish Room at Kingston Lacy', National Trust, www.nationaltrust.org.uk, accessed 3 January 2018.
5 'Memorandum about the Doors in the Spanish Picture Room', Dorset History Centre, D-BKL/H/J/2/1/18.
6 Giles Worsley, 'The Origins of the Gothic Revival: A Reassessment', *Transactions of the Royal Historical Society*, 3 (1993), p. 107.
7 Alice Friedman, 'Did England Have a Renaissance? Classical and Anticlassical Themes in Elizabethan Culture', in *Cultural Differentiation and Cultural Identity in the Visual Arts*, ed. Susan J. Barnes and Walter S. Melion (London, 1989), p. 105.
8 Maurice Howard, 'Classicism and Civic Architecture in Renaissance England', in *Albion's Classicism: The Visual Arts in Britain, 1550–1660*, ed. Lucy Gent (New Haven, CT, 1995), p. 29.
9 Jonathan Bate, 'The Elizabethans in Italy', in *Travel and Drama in Shakespeare's Time*, ed. Jean-Pierre Maquerlot and Michèle Willems (Cambridge, 1996), p. 56.
10 Ralph Houlbrooke, *Britain and Europe, 1500–1780* (London, 2011), p. 89.
11 Andrew Hadfield, *The English Renaissance, 1500–1620* (Oxford, 2001), p. 11.
12 Maurice Howard, *The Early Tudor Country House* (London, 1987), p. 8. Sara James describes these buildings as 'fundamentally Gothic with a classical overlay'. Sara N. James, *Art in England: The Saxons to the Tudors, 600–1600* (Oxford, 2016), p. 246.
13 Christy Anderson, 'Learning to Read Architecture in the English Renaissance', in *Albion's Classicism*, ed. Gent, p. 269.
14 Nicholas Cooper, *Houses of the Gentry, 1480–1680* (New Haven, CT, 1999), p. 20.
15 Malcolm Smuts writes, 'Even the most outspoken Elizabethan proponents of native traditions . . . never attempted to escape the influence of antiquity. On the contrary, they regarded the attainments of Greece and Rome as models for what they hoped to achieve

using English materials, and drew eclectically on both ancient and medieval traditions ... Builders of country houses saw nothing odd about using columns and pediments to decorate facades that were anything but classical in overall design.' R. Malcolm Smuts, *Culture and Power in England, 1585–1685* (Basingstoke, 1999), p. 95.
16 Friedman, 'Did England Have a Renaissance?', pp. 95–6.
17 Loggias were 'one of the most important and immediately recognizable Renaissance architectural forms'. Paula Henderson, 'The Loggia in Tudor and Early Stuart England: The Adaptation and Function of Classical Form', in *Albion's Classicism*, ed. Gent, p. 109. To an Elizabethan visitor, writes Matthew Johnson, Dudley's loggia would have been seen as 'a near-perfect copy of a piece of Italian architecture'. By the time of Elizabeth's 1575 visit, Leicester had converted the garden to the Italian style as well, including the addition of a white marble fountain carved with scenes from classical mythology. Matthew Johnson, *Behind the Castle Gate: From Medieval to Renaissance* (London, 2002), p. 150.
18 'Ambulatory 20 Yards Southwest of Horton Court', Historic England, https://historicengland.org, accessed 19 August 2018.
19 The earliest known English loggia of this type was on the gatehouse at Dingley Hall in Northamptonshire (1558–60).
20 James, *Art in England*, p. 285.
21 Johnson, *Behind the Castle Gate*, p. 150.
22 Elizabeth Goldring, *Robert Dudley, Earl of Leicester, and the World of Elizabethan Art: Painting and Patronage at the Court of Elizabeth I* (New Haven, CT, 2014), pp. 52–3.
23 Mark Girouard, *Robert Smythson and the Elizabethan Country House* (New Haven, CT, 1983), p. 41.
24 David Burnett, *Longleat: The Story of an English Country House* (London, 1978), p. 27.
25 For a detailed discussion of Longleat's design, see Girouard, *Robert Smythson*, pp. 68–76.
26 Other contemporary houses, including Kirby Hall in Northamptonshire (1570) and Holdenby Hall in Northamptonshire (1571), also displayed the classical orders in the 'correct' way.
27 Keith Thomas, 'English Protestantism and Classical Art', in *Albion's Classicism*, ed. Gent, pp. 225–6. Friedman notes that 'the great hall was a crucial part of any Elizabethan country house design: it was a resonant survival from the medieval past and symbolized both the owner's knightly status and his family's traditional power over the land.' Friedman, 'Did England Have a Renaissance?', p. 101.
28 Jill Husselby, 'The Politics of Pleasure: William Cecil and Burghley House', in *Patronage, Culture and Power: The Early Cecils*, ed. Pauline Croft (New Haven, CT, 2002), p. 27.
29 Worsley, 'Origins of the Gothic Revival', p. 106.
30 Husselby, 'Politics of Pleasure', p. 32.
31 For Flemish and Dutch influence on early modern English culture, see Lisa Jardine, *Going Dutch: How England Plundered Holland's Glory* (London, 2008); Walter S. Melion, *Shaping the Netherlandish: Karel von Mander's Schilder-Boeck* (Chicago, IL, 1991); and Marjorie Rubright, *Doppelgänger Dilemmas: Anglo-Dutch Relations in Early Modern English Literature and Culture* (Philadelphia, PA, 2014).
32 Friedman, 'Did England Have a Renaissance?', p. 101.
33 Girouard writes that 'Wollaton's flaunting classical and Flemish outer garments should never blind us to the essentially late-gothic roots of its main structure.' Mark Girouard, 'Elizabethan Architecture and the Gothic Tradition', *Architectural History*, 6 (1963), p. 32.
34 Girouard, *Robert Smythson*, p. 32.
35 David Adshead, 'Introduction', in *Hardwick Hall: A Great Old Castle of*

Romance, ed. David Adshead and David A.H.B. Taylor (New Haven, CT, 2016), p. xiv.
36 Girouard, 'Elizabethan Architecture and the Gothic Tradition', p. 30. Though the famous description of Hardwick is often quoted today as 'more glass than wall', Mary Lovell argues that in its original form the word 'window' was used. Mary S. Lovell, *Bess of Hardwick: First Lady of Chatsworth* (London, 2005), p. 410.
37 Lucy Gent, 'Introduction', in *Albion's Classicism*, ed. Gent, p. 2.
38 Worsley, 'Origins of the Gothic Revival', p. 106.
39 Catherine Belsey, 'Afterword: Classicism and Cultural Dissonance', in *Albion's Classicism*, ed. Gent, p. 427.
40 Christy Anderson, *Inigo Jones and the Classical Tradition* (Cambridge, 2007), pp. 137–9.
41 See Timothy Mowl and Brian Earnshaw, *Architecture without Kings: The Rise of Puritan Classicism under Cromwell* (Manchester, 1995), pp. 48–59. Nigel Silcox-Crowe argues that the building of Coleshill did not start until 1657 and hence Jones could have had nothing to do with its design. See Nigel Silcox-Crowe, 'Sir Roger Pratt, 1620–1685: The Ingenious Gentleman Architect', in *The Architectural Outsiders*, ed. Roderick Brown (London, 1985), pp. 1–20.
42 Quoted in Giles Worsley, *Inigo Jones and the European Classicist Tradition* (New Haven, CT, 2007), p. 83.
43 Ibid., p. 86. The attribution of Wilton remains controversial. See Mowl and Earnshaw, *Architecture without Kings*, pp. 31–47; and H. M. Colvin, 'The South Front of Wilton House', *Archaeological Journal*, III (1954), pp. 181–90.
44 The Brutus legend, 'linked as it was to the Golden Ages of Troy and Rome, underpinned Jones's introduction of what would otherwise have been a foreign and new style of architecture'. Vaughan Hart, *Inigo Jones: The Architect of Kings* (New Haven, CT, 2011), p. 43.
45 Anderson, *Inigo Jones and the Classical Tradition*, p. 146.
46 'The "defacing" of the cathedral's Corinthian portico and the toppling of its statues . . . testify to the popular identification of Jones's architecture with royal authority.' Hart, *Inigo Jones*, p. 127.
47 John Summerson, *Inigo Jones* (Harmondsworth, 1966), p. 137.
48 Robert Tavernor, *Palladio and Palladianism* (London, 1991), p. 145.
49 Anderson, *Inigo Jones and the Classical Tradition*, p. 4.
50 Quoted in Peter N. Lindfield, *Georgian Gothic: Medievalist Architecture, Furniture and Interiors, 1730–1840* (Woodbridge, 2016), p. 45.
51 Mowl and Earnshaw, *Architecture without Kings*, p. 81.
52 A. A. Tait, 'Post-Modernism in the 1650s', in *Inigo Jones and the Spread of Classicism: Papers Given at the Georgian Group Symposium 1986* (London, 1987), p. 23.
53 Examples can be found at Chatsworth (1687–96), Burghley House (c. 1688–98), Hampton Court (1690), Petworth House (1692), Buckingham House in London (c. 1705), Burley-on-the-Hill in Rutland (c. 1708), Hanbury Hall (c. 1710) and Drayton House (c. 1712).
54 Giles Worsley, *Classical Architecture in Britain: The Heroic Age* (New Haven, CT, 1995), p. 73. A rare example of a fully Baroque interior in England was Nicholas Hawksmoor's work at Easton Neston in Northamptonshire (1702).
55 James Lees-Milne, *English Country Houses: Baroque, 1685–1715* (London, 1970), p. 10; and Giles Worsley, 'Wren, Vanbrugh, Hawksmoor and Archer: The Search for an English Baroque', in *Circa 1700: Architecture in Europe and the Americas*, ed. Henry A. Millon (New Haven, CT, 2005), p. 99.
56 Jeremy Musson, *The Country Houses of Sir John Vanbrugh: From the Archives of Country Life* (London, 2008), p. 40.
57 Worsley, 'Wren, Vanbrugh, Hawksmoor and Archer', p. 109.

58 Musson, *Country Houses of Sir John Vanbrugh*, p. 89.
59 Worsley, 'Wren, Vanbrugh, Hawksmoor and Archer', p. 110.
60 Hart writes that in his use of the forms of Elizabethan architecture, Vanbrugh was expressing 'his desire to find a truly national basis for an architectural vocabulary of forms which were distinct from foreign influence'. Vaughan Hart, *Sir John Vanbrugh: Storyteller in Stone* (New Haven, CT, 2008), p. 48. See also Giles Worsley, 'Sir John Vanbrugh and the Search for a National Style', in *Gothic Architecture and Its Meanings, 1550–1830*, ed. Michael Hall (Reading, 2002), pp. 97–132.
61 See Timothy Mowl, 'Antiquaries, Theatre and Early Medievalism', in *Sir John Vanbrugh and Landscape Architecture in Baroque England, 1690–1730*, ed. Christopher Ridgway and Robert Williams (Stroud, Gloucestershire, 2000), pp. 71–92.
62 Quoted in Hart, *Sir John Vanbrugh*, p. 73.
63 Musson, *Country Houses of Sir John Vanbrugh*, p. 120.
64 Ibid., p. 134.
65 Worsley, 'Wren, Vanbrugh, Hawksmoor and Archer', p. 114. Hart concurs: 'Vanbrugh's eclectic style gave expression to his love affair with medieval military architecture and with Britain's history and traditions, whilst remaining grounded in the by then well-established classical canons of proportion, symmetry and order ... Vanbrugh clearly identified this liberal mix as a quintessentially British style of architecture suited to national liberties and Whig ideals.' Hart, *Sir John Vanbrugh*, p. xi.
66 See Kerry Downes, 'The Publication of Shaftesbury's "Letter concerning Design"', *Architectural History*, 27 (1984), pp. 519–23.
67 Barbara Arciszewska, 'A Villa Fit for a King: The Role of Palladian Architecture in the Ascendancy of the House of Hanover under George I', *Canadian Art Review*, 19 (1992), p. 42.
68 Elizabeth Angelicoussis, 'Walpole's Roman Legion: Antique Sculpture at Houghton Hall', *Apollo*, CLXIX/562 (February 2002), p. 24.
69 Ibid.
70 Ibid., p. 31.
71 'Designs for Houghton Hall, Norfolk', Royal Institute of British Architects, www.ribapix.com, accessed 19 October 2018. Nikolaus Pevsner commented that 'these domes have no parallels among Georgian Mansions ... They add a continental warmth and opulence to the cool perfection of the rest.' Nikolaus Pevsner and Bill Wilson, *Norfolk 2: North-West and South*, The Buildings of England, 2nd edn (New Haven, CT, 2002), p. 429.
72 Anderson, *Inigo Jones and the Classical Tradition*, p. 2.
73 'British classicism, positioned at the nexus of the indigenous and the foreign, was tied from the very beginning with the discourse of national identity.' Barbara Arciszewska, 'Classicism: Constructing the Paradigm in Continental Europe and Britain', in *Articulating British Classicism: New Approaches to Eighteenth-Century Architecture*, ed. Barbara Arciszewska and Elizabeth McKellar (Aldershot, 2004), p. 14.
74 Colen Campbell, *Vitruvius Britannicus or the British Architect, Containing the Plans, Elevations, and Sections of the Regular Buildings, both Publick and Private, in Great Britain* (London, 1715), vol. I, Introduction.
75 'The nationalistic bias of the eighteenth-century Palladians had eventually elevated [Jones] to a position counterbalancing the "papist" Palladio himself.' Arciszewska, 'Classicism', p. 16. There was some truth to this. Clive Aslet writes that the Palladian revival was 'misnamed: it might just as well have been called an Inigo Jones Revival.' Clive Aslet, *The Story of the Country House: A History of Places and People* (New Haven, CT, 2021), p. 92.
76 Robert Fermor-Hesketh, 'Conclusion', in Jan Morris, Charles Allen, Gillian Tindall, Colin Amery and Gavin Stamp, *Architecture of the British Empire* (London, 1986), p. 206.

77 John Harris, *The Palladian Revival: Lord Burlington, His Villa and Garden at Chiswick* (New Haven, CT, 1994), p. 26.
78 Ibid., pp. 106–7.
79 James J. Cartwright, *The Wentworth Papers, 1705–1739* (London, 1883), p. 79.
80 Robert Hewlings, 'The Classical Leviathan: Wentworth Woodhouse, South Yorkshire, The Home of Mr and Mrs Newbold, Part 1', *Country Life*, CCIV/7 (17 February 2010), p. 52.
81 Dylan Wayne Spivey, 'From Baroque to Palladian: The Two Faces of Wentworth Woodhouse', *Palladiana: Journal of Center for Palladian Studies in America* (Fall 2020), https://palladiancenter.org.
82 Centre for Buckinghamshire Studies, D/DR/5/1.
83 Centre for Buckinghamshire Studies, D/DR/5/2.
84 Centre for Buckinghamshire Studies, D/DR/5/3.
85 Centre for Buckinghamshire Studies, D/DR/5/6.
86 Centre for Buckinghamshire Studies, D/DR/5/11.
87 Ibid.
88 Centre for Buckinghamshire Studies, D/DR/5/21.
89 See Jeremy Black, *The British Abroad: The Grand Tour in the Eighteenth Century* (Stroud, Gloucestershire, 1997); Claire Hornsby, *The Impact of Italy: The Grand Tour and Beyond* (London, 2000); Rosemary Sweet, *Cities and the Grand Tour: The British in Italy, c. 1690–1820* (Cambridge, 2015); and Andrew Wilton and Ilaria Bignamini, eds, *Grand Tour: The Lure of Italy in the Eighteenth Century* (London, 1996).
90 Holbech commissioned two additional paintings by Canaletto while the artist was in England from 1746 to 1750.
91 *Farnborough Hall, Warwickshire* (Swindon, 1999), p. 4.
92 Windham's Grand Tour Cabinet survives virtually intact. Oliver Garnett, *Felbrigg Hall, Gardens and Estate* (Swindon, 2016), pp. 14–17, 40 and 42–3.
93 Oliver Garnett and Diana Owen, *Petworth: A Souvenir Guide* (Swindon, 2006), p. 16.
94 Christopher Rowell, *Uppark* (Swindon, 1995), pp. 17–23.
95 Peter Tuffrey, *Yorkshire Country Houses* (Bradford, 2017), pp. 41–3.
96 [Edward Coke,] 7th Earl of Leicester, *Holkham* (Coventry, 2004), pp. 9–10 and 15–16.
97 Nikolaus Pevsner and Bill Wilson, *Norfolk 1: Norwich and North-East*, The Buildings of England, 2nd edn (New Haven, CT, 1997), p. 554.
98 Rosemary Baird, *Goodwood: Art and Architecture, Sport and Family* (London, 2007), pp. 17–19.
99 Quoted in Jason M. Kelly, 'Riots, Revelries and Rumor: Libertinism and Masculine Association in Enlightenment London', *Journal of British Studies*, 45 (2006), p. 777.
100 Jason M. Kelly, 'Sir Francis Dashwood: Connoisseur, Collector and Traveller', *Art and the Country House*, www.artandthecountryhouse.com, accessed 15 November 2018.
101 Ibid.
102 'The House: The Statue Gallery', Newby Hall, www.newbyhall.com, accessed 30 July 2018.
103 Mark Girouard, 'Ambrose Phillipps of Garendon', *Architectural History*, 8 (1965), pp. 25–38.
104 'Robert and James Adam Office Drawings', Sir John Soane's Museum Collection, http://collections.soane.org, accessed 17 July 2018.
105 Asprucci never came to England, and so the architect brothers Francis and Joseph Sandys supervised the construction process.
106 Quoted in Rebecca Campion, '"Antiquity Mad": The Influence of Continental Travel on the Irish Houses of Frederick Hervey, the Earl Bishop, 1730–1803', in *Travel and the British Country House: Cultures, Critiques and Consumption in the Long Eighteenth*

Century, ed. Jon Stobart (Manchester, 2017), p. 29.
107 John Martin Robinson, *The Regency Country House: From the Archives of Country Life* (London, 2005), p. 118.
108 Peter Mandler, *The Fall and Rise of the Stately Home* (New Haven, CT, 1997), pp. 31–2.
109 Joseph Nash, *Descriptions of the Plates of the Mansions of England in the Olden Time* (London, 1849), vol. I, p. 2.
110 Baroness de Calabrella, ed., *Evenings at Haddon Hall: A Series of Romantic Tales of the Olden Time* (London, 1860), p. 1.
111 See Mandler, *Fall and Rise of the Stately Home*, pp. 58–61.
112 *Charlecote Park, Warwickshire* (Swindon, 2005), p. 3.
113 Devon Heritage Centre, 2547M/E/19.
114 Ibid.
115 Devon Heritage Centre, 2547M/E/37.
116 Devon Heritage Centre, 2547M/E/19.
117 Ibid.
118 Mark Girouard finds that there were more gothic than Jacobethan houses prior to 1870, and thereafter the 'situation was reversed'. My own sample finds a larger number of Jacobethan houses throughout the nineteenth century, but this may be a matter of classification, for in many cases the line between 'gothic' and 'Jacobethan' was blurred. For comparison purposes, Girouard's sample contained 500 houses that were built or rebuilt between 1835 and 1889; my database lists 975 houses for that period. Mark Girouard, *The Victorian Country House*, new edn (New Haven, CT, 1979), p. 53.
119 Centre for Buckinghamshire Studies, D/GR/18/26.
120 Girouard, *Victorian Country House*, p. 293.
121 Mark Girouard describes it as a '*nouveau-riche* style', which came to be associated with 'the new commercial and industrial rich' so that 'the older families gradually dropped it'. Ibid., pp. 292 and 294.
122 Hannah Rothschild, *The Baroness: The Search for Nica, the Rebellious Rothschild* (London, 2012), p. 59; and John Harris, *Moving Rooms* (New Haven, CT, 2007), pp. 65–6.
123 Girouard, *Victorian Country House*, p. 300.
124 Rothschild, *Baroness*, p. 62.
125 Quoted in Nicola Ann Pickering, 'The English Rothschild Family in the Vale of Aylesbury: Their Houses, Collections and Collecting Activity, 1830–1900', DPhil, King's College London, 2013, pp. 353 and 425.
126 Lauren M. E. Goodlad, 'Trollopian "Foreign Policy": Rootedness and Cosmopolitanism in the Mid-Victorian Global Imaginary', PMLA, 124 (2009), p. 439.
127 For antisemitism in Britain, see David Cesarani, ed., *The Making of Modern Anglo-Jewry* (Oxford, 1990); David Feldman, *Englishmen and Jews: Social Relations and Political Culture, 1840–1914* (New Haven, CT, 1994); Tony Kushner, *The Persistence of Prejudice: Antisemitism in British Society during the Second World War* (Manchester, 1989); and Thomas Weber, 'Anti-semitism and Philo-semitism among the British and German Elites: Oxford and Heidelberg before the First World War', *English Historical Review*, 118 (2003), pp. 86–119.
128 Tom Stammers, 'How the Jewish Aristocracy Reinvented the European Country House', *Apollo*, 7 (March 2022), available at www.apollo-magazine.com, accessed 17 October 2022.
129 Rothschild, *Baroness*, pp. 62–3.
130 Claire Hirshfield, 'The Anglo-Boer War and the Issue of Jewish Culpability', *Journal of Contemporary History*, 15 (1980), pp. 619–20.
131 See Panikos Panayi, *The Enemy in Our Midst: Germans in Britain during the First World War* (Oxford, 1991).
132 Maud Messel's objection may have been not because of the house's Germanic appearance but because it was ugly. Ludwig Messel's grandson Rudolph Putnam Messel later described it as an 'architectural freak' and his cousin Oliver Messel, the famous stage designer, called

it 'exceptionally hideous'. John Hilary, *From Refugees to Royalty: The Remarkable Story of the Messel Family of Nymans* (London, 2021), pp. 92 and 111.
133 Quoted ibid., p. 112.
134 Ibid., p. 113.
135 For a comprehensive review of Devey's career, see Jill Allibone, *George Devey: Architect, 1820–1886* (Cambridge, 1991).
136 Andrew Saint, *Richard Norman Shaw*, rev. edn (New Haven, CT, 2010), p. 52.
137 Charles Locke Eastlake, *A History of the Gothic Revival* (London, 1872), p. 342.
138 Alun Howkins, 'The Discovery of Rural England', in *Englishness: Politics and Culture, 1880–1920*, ed. Robert Colls and Philip Dodd, 2nd edn (London, 1986), pp. 85–111.
139 Martin Wiener, *English Culture and the Decline of the Industrial Spirit, 1850–1980*, 2nd edn (Cambridge, 2004), p. 52.
140 Stephen Daniels, *Fields of Vision: Landscape Imagery and National Identity in England and the United States* (Princeton, NJ, 1993), p. 209.
141 Howkins, 'Discovery of Rural England', p. 88; and Daniels, *Fields of Vision*, p. 214.
142 Sheila Kirk, *Philip Webb: Pioneer of Arts and Crafts Architecture* (Chichester, 2005), pp. 102–3. Malcolm Chase writes, 'this gently undulating green, and unsevere landscape dominated the conception of the ideal England.' Malcolm Chase, 'This Is No Claptrap, This Is our Heritage', in *The Imagined Past: History and Nostalgia*, ed. Malcolm Chase and Christopher Shaw (Manchester, 1989), p. 143. Stephen Daniels writes that 'the image of England as vernacular, agrarian, home-counties countryside is a recent, largely twentieth-century development.' Stephen Daniels, 'Envisioning England', *Journal of Historical Geography*, 17 (1991), p. 98. See also Catherine Brace, 'Finding zEngland Everywhere: Regional Identity and the Construction of National Identity, 1890–1940', *Ecumene*, 6 (1999), pp. 90–109.
143 Ian Macdonald-Smith, *Arts and Crafts Master: The Houses and Gardens of M. H. Baillie Scott* (New York, 2010), p. 24.
144 Kirk, *Philip Webb*, p. 80.
145 John Aplin, *The Letters of Philip Webb* (Abingdon, 2015), vol. 1, pp. 237–8.
146 Paul Readman, 'The Place of the Past in English Culture, c. 1890–1914', *Past and Present*, 186 (2005), p. 165.
147 Ibid., pp. 179 and 181.
148 Peter Mandler, 'Against "Englishness": English Culture and the Limits to Rural Nostalgia, 1850–1940', *Transactions of the Royal Historical Society*, 6th series, 7 (1997), p. 155.
149 Quoted in Clive Aslet, *The Last Country Houses* (New Haven, CT, 1992), p. 141.
150 Quoted ibid., pp. 141–3.
151 Readman, 'Place of the Past', pp. 149–50.
152 Mary Ann Caws, *Vita Sackville-West: Selected Writings* (New York, 2002), p. 193.
153 Aslet, *Last Country Houses*, pp. 146 and 153.
154 Ibid., p. 155.
155 Mandler, 'Against "Englishness"', p. 170.
156 See, for example, Sam Knight, 'Britain's Idyllic Country Houses Reveal a Darker History', *New Yorker*, 16 August 2021, www.newyorker.com.

Conclusion

1 Nikolaus Pevsner, 'Building with Wit: The Architecture of Sir Edwin Lutyens', *Architectural Review* (5 April 1951), available at www.architectural-review.com, accessed 17 October 2022.
2 Quoted in David Cole, *Sir Edwin Lutyens: The Arts and Crafts Houses* (Melbourne, 2017), p. 28.
3 William Whyte, 'The Englishness of English Architecture: Modernism and the Making of a National International Style, 1927–1957', *Journal of British Studies*, 48 (2009), pp. 441 and 444.
4 Cole, *Sir Edwin Lutyens*, p. 59.
5 Ibid., p. 165.
6 Elizabeth Wilhide, *Sir Edwin Lutyens: Designing in the English Tradition* (New York, 2000), p. 24. Similarly, Gavin Stamp

asserts that 'there is no easy chronological sequence in Lutyens's use of different styles': 'He had been using classical elements, and playing games with them, much earlier – almost from the beginning.' Gavin Stamp, *Edwin Lutyens's Country Houses: From the Archives of Country Life* (London, 2001), p. 26.
7   Ibid., pp. 26–7.
8   Ibid., pp. 80 and 99.
9   William Rothenstein, *Twenty-Four Portraits* (London, 1923), p. 60.
10 Stamp, *Edwin Lutyens's Country Houses*, p. 21.
11 Lawrence Weaver, *Small Country Houses of To-Day* (London, 1919), vol. II, p. vii.
12 Robert Grant Irving, *Indian Summer: Lutyens, Baker and Imperial Delhi* (New Haven, CT, 1981), p. 102.
13 Ibid., pp. 105–6.
14 Ibid., p. 101.
15 Stamp, *Edwin Lutyens's Country Houses*, p. 183.
16 Quoted ibid., p. 183.
17 Ibid., p. 142.
18 'Although, at first sight, Castle Drogo appears unique amongst his work, it is very typical of Lutyens in its basic plan type, his attitude to historical styles and his general approach to design.' Peter Inskip, 'The Compromise of Castle Drogo', *Architectural Review*, 45 (1979), p. 220.
19 Stamp, *Edwin Lutyens's Country Houses*, p. 158.
20 Julius Drewe's two other sons, Basil and Cedric, also fought in the war, but survived.
21 Stamp, *Edwin Lutyens's Country Houses*, p. 142; and Siân Evans, Bryher Mason and John Rippin, *Castle Drogo, Devon: A Souvenir Guide* (Swindon, 2009), p. 13.
22 The room included the wooden cross that had been erected as a temporary marker for Adrian Drewe's grave, until the Commonwealth War Graves Commission installed a permanent stone one after the war was over. 'Adrian Drewe's Memorial Room and Grave Marker', National Trust, www.nationaltrust.org.uk, accessed 12 October 2020.
23 'With the truncation, Castle Drogo is treated as a residual fragment of a larger building, and the rest of the house and courtyard exist only by implication.' Inskip, 'Compromise of Castle Drogo', p. 26.
24 See Paul Fussell, *The Great War and Modern Memory*, new edn (Oxford, 2013); and Jay Winter, *Sites of Memory, Sites of Mourning: The Great War in European Cultural Memory* (Cambridge, 1998).
25 Simon Martin, *The Mythic Method: Classicism in British Art, 1920–1950* (Chichester, 2016), p. 10.
26 Ana Carden-Coyne, *Reconstructing the Body: Classicism, Modernism and the First World War* (Oxford, 2009), p. 2.
27 Wilhide, *Edwin Lutyens*, p. 49.
28 Winter, *Sites of Memory, Sites of Mourning*, p. 108.
29 Jeremy Gould, 'Architecture in Devon, 1910–1958', in *Going Modern and Being British: Art, Architecture and Design in Devon, c. 1910–1960*, ed. Sam Smiles (Exeter, 1998), p. 17.
30 Inskip, 'Compromise of Castle Drogo', p. 31.
31 Oliver Bradbury, *Sir John Soane's Influence on Architecture from 1791: A Continuing Legacy* (Farnham, 2015), p. 340.
32 Quoted in Martin, *Mythic Method*, p. 17.
33 Alastair Curtis, 'Paul Nash: Going Modern, Being British', *1843*, 26 October 2016, available at www.1843magazine.com, accessed 17 October 2022.
34 Evans, Mason and Rippin, *Castle Drogo*, p. 21.

FURTHER READING

Airs, Malcolm, *The Making of the English Country House, 1500–1640* (London, 1975)
—, *The Tudor and Jacobean Country House: A Building History* (Stroud, Gloucestershire, 1995)
Aslet, Clive, *The Last Country Houses* (New Haven, CT, 1992)
—, *The Arts and Crafts Country House: From the Archives of Country Life* (London, 2011)
—, *The Story of the Country House: A History of Places and People* (New Haven, CT, 2021)
Barczewski, Stephanie, *Country Houses and the British Empire, 1700–1930* (Manchester, 2014)
Christie, Christopher, *The British Country House in the Eighteenth Century* (Manchester, 2000)
Coffin, David R., *The English Garden: Meditation and Memorial* (Princeton, NJ, 1994)
Cooper, Nicholas, *Houses of the Gentry, 1480–1680* (New Haven, CT, 1999)
Dooley, Terence, and Christopher Ridgway, eds, *The Irish Country House: Its Past, Present and Future* (Dublin, 2015)
Gent, Lucy, ed., *Albion's Classicism: The Visual Arts in Britain, 1550–1660* (New Haven, CT, 1995)
Girouard, Mark, *The Victorian Country House*, new edn (New Haven, CT, 1979)
—, *Robert Smythson and the Elizabethan Country House* (New Haven, CT, 1983)
—, *Elizabethan Architecture: Its Rise and Fall, 1540–1640* (New Haven, CT, 2009)

Glendinning, Miles, and Aonghus MacKechnie, *Scotch Baronial: Architecture and National Identity in Scotland* (London, 2019)
Gomme, Andor, and Alison Maguire, *Design and Plan in the Country House: From Castle Donjons to Palladian Boxes* (New Haven, CT, 2008)
Goodall, John, *The English Castle* (New Haven, CT, 2011)
Gow, Ian, and Alastair Rowan, eds, *Scottish Country Houses, 1600–1914* (Edinburgh, 1998)
Hall, Michael, *The English Country House: From the Archives of Country Life, 1897–1939* (London, 2001)
—, *The Victorian Country House* (London, 2009)
—, ed., *Gothic Architecture and Its Meanings, 1550–1830* (Reading, 2002)
Harris, Eileen, *The Country Houses of Robert Adam* (London, 2008)
Harris, John, *The Palladian Revival: Lord Burlington, His Villa and Garden at Chiswick* (New Haven, CT, 1994)
Hart, Vaughan, *Sir John Vanbrugh: Storyteller in Stone* (New Haven, CT, 2008)
—, *Inigo Jones: The Architect of Kings* (New Haven, CT, 2011)
Howard, Maurice, *The Early Tudor Country House* (London, 1987)
—, *The Building of Elizabethan and Jacobean England* (New Haven, CT, 2007)
Johnson, Matthew, *Behind the Castle Gate: From the Middle Ages to the Renaissance* (London, 2002)

Further Reading

Kelsall, Malcolm, *The Great Good Place: The Country House and English Literature* (New York, 1993)

Lees-Milne, James, *English Country Houses: Baroque, 1685–1715* (London, 1970)

Lindfield, Peter N., *Georgian Gothic: Medievalist Architecture, Furniture and Interiors, 1730–1840* (Woodbridge, 2016)

Macaulay, James, *The Classical Country House in Scotland, 1660–1800* (London, 1987)

McKean, Charles, *The Scottish Chateau: The Country House of Renaissance Scotland* (Stroud, Gloucestershire, 2001)

Mandler, Peter, *The Fall and Rise of the Stately Home* (New Haven, CT, 1997)

Matless, David, *Landscape and Englishness* (London, 1998)

Miers, Mary, *Highland Retreats: The Architecture and Interiors of Scotland's Romantic North* (New York, 2017)

Mowl, Timothy, and Brian Earnshaw, *Architecture without Kings: The Rise of Puritan Classicism under Cromwell* (Manchester, 1995)

Musson, Jeremy, *The English Manor House: From the Archives of Country Life* (London, 1999)

——, *The Country Houses of Sir John Vanbrugh: From the Archives of Country Life* (London, 2008)

Porter, Bernard, *The Battle of the Styles: Society, Culture and the Design of the New Foreign Office, 1855–1861* (London, 2011)

Raven, James, ed., *Lost Mansions: Essays on the Destruction of the Country House* (Basingstoke, 2015)

Readman, Paul, *Storied Ground: Landscape and the Shaping of English National Identity* (Cambridge, 2018)

Ridgway, Christopher, and Robert Williams, eds, *Sir John Vanbrugh and Landscape Architecture in Baroque England, 1690–1730* (Stroud, Gloucestershire, 2000)

Robinson, John Martin, *The Regency Country House: From the Archives of Country Life* (London, 2005)

Rowley, Trevor, *The English Landscape in the Twentieth Century* (London, 2006)

Stamp, Gavin, *Edwin Lutyens's Country Houses: From the Archives of Country Life* (London, 2001)

Stobart, Jon, ed., *Travel and the British Country House: Cultures, Critiques and Consumption in the Long Eighteenth Century* (Manchester, 2017)

Strong, Roy, Marcus Binney and John Harris, eds, *The Destruction of the Country House* (London, 1974)

Thomas, Andrea, *Glory and Honour: The Renaissance in Scotland* (Edinburgh, 2013)

Thompson, M. W., *The Decline of the Castle* (Cambridge, 1987)

Tinniswood, Adrian, *The Polite Tourist: Country House Visiting through the Centuries* (London, 1989)

Townshend, Dale, *Gothic Antiquity: History, Romance and the Architectural Imagination, 1760–1840* (Oxford, 2019)

Tyack, Geoffrey, ed., *John Nash: Architect of the Picturesque* (Swindon, 2013)

Wilson, Richard, and Alan Mackley, *Creating Paradise: The Building of the English Country House, 1660–1880* (London, 2000)

Worsley, Giles, *Classical Architecture in Britain: The Heroic Age* (New Haven, CT, 1995)

——, *England's Lost Houses* (London, 2002)

——, *Inigo Jones and the European Classicist Tradition* (New Haven, CT, 2007)

ACKNOWLEDGEMENTS

I finished a draft of this manuscript in March 2020, right as the Covid-19 pandemic began to sweep across the world. Like most people, I assumed that the disruption would be relatively brief, and that only a few months would elapse before I would be able to return to the United Kingdom to finish the research required for the revisions that the publisher and I had agreed upon. That, of course, did not happen, and after months elapsed with no end to travel bans in sight, I concluded that it would be necessary to rewrite the book in a different way. It thus became data- rather than archive-driven. I used the massive database of country houses which I had amassed in the course of my previous research to expand significantly the range of statistical analyses. Frustrating as it was at the time, this alteration was ultimately beneficial in moving the book away from its original Brexit-dominated conception towards a broader consideration of English national identity.

This is not, therefore, a book based upon archival research, but it does contain some references to archival sources. I visited several county archives, and I would therefore like to thank the staffs of the Berkshire Record Office, the Centre for Buckinghamshire Studies, the Cornwall Record Office, the Devon Heritage Centre and the Dorset History Centre. I would also like to thank the staff of the British Library, where much of the writing of this book took place. It continues to amaze me that I can get more work done in a week in the British Library than I can in months at home. It was wonderful to at long last return there in the spring of 2022.

On a more personal level, my professional debts to those who have supported my career are long and extensive. Sir David Cannadine and Dame Linda Colley have served as mentors and inspirations since I was an undergraduate at Columbia (in David's case) and a PhD student at Yale (in Linda's). John MacKenzie and Nigel Dalziel invited me to an amazing conference at The Burn, where I presented some of my research and enjoyed one of the friendliest and liveliest academic environments I have ever encountered. A good time, it is safe to say, was had by all. John and Nigel later hosted me in their home, and drove me all over northeastern Scotland so that I could try and determine whether the Scottish Renaissance really did differ from its English counterpart. (They will be pleased to learn that I believe it did.) Other colleagues played a less direct role in the writing of this book, but their support and friendship has been no less vital: Mou Banerjee, Dane Kennedy, Philippa Levine, Susan Pennybacker and Michelle Tusan all need to be mentioned in this category. And finally, no accounting of my professional debts would be complete without an acknowledgement

Acknowledgements

of the role my Clemson colleagues play in making my professional existence a happy and (I hope) productive one: Abel Bartley, James Burns, Vernon Burton, Elizabeth Carney, Caroline Dunn, Stephanie Hassell, Bill and Sue Lasser, Linda Li-Bleuel, Steve Marks and Lee Wilson deserve particular thanks.

The writing of this book has occurred at a point in my life when I am feeling more aware of the importance of long and close friendships, because I am now at an age where some of them have proved very lasting indeed. On this side of the Atlantic, Christa Smith has been a joyful companion on travels to the Canadian Rockies, the Grand Canyon, the Women's March in Washington, DC, and Walt Disney World, and at home she has been a stalwart, reliable and most of all tremendously fun friend. I could not hope to find a better friend than Rachel Moore, who is always there to listen, support or make me laugh. She is the strongest woman I know. Her two boys, Elijah and Marcos, are the nephews that my husband and I have never had. It has been a delight watching them grow up, and I very much look forward to remaining a part of their lives in the future.

No acknowledgements could be complete without thanking the two most important people in my life. It has been wonderful having my mother, Patsy Barczewski, living nearby for the last eight years, and equally wonderful seeing her thrive. Long may she reign as the trivia champion of her retirement community. My husband, Michael Silvestri, continues to be both an ideal colleague and my best friend. He has once again provided consultation, support and advice, and has diligently edited the manuscript in order to save me from embarrassing errors. (Any that remain are certainly not his fault.) Our three dogs, Bear, Ellie and Lizzie, provided minimum disruption (on some days, anyway) and maximum joy while this book was being written.

Finally, this book is dedicated to the family that has sustained and supported me over what is now approaching a quarter-century of research travel to London. I asked John Moisson to edit the manuscript because I thought he would be good at it; I had no inkling of just how correct that supposition would prove. John devoted himself to the task with an astonishing degree of patience, care and skill, and I will forever be grateful for his generosity of time and attention, as well as for his wit and humour throughout. His interventions dramatically improved the prose; the finished manuscript displayed with Microsoft Word's 'track changes' in place was an impressive array of black (my original), blue (John's suggestions) and red (my reconciliation of the previous two), with the final text truly a collaborative effort. Any remaining unwieldy language – or confusion over British and American usages of 'that' and 'which' – is entirely my responsibility. Beyond his editorial role, John's friendship was massively sustaining during those long months of pandemic isolation, and I shall always be extremely grateful to him. He made me laugh at times when it was hard to remember that life could be funny.

Although they did not play quite such a direct role in shepherding this book into print, the rest of the Moisson family have been vital sources of hospitality and support. I have come in recent months to know Kate much better, and I hope to experience even more of her wisdom, strength and empathy in the future. Ed and Claire have been friends through good times and bad, and have made the former better and the latter more bearable. They have been there to provide support whenever I have needed them, including during the stressful last weeks of finishing this book. Their son William is a joy to be around, at Fulham football fixtures and in all other contexts; it has been a delight to watch him grow into such a lovely young man who has clearly inherited the familial characteristics of kindness and an excellent sense of humour. As they are English, I will not embarrass the Moissons with fulsome American-style declarations of my feelings, but I hope that the dedication of this book goes some way towards expressing how much their friendship means to me.

PHOTO ACKNOWLEDGEMENTS

The author and publishers wish to express their thanks to the below sources of illustrative material and/or permission to reproduce it:

Alamy Stock Photo: pp. 130 (VTR), 131 (The Picture Art Collection), 202 (Dennis Hardley), 279 (SJ Images); Stephanie Barczewski: pp. 43, 62, 89; Bigstock.com: pp. 101 (khrizmo), 153 (jeffbanke), 164 (Stock_Photography), 263 (Hinksy), 296 (donsimon); Cheshire Archives and Local Studies and Chester History and Heritage, Cheshire Image Bank/www.cheshireimagebank.org.uk (used with permission): p. 103; Dreamstime.com: p. 76 (© Acceleratorhams); Flickr: pp. 193 (photo Hanna Jeffery, CC BY-SA 2.0), 200 (photo Caroline Legg, CC BY 2.0), 210 (photo Tom Parnell, CC BY-SA 2.0), 272 (British Library, public domain); Folger Shakespeare Library, Washington, DC (CC BY-SA 4.0): p. 94; Getty Images: p. 169 (David Goddard); Library of Congress, Prints and Photographs Division, Washington, DC: pp. 205, 231 (photo Carol M. Highsmith); from F. O. Morris, ed., *A Series of Picturesque Views of Seats of the Noblemen and Gentlemen of Great Britain and Ireland* (London, Edinburgh and Dublin, 1880), photos Getty Research Institute, Los Angeles: pp. 166 (vol. V), 238 (vol. III); © National Trust Images: pp. 48 (Arnhel de Serra), 65 (Andrew Butler), 124 (Robert Thrift), 127 (Robert Morris), 134 (John Hammond), 143 (John Hammond), 227 (James Dobson), 234 (John Bethell), 235 (Dennis Gilbert), 254 (Derrick E. Witty), 260 (Chris Lacey), 284 (John Hammond), 285 (John Hammond), 303 (James Dobson), 311 (Charlie Waite), 314 (top and bottom; Dennis Gilbert), 315 (James Mortimer); from W. H. Bernard Saunders, *Legends and Traditions of Huntingdonshire* (London, 1888), photo University of California Libraries: p. 276; Shutterstock.com: pp. 37 (wolfman57), 45 (Andrew Roland), 80 (Shelli Jensen), 102 (Helen Hotson), 109 (bottom; Leon Griffiths), 120 (Carole MacDonald), 129 (Kit Leong), 180 (Wirestock Creators), 203 (MichaelY), 206 (essevu), 212 (Shelli Jensen), 261 (Ruben Perez Gil), 264 (Wayne Midgley), 266 (stuartlambertphotography), 267 (abcbritain), 275 (top; Leonid Andronov), 275 (bottom; Petr Kovalenkov), 288 (Raedwald), 304 (Lilly Trott); Wikimedia Commons: pp. 150 (photo Kognos, CC BY-SA 4.0), 181 (photo Chris Andrews, CC BY-SA 2.0), 185 (photo Neville Young, CC BY-SA 4.0), 191 (photo Julia Cymru, CC BY-SA 4.0), 197 (photo Prussianblues, CC BY-SA 3.0), 211 (photo GentryGraves, CC BY-SA 4.0), 247 (photo Trenchspike, CC BY-SA 4.0), 293 (photo Boddah, CC BY-SA 3.0); Yale Center for British Art, New Haven, CT: pp. 68, 109 (top), 112, 156, 290, 291, 292.

INDEX

Page numbers in *italics* indicate illustrations

Abbey House 312
Abbotsbury Abbey 75, 76
Abbotsford 207
Acland, Arthur Henry Dyke 292–3
Act of Indemnity and Oblivion (1660) 117
Act of Union (1707) 186, 202
Act of Union (1801) 246
Adam, Robert 68, 204, 213, 233, 282, 287
Adam, William 202, 204
Adare Manor 247
Adderley Hall 298
Adlington Hall 125
Akeley Wood 298
Albright Hussey 99
Allerton Manor 106
Allington Castle 53
Alloa Tower 203
Althorp House 111, *112*
American colonies 229–30, 239
Americans, indigenous 217–29
Ampthill Plantation 230
Angelsey Abbey 249
Anglo-Boer War (Second) 297
Anne, Queen 133–4, 144
antisemitism 296, 297
Arbury Hall 142
Ardkinglas 209, *210*
Artari, Giuseppe 145

Arts and Crafts style 300–304, *301*
Ascott House 298
Ashburnham Place 234
Ashby St Ledgers 303
Ashley-Cooper, Anthony, 3rd Earl of Shaftesbury 277
Ashley-Cooper, Sir Anthony 76
Ashridge Park 160
Astor, William Waldorf 303–4
Atterbury Plot 144
Audley End 65, 249
Australia 239, 243

Baberton House 199
Bach-y-Graig 190
Bacon's Castle 230
Baconsthorpe Castle 101, *102*
Baddesley Clinton 36, *37*, 39, 46
Badminton House 113, 190
Badsworth Hall 106
Bailiffscourt 303
Baker, Herbert 309, 310
Baldwin, Stanley 18
Ballyscullion 288
Balmoral Castle 207
Bankes, William John 252–5
Barlings Abbey 56
Barningham Hall 289

Baroque 143, 146, 151, 273–7, *274*, 281
Barry, Charles 165, 208, 252
Barton Hall 90
Basildon Park 234, *235*
Basing House 94–5, *94*, 99
bastles 184
Batsford guidebooks 18
Battersea Manor 139
Bavington Hall 140
Bayham Abbey 155
Beauchamp Court 66
Beaulieu Abbey 64
Beaupré 190
Bellamont Forest 246
Bellinter House 246
Belmont House 248
Belton House 201
Belvoir Castle 160, 162, 249, 289
Berwick-on-Tweed 185
Betteshanger House 298
Bindon Abbey 151, 158
Binham Priory 67, *68*
Blair, Tony 11
Blanchland Abbey 66
Blathwayt, William 127–8
Blenheim Palace 273–4
Bletchingley Manor 53
Bletchington Manor 99
Blomfield, Reginald 302
Blore, Edward 160
Boarstall Manor 93–4
Boconnoc House 93

382

Index

Bolsover Castle 199
Bolton Abbey 63
Bolton Castle 52
Bonaparte, Empress Josephine 162
Bonaparte, Napoleon 163
Boscawen, Edward 233
Bottesford Preceptory 64
Boughton House 133
Bourton House 85
Boyle, Richard, 3rd Earl of Burlington 141, 146, 281
Boyne Castle 196
Boyne, Battle of the 125
Brackenhill Tower 185
Brampton Bryan Castle 113
Brancepeth Castle 55
Brandon, Charles, 1st Duke of Suffolk 56
Bretby Hall 84
Brettingham, Matthew 286
Brexit 7–8, 11–12, 170
Brick House 230
Bridgwater Manor 95
Bromham Manor 67, 111
Broomwell House 162
Brown, Capability 155
Broyle Place 66
Bruce, Sir William 200–201
Bryce, David 168, 208
Brymbo Hall 191, 192
Brynkir 192
Buckland Abbey 64, *65*
Bulstrode Park 124
Burghley House 262, *264*, 274
Burke, Edmund 35, 236
Burn, William 168, 208, 210, 294
Burton Agnes Hall 190
Burton Constable Hall 97, 248, 284
Bushwood Hall 81
'Bye Plot' (1603) 79
Byfleet House 269
Byland Abbey 63

'cabinets of curiosities' 222
Cadhay House 113
Caerlaverock Castle 196
Caerphilly Castle 193
Caldecote Hall 92
Callaly Castle 145
Cameron, David 7
Campbell, Colen 146, 202, 231, 278–9, 280–81, 286
Campden House 92, 111
Canons Ashby 216–18, 223
Cardiff Castle 213
Carew Castle 190
Carew Manor 53
Carnegie, Andrew 208
Cassells, Richard 246
Castell Coch 213
Castle Ashby 97, 101
Castle Campbell 196
Castle Drogo 310–17, *311*, *314–15*
Castle Howard 273
Castle Stuart 199
Castlemartyr Castle 245
castles 85–6, 158–9, 166, 178–9
Castletown House 246
Catesby, Robert 46, 79, 81
Catholicism (English) 43–4, 121–2, 140, 158
Caus Castle 112
Cecil, William 189, 262
Cefnamlwch 190
Cerne Abbey 64
Charborough Park 110, 111, 125
Chargate 274
Charlecote Park 106–7, 291
Charles I 82, 88, 97, 108, 122, 270
Charles II 100, 107, 117, 121, 125, 143
Charles Pinckney House 230
Charleville Castle *247*
Chastleton House 79, *80*, 142, *143*, 144, 190
Chatsworth House 22, 95, 98, 129
Cheeseburn Grange 140
Chéron, Louis 133
Chevening House 269, 271
Chideock Castle 46

China 249
Chirbury Hall 66
Chiswick House 141, 281
Church Hill House 300
Cirencester Park 146
classicism (English) 145–6, 231, 233, 240–42, 256, 262, 264–5, 268, 269–72, *271*, 280, 294, 308, 312
Claydon House 114, 250
Clayhill House 66
Clifford Manor 107
Clifton Hall Tower 136
Clifton Maybank 291
Clopton House 81
Clouds 300
Cobbett, William 17
Cobham Hall 53, 78
Cockle Park 184, *185*
Coke, Thomas, 1st Earl of Leicester 286
Colcombe Castle 53
Cole Orton Hall 234
Coleshill 201, 246, 269, 271, 272
Compton Wynyates 97, 101
Constable, John 299
continuity 29–30, 35–6, 38, 159
Cooling Castle 53
Corfe Castle 108–10, *109*
Cornbury House 99
Cornbury Plot 144
Cors-y-gedol 190
Cotehele 26
Cotman, John Sell *103*
Cotswolds 17
Coughton Court 80
Coupland Castle 184
Cowdray House 95
Craighall Castle 202
Craigievar Castle 199
Craigmillar Castle 200
Craignethan 196
Craigston Castle 196
Crichton Castle 196, *197*
Cromwell, Oliver 85, 94, 120
Cromwell, Thomas 53, 58, 59, 64, 66

Crooksbury 308
Culloden Tower 149, *150*
Curwen, Margaret 122
Cyfarthfa Castle 213

Dalston Hall 184
Dalton, Hugh 25
Dashwood, Sir Francis 286–7
Daylesford 235–6, 237
Dance, George 233–4
Daniell, Thomas 237, 238
Danny 143
Dawley Hall 139
'Debatable Lands' 188
Declaration of Arbroath 176
Denne Hill 298
Desart Court 246
Devey, George 209, 298
Devizes Castle 111
Dewlish House 249
Dilston Hall 137
Dilston Tower 184
Dissolution of the Monasteries 32, 36, 54, 57–71, *62*, 151, 166
Dodington Hall 223
Donington Hall 112
Dore Abbey 153
Downton Abbey 11–13, 20, 305
Drake, Francis 225
Drax Hall 230
Drayton Hall 230, *231*
Drochil Castle 196
Drumlanrig Castle 200
Drybridge House 212
Duchy of Cornwall 53, 63
Duddo Tower 184
Dudley Priory 155
Dudley, Robert, 1st Earl of Leicester 259–61
Dunham Massey 122
Dunkeld Castle 201
Dunluce Castle 245
Dunnichen, Battle of 174
Dunrobin Castle 206, 207
Dutch influence (on country houses) 126–8

Dyrham Park 127–8
Drewe, Julius 310–11
decline (national) 22–3, 299

Easby Abbey 63
East Cowes Castle 160
Eastbury Park 274
Eastlake, Charles 298
Eastnor Castle 160, 249
Eastwood Hall 93
Eaton Hall 159, 201
Eccleshall Castle 82
Eccleston Hall 140
Edgbaston Hall 122
Edinburgh Castle 199
Edward I 175, 182, 183, 213
Edward III 183
Edwinsford 191, 192
Egglestone Abbey 152
Eilean Donan Castle 209
Elgin Tower 210
Elizabeth I 36, 48, 49, 54–5, 185, 247, 257
Ellesborough Manor 53
empire (British) 7, 8, 32, 216–51, 309
Endsleigh House 289
English Civil War 31, 32, 45, 77–8, 81–102, 121, 122–3, 153, 166
financial impact of 102–7
memory of 114–18
English landscape style 151
Erddig 27
Esher Place 146
Eslington Hall 137

Falkland Palace 195
Farnborough Hall 107, 283, *284*
Fawley Court 92
Felbrigg House 283–4, *285*
Fellowes, Julian 12
Fenwick Hall 230
Ferniehurst Castle 186
Ferrey, Benjamin 293
First World War 31, 309, 312
FitzOsbern, William 178

Flamborough Castle 52
Flemish influences 196–7, 265
Flitcroft, Henry 156
Folly Farm 308
Fonthill Abbey 160, 210, 249
Forde Abbey 66, 152, *153*
forfeiture (of property) 50–51, 138–9
Forster, E. M. 23
Foulkes, Samuel 49
Fountains Abbey 63, 64, 155, *156*, 157
'four nations' history 9
France, England's rivalry with 278
French influences 195, 207, 263, 265–6, 273, *275*, 294–6, *294*
French Revolution 32, 158–65, 166, 288, 289, 305

garden-city movement 24
Garenton 287
Garnet, Henry 44, 46, 80
Gayhurst Hall 104
Gayton House 125
George I 277
Gibbons, Grinling 49
Gibbs, James 114, 144, 145, 146, 148, 202, 278–9
Gifford Hall 85
Gilpin, William 157
Gisborough Hall 155
Gledstone Hall 308
Glen Andred 298
Glen Tanar 208
Glenborrodale Castle 208
Glenvoe Castle 213
Glorious Revolution 31, 32, 121–35, 146, 147, 201, 273, 277
Glyndwr, Owen 175, 180, 182
Gnoll Castle 213
Godinton Hall 162
Godolphin House 100
Godstow House 77, 83
Goldings 298
Goodrich Court 160

384

Goodwood House 126, 286
Gothic style 146–51, 159–60, 163–6, 198, 242–3, 256–7, 262, 263, 265, 268, 289, 293, *294*
Government House (Calcutta) 231
Governor's House (Annapolis) 230
Governor's Palace (Virginia) 230
Gowers, Sir Ernest 26
Grafton Manor 79
Grand Tour 32, 158, 278, 283–8
Great Dixter 303
Great Stanmore Manor 235
Greatford Hall 55
Green, The 149
Greenlands House 83
Gresley Hall 66
Grimsthorpe Castle 274
Gunpowder Plot 46, 49, 79–81, 119

Haddon Hall 289–90, *291*
Hagley Hall 149
Hailes Abbey 60
Haines Hill 106
Hall Place 298
Hall, Edward 258
Halton House 295
Hampton Court (Herefordshire) 111
Hampton Court (Richmond) 258
Hanbury Hall 133
Hangleton Manor 66
Hanoverian Succession 202
Hardinge, Charles, 1st Baron Hardinge 309
Hardwick Hall 95, *267*, 268, 274
Hardy, Thomas 299
Harlaxton Manor 161
Harley, Robert 113
Harrowden Hall 81
Hartlebury Manor 99
Harvington Hall *45*
Hastings, Warren 235–6, 237

Hatchlands Park 233
Hatfield House 249
Hatherley, Owen 28
Hazlitt, William 289
Heathcote 308
Hellifield Peel 52
Henblas 192
Hengrave Hall 84
Henry VII 5 8
Henry VIII 51, 52, 53, 54, 56, 58, 63, 257
heritage (English national) 10, 28
Herrera, Juan de 191
Hervey, Frederick Augustus, 4th Earl of Bristol 287–8
Hetton Hall 184
Hever Castle 303, *304*
High Ercall Hall 91, 116
Highclere Castle 305
Highcliffe Castle 161, *164*
Highland Clearances 208
Highnam Court 98
Hill Bark 102, 289
Hillesden House 85
Hindlip Hall 45, 46, 80
Hinton Priory 64
Historic Buildings and Ancient Monuments Act (1953) 26
Holbeche House 81
Holdenby House 88
Holkham Hall 232, 286
Holland, Henry 112
Holme Lacy 153
Holyrood Palace 199, 201
Honingham Hall 148
Hooke, Robert 126
Hopetoun House 201
Horsenden Manor 99
Horton Court 260
Houghton Conquest 269
Houghton Hall 277, *278*
Houndhill Manor 100
House of the Binns 199
Howley Hall 90
Huddington Court 81
Hugo, Victor 162
Huntsham Court 292, *293*

Hurlands 300
Hussey Tower 53
Hussey, Christopher 9, 24, 297
Hutton in the Forest 100, *101*
Huttonhall 186

Ickworth 287, *288*
iconoclasm 81–2
Ince Castle 100
India 233–9, 248, 309–10
Indo-Saracenic style 243–4
industrialization 16
interwar years 17
Inveraray Castle 204, *205*
Ireland 50, 244–8, 250
Ishiguro, Kazuo 20–21
Italian influence 196, 252–3, 261–2
Italianate style 294

'Jacobethan' style 293, *294*
Jacobitism 31, 32, 123, 125, 135–45, 149, 201, 203
James I 78, 79, 101, 119, 186, 199
James II 121, 122, 123, 124, 125
James of St George 183
Jeffreys, George 124
Jekyll, Gertrude 308
Jervaulx Abbey 63
Jesuits 44
Joldwynds 300
Jones, Inigo 65, 152, 200, 245, 252, 269–72, *270*, 281

Keck, Anthony 213
Kedleston Hall 231
Kelburn Castle 202
Kenilworth Castle 81, 87, 259–61, *261*
Kent, William 146, 148
Kerr, Robert 294–5
Kerr, Sir Robert 198, 199
Kett's Rebellion 54
Killhow 210
Kimbolton Castle 133, 274–5, *276*
King's House (Salisbury) 223

King's House (Spanish Town) 231
King's Weston House 274
Kingston Lacy 108–10, *109*, 252–5, *254*
Kingston Manor 66
Kinloch Castle 208
Kinross House 201, *202*
Kirkandrews Tower 184
Kirkstead Abbey 56
Kirtlington Park 144
Knole 85, 302

Labour government (1945–51) 25–6
Laguerre, Louis 129–31, *130*, 273
Lambay Castle 311
Langley Castle 137
Lanhydrock House 84
Lastingham 52
Lathom House 89
Launde Abbey 64
Leadbetter, Stiff 282–3
Leasowes, The 157
Leckhampstead House 105–6
Lee Priory 160
Lees-Milne, James 20, 27
Leicester Abbey 64, 77
Leigh Court 99
Leighton Hall 136, 140
Lennox, Charles, 1st Duke of Richmond 125–6
Lennox, Charles, 2nd Duke of Richmond 286
Leonardo da Vinci 196
Leoni, Giacomo 282
Leslie House 201
Lethaby, William 302
Levens Hall 223
Lewes Priory 59, 66
Leyswood 298
liberty 147–8, 157, 166
Lilleshall Abbey 77
Lindisfarne Castle 311
Lindsay, David 296
Linlithgow Palace 194
'Little Englandism' 29

Little Moreton Hall 102, *103*, 289
Little Thakeham 308
Littlecote House 290
Llanover House 213
Llanvihangel Court 190
Llewelyn the Great 174
Lloyd Wright, Frank 307
Llwynywormwood 192
loggias 260
Longleat 262, *263*
Lorimer, Robert 209
Loseley Park 67
Loudon, J. C. 162
Louis XIV 49, 162
Low Hall 138
Lowther Castle 160, 163
Lullingstone Castle 144
Lulworth Castle 192
Lumley Castle 276
Lutyens, Edwin 303, 307–16
Lydford Grange 45
Lyme Park 142
Lyttleton, George 149

Macharioch Castle 209
MacLaren, James 209
Macmillan, Harold 26
Mackworth Castle 265
Madresfield Court 99
'Main Plot' (1603) 78–9
manor houses 36–8
Mar Lodge 209, *211*
Mar's Walk 196
Marie Antoinette 162–3
Markenfield Hall 213
Marshcourt 213, 308
Mary I 53, 257
Mary II 131–2
Mason, William 157
Mathew, Robert 91
May, Hugh 126
Medmenham Manor 53
Melchet Park 237
Melville Castle 204
Mersham Hatch 287
Merton Abbey 153
Messel, Leonard 297
Messel, Ludwig 296–7

Milcote House 92
Miles Brewton House 230
Miller, Sanderson 149
Minsterley Hall 112
Minterne Magna 302
Monmouth Rebellion 124, 125, 137
Montacute House 290–91, *292*
Moore Abbey 245
Morton, H. V. 17
Mottisfont Abbey 64
Mount Airey 230
Mount Surrey 54
Mounton House 213
Mulgrave Castle 52
Mylne, Robert 202, 204
mythology (classical) 131–4, 144–5, 278

Napoleonic Wars 163
Narford Hall 286
Nash, John 160
Nash, Joseph 289
Nash, Paul 313, 315
Nashdom 308
National Trust 10, 20, 24, 25–6, 27, 301, 305
Neo-Georgian style 304, 308
Neo-Palladian style 32, 143, 145–6, 202, 230–31, 233, 277–83, *282*
    Irish 246
Nerquis 192
Nesfield, William Eden 298
Netherwitton House 138
Netley Abbey 64–5
New Delhi 309, 316
New Labour 11
Newark Park 67
Newby Hall 287
Newstead Abbey 65, 73
Ney, Michel 162
Nonington 298
Nonsuch Palace 67, 258
Norman Court 234
'Norman yoke' 158
nostalgia 11, 13, 18–19, 152, 154–5

Nunnington Hall 142, 143–4
Nymans 296–7

Oakleigh 299–300
Offa's Dyke 173
Oglethorpe, James Edward 135
Okehampton Castle 53
'Old Scots' style 209
Oldmixon, John 147
Opium War (First) 249
Orleans House 145
Oulton Park 142
Overstrand Hall 308
Owen, Nicholas 44–5, 80
Oxburgh Hall 36, 39, 97, 142

Padley Hall 45
Paine, James 231, 233, 283, 284
Palace of Westminster 165
Palgrave, Francis 163
Palladio, Andrea 191, 230, 231, 233, 264, 276, 281, 286, 287, 288
Panmure House 201
Papists' Estates Act (1716)
pastoral tradition in England 16
Peacham, Henry 258
Pearce, Edward Lovett 246
pele towers 183
Pelligrini, Giovanni Antonio 133
Penheale Manor 312
Penrhyn Castle 213
Penshurst Place 298
Perpendicular style 164–5, 171, 242, 258, 260, 266–7
Petworth House 47, 48, 284
Pevsner, Nikolaus 307
Phillips, Amyas 303
Phyllis Court 116
picturesque 156–7
Pilgrimage of Grace 47, 48, 51–3, 55, 56, 57, 58, 63, 122
Pinkie House 196–7
Pipewell Hall 66
Plas Clough 190
Plas Dinam 213

Plas Teg 190–91
Playfair, James 204
Pocahontas 219
Polesworth Hall 66
Pontefract Castle 52
Popish Plot 123
Portinari, Giovanni 59
Portumna Castle 245
Poundisford Park 67
Powell, Enoch 14
Powerscourt House 246
Powis Castle 181, 190, 239
Pratt, Sir Roger 110–11, 126, 201, 246, 252, 269
Preston Hall 107
Price, Sir Uvedale 157
priest holes 42–7, *43*, 71–2
Prior Overton's Tower 265
Priory Hall 152, 155
Proctor, Sir Stephen 119

Queen Anne style 304, 308

Raby Castle 55
Radclyffe, James, 3rd Earl of Derwentwater 137
Raglan Castle 113, 190
Ragley Hall 113, 211
Ralegh, Sir Walter 78, 219, 223, 225, 228–9
'Recording Britain' 18
Red Lodge 223
Reformation (English) 30, 39–40, 70–74, 78, 157
Reivers 177, 183
Renaissance influences 193–5, 196, 258, *259*, 262
Renishaw Hall 98
Rennie Mackintosh, Charles 209
Restoration 121
Rhual 192
Rickman, Thomas 164
Rievaulx Abbey 63, 155
Ringmore 210
Ripley Castle 119, *120*
Rising of the North 47, 48, 54–5, 56, 119
Roche Abbey 155

Rococo style 143, 246
Rokeby Park 232
Romanticism 16, 17, 205
Rome, ancient 232–3, 241, 278–9
Rotherwas Court 113–14
Rothschild, Baron Ferdinand de 295
'Rough Wooing' 63, 177
Rounton Grange 300
Rousham House 100, 146
Royal Fort House 115
Royal Pavilion (Brighton) 248
Ruperra Castle 192, *193*
Rupert, Prince 92, 96, 115
Russborough House 246
Ruthin Castle 213
Rye House Plot 128
Rysbrack, John Michael 278

Sacheverell, Thomas 133, *134*
Sackville-West, Vita 103, 302
St Alban's Court 298
St Fagan's Castle 192
St John, Henry, 1st Viscount Bolingbroke 139
St John's Abbey (Colchester) 77
St Mary's Abbey (York) 63
St Nicholas Abbey 230
St Osyth's Abbey 77
Samuel, Raphael 24, 27–8
Sandbeck Park 155
Sandgate Castle 67
Sandon Hall 168, *169*
Scarborough Castle 97
Scarborough, John 49
Scotland 31, 172, 174, 175, 176–7, 194–211
Scottish Baronial style 168–70, 198, 207–8
Scottish Borders 173, 176, 181, 183–8
Scruton, Roger 11, 14
Seaton Delaval Hall 274, 276–7
Second World War 24, 31
Seeley, J. R. 241

sequestration 105–6
Seringapatam, Battle of 248
Settrington House 52
Seven Years War 233, 248
Sezincote 237, *238*, 248
Shardeloes 282–3
Shaw, Richard Norman 209, 213, 298
Sheffield Castle 88
Shelford House 117
Shell guides 18
Shenstone, William 157
Sherborne Castle 78
Shillingstone Manor 79
Shirley-Eustis House 230
Shirley Plantation 230
Shotover Park 146, 147, 149
Shugborough House 249
sieges 91–5
Sissinghurst Castle 103–4
Sizergh Castle 122–4
Slaidburn 52
Smeaton Manor 300
Smirke, Robert 160, 161
Smith, James 202
Smythson, Robert 80, 256, 262, 267, 269
Snelston Hall 162
Soane, Sir John 313
Society of Dilettanti 286–7
Sopwell Priory 65
Southover Grange 66
Spye Park 111
Stainborough House 281
Standen 300, *303*
Stapleton Castle 83
Staveley Hall 98
Stella Hall 138
Stenton House 230
Stirling Castle 194, 195
Stoke Park House 269
Stokesay Castle 179–80, *180*
Stone Cross 210
Stonegarthside Hall 188
Stoneleigh Abbey 62
Stourhead 156
Stowe 146, 148, 149

Stratton Park 234
Strawberry Hill 148
Strensham Manor 92, 99
Stuart, Charles Edward 142
Stuart, James Edward 142, 144
Stuart, Louisa Maria Theresa *124*
Studley Royal 155
Sudeley Castle 66, 98
Summerhill House 246
Sutton Scarsdale Hall 98
Sykes, Sir Francis 234–5
Syon Abbey 68

Talgarth Tower *181*
Talman, William 26, 127
Taplow Court 294
Tattershall Castle 56
Temple Newsam 52
Thame Abbey 66
Thatcher, Margaret 10
Thirlstane Castle 200
Thompson, E. P. 15
Thornhill, Sir James 133–4, *134*, 273
Thornton Abbey 154
Thynne, Sir John 262
Tilty Abbey 57
Tipu Sultan 239, 248–9
Titchfield Abbey 61, 64
Tiverton Castle 53
Toddington Manor 165, *166*
Torksey Castle 85
Tortington Place 67
Tradescant, John 222
Traquair House *203*
Tredegar House 211, *212*
Tredwstan Court 194
Trefecca Fawr 194
Trefusis House 210
Trerice 265
Trevalyn Hall 190, *191*
Tring Park 126, 295

Unionism (Irish) 246–7
Uppark 128, *129*, 284
Upstairs, Downstairs 20
urbanization 16

Vanbrugh, Sir John 133, 204, 273–7
vernacular revival style 298–300, *299*
Verrio, Antonio 129–32, *131*, 273
violence 41–2, 46–7, 50, 90–91
Vredeman de Vries, Hans 191, 197
Vyne, The 107

Waddesdon 295, *296*
Wadhurst Hall 312
Wales 171, 189–94, 211–14
Wallington House 141
Walpole, Horace 104, 148, 286–7
Walpole, Sir Robert 146, 278–9
Wanstead House 286
Wardour Castle 112, 158, 256–7
Wars of the Roses 48
Wat's Dyke 173
Wattlesborough Castle 181
Waugh, Evelyn 23
Weaver, Sir Lawrence 39, 184, 309
Webb, Philip 300, 303
Wells, H. G. 38
Welsh Marches 172–3, 174, 175, 177–83
Wenlock Priory 111
Wentworth Castle 144
Wentworth Woodhouse 281
West Wycombe 286–7
Westbrook Place 135
Weston Hall 101
Westover Plantation 230
Westwood Manor 223, 226, *227*
Whitelocke, Bulstrode 92, 116
Widdrington Castle 138
Wiener, Martin 17
Wigglesworth Hall 52
Wightwick Manor 102, 289

Index

William I 174
William III 122, 124, 125, 128, 129, 133, 246
Williams, Raymond 15–16
Willinghurst 300
Wilton Castle 52
Wilton House 65, 193, 269
Wimpole Hall 149
Windebank, Sir Francis 106
Windsor Castle 273
Wing Manor 97
Wingerworth Hall 98

Wingfield Manor 98
Wingfield, Samuel 107
Winton House 199
Wintour, Robert 79, 81
Woburn Abbey 152, 155–6
Wolfeton House 223, 228–9
Wollaton Hall 264–5, *266*, 274
Wombridge Priory 64
Woodstock Manor 99
Wootton Lodge 98
Wordsworth, William 16, 160

Wormleighton Manor 111–12
Wren, Sir Christopher 126, 271, 302
Wright, Patrick 10
Wroxton Abbey 66
Wyatt, James 159–60
Wyatt's Rebellion 53
Wymondham Abbey 54
Wyvis Lodge 209

Yarnton Manor 102